1986

Romanticism and its Consequences:

Emergent Culture in the Nineteenth Century

1790-1912

I

The Birth of Romanticism:

Cultural Crisis 1790-1815

The Birth of Romanticism

1790 – 1815

by

Morse Peckham

The Penkevill Publishing Company
Greenwood, Florida

ISBN 0—913283—16—9
Printed in the United States of America

Dedicated to

Gordon Lindstrand

CONTENTS

Prologue

xi

Chapter I

The Enlightenment's Bequest of Incoherence

1

Chapter II

Romantic Beginnings 1794-1800

63

Chapter III

Emerging Romantic Styles 1801-1809

143

Chapter IV

Romanticism Confirmed 1810-1815

263

Appendix I

Music and Meaning

345

Appendix II

The Argument of *Explanation and Power*

358

Appendix III

Intention and Interpretation

367

Appendix IV
Chronological Table
375

Index of Persons, Titles, and Places
387

Index of Paintings: Titles and Locations
397

Subject Index
401

Prologue

This volume is the first of a proposed series of five volumes. My aim is to identify and trace the emergent culture of what I believe to be best understood as the Romantic tradition and its superimposition upon the culture of the Enlightenment, itself superimposed upon the culture of medieval and renaissance Western Europe. Specifically, the problem to be dealt with and moved toward is the emergence in the first decade of the twentieth century, more precisely in the years 1907 and 1908, of what is still called Modernism, in literature, philosophy, painting, sculpture, architecture — and in time even the dance and the decorative arts.

The first and most striking attribute of the sudden emergence of Modernism is that initially the leaders, such men as Picasso, Matisse, Loos, and Schoenberg, were not aware of each other. The emergence of Modernism is thus one of the most extraordinary examples in history of cultural convergence, the simultaneous and independent appearance of similar cultural innovations. As we look back today, we can see signs of what was about to happen, but at the same time the break with the preceding styles in the various arts and in philosophy as well was so sharp and complete as to meet initially with shock, incomprehension, and rejection, a reaction that is still widely to be encountered. If we examine, for example, the paintings by Picasso in the two or three years immediately preceding the first work in what is inadequately known as Cubism, we can see a progressive simplification, a progressive abandonment and stripping away of the whole tradition of Western painting. The culmination, or close to the culmination, of this movement, was a painting of a naked youth leading a horse, an emblem of energy under control, but without the appurtenances of cultivated equitation, that is, of cultural tradition. And this painting was followed by a self-portrait, a naked torso, Picasso himself stripped bare of the costume of tradition. At almost exactly the same time Adolf Loos was creating a house in Vienna from which all ornamentation, everything traditionally identified as architecture, was eliminated, stripped off, abandoned. And at the same time in the same city Schoenberg was abandoning the whole system of the rules of how to compose music. Almost immediately he found himself unable to compose anything more than at most a minute long, unless he controlled the compositional process by responding to a text.

These instances are enough to open up to examination and consideration the second striking attribute of the appearance of Modernism, the fact that such a break with tradition, such an abandonment, such a stripping away of cultural tradition, was unique in the history of culture, not merely in the history of Western or Mediterranean culture, but in the history of any culture. The nearest thing would be the Japanese wholesale adoption of China's Tang culture in the Heian period, or the similar wholesale adoption of Western culture in the nineteenth century. These too were the results of the decisions of only a few individuals, but they were the decisions of individuals in governmental power, not of individuals on the social periphery, individuals at the time of no economic importance, let alone political; they were political and economic decisions. And they did not involve an abandonment of traditional Japanese culture but were rather both an imposition or addition, and a synthesizing with Japanese cultural forms and styles. It is unquestionable that the cultural innovation which we still call Modernism is unique in world history. There is nothing in the cultural history of Western Europe that so demands and so resists explanation.

Yet just as it is possible to see signs of a coming change in the work of the months or several years immediately preceding the breakthrough into Modernism by two or three artists, so it is possible to look before and after those crucial years of 1907 and 1908 and begin to comprehend what had happened, and to do so from a wider perspective.

In recent years a deeply searching and richly rewarding disturbance has emerged in the academic world and by now, spreading beyond that world, has begun to attract the attention of a non-academic public interested in ideas and the arts. This is a public convinced that what affects the general pattern of our thinking and also has an impact upon the arts is of importance, even of the highest importance; for sooner or later such a powerful emergent in these realms will have a political impact. The name for this disturbance is "deconstructionism."

It is not necessary here to attempt a full account of the thinking of the principal figure in that emergent movement, the French philosopher Jacques Derrida, whose most famous work is *Of Grammatology*, published in French in 1967 and in translation in this country in 1976. It is enough to give a couple of examples of his ideas and their implications. One of his central notions is that of "the metaphysics of presence": how we respond to a word or a configuration is not determined or demanded by that word or configuration. Its "presence" as something which impels us to thought or action is metaphysical — not physical. *We* supply the "presence" which impels us. For example, one factor in our responses consists of "traces" of our previous behavior in response to that word or configuration or similar words or configurations.

From this metaphysics of presence arise all sorts of questions. What holds words together in sentences? And what holds sentences together? Is it only the metaphysics of presence, or groundless belief that words and sentences naturally hold together as we hear them or as we utter them? Such questions lead to the idea of "logocentrism"; the notion that our conviction that an absolute or ultimate level of linguistic meaning subsumes and justifies any verbal construction we may create is no more than illusion. It is as sensible to say that a discourse is not a coherent structure, no matter what its claims or pretensions, as it is to say that it is a coherent structure. The incoherence of *any* text can be demonstrated. To use old-fashioned terms, a discourse is coherent only because someone wills its coherence. Or, to be a bit more modern, a discourse is held together by a human interest. Whatever construction we may create linguistically and impose on the world is arbitrary, and examination will always reveal that, no matter what its pretensions, it is fundamentally as incoherent as it is arbitrary.

We believe that our language gives us the world, but it gives us only a dream of the world, a dream that is arbitrary and, as history shows, evanescent. The effect and the unpalatable lesson — unpalatable, at least, to most people, yet quite possibly almost wildly optimistic — of "deconstructionism" is that the very foundation on which the most extreme skepticisms of European thinking have been built, language itself, is not a foundation at all; it is a quagmire, a quicksand, it is something that on examination evaporates into a wisp of mist, into a nothingness. Yet such a notion can be optimistic if we think of how often a European claim to have arrived at a "truth," that is, a linguistic construction deserving of "belief," has brought about the most hideous and destructive consequences, so dreadful that there is some justice in calling, as has happened, the white race of Europe the cancer of mankind. The deconstruction of our ultimate resource, language, our very mode of being, may at least make us more modest and less murderous.

In the same years, the 1970s, in which Derrida's deconstructionism was emigrating from France — and disturbing and exciting, sometimes to trivial results, American academic purlieus — a native development was shaping itself and rearing into prominence. It was American because to a considerable degree it emerged from the tradition, in recent decades neglected by American academic philosophy, of American pragmatism. This innovation in American philosophy is the work of the philosopher Richard Rorty, whose book *Philosophy and the Mirror of Nature,* published in 1979, was reviewed in a journal of great prominence under the title "The End of Philosophy." And indeed Rorty's work does mark the end of philosophy as it has been practiced for two and a half millenia.

Rorty dethrones philosophy, known for ages as the Queen of Thought, as the absolute level on which mind can ultimately resolve problems and unveil apparent incoherence to reveal an absolute coherence of intellectual construction. It is fair enough to say that he reveals the history of philosophy as how each philosophical stage, thought to be a development, merely deconstructs its predecessor and is in turn deconstructed by its successor. Rorty is sympathetic to Derrida, and turns philosophy into a great conversation which perhaps in itself accomplishes nothing but serves, like a wind-propelled source of intellectual energy, merely to keep us going.

Nor can I forbear saying that my own work is culturally convergent with that of Derrida and Rorty. By "cultural convergence" I mean that all three positions were arrived at independently of any knowledge of the others. During the same decade of the 1970s I examined language not with the tools of philosophy but as behavior, a study culminating in my *Explanation and Power: The Control of Human Behavior*, published in 1979. My position proposes that the meaning of any verbal and non-verbal configuration is the response to that configuration, a notion virtually equivalent to Derrida's "metaphysics of presence"; that in the long run all meanings of either words or configurations are stabilized by force; that explanation attempts to circumvent the use of force and is thus the foundation of civilization; that it also, being meaning, is ultimately sustained by force; and that the attempt to stabilize explanations of man and the world and to maintain such explanations by pure political power has again and again crucified mankind.

It is beginning to look as if "deconstructionism" instead of being the name of an academic intellectual fashion is coming to be the designation of an emerging cultural era. It is more than likely that it is a more accurate name for "post-modernism." And those of us who are historically-minded are bound to wonder how such an extraordinary cultural development has come about. Now if we look back, in an almost random way, we can see anticipatory hints of what has happened so recently. In the 1920s, for example, there emerged surrealism, a movement that affected a group of artists and writers and even today, particularly among the striking new writers of Latin America, is still powerful.

The surrealists, of whom Salvador Dali is merely the most famous, claimed to release the unconscious. But since we can really know nothing about the unconscious, or even be sure there is such a thing, we can ignore that claim of the surrealists and think about what in fact they did. And what they accomplished was of great interest for what was to follow. By relaxing what were revealed to be the conventional modes of organizing and relating the verbal and visual categories with which we fancy we are related to the world, they showed that those modes were indeed not natural, not logical — that is, necessary and native to the mind, innate to the very immanent structure of language and visual signs — but arbitrary and more than arbitrary, oppressive.

Looking back a little further into the years directly after the First World War, we can see now that James Joyce was using his *Ulysses* to show that language is the labyrinth in which, like sacred monsters, we live and have our being, a revelation he was to make more vivid in *Work in Progress,* which was to become, in time, *Finnegans Wake.* And in the same years, T. S. Eliot was deliberately showing that language as we know it is a heap of ruins, and Ezra Pound was calling European high culture an "old bitch gone in the teeth."

Moving further back we can see in the pre-war experiments of Gertrude Stein the heroic effort, admittedly almost unreadable, to show that we are free to put words together in entirely novel ways, and thus perhaps to force new meanings into existence. She was of course inspired by what we have already encountered, the breakthrough into Modernism in the analytic Cubist paintings of Picasso and Braque, that ravishing monochromatic style of 1907 and 1908, which revealed the freedom of the artist to create visible reconstructions of the visual language of painting; for that language, to use the word metaphorically (semiotic system would be more accurate), is ultimately arbitrary and a free creation of the human imagination. Contemporary with them, and culturally convergent in the same years, was the music of Arnold Schoenberg, who abandoned the idea of tonality as something given by nature or by logic and instead demonstrated that music can be made by the freest juxtaposition of tones and chords, a juxtaposition controlled only by the feeling of the composer for the sound that, for him, is in a particular situation "right."

Beyond, historically, these artists we can see the figure of Nietzsche, the great nihilist, the nineteenth-century figure in whom deconstructionism has shown great revivalist and revitalizing interest; the philospher who called for the transvaluation of all values, who saw a failure of European culture so complete that only an unimaginable cultural transcendence was possible. And unimaginable is here the correct word, for Nietzsche said that he could not be understood by what he said but only by what was unsayable, to be experienced by responding to the empty spaces between his aphorisms. That conviction allied him with his contemporaries in the last decades of the nineteenth century, the Symbolists. These were the painters and writers whose astonishing achievement was to create works which elicited from the reader or the observer the greatest possible experience of the meaningfulness of what they were responding to, yet with the total inability to say what that meaning might be. They analyzed out from human behavior the pure experience of meaningfulness. Like Nietzsche, the Symbolists, of whom Stéphane Mallarmé was the greatest, tore language loose from the world.

And we can go further back still to the early 1880s and watch Monet turn Impressionism into something else, something that can only be rightly named by using a term that emerged much later, Expressionism. Or, to put it another way, when Nietzsche was tearing language loose from the world, Monet, with equal analytic enterprise, was tearing color loose from the world and loose from the traditions of painting. What he was doing showed the same tendencies that had already emerged in the early stage of Impressionism and was to achieve its fullest manifestation in the work of Vincent Van Gogh, the emergence of the brush stroke as a supremely important element in the visual design of a painting. It was an analytic emergence of the trace of the basic activity of painting, the application of a paint-laden brush to canvas.

In those same 1870s of the emerging brush-stroke, evident, for example, in the late painting of the Barbizon painter, Charles Daubigny, the philosopher Hans Vaihinger, still in his twenties, was drafting his "philosophy of as if," not to be published until 1911. We have to act, he claimed, *as if* the statements of science or morals were in fact true. And in these years the similarly directed American pragmatism was beginning to gather itself together. In the preceding decade of the 1860s Richard Wagner had anticipated Vaihinger in *Die Meistersinger*. We live by illusions, Wagner's hero Hans Sachs comes to realize, and if we wish to do a great thing we must fearlessly manipulate those illusions. This was Wagner's solution to the conundrum with which in 1857 he revised the ending of *Der Ring des Nibelungen*. The Gods are dead. Their attempt to create a hero to carry out their will, their ultimately deceitful and dishonest will and incoherent will, has failed. They go up in flames, leaving men without gods. In his analysis of power Wagner came to the end of ideology, to the end of any belief that there is an absolute, transcendent, metaphysical reality in which human problems can be solved, or from which human behavior can be imagined to be controlled.

It is possible to go back even further, but this movement backward for well over a hundred years from our contemporary culture of deconstructionism to the bleak vision of Richard Wagner — of man without his beliefs, and beliefs that have become illusions — is enough to reveal a pattern. It is the pattern according to which European culture, and by that of course I mean North and South American culture as well — wherever the culture of Europe has spread — has consisted of the continuous analytic striving of the emergent and innovative thinkers and artists during this period of, by now, very nearly two centuries.

Everything in European culture has not only been questioned. It has been rigorously analyzed, verbally and non-verbally, in painting and music, in architecture and the dance, as well as in thought and language. The whole sweep of that cultural emergence has been the *analytic dismantlement of the superstructure of Western culture.* Once we have seen that, if we continue to consider the problem historically, to gain through history some insight into where we are now, some grasp of the culture of deconstructionism, we are bound to ask: When did that analytic dismantlement begin, and why? Can we account for it? If we can, then we will have an explanation for the conundrum with which this "Prologue" opened, the emergence of Modernism.

This first volume is the attempt to discover those beginnings and to propose an explanation of why that dismantlement emerged in European history. To do so we must look not merely at political thought, or philosophy, but also at literature, painting, music, architecture, for those too are modes of thought, of the structure of our thinking about the world, and therefore revelations of our dismantlement of that structure. That tradition of analysis is, I maintain and will endeavor to show, the *tradition of Romanticism,* which emerges in the 1790s; here the "birth of Romanticism" means not only the birth of what is usually called Romanticism but also of the current stage of the Romantic tradition, post-modernism or deconstructionism. To understand the emergence of Romanticism we must first see what it emerged from, the Enlightenment. We begin, therefore, with the culminating figure of Enlightenment culture, Immanuel Kant, and with his opponent, Johann Gottfried von Herder. Our distant goal, or terminus, is the first performance of Arnold Schoenberg's *Pierrot Lunaire* in Berlin's Choralion-Saal on October 16, 1912. With at least poetic truth and a certain dramatic fitness one can say that that occasion marked the successful, the triumphant establishment of Modernism. As I hope to show, Modernism was the first response at all adequate to the demand of the initial and precipitating problem of Romanticism, to the cultural crisis from which Romanticism was born, the twenty-five years from the Fall of the Bastille to the battle of Waterloo.

Chapter I

The Enlightenment's Bequest of Incoherence

Immanuel Kant (1714-1804) vs. Johann Gottfried von Herder (1744-1803)

The year 1790 saw the publication of the last of Immanuel Kant's three great critiques, *Kritik der Urteilskraft*. The title is usually translated as *Critique of Judgment*, although that translation neglects the force of *kraft*, or power, or mildly, ability. What the word emphasizes is that judgment is an act, an imposition of the mind upon the world. The third *Critique* had been preceded by *Kritik der reinen vernunft* (*Critique of Pure Reason*), published in 1781 and revised 1787, and *Kritik der praktischen Vernunft* (*Critique of Practical Reason*), published in 1788. Few works of philosophy have been considered so immensely important, and few, at least since Plato and Aristotle, have been so thoroughly dissected. The results, as is to be expected with any work acutely examined by means of powerful methods of analysis, have been discoveries of incoherences and missing arguments and unsolved problems. Whether these faults are really there is uncertain and must remain uncertain, for it is now impossible, at least for anyone with any philosophical training — and only such people can read Kant at all — to consider Kant in a manner free from all that has been done to him during the last two hundred years. Consequently any attempt by anyone to say what Kant was really getting after is bound to elicit a reply from someone else with equally powerful claims that that was not at all what Kant was up to. Nevertheless professional philosophers continue to make noble and large-scaled efforts to settle the problem, although the state of philosophy today should make it quite obvious to anyone that no philosophical problem, let alone the Kantian problem, can be settled.

It would seem not only idle but even dangerous, then, to begin a discussion of the condition of European high culture with an attempt to say plainly why Kant thought he had brought about a Copernican revolution in philosophy. Yet the effort must be made; for not only did philosophers in the 19th century launch themselves from Kant, but a great many writers of all sorts as well. We must try to gain some notion, however approximate, of why Kant had such an impact upon European culture, and yet also why so many serious people at a high cultural level concluded that, in spite of the immense and extraordinarily demanding effort Kant had made to solve the basic problems of philosophy, the results were unsatisfactory. The issue was one of the highest importance. Clearly Kant was one of the greatest of philosophers, but just as clearly he was not interested in philosophy for philosophy's sake, in spite of the fact that he was the first truly professional philosopher; his effort was rather to determine the condition of man in the world and the relation of man to the world in which he finds himself. That man in the course of history had indeed found himself among other objects in the world, had indeed managed, through philosophy, *to get his own attention,* was what Kant was mostly deeply interested in.

Having found himself, what according to Kant had man found? Simply, that self-discovery is itself the essence of the historical process. Hence there must be historical consequences. Man has a future.

But what does that future hold? Fortunately it is possible to dispense with the grandiose panoply of the three critiques, the three analyses of reason, pure and practical, and judgment (very much the same thing). After all, that immense structure, quite old-fashioned (even medieval) in many ways, was designed to impress philosophers, a class of individuals notoriously and professionally difficult to convince of anything, and perhaps designed above all to impress Kant himself with his own philosophical competence. It is possible to dispense with all that because, happily, Kant said quite simply and clearly what his Copernican revolution amounted to. Anyone who has ever heard of Kant probably knows that he maintained that the mind cannot know the *ding-an-sich,* the thing-in-itself, the world as it really is. The explanation for this is that the reason, the highest of the various faculties of the mind (such as sensibility, understanding, imagination, judgment, intuition, and so on) has only a regulatory function in relation to those faculties. It can control what the mind does with those faculties, but it cannot of itself say anything about the world, or indeed about the transcendent — that is, about God. What this amounts to Kant himself stated clearly. Human beings know the world only in terms of human interests. We cannot know the world from any transcendent position, any position that transcends, rises above, looks down upon, is separate from, human interests. Thus we cannot say that there is any divine purpose to human history, but only what man's self-discovery can, it is to be hoped, accomplish.

Coming at the end of two and a half centuries of scientific advance, Kant was above all interested in understanding science and how scientific advance is possible. So he postulated in man an innate capacity for invention, but he also saw individual human beings as egotistic, interested above all in their own individuality, a necessary consequence of self-discovery. He saw individuals as basically unsocial but as gradually coming to the realization that unsociability could be fulfilled only by sociability. He saw as the necessary result a condition of universal peace, a condition in which the competition of inventiveness leads not to war but to a condition in which the pure reason regulates all behavior. It leads to a condition in which the irrational, perhaps best understood as self-destructive inventiveness, or asocial inventiveness, is finally eliminated. The reason, then, can convert egotistic and individualistic unsociability into a sociability which does not compromise either egotism or individualism: does not, that is, compromise man's competitive inventiveness. Man, then, can know nature only in terms of human interests, even though man is a product of nature. Between reason and nature there is an uncrossable abyss.

One man mounted a powerful attack upon Kant, an attack that seems more impressive now than it did in the 1790s when it was dismissed with contempt, the usual philosophical polemic strategy, by Kant and his followers. Yet in this disagreement with Kant, it can be said with some justice that Johann Gottfried Herder had the better of the argument. He attacked Kant on three points. To begin with, he asserted that Kant was guilty of reifying or hypostatizing such words as reason, understanding, and the rest of Kant's facultative assemblage. That is, Herder maintained, Kant had mistakenly asserted that such words refer to actual entities. Herder had behind him a profoundly original conception of language. According to theologians language had been a gift of God, implanted in man by divine power. According to rationalistic philosophers, language had emerged from the operations of the mind. Not so, Herder maintained. Language, he asserted, had emerged from the interaction of primitive human beings. It had neither a divine nor a metaphysical origin. It was a product of nature. Furthermore, he maintained, in talking about the mind Kant was merely talking about covert verbal behavior, man talking silently to himself, thus reiterating a notion first proposed in the seventeenth century. Kant's faculties, then, were but linguistic modes, or, one might say, rhetorics. There are no mental faculties, then. When a man does anything, whether he is engaged in a nonverbal action or in a verbal action, the whole man is involved. Finally, Herder made an extraordinarily acute point, one which is an important guide to the whole enterprise of the Enlightenment. He insisted that Kant, in talking about the irrational, was only re-introducing by the back door the Christian concept of original sin. These were the most powerful arguments he made in his campaign against Kant, particularly in two books, the *Megakritik* of 1799 and the *Kalligone* of 1800.

Herder's experience in life had been as different from Kant's as could be, and his intellectual life was even more strikingly antithetical. He came from the same part of Europe as Kant, the Eastern Baltic, and indeed had studied under Kant in Königsberg. But whereas Kant spent his entire life in Königsberg, Herder had wandered to Western Europe, to France, to various places in Germany, and had ended up in Goethe's Weimar, a town and a culture to which we shall return. Even so, his greatest work was published in Riga, *Ideen zur Philosphie der Geschichte der Menscheit* (*Ideas for the Philosophy of the History of Mankind*), published in four parts from 1784-1791, and its successor, highly miscellaneous in content, *Briefe zur Beförderung der Humanität* (*Letters on the Advancement of Humanity*) 1793-1797. In the first of these he shows an astonishing erudition, a knowledge most unusual for his time of areas of the world outside Europe. The work was designed to continue in the most inclusive manner the basic notion of his ideas about language. Man had emerged from nature, had links with non-human organic nature, had moved through primitive life to historical life, to civilization. But above all, each race and each nation has had its own character. Its achievements are not to be understood or judged by supra-cultural standards of European rationality, but in terms of the situation from which it had emerged, including geography and climate, and the cultural situation which it had created. Each culture, past or present, has its own unique character, and it must be understood in terms of that uniqueness. What Herder offered was a remarkably full-blown cultural relativism. But at the same time, as the *Letters* make clear, he was at one with Kant in his distinction between mankind and humanity. In man there is an essence, humanity, founded upon nature and derived from it — an essence which is primarily social in character and which moves steadily in spite of ups and downs toward a progressive future. There is a purpose or teleology in history, and that purpose is freedom and progress, a progress to be measured in man's adaptation to the nature from which he had emerged. And so the antithesis between Kant and Herder resolves itself into an antithesis between nature and reason, Kant, as we have seen, on the side of a reason which separates man from nature, Herder on the side of man's progressive understanding of his place in nature; this understanding through culture and cultural relativism of his destiny was one of freedom and happiness through his progressive mastery not of nature but of his oneness with nature.

It was once asserted that the Enlightenment was the Age of Reason, and that Herder was therefore an anomaly in the 18th century. But we can no longer accept that simplicity. Rather we can see Herder as much a man of the Enlightenment as was Kant, and we can also see that by the end of the 18th century the Enlightenment had developed within itself a profound incoherence. To understand that incoherence is to be able to understand both the French Revolution and that re-action against it — that heroic effort to transcend the incoherence of the Enlightenment, that effort which for want of a better term is known as Romanticism, a term which by an awkward and misleading convention merely subsumes the individuals who made that effort but is not to be thought of as in itself giving any information about them at all, except that they made that effort of cultural transcend-ence. But in order to   understand that incoherence and how it emerged and why, it is necessary to turn back to the early fifteenth century and examine the intellectual revolution that then took place.

To begin with, we may take a cue from Kant. If we know the world only in 'terms of human interests, we know it only in terms of cate-gories human beings have developed. Thus whatever we may encounter, we have to interpret it in terms of those categories. During the middle ages the world was interpreted in categories derived from the Bible by theological speculation and derived by philosophy from melting together the Greek and Roman tradition of thinking about the world with Judaeo-Christian modes. In interpreting the documents of Roman history, for example, medieval thought judged Cicero to be a bad man. The explanation was that he was a defender of the Roman Re- . public against Caesar, Antony, and Octavius, the last of whom was destined to found the Roman Empire and on Antony's urging had Cicero killed. But medieval theory saw the Roman Empire as divinely instituted to provide protection for the coming Christian Church and to be, in the course of time, its secular arm. So, it followed, Cicero was a bad man because he was an enemy of the will of God.

In the early 15th century, however, certain historians of Florence began to consider this problem differently. They pointed out that Cicero could scarcely have known of the future Roman Empire or of its divinely assigned task. On the contrary, having been born in 106 B.C. he rightly defended the Republic. The Republic was what he had been born into and what he had been brought up to help sustain by means of his legal profession. The values of the Republic were his values, and he could have known no other. He could see Caesar, Antony, and Octavius only as men who were aiming at the destruction of what he most valued. In maintaining as best he could those Republican values at a time of great political difficulty and disturbance he was clearly to be judged to be a good man, even a noble man, though with understandable failings. This reversal of the traditional judgment of Cicero was a cultural re-direction of the utmost importance. Something in the world — and Cicero was judged to have been something in the world, not just a name in documents — was no longer to be judged by theological-philosophical categories, but, rather, in relation to the situation of which that something is a part and from which it emerges. This new mode of interpreting the world was the heart of that cultural revolution we call the Renaissance; that mode is a very complex notion, and high culture ever since has been devoted to comprehending what is at stake in such interpretation.

What was involved can be understood by examining the early 15th century invention, also in Florence, of "scientific" perspective, first theoretically mastered by Brunelleschi and first used by his friend Masaccio in his huge fresco of the Trinity in Florence's Santa Maria Novella, painted in 1427. "Scientific" perpective makes it possible to render a scene from a single point of view rather than, as had been the case with the preceding devices for indicating spatial regression, from multiple points of view. What this does is to give the artist control over the situation he is painting. The movement toward such situational interpretation appears in paintings of lives of saints. In the early 15th century painters began to abandon a mode of painting in which several incidents of a saint's life were presented in the same landscape setting or interior or at times both. Now began the attempt to present the saint in a setting in which he might have lived, and in each setting but a single incident. Or, when the painter decided on a scene from the classic world, either historical or mythological, he no longer presented the actors in medieval costumes and medieval architecture, but attempted to present them in classic costumes and architecture.

The implications of the new way of painting emerge when one considers that the new conception of perspective was indeed "scientific," that is, mathematical, based on solid geometry. So in situational interpretation two factors are at work — the factors or elements in the situation and a rationally determined control over those elements. But that rational control is necessarily selective. The painter could no longer paint two configurations simultaneously if his single point of view concealed one behind the other. He could no longer simply place the concealed figure above the visible figure, so that both were given in the painting. To use Kant's notion — who was primarily interested in understanding why science had been so successful — this cultural transcendence of the Renaissance was an enormous step forward in man's self-discovery.

A parallel cultural event was the emergence of what has long since been known as Renaissance Humanism, which has been accounted, with fair accuracy, as the scientific attempt to understand the Greek and Roman texts. It has been called, along with various other epithets that have been used to describe it, the Revival of Learning. Like the historians who thought anew about the problem of Cicero, the first great humanist, Lorenzo Valla (1407-1457) began to think in terms of the situation in which an event or document or artifact originally appeared. Only he was more radical and thorough than his historical predecessors. He faced the problem of how one should properly interpret a text, insisting that his medieval predecessors had misinterpreted the texts of Roman culture. It came down, he thought, to determining the meaning of a word, and to do that one had first to understand the history of the word, its use as could be best determined in a variety of texts, and then its use in the particular text one was working with. But to control one's interpretation of that word one had to examine other texts of the same period, that is, of the situation from which the text in question emerged. This "situationism" was the origin of what has come to be called the philological-historical method of literary and historical and legal scholarship. It was, like perspective, an important step in man's self-discovery, and of the same kind. One no longer applied naively and without question the categories one had learned, but instead one had to become aware of the categorical determinants of one's interpretation, and above all one had to create by scholarship new and more appropriate categories, categories derived from, one hoped, the generating situation of both word and text, just as in using or responding to perspective one became self-conscious of the rational determinants of interpretation. Humanistic scholarship had to be rational; one was faced with a set of documents, or texts, as a set to which new documents were constantly being added. One had to limit, somehow, the set of documents to be studied, and one had to limit the modes of interpretation one employed. Selection was essential, as in perspective painting, and that selection had to be rationally controlled by fresh principles of philology and history.

From that Renaissance cultural context of situational interpretation emerged not only humanistic scholarship but also modern science. In the 15th century the great effort was the improvement of mathematical tools for the purposes of scientific investigation, and in the 16th century those tools had become so refined that it could be demonstrated that the sun did not go around the earth, but rather that the earth and other planets go around the sun. And from that situation evolved in the 17th century the experimental method, still crude and unrefined, but usable and capable of producing astonishing results, changing the whole conception of the world. So dumbfounding were the discoveries of Galileo and the other early scientists, we now see that a more exact definition of the experimental method is needed. It amounts to this: do not ascribe truth to a sentence merely because it has been, it is claimed, logically deduced from sentences of more general purport, but do so if, and only if, the sentence can give you directions for so manipulating the physical world that you can interpret the sentence as having predicted the consequences of that manipulation. What this amounts to is another transformation of situational thinking. Briefly, consider the object in question in terms of the situation in which you find it, but control that consideration by a rationally constructed hypothesis.

The results of this mode of situational interpretation were so spectacular that it is not surprising that cultural history has emphasized the scientific strain in the culture of the post-Renaissance era. Above all, philosophy was necessarily concerned with the consequences of science for epistemology. The relation of the mind to the world had to be completely rethought, and in the middle of the new 17th century Descartes sat down and tried to think it through from scratch. Kant, as we have seen, was still working on it in the 1780s, and, in following the tradition of concentration upon the rational control of situational thinking, devoted himself, as had his predecessors, to trying to understand how the reason works — that reason which controls or regulates our interpretations of the world.

But Herder, however, like his great early 18th-century predecessor, the Neapolitan Giambattisto Vico (1668-1744), whose writings he may or may not have known, was working in the other tradition of situational thinking, the situation itself. Until fairly recently it was considered quite puzzling that Vico and then Herder, apparently quite independently, each arrived at a theory of human culture. It seemed to have come out of nothing at all, out of their sheer genius. But now we know better. We know that cultural history has erred in concentrating on the scientific and philosophical developments from 1400 to 1800, and that the philological-historical tradition was just as important. Now it appears that the most significant development was in the legal studies of certain Frenchmen in the 16th and 17th centuries, a tradition of historical legalism with which Vico, trained as a lawyer, was quite familiar. Culture in this sense means merely the humanly created situation in which human beings find themselves, from which they emerge, and which controls what they can think and do, which is even the limiting frame for innovation and invention. But both Vico and Herder saw that culture emerged from nature, that indeed it was a manifestation or emanation of nature. Hence arose an ambiguity, or a confusion, in understanding the cultural developments during the centuries which led up to and culminated in the Enlightenment.

In the documents of that period, "nature" can mean the physical nature over which science was extending its control, a nature which was utterly remote from the ordinary concerns of human beings — astronomy, physics, chemistry, optics, and in the middle of the 18th century, electricity. And all of these were still in a fairly primitive condition. It was not, for example, until well into the 19th century that the universe could be understood as not packed solid to infinity with solar systems but, rather, as inhabited by vast constellations of suns, or island universes, separated by enormous empty space. On the other hand, "nature" meant "human nature," the nature of artifacts, texts, social interaction, and in time — a most important matter for understanding the late 18th century — the physiological nature in which man's mind or self-consciousness or soul or whatever found its place and from which it had emerged. One "nature" was interested in the rational control of the interpretational act; the other "nature" was interested in the situation which was being interpreted, and above all in the emergence of rational control from a cultural situation.

From what has been called here situational interpretation, then, emerged the late Enlightenment incoherence of reason and nature. The disagreement between Kant and Herder emerged from the inherent complexity and hidden difficulties and problems of situational interpretation. That disagreement survives today, for example in the arguments about whether a given bit of behavior can be traced to heredity or environment. Or in the current quarrels over whether human behavior is under genetic control or under cultural control or, indeed, whether it is even possible to decide that question, since any decision must be a cultural product.

In the 1790s there were very few people as intellectually sophisticated as Kant and Herder. Perhaps there were none. These two were virtually unique. They had followers, of course, as well as predecessors, but their followers only quarrelled with each other, with no understanding that they really had the same quarrel, that their disagreements had emerged from two disparate traditions of understanding the same problem. Moreover at a lower level of culture and intellectual sophistication there was not even a quarrel. Reason and nature were naively identified. Or rather, it was believed that in political, religious, and general social arrangements reason had gone astray from nature, and that the great human task was to restore the identity of reason and nature.

What had happened was the secularization of European culture at the high cultural levels. The religious tradition asserted that ours is a fallen world, and that man has inherited from the rebellion of Adam a sinful nature. He could be restored to his original innocence only after death, in heaven — if he was either good or, if a Calvinist, lucky. However, astronomy and mathematics had demonstrated that ours is not a fallen world, and that a creative deity, if there had been one — and more and more people were beginning to doubt even that — had created a mathematically perfect, or at least a rationally comprehensive, universe. Deity had set up natural laws which man can discover by the sheer power of human reason, most splendidly confirmed by modern science. It followed that man is not a fallen creature, inherently and by inheritance from Adam evil, but an innocent creature, a good creature. Nature is the creation of God, and Man is the creation of nature. As Herder had shown, language itself emerges from the "naturally" social interaction of human beings. Man's social arrangements had become oppressive and tyrannous because of the attempt to control inherent human evil, which did not exist, and because of the effort of men who believed in that inherent evil to take advantage of their fellow men by exploiting that evil in themselves and others.

Man, then, had misinterpreted his relation to the situation in which he finds himself. This was what lay behind the 18th century adulation of the world of Greece and Rome. To be sure, those ancient men may not have had the knowledge that modern science has given us, but on the other hand they were innocent of the notion of original sin. They felt at home in the world. They were at one with the situation from which they had emerged and in which they lived. Hence their ease and their greatness. For many 18th century thinkers the classic world was a secularized substitution for the rejected Christian paradise. It followed that man's self-conscious mastery of reason would make it possible to create a social reality in which reason and nature would be unified. As we have seen, even Kant could not resist that vision. Heaven lay in the future, on earth, in nature; and the 18th century was filled with Utopian visions.

One of the most important corollaries of this secularized thinking emerged in the early 18th century and became of the highest importance about the middle of the century: newly emergent values of feeling, emotion, sentiment, and sensibility which quickly came, for example, to dominate the arts. The European moral tradition had been repressive, even stoic. On the one hand was the ascetic tradition, the Puritan tradition, the repression and control of emotions, for they led to an indulgence in the natural world, the fallen world, and to the neglect of the sole object of man, his rescue from sin and his restoration to innocence in heaven, after death. On the other hand in so far as man was social and public he required every possible aid in architecture, furniture, clothing, enormous wigs, elaborate public and courtly ceremony — all to sustain in a noble and stately behavior a magnificence of repression, a magnificence itself an emblem of the magnificence of the creative deity, and of that deity's authority.

But emergent natural thinking now saw all this splendor as an artificial aid to priestcraft and tyranny. It was seen for what it indeed was, a strategy to contain and restrict emotion. But are not emotion and feeling and sensibility and the rest natural products of the body's response to the world through the senses, and is not the quivering of the senses a proper guide to man's relation to his situation? Emotional lability became the culture of the present, the mid-18th century, the century of the new culture, the natural culture. It became rational to enjoy, even rapturously, the irregularity of the unfallen natural world, which gardens should imitate. It was unnatural and pseudo-rational to enjoy gardens laid out in mathematical perfection. A garden should be a reflection or at most an intensification of the natural situation in which it was created. It should not be a mathematical emblem of a transcendent paradise. All of the natural world is the unfallen Garden of Eden, and our response to it should be one of sensibility, of sentiment, of feeling, of emotion. And we should dress accordingly, in clothes fitted to the natural contours of the body, and we should dispense with wigs. Hence the great task of man is to create anew, or to newly create, a social world in which reason and nature are one, and the dynamic power to achieve that world could be found by releasing the passions of man from artificial and unnatural and tyrannous restraint. And that is exactly what the intellectual leaders, or ideologues, of the French Revolution set out to do.

Against the background of five years of the French Revolution, from the fall of the Bastille in 1789 to the death in 1794 of that great doctrinaire of reason and nature Robespierrre under the knife of his beloved guillotine, the quarrel between Herder and Kant took place. The most salient consequence of those five years, the consequence that leaps out, was that the ideologically controlled attempt to create a social world both natural and reasonable, a world in which man would regain the liberty, the equality, and the fraternity which nature had originally given him, led directly to the Revolutionary Terror. It became clear to at least a few thoughtful Europeans that the only way to free mankind was to kill all the people who did not accept an ideology of how to achieve that freedom. The Terror came to an end simply because there was no way to limit it, no way derivable either from nature or reason, and certainly not derivable from the release of passions from repression. At first most European intellectuals and artists welcomed the French Revolution. It meant that something could be done about a socio-political system that was becoming increasingly unacceptable. But by 1795 most of these intellectuals and artists were appalled at what had happened, and even more appalled by the development in France of an increasingly narrow dictatorship, finally emerging in the military dictatorship of Napoleon. This heir to the Revolution ended up by helplessly indulging in a magnificent but garish and vulgar parody of the old regime, including everything from a restored court ceremonial to dynastic alliances. But Napoleon was the true heir of the Revolution because he had learned the Revolution's terrible lesson: a population can be ideologically and rationally controlled, and that rational control must be maintained by extremes of force and an arbitrarily monitoring secret police. Whoever does not define the situation as the ideology does must be killed or otherwise rendered ineffective. Napoleon's secret police were the heirs of the Revolution's Committees of Public Safety, those surveilling watch-dogs of the imagined People.

What the descent of the sublime French Revolution into the degradation of the Terror meant, and means, was that the categories which man creates to understand and control the situations of the world can neither exhaust the attributes of any situation nor can set up limits to that situation except arbitrarily, as in the arbitrary limits set up in the experimental laboratory. Thus Reason and Nature can never be reconciled. Or to put it in another way, between subject and object, between mind and world, there is an irresolvable tension. Is there then a Kantian abyss between the knower and the unknowable thing-in-itself? Not quite, for the one criticism of his system that Kant found interesting was the suggestion that that unknowable thing-in-itself is simply what we do not yet know. Here was an obscure recognition that no situation which we investigate has rationally determinable limits or boundaries.

But it is not to be maintained that very many at the time fully understood this, or indeed that anyone then did. Still, here and there in Europe, a few artists, a few thinkers, perhaps initially fewer than twenty, understood the most important lesson of the French Revolution and of the Terror. Something was seriously wrong, seriously in error, seriously, fundamentally mistaken in the very structure of European intellectual and artistic culture, at its very highest and most intellectually and artistically sophisticated level. European culture had to be thought through from its foundations. Whatever was wrong had to be transcended. These few individuals were the individuals we call the Romantics.

Joseph Haydn   It is not enough to understand the philosoph-
(1732-1809)   ical and ideological situation against which the
first Romantics struggled and which they endeavored to transcend. To grasp what the Romantic artists were trying to do, it is necessary to comprehend the stylistic character of the non-verbal arts of the Enlightenment in the 1790's — architecture, painting, and music. It is useful to begin with music, for the later compositions of Joseph Haydn present with striking clarity the cultural character of the period.

First, however, one must examine the musical development of the last half of the 18th century, a period marked by the concentration of instrumental music on what has now come to be known as the

Sonata style and still more generally called the Classic style. The origins of that style are not entirely clear, but for the present purposes it is enough to say that its character began to emerge and to be clarified in the 1750s, particularly in the work of Carl Philipp Emanuel Bach, from whom Haydn averred that he had learned more than from anyone else. Baroque music and even its immediate successor, *style galant,* was controlled by the notion of *affekt.* The idea was that each movement should be completely dominated by a single emotional character. But the word "emotional" and the term "emotional expression" are not sharp enough to grasp what music is concerned with. Music, like all the arts, like all language, is an interpretation of the world. Yet, except when it deliberately reproduces non-musical sounds, music can be more precisely characterized as an interpretation of emotional response to the world. But for this we need an understanding of the word "emotion" marked by as much precision as possible.

We live in an interpreted world. Perception itself is an act of selective and structuring interpretation; it has recently been compared to a scientific hypothesis. Every perception (i.e., interpretation) has two aspects, the cognitive and the emotive, but neither can be understood without recognizing that both are aspects of culture regarded as instructions for behavior; but culture continuously modified by the individual's interpretations. As instruction, culture requires that two questions, as it were, be asked about every stimulus field; first, What is it? and second, How should I regulate my response to it? The answers to the first question are cognitive; the answers to the second are emotive — that is, the response takes the form of having an effect upon and modifying the physical system, specifically the musculature. And this modification in turn has an effect upon the cognitive processes by becoming part of the stimulus field to which the brain is responding. These emotive responses to the stimulus field interpret it first, culturally, as either guidance or hindrance: and second as a stimulus field toward which a level of aggression ranging from high to low is appropriate. By aggression is meant here that the organism has no choice but to manipulate the stimulus field, including its own body, to what it cognitively judges to be its benefit. (The choice of what to manipulate, the field or the body, is a cognitive-emotive activity.)

What music does is to use the intonation which is part of all linguistic behavior and, in animal behavior, preceded the existence of language, to indicate semiotically, that is, by means of a culturally conventionalized sign system, guidance and hindrance by the regularity and irregularity of rhythm; and since the early 17th century, in a great enrichment of musical semiosis, by the distinction between major (guidance) and minor (hindrance) keys. The level of aggression is semiotically indicated by the movement from low pitch to high, by the level of volume, and by tempo, from slow to fast. In combination these musical elements make possible a "language" of emotions of infinite richness and of the utmost precision. As Mendelssohn said, music is more precise than language itself. For example, music can signify emotional changes with a rapidity totally unavailable to language. The precision of music was wonderfully increased by the musical style of the late 18th century.

[It is obvious to me that a great many readers will find the above account either too concise to be comprehensible or quite unacceptable, since they cannot countenance the notion that music has, or can be said to have or bear, "meaning." I have added an Appendix in which I attempt to show why both the position that music is meaningful and the position that it is not meaningful are, at least in their usual form, deficient, and also to propose an explanation of the meaningfulness of music, or more precisely, an explanation of why meaning is so widely, almost universally, ascribed to music — an explanation that will, I hope, be found less deficient than the usual positions on this difficult and vexing subject.]

As we have seen, until the middle of the 18th century the dominating morality was the ascetic or stoic or socio-political control of the emotions, a morality which controlled the decisions of all artists in painting, architecture, literature, costume, interior decor, and so on. In music the 17th century theory of affects meant that one emotion controlled all other emotions, in the sense that when one affect was dominant, any other emotion was scarcely permitted to appear. In opera, for example, an aria presented the character's emotional response to the situation, and it was an exploration of that single response. It was externally dramatic. It examined the character's interpretation of the behavior of the character to whom the singer was responding as either hindrance or guidance — or of the character's own behavior. But it was not internally dramatic; it did not present an alteration or shifting from one interpretation to another. It was emotionally stable.

A change began to come over music, however, in the years before the middle of the century. This was the development of the style called *Empfindsamkeit,* the German for sentiment or sentimentalism. Its master was Carl Philipp Emanuel Bach. It expressed the new morality, the morality of nature, of irregularity, of emotional lability. In the literature and poetry of the time the shedding of tears became a positive value, and the music of *Empfindsamkeit* was designed to elicit tears from an audience, an audience to be sure already prepared to weep. The man of feeling became an ideal type, a man so responsive to the quivering of his senses that he burst into tears at the slightest provocation or, better, at the slightest opportunity. From this culture of emotional lability emerged the 18th century sonata and the classic style, both rebellions against the rational control of emotional response.

The key word of this new moral culture was *adaptation* or, in another form, *adaptability,* specifically adaptability to one's own physiological organism. For the artist the new morality of adaptability had a further instruction. He had to create in such a way that the audience experienced a reduction in the output of cognitive energy required to make a perceptual accommodation and adaptation to the work. The classic style, then, may be understood as a clarification of the style of *Empfindsamkeit.* Although the word is German, principally because German musicology dominated musical theory so long, that development can be seen as well in the music styles of England, France, and Italy. By a historical accident the two greatest masters of the classic style were from the Germanic culture area. Both Mozart and Haydn were Austrian, and the classic style reached its highest level in Vienna, even though, as we shall see, the culminating works were written for London.

The first musical consequence of the new morality for interpreting the world and presenting that interpretation in music was that a movement of an instrumental work should no longer be dominated by a single affect but should shift rapidly from one affect to another. In the keyboard sonatas of C. P. E. Bach this meant frequent changes of key, apparently quite willful, and a melodic line extravagant and even at times wildly bizarre. The new morality of music had not yet been extended to the audience. In the 1760s Christoph Willibald Gluck, setting out to reform opera in accordance, he said, with nature, presented his first such work in Vienna, *Orfeo ed Euridice* (1762), using once again the subject of the first operas to have survived from the beginning of the 17th century. Now the aria became internally dramatic, presenting the ebb and flow of emotion with shifts from despair to hope and back again; within the same aria the character interpreted his situation as both guidance and hindrance. But Gluck was also guided by the ideas of the beautiful and of the sublime — ideas which did not suppress emotional lability but rather organized it to the moral need of the audience for easy adaptation. Formally, this meant a movement towards continuity rather than the extreme formal discontinuity of *Empfindsamkeit*.

Gluck also made an important step toward formal clarification by intensifying the polarity between the major and minor modes, beyond Baroque style and *Empfindsamkeit*. Further, he greatly reduced the frequency of key changes. Indeed, he was even accused by older composers of harmonic incompetence, that is, by men who did not understand what was happening in the cultural situation. The polarity of major and minor meant an increased precision in determining whether the interpretation of emotion was a judgment of guidance or hindrance; together with the reduction of frequency of key changes it lowered the demands on the audiences for cognitive energy. The latter also made it possible to contemplate and respond to an interpretation before another interpretation took its place. In the 1760s, the decade of Gluck's reforms, Haydn in remote Eszterház near Hungary was making the same developments in symphonies, chamber music, and solo instrumental works. Engaged in instrumental composition, Haydn began to establish the pattern of the sonata form: first an allegro, then an andante or adagio, then a faster movement in the minuet, and a still faster one in the fourth movement — or a three-movement plan, fast-slow-faster. But these tempo indications, though commonly used, are not enough to indicate what was going on in the sonata, which by the end of the century dominated almost all musical forms.

The first-movement plan came to be characterized by (1) a presentation of thematic material which moved harmonically from the tonic (whatever key the movement began with) to the dominant (the key of a fifth above the tonic); (2) the repetition of the material; then (3) a development of the thematic material, or some of it, in various keys (sometimes more interestingly called the argument); finally (4) a repetition of the opening presentation entirely in the opening key, that is, the tonic. But this is not in fact much of a change, for the scale of the dominant has only one note different from the scale of the tonic. It has been suggested that 18th century ears were more subtly attuned to key changes than ours, but this is doubtful. Key change was simply made barely perceptible in accordance with the principle of reducing the demand on the adaptive perceptual energy of the audience. This fairly elaborate plan of the first movement in a sonata meant that the first movement presented the highest level of emotional lability. The second movement, modelled on the Gluckian operatic aria, reduced that level. A common plan was the presentation of a melody in the major, followed by a second melody in the minor, followed by a repetition, with variation, of the first melody once again in the major. The third movement reduced the emotional lability still further, for it was a dance, a minuet, again a three-part form: a tune, another tune in a contrasting key, and a repetition of the first tune. But each section of each tune was repeated, again and again. Such repetition further reduced the demands upon the accommodation of the audience, but to our ears it can often become tiresome. The fourth movement was faster, but ordinarily far less elaborate than the first, even when it was written in the first-movement form. There was more repetition than in the first movement, and it had a more consistent emotional character than any of the first three movements. It tended to be lighter and easier, moving rapidly with little or no hindrance and with little harmonic change.

The best word to describe it is "frolicsome." But there was a further difference among the movements. Each movement tended to be shorter than the preceding movement. Thus the task of the audience became progressively easier as the work proceeded, so that toward the end it had so little of a task that it was virtually instructed to relax and take it easy.

Music, in short, was conceived of as civilized entertainment, and the smaller the audience the more serious was that entertainment. Thus Haydn's piano sonatas have been called his most personal music. That may be doubted; rather for an audience of one, in which the performer is the audience, or for an audience of but a few, a more serious and perceptually demanding and even troubling experience was possible. For such listeners are isolated and psychically protected; isolation and such protection are the conditions for sustained problem exposure.

In the 1790s the music of Haydn underwent a striking change, a change that makes it more accessible to today's taste. Indeed, until recently most of Haydn's music known even to cultivated musicians and music-lovers was written in the 1790s. To understand this change it is necessary to consider how the composer had spent the preceding thirty years. In the 1750s Haydn was a free-lance composer in Vienna, leading a life which was necessarily, under the social conditions of the mid-18th century, a very difficult one financially. But in 1760 or 1761 he entered the service of Prince Esterházy. The Prince was one of the greatest noblemen of Europe. His enormous estates were in what is now eastern Austria and western Hungary, south-east of Vienna, and there he maintained two residences, Eisenstadt and Eszterház. These were palaces with vast formal gardens and all kinds of other buildings, including dormitories and apartments for servants, and even, in time, the Prince's own charming opera house. The staff was huge, including everything from chamberlains and musicians down to stable-boys. The Prince lived on a scale surpassed by only a few European monarchs. In 1761 Haydn became his Kapellmeister, in charge of all musical activities, instrumentalists, choruses, church music, operas, theater. But Haydn's title should not mislead us. He was a servant, and wore the Prince's livery. He wrote music to order, for whatever occasion the Prince had in mind. The Prince played the baryton, a now obsolete instrument of the string family, and for the Prince's delectation Haydn composed 33 sonatas for one or two barytons. In the 1770s and the 1780s he was required to compose a number of operas, though either his talent for opera or his interest was limited. In 1785 he was at last permitted to compose on commission for other noblemen and for music publishers in Vienna and elsewhere. That was possible because he already had a European reputation, since he had been permitted to publish much of the music he wrote for his Prince. In 1789 Prince Nikolaus Esterházy died, and his successor Prince Anton had little interest in music. Haydn was continued on full salary, but was permitted to move to Vienna. But he did not stay there long. In 1789 Johann Peter Salomon, a concert manager in London, heard that Prince Nikolaus was dead and that Haydn was free. Salomon at once left for Vienna. In December, 1790, Haydn set out for London, to give a series of concerts of music written especially for London audiences. A highly significant decision was to go from Vienna down the Rhine and through the Low Countries. Paris had to be avoided because of the disturbances there from the French Revolution.

During his London residencies in 1791-1792 and 1794-1795 the music that Haydn composed, symphonies and piano trios, even an opera for various reasons unperformed, rose in a short time to a new level. In the 1780s there was little development in his style, not surprising for a composer in his fifties, more or less isolated in remote Hungary. His style was on a plateau. When he first set off for London he was half way into his fifty-ninth year. What happened was an extraordinary renewal of his musical energies, in itself one of our best indicators of the cultural situation in the 1790s. His music becomes more serious, more passionate. Amusement becomes gaiety, at times almost demonic. For symphonies he uses a slow introduction, often in the minor, consciously sublime, presenting a struggle against powerful hindrance. In quiet slow movements there are sudden outbursts, volcanic in the energy released and in the aggressiveness displayed. Or at times there is just the opposite. In certain symphonies and in some of the wonderful piano trios and string quartets, particularly the last ones of 1795 and 1796, the emotional interpretation is sustained depression, unrelieved hindrance against which no aggressive attack seems possible. At the same time the harmonic, melodic, and instrumentational inventiveness reveals an imagination and power which could not have been predicted from his earlier music. If one listens in chronological order to each major genre — quartets, trios, piano sonatas, symphonies — from the beginning of his musical career, one is constantly charmed, delighted, even enchanted, almost always at least entertained. But on arriving at the music of the 1790s one is moved and astonished. The last movements are no longer merely frolicsome but often almost manic in their presentation of unbroken energy and aggressiveness. At the same time, however, this music is formally clearer, more moving because it is easier to follow. Its passion is in part made possible by formal clarification and simplification. Perhaps Haydn had learned something from Mozart, who died in 1791. But even Mozart, so far ahead of Haydn in the 1780s, had rarely risen to the passionate intensity of Haydn's most powerful music of the 1790s.

What had happened? For the first time in his life Haydn was a free man, not the servant of a prince. Even when a new Prince Nikolaus Esterházy, the son of Prince Anton, asked Haydn in 1795 to resume his duties as Kapellmeister, he spent little time on the Esterházy estates, partly because the new prince spent as much time in Vienna as in Eisenstadt, the more distant Eszterház having been given up. For Eisenstadt Haydn composed only a few masses; his greatest energies went into writing *The Creation* and *The Seasons* for performance in Vienna, oratorios of a new level of sublimity, passion, and beauty — and clarity. He was at last free and independent. And now in 1790 came a recognition such as he had never received. He was invited to London, the capital of the freest country of Europe, the political ideal of innumerable Enlightenment political and social thinkers for more than three-quarters of a century. He could compose as he wished for the most sophisticated and cosmopolitan audience in Europe. He was completely successful. Oxford gave him an honorary degree, and royalty attended his concerts and received him. He experienced an ascription of value such as he had never enjoyed and had never anticipated, and he received it as a free and independent artist in the home of what freedom Europe could then offer.

My repetition of the word "free" is not by chance. For Haydn's London experience took place against the background of the French Revolution. We have seen that the artists and intellectuals of Europe welcomed enthusiastically the opening years of the Revolution. As the English politician Charles James Fox said, it was much the greatest event in history and much the best. Its leaders established a new mode of heroism, a mode in which European civilization has never forgotten and which has spread, for good or ill, throughout the entire world. The Iranian Revolution of 1978-1979, for example, would not and could not have happened without the model of the French Revolution of nearly two hundred years before. Heroism in the past had always been in the service of the *status quo,* the dominating ideology and socio-political arrangements. Even the Reformation heroes had been only a partial exception; the Reformation was but the reform of an ideology, though many of the French Revolutionary heroes thought of Luther and the others as, to a certain extent, models. But now there was a revolution in which the heroes were in the service of a new ideology — at least they thought it was new. They were heroes of an attack upon the *status quo.* They were proof that something could be done about a set of social arrangements which had kept Haydn all of his life in the status of a servant. The new Prince Nikolaus had to ask Haydn to resume his duties, and Haydn did so on his own terms. A man of the Enlightenment, he remained an Enlightenment musician until the end of his career and the composition of *The Seasons,* finished in 1801. After that he set a number of folk songs for a Scottish publisher, and that was all. He did not transcend Enlightenment culture, but like the greatest artists of the 1790s and the period's greatest political figures, he showed that a great leap is possible. In the 1790s Haydn became a hero of individual freedom. The Romantic composers could not have reached for a transcendence of European musical culture had not Haydn's great leap been their inspiration, their ideal, and their model.

Wolfgang Amadeus Mozart   On January 26, 1790, *Cosi fan tutte, ossia*
(1756-1791)   *La scuola degli amanti,* commissioned by
                            the Emperor Joseph II, received its first
public performance (Burgtheater, Vienna). It was the third and last
of the opera libretti Lorenzo da Ponte had written for Mozart, the
only quite original one and the only one of Mozart's operas the social
milieu of which was the middle class. Both the previous Da Ponte
operas (*Don Giovanni* and *Le nozze di Figaro*) had for their Enlightenment theme the dissoluteness and self-indulgence of a noble and his
defeat. *All Women Behave Alike* (an awkward title without the succinctness of the Italian) narrows the social perspective and concentrates upon the problem of emotional lability. One of Jane Austen's
titles, *Sense and Sensibility,* would do very well as a title for this
opera. An elderly Neapolitan officer wagers two of his younger colleagues that their sweethearts are fickle, as are all women. The young
officers pretend to be called away for military service but return disguised as Albanians and set out to woo each other's fiancée. And
they succeed. The girls, who had each sworn undying fidelity, fall
in love all over again. The masquerade is abandoned; the girls are
embarrassed; but all is forgiven. The lovers return to their original
partnerships. And in the final sextet we are told, "Happy the man
. . . who guides himself by reason."

But the question is, What should one be reasonable about? What
is the enemy of reason? Even if the libretto is not crystal clear, the
music clarifies. This is not a cynical work about women's fickleness.
It is about natural susceptibility, about sensibility, or, in its 18th
century sense, sentimentalism, not something to be condemned but
a trait of human behavior to be accepted and even admired as natural.
Mozart's instrumental music, even more than Haydn's since Mozart
was younger, evinces that sensibility of the classic style, and may be
heard very well in his two last instrumental works: the piano concerto
K. 595, completed in January, 1791, with it sudden alterations between
major and minor and its strange harmonic developments in the first
movement, and the clarinet concerto K. 622, written in October,
1791, with its gentle melancholy.

It has been suggested that the arias of the heroines of *Cosi fan tutte* are parodies because of their exaggerated emotionality. And the opera is usually played that way. But such a judgment is to misunderstand the sensibility of the late 18th century. The girls are truly suffering, but what is suggested is that they are suffering because they think they ought to. They are submitting to a cultural mode of their time. The point of the opera is not that they should be reasonable but rather that it is reasonable to expect young people to guide their emotions by a cultural norm, and also that that cultural mode is itself "natural." The work should not be played as farce but as a serious consideration of a recently recognized pattern of behavior, a pattern justified by what human beings are really made of, what truly controls them, their emotional susceptibility. The charm and enchantment of the music should govern the performance. The work is civilized; it is both compassionate and witty. Nor should the unhappiness of *Così fan tutte's* two young men be considered as absurd. We can be amused, but the amusement should be affectionate. The work is concerned with emotional sincerity, with the difficulties such sincerity can bring about, and with the moral requirement to be reasonable about those difficulties.

Mozart's two final operas were composed in the summer of 1791. *La Clemenza di Tito* may have been planned earlier, but it was completed for the coronation of the new German Emperor, Leopold II, as King of Bohemia, and first performed in Prague on September 6, 1791 (National Theater). *The Magic Flute* was mostly written before its companion but not completed until shortly before its first performance in Vienna (Theater auf der Wieden, September 30, 1791). The ideological contrast between these two works is immense. Pietro Metastasio (1698-1782) became court poet at the imperial court in Vienna in 1729, and in 1734 he wrote the libretto of *La clemenza di Tito* for Antonio Caldara (c. 1670-1736), an imperial court composer who had come to Vienna from Italy in 1716. Metastasio was concerned with giving literary dignity to opera libretti, and his success is indicated by the repeated setting of his libretti until the opening years of the 19th century. This libretto had been set by fourteen composers before Mozart took it up, perhaps because the most recent setting had been in 1771. It was used once again as late as 1798.

Mozart, however, did not use Metastasio's text unchanged. It was modernized by Caterino Mazzola, court poet of Saxony, a friend of Da Ponte's and recent arrival in Vienna. His aim was to provide more arias, carved from Metastasio's recitatives; that is, to give greater emotional variety to the work in accordance with contemporary taste. The result was certainly less formal and stoic than the original, but the theme remained the same. The story is simply of how Titus forgave a friend who, surrendering to passion, had attempted to assassinate him.

La clemenza di Tito is Baroque in its morality. Passion is reprehensible, and is presented as reprehensible in the two characters infected by it. But the theme is weightier than that, for the man who restrains his passion is an absolute monarch. It is Metastasio's conviction, as it was of most of his contemporaries, that an absolute monarchy is the ablest as well as the most rational form of political organization: an ideal monarch can rise above the failings of lesser mortals. The noble Roman Emperor Titus, then, was an ideal for all monarchs and a justification for absolute monarchy. As we have seen, that notion survived the French Revolution and Napoleon gave it as grand and convincing an exemplification as he could manage. Musically, this work of Mozart cannot be mistaken for an *opera seria* (the serious opera of the aristocracy) of the first half of the century, but it preserves the fundamental plan that each aria is not an exploration and modification and transformation of an emotional state but a meditation upon a single emotional condition and its moral justification. It was to remain popular for another forty years, so long as the absolutist reaction to the French Revolution remained in power and controlled what went on in opera houses. After that it virtually disappeared.

The Magic Flute is an entirely different matter. Ideologically it presents exactly the opposite judgment of absolute monarchy. The producer and singer, Johann Josef Schikaneder (1751-1812) composed the libretto in the tradition of Viennese popular musical comedy (*Singspiele*) — fairy-tale plots and spectacular productions. But it was far more than that, and far more serious. Joseph II, the best of the Enlightenment despots, had died in February, 1790, after having, in the preceding January, withdrawn all his reforms. Like all European monarchs, he was frightened by the French Revolution. To keep Enlightenment ideals before the public, and in the theater, was the problem Schikaneder and Mozart faced. Their solution was to set the story in ancient Egypt and to build the work around Masonic rituals and ideas, for not only were librettist and composer Masons but Joseph II had himself been a member of a Masonic lodge.

In the course of the Enlightenment two organizations emerged which had as their goal the reform of socio-political structure in accordance with the ideals of reason and nature and the coalescence of these antithetical ideals. These were the Masons and the Society of the Illuminati. The latter originated many of the ideas which were adopted in France and which the French revolutionaries attempted to put into effect. However, it must be recognized that the idea of a semi-secret organization in service to an ideology was not an original idea with either of these groups. Their model was the Society of Jesus, the Jesuits, founded in the 16th century to effect the spiritual (religious and moral) control of the papacy over the population of the world, beginning with Europe. Their immediate aim was the recovery for Roman Catholicism of these segments of the European population which had seceded to the various sects of Protestantism. The authority for the Jesuit ideology was revelation as interpreted by the Catholic Church. The Enlightenment ideal of the coalescence of nature and reason, in spite of its rejection of original sin, was basically a mere secularization of revelation. Since God had created both reason and nature, there could be no disjuncture between the two. That was the Deistic notion, whereas the atheistic notion merely did away with God. Even Robespierre was a Deist.

The Jesuit *modus operandi* was to infiltrate into centers of power and through education, moral intimidation, and seduction to gain control over the power-wielding and decision-making class, the monarchs and nobility of Europe, including the higher levels of the Church hierarchy. The history of the Jesuits is an exemplification of the adage that nothing fails like success. They became so powerful and wealthy that they resisted not only the spread of the emerging Enlightenment ideals and policies but distorted the operation of the very Church to which they were supposed to be in service and interfered with the monarchies. In 1764 they were expelled from Portugal and in 1767 from Spain; in 1773 Pope Clement XIV suppressed the Jesuit order. It is particularly significant for understanding *The Magic Flute* that Maria Teresa of Austria and her son Joseph II, co-regents from 1765 to 1780, withdrew their support from the Jesuits.

What the Masons and the Illuminati learned from the Jesuits is that a small number of individuals dedicated to a clear, consistent, reductionist, and simplistic ideology can be organized into a wide-spreading network of lodges or, in the terminology of the 19th century, cells, and from these centers can infiltrate the centers of power and ideology, such as educational systems, and seize control. The Jesuits established the pattern of bringing about a value revolution from behind the scenes. Their aim was to free man from sin; it was, then, anti-authoritarian. In practice, however, they both discovered and revealed that authoritarianism, not infrequently violent, fraudulent, subversive, and treacherous, is the means whereby freedom from sin is both established and maintained. The efforts of the Masons and the Illuminati to establish socio-political freedom were also anti-authoritarian, but the French Revolution repeated the experience of the Jesuits: violent authoritarianism is necessary to establish socio-political freedom and necessary to maintain it. Furthermore, the more innovative an ideology thus established, and the more it is in disagreement with the dominant ideology, the more violent its authoritarianism must be. It must always be remembered that Enlightenment ideology was entertained by only a very small segment of the European population, though not so tiny a segment as the Romantics were to be. Moreover, as the French Revolution developed, it became apparent that ideological and political control over a culture is not enough. Far more important, and far more basic, is economic control. And that is why, for example, the most radical of Revolutionary ideologists, Françoise-Emile Babeuf (1760-1797), proposed the destruction of the superstructure, political, economic, and cultural, and the reduction of the lives of all men to the simplest kind of agricultural economy.

The Jesuits also established another pattern of behavior of highest importance to both the Illuminati and the Masons, the pattern of induction into service. Recruits must be carefully chosen. They must be individuals susceptible to ideological manipulation, individuals too young to be ideologically committed or individuals ideologically dissatisfied. When such individuals have been brought to the proper level of ideological development, they are ready to be inducted into the organization — into a lodge or cell. To be successful, that induction must be a true ritual of initiation; it must be both terrifying and exalting; and it must include an oath of absolute, life-long allegiance to the ideology of the organization.

Mozart was writing his new opera in June, 1791, the month in which Louis XVI fled, was apprehended in Varennes, and was returned to Paris under guard. On September 14, between the premiers of *La clemenza di Tito* and *Die Zauberflöte,* Louis accepted the revised and completed constitution of France. On September 30, the date of the latter opera's premiere, the French National Assembly dissolved itself to make way for the Legislative Assembly, the supreme power under the new constitution. And this coincidence was not inappropriate, for the theme of *The Magic Flute* is the triumph of reason (the sun) over the tyranny (the night), the world of irrational authoritarian monarchy, a form of government which maintains itself by fraud and violence.

At the opening of the opera the Queen of the Night presents herself as the victim of the Priest of the Sun, Sarastro, who has, how we do not know, spirited away her daughter, Pamina. These then are the two principal antagonistic forces. Tamino and his love Pamina are the still naive and uncommitted youths whom the Queen wishes to seduce into her control. She gives Tamino the magic flute, which will protect him from harm. The flute, or music itself, is the old symbol of natural harmony and beauty; but the Queen has stolen it from the Temple of the Sun. Tamino and Pamina are both princes, potential inheritors of power. It is essential for the triumph of virtue and reason that they come under the beneficent control of Sarastro, whose world is not identical with that of Masonry but which uses certain Masonic emblems to identify itself with the enlightened spirit of Masonry. (That George Washington was a Mason was of the highest importance to European Masonry, whose members saw themselves as the planners and builders of a new social order.) Papageno and Papagena are emblems of natural man, essentially good in spite of moral weaknesses and redeemable to the forces of light. This potentiality is signified by Papageno's bells, a less organized form of music than a flute. Monostatos, the servant of Sarastro, betrays him, to demonstrate the seductive power of darkness and the potentiality of man to do evil; but what undermines him is his lust for Pamina, whom Sarastro has put in his charge. This touch brings out the sexual puritanism implicit in the Enlightenment, a usual attribute of reolutionary ideologies, intensified after a brief spell of sexual freedom if revolutionaries are successful in seizing power. Moreover, Monostatos' treason to his master and his seduction by the Queen of Night exemplify one of the major motives of the opera, the superiority of men over women. This anti-feminism is one of the inheritances of the Enlightenment from its source, Christianity, and a further indication that the Enlightenment was a secularization of Christianity. Only later in the 1790s did the equality of women become even a minor motive in Enlightenment ideology.

In the second act Tamino once again receives the flute, but this time from a beneficent source, the Three Boys in the service of Sarastro, who is the exemplar of reason and virtue. Tamino and Pamina pass through their initiatory trials — the terrifying — and are received in the temple of the Sun — the exalting; but not before Papageno and Papagena are united under the beneficent rule of Sarastro, to signify the union of nature and reason; and not before the Queen of the Night, her followers, and Monostatos are defeated in their attack on the Temple and plunged into a nether world of darkness. In the final scene Sarastro appears raised upon the altar of the Temple of the Sun. He hails the sun's power to drive away the night — the night of fraudulent power. The chorus celebrates the initiates, who have transcended the night and become emblems of beauty and wisdom.

In spite of its superficial complications and apparent confusions, the theme of *The Magic Flute* is as clear as one could wish. It is the conflict between malignant, destructive, and artificial forces, and virtuous, reasonable, and natural forces. The queen is all the monarchs of Europe, monarchy itself, but Sarastro is the chief of a band of beneficent and redeeming brothers. All well and good, but the conflict can also be understood as that between malignant authority and beneficent authority. Sarastro has Monostatos lashed. Here was the problem which the Enlightenment tradition has never solved. Are there limits to the power of beneficent authority; or is the power of beneficent authority unlimited? Robespierre was the Sarastro of the French Revolution. To maintain his beneficence he directed the Terror to its climax, and himself became the victim of the Terror. His heir was Napoleon.

Luigi Cherubini   Mozart died before anti-Revolutionary pow-
(1760-1842)   ers took arms against Revolutionary France.
                     Haydn was able to keep his distance, though
he was by no means unaffected by it. But were his masses, his oratories of the creation and of the seasons, the themes of which were the beneficence of the Christian creator, inspired by his response to the Terror? Was his librettist, the librarian of the Imperial Library, celebrating the virtues of the *ancien régime*? It may be so. One opera composer, however, lived through the Revolution itself and maintained the values of the Enlightenment, while at the same time responding to the passions released in Paris. That was Luigi Cherubini. For fifteen years, from 1773 to 1788, he was a typical successful itinerant Italian opera composer, providing *opere serie* and *opere buffe* for Florence, Venice, Rome, Livorno, Mantua, London, and Paris. Under the impact of the Revolution, however, he presented on July 18, 1791 (at the newly built Théâtre Feydeau, Paris), a new kind of opera, *Lodoïska*. True it was a rescue opera (an already established type in which an innocent person is delivered from prison), but its novelty was its combination of *opera seria* grandeur, *opera buffa,* the spoken dialogue and comic roles of the French comic opera, harmonic and instrumental resources never appearing in opera before, which Cherubini had learned from Haydn, and an attempt to present richly and realistically developed characterizations. It has been called a Romantic opera, because of these elements and because it was set in remote Poland, and it *was* a romantic opera — but only in the 18th century sense of that word.

To understand what Cherubini and his librettist had accomplished we must look back again to the 1750s and the 1760s, when the "natural" culture of emotional lability emerged, the culture of feeling, of sentimentalism, a period when Laurence Sterne presented characters of quivering sensibility in *Tristram Shandy* (1760-1767) and himself as such a man in *A Sentimental Journey* (1768), shortly to be followed by Henry Mackenzie's *The Man of Feeling* (1771). Two other terms emerged from that period, both nearly interchangeable with "feeling" and "sentiment" — the words "picturesque" and "romantic." The former subsumed the visual equivalent or symbolization of "feeling"; the irregular in landscape, the "natural." (We shall return to this in considering the painting of the 1790s.) "Romantic" meant the use of themes and settings from the middle ages and the early Renaissance, for these were the ages of the romances, stories in verse and prose centering on the courts of Arthur and Charlemagne and a medieval version of Troy. The morality of such literature was not that of the Classic world, nor was its unstable emotionality, its wildness and supernaturalism, its extreme imaginative freedom, and the license it gave its writers to mix what the classicism of the 17th and early 18th century kept carefully separated. The use of the term "romantic" justified the culture of natural emotional lability by giving it a historical locus and origin, one not only closer to natural man than the sophisticated culture of the ancient world as 16th, 17th, and 18th century Europe comprehended it, but also it was Christian, not pagan. Gothic architecture once again began to be admired; Goethe's enthusiastic response to the Gothic splendor of the Strasbourg cathedral was typical of the time, especially since he thought of the Gothic style as German, and his response to it, as a German, was natural to his race and his culture. Indeed Germans long maintained that Germany had invented Gothic architecture. The Gothic, with its extravagance, its mixture of light and darkness, its colored windows, was the equivalent of the picturesque in landscape. Moreover — and particularly important for comprehending Cherubini's achievement — was the revaluation of Shakespeare, first in England and then in Germany.

Cherubini spent almost two years in England (1784-1786), but he

was not culturally isolated, having been admitted to the intellectually and artistically sophisticated circle of the Prince of Wales, to be
a poor regent and a poor king as George IV, but a highly gifted and
culturally sensitive interior decorator, and a devotee of the picturesque.
His taste was representative of the time; he was interested in Chinese,
Indian, and Arabian architecture and art. He possessed a typical taste
for the exotic which accompanied the taste for the Gothic and was
equally emblematic of the movement of advanced European taste
out from under the overwhelming domination of the classic and toward what was thought of as the natural. It was at this time, it will
be remembered, that Herder was developing his notions of culture,
justly recognized now as an early form of cultural anthropology.
And Herder too was engaged in the revaluation of Shakespeare, whom
he recognized in the 1770s as the European equivalent of Homer.
Shakespeare was no longer thought of as a half barbarian, ignorant
of the eternal values of the classic theater, but as a great genius, the
master of a different conception of theater, one as valid as that of classicism and far more natural. He was the great predecessor and model
of the culture of natural emotional lability. When Cherubini and his
librettist set *Lodoïska* in Poland they were responding to the tradition of exoticism and to the Shakesperian model of the mixture of
the genres of tragedy and comedy, of exalted feeling and buffoonery.
And in the operatic figure of the rescuing Tartar chief, the barbarian
whose devotion to nobility, morality, and justice made him superior
to the aristocratic villain, they presented the virtuous natural man.

   Lodoïska created new possibilities for opera, and Cherubini's next
opera was even more adventurous, *Eliza ou Le voyage aux glaciers
de Mont Saint-Bernard* (Théatre Feydeau, December 13, 1794). Unlike his Italian musical colleagues in Paris, Cherubini dedicated himself to the Revolution. After a retreat to Normandy in 1793, where
he worked on *Eliza,* he returned to Paris and became an officer and
teacher in the newly founded Institute Nationale de Musique. The
plot of *Eliza* has little significance. It is a tale of an Italian painter
who believes that he has lost his beloved, first through the objections
of her father and then through her alliance with someone else after
her father's death. But this is all a misunderstanding, not cleared

up until the hero is buried in an avalanche, is rescued and thought dead, but revives under the lamentations of his beloved. The plot was only an excuse for the time as contemporary, and the setting, the Alps, one already used in André Grétry's opera on William Tell (April 9, 1791). Here is the picturesque in all fullness, and the pass of St. Bernard provides a realistic justification for travelers, a postman and mule-driver, or freight carrier, who sings folk songs, and a chorus of Savoy peasants on their way to Paris, the city of equality and the capital of the French, who were triumphant everywhere. The servants of the hospice of St. Bernard are also full of benevolence, as is the prior, who saves the hero from desperation and leads him to the hospice as night falls, an exit that was a splendid invention in the picturesque mode. In the hero and the heroine we have a man and a woman who are all feeling; in the prior a man all benevolence; in the peasants and hospice servants the natural goodness of sentimental realism. In the setting we have both the beauty of nature — called "*romanesque*" (romantic) by the painter — and also the terrifying and awe-inspiring sublime in the snow peaks of the backdrop and in the avalanche which precipitates a tragedy converted into a happy ending.

And except for that ending the music more than rises to *Lodoïska's* themes. The hero is exalted by the landscape, which he conceives as the visual and natural equivalent of his passion for Eliza. The music of his aria on his love offers an emotional range unknown even to the *opera seria* and certainly not reached by Mozart. It is far more akin to the intense slow movements of Haydn's instrumental works in the 1790s, and in fact so reminds one of Berlioz that one remembers how much Berlioz admired Cherubini. Once again the events of the Revolution are pertinent. *Eliza* was presented not long after the closing of the club of the Jacobins — the extreme radicals, leaders of the Terror — and only five months after the guillotining of Robespierre. It was written, then, during the Terror, and it is clear that Cherubini was responding to what the Revolution and the Terror had revealed, a range of human emotion and violence coupled with an equally extreme moral rectitude. Revolutionary Paris opened up new possibilities and actualities of human exaltation and terroristic degradation.

But what Cherubini accomplished in *Eliza*, a work of great beauty and power, was surpassed in his next work, *Médée*.

The story of Medea had been often used in *opera seria*, but it is a mistake to assume that Cherubini's opera was a continuation or revival of the *opera seria* conventions and style. In a tragic opera Cherubini again combined different traditions in an even more striking Shakespearean manner than hitherto. The work uses speech, melodrama (spoken dialogue accompanied by music), recitative, aria, ensemble, and chorus. This scheme gave him a greater emotional range, in particular a greater range of volume, than had been available. Since *Médée*'s revival in 1953 recitative with orchestra has almost always been substituted for spoken dialogue and the melodramas (ordinarily in the 1850s version of Franz Lachner), and this re-arrangement gives a false notion of what Cherubini accomplished. Clearly what he was interested in was the emergence of emotional violence from common interaction. The very opening reveals this, for Glauce, waiting to be the bride of Jason, fears the power of Medea; but only after a long recitative and aria of increasing emotional intensity does she mention Medea and reveal the cause of her fear. The repression of a terrible anxiety and knowledge of Medea can no longer by maintained. This scene is a concentration of the plan of the opera. Just as Glauce endeavors to repress her anxiety and her fear in order to experience her happiness at marrying Jason, so Medea represses her rage in order to achieve her revenge — the murder of Glauce, the murder of her two children, and the firing of the temple in which she has taken refuge. Her rage and her revenge are ultimately self-destructive.

Médée was first presented on March 13, 1797 (Théatre Feydeau) at a time when the Directory had been in existence for a year and a half, had established its power, and was experiencing the triumph of French military might, most splendidly in Italy, commanded by Napoleon. It was a time when what the Revolution and the Terror had revealed about humanity could be transformed into theater. The music of Cherubini, placed against the music of its time and the music of the European tradition, presented a violent aggressiveness hitherto unknown in music, whether theatrical or instumental. And just as the revolutionary release of violent aggressiveness out of a condition of repressed outrage reached its climax in the Terror of Robespierre and ended in self-destructiveness, so also ended the violent trajectory of Medea's life. In the Terror the Revolution was devouring its children, and Medea murdered hers. *Médée* transformed into art what the Revolution had revealed about humanity and the human condition. The Enlightenment had sown the wind and reaped the whirlwind. The Directory and Napoleon subdued that whirlwind, but the possibility of its rebirth haunted the 19th century and indeed still haunts the 20th. *Médée* revealed in an individual a fearful human potentiality. This revelation of human behavior was the result of a prodigious effort to unify nature and reason, world and mind. Jason betrayed Medea, the natural barbarian, and both the old regime and the regime of Enlightenment ideology had betrayed European man. And both, as well as Medea, had betrayed themselves. That reversal, that duplicity within human emotions and conduct, was what the Romantics of the 19th century had to come to terms with. That is what they had to transcend.

In Cherubini's final successful opera, *Les deux journées, ou le porteur d'eau* (January 16, 1800, Théatre Feydeau), set in the 17th century, a man of the people, a Savoyard, saves the aristocratic President of the Paris Parlement, the friend of the people, from the murderous plans of Mazarin, the successor to Richelieu. It was one of the numerous efforts to reconcile the upper-class power elite and the people, an effort that was to be the central concern of nineteenth century politics and economics. No government, whether democratic, socialist, or fascist — all Enlightenment ideologies — has yet effected that reconciliation.

Jacques-Louis David
(1748-1825)

Among the many artists who, for one reason or another, sided with the Revolution, few did so with the commitment of Jacques-Louis David, who voted for the death of Louis XVI in January, 1793, attacked and helped destroy the Academy of Art as a creature of the monarchy, and helped found the new Institute which took its place. He designed the pageantry of the Revolutionary celebrations and festivals, was a member of the Committee of Public

Safety, signing any number of condemnations to the guillotine, and after the death of Robespierre was himself imprisoned for a time. He was also the most important French artist of the late 18th century. In the 1790s his style finally achieved the consummation toward which he had been moving since his first return from Rome in 1780. David's movement was steadily toward an extreme clarification of a painting. His ideology was that of the Enlightenment at its most radical. The object of painting was to provide easily grasped examples of heroic virtue devoted to the purity of the social order. For this reason he was the leader in the general tendency towards the reduction of complexity within the frame of a painting. The object was that the spectator should be inspired by the virtuous morality of the work with the utmost immediacy, with the least loss 'of perceptual adaptation. One aspect of this movement was the steady reduction of color. Thus the settings of gray stone for "The Oath of the Horatii" (1784, Louvre), "The Death of Socrates" (1787, Metropolitan, New York), and "Brutus and his Dead Sons" (1789, Louvre) are extremely simple, primitivistic, and, classic. In these settings, indeed, he designed an architecture at least as radical in its simplification as the work of Claude-Nicolas Ledoux (1736-1806), who in the 1780s was building the monumental custom-gates of Paris as nearly pure cubes and cylinders, and as the geometrically even purer paper architecture of Etienne-Louis Boullée (1728-1799), to whom we shall return. The placing of the human figures in these paintings was as simplified as the architecture. Instead of the deep recession filled with gradually diminishing figures typical of the history paintings of the 17th and 18th centuries, the space was shallow and the figures arranged across the fore-stage as on a classic frieze.

This isolation of the figures against an almost neutral background still left color for their costumes. The next step was to eliminate color, and this he virtually accomplished in the 1790s. Probably in January or February, 1792, he painted a portrait of the Marquise de Pastoret. Except for pinks in the cheeks and lips and the ivory of the breast and left arm, the painting is entirely in white, light brown, and grayish green. It is one of David's many portraits of the period which are assumed to be unfinished, and perhaps they are. Perhaps they are

Jacques-Louis David
La Marquise de Pastoret
reproduced by permission of the Art Institute of Chicago

unfinished because of the slowness with which he worked and the rush of events during the first five years of the Revolution. But perhaps there is another explanation. There is in this portrait, for example, no hint of background furniture, draperies, or architecture. The Marquise is placed in undefined space. Part of the back of her chair is visible and in the right foreground is the end of a cradle in which appears a glimpse of her infant son. Thus the sculpturesque effect of the figure, already apparent in the paintings of the 1780s, is emphasized. Furthermore the precedent of Michelangelo's famous incomplete Slaves provided a justification for not finishing a work of art. An unfinished work forces the observer to wonder why, to turn his attention to the artist and his situation. And this painter was deeply engaged in the endeavor to create a society in which what was believed to be the simple truth of human nature would find its proper and unrepressed sphere of action. Thus the Marquise is not only clothed in the simplest of dresses, worn carelessly, but she is also engaged in sewing, presumably something for her child. Her very hair is loosely hanging and a little disordered. A member of the aristocracy is presented in her purest humanity of fostering motherhood, is reduced to the level of a woman of the people.

On July 13, 1793, the day before the fourth anniversary of the storming of the Bastille, a 24-year-old woman of Normandy assassinated Jean Paul Marat, who with Danton and Robespierre had overthrown the moderate Girondins and started the Terror. Charlotte Corday was a child of the late Enlightenment, a product of precisely the same cultural situation which produced David's pictures of the 1780s, the worship of the noble Greeks and Romans devoted to public virtue. Many of the Girondins fled to Normandy, where Mlle. Corday heard them speak and mingled with them. Unlike David she saw a moral disparity between the principles of the Revolution and the Terror. She came to Paris, killed Marat in his medicinal bath —although he was already dying — and was herself guillotined three days later, ascending the scaffold unperturbed, and without assistance placing herself under the knife. In memorializing Marat, David created his greatest surviving picture.

"The Death of Marat" was presented to the Convention on November 14, 1793. Returned to David on February 10, 1795, after he had been released from prison, for a time it was in the studio of the painter of Napoleon's triumphs, Baron Gros. There it was covered with a coat of white paint. Eventually David's nephew bequeathed it to the Brussels Museum of Fine Art (1893) in recognition of the refuge Brussels had granted David at the time of the restoration of the monarchy in 1815. These adventures reveal the extreme contentiousness of the picture and the act of painting it as a political act. On the other hand, Charlotte Corday became a heroine to those who saw the Terror as a betrayal of the Revolution. She has been hailed as an angel of assassination.

The picture is the most advanced example of pictorial reductionism that David had yet achieved or was ever to achieve. Except for the head with its turban-like dressing, and the naked chest and arms of Marat, it is composed almost entirely of explicit and implicit rectangles. In the right foreground is an up-ended box on which sit a round inkwell, a feather pen, a letter, and what may be a piece of revolutionary paper money. Behind, extending across the painting and cut off at either end, is Marat's bath, lined by a sheet, which forms two implied rectangles at the left. It is covered almost to Marat's chest by a board, itself covered with a rectangular green blanket. Beyond is again undefined space, as in the "Marquise de Pastoret." The values of the composition arrive at further simplification by means of an implied line from the upper left corner to the lower right, dividing the painting into two equal triangles. The predominating colors — brown, brownish flesh, cream and green for the configurations, and shading from black to an undefined mixture of greens and browns in the background — is relieved only by small spots of blood from the chest wound, seen on the sheet and in the bath water.

In Marat's left hand is a letter from Corday. An oddity of the picture is that Marat's head, presumably the center of interest, is far to the left, and is balanced by the much smaller but powerful configuration of the ink-well, the curve of which echoes the curve of Marat's mouth and eyelids. Is this merely a formal device of composition, or are we to make more of it? An inkwell, with its pen, is the instrument of civilized communication, but here its juxtaposition with Charlotte

Corday's letter, the letter with which she succeeded on her third attempt to see Marat, suggests correspondence as an instrument of betrayal. Does David wish to suggest the ambivalence of the civilization which man has created, the destructiveness of man's departure from nature and the corruption of his reason? Charlotte Corday interpreted her act as heroic and virtuous, carried out for the public good and for the Republic. Did David see a parallel between the reductionism of the Terror and the reductionism in the decision of Charlotte Corday? Did he grasp that both derived from the same ideology, one that appeared coincidentally in his own work and his own reductionism? Certainly years later during his post-Napoleonic exile in Brussels his style shows a complexity and irony it had never before exhibited. That ink-well raises strange questions.

Henry Fuseli   A similar reductionism is to be found in the ar-
(1741-1825)   tistic development of the Swiss-English painter and
                   book illustrator Henry Fuseli (born Johann Heinrich
Füssli). He began to work in his unique style in the late 1760s and established it in Rome in the 1770s. The first subjects of his new style were taken from Greek tragedy, but he soon turned to Dante, Shakespeare, and Milton. But no matter what the literary source, his choice of subjects was almost invariably the horrific. It was not merely that he was influenced by the *terribilità* of Michelangelo. He was far more terrible. Repeatedly his figures rear up defiantly with arms and legs outflung in aggression and attack, or they hurl themselves backwards in terror, as Macbeth before the witches or Hamlet before his father's ghost. His originality lay in his extending the sublime to subsume the terrible and the fearful and the horrible. The same cultural strain during the 1780s and the 1790s was to yield the Gothic novel, a genre that accomplished a descent to a lower cultural level of the culture of feeling, rationally extended to its most extreme modalities, specifically that of the frightful. At a higher cultural level this strain was responsible for the sublime and powerful minor key introductions to Haydn's late symphonies. Probably the earliest manifestation, however, is to be found in Giambattista Piranesi's prints of fantastic imaginary *Prisons* (1745-1761).

In the 1790s Fuseli devoted himself principally to subjects from the works of Milton. And stylistically they are as extreme in their reductionism as the works of David appearing at the same time. But unlike David's, the configurations of Fuseli are not precise and hard. Rather, the figures melt into an undifferentiated dark and often black background, so that the figure emerges from nothingness — from empty, undefined space. "Loneliness at Dawn," an illustration for Milton's pastoral elegy "Lycidas," shows a sleeping figure bent over itself and leaning against a rock (1794-1796). In the mist is a barely visible and half-monstrous dog, and the undifferentiated background reveals only a sliver of a moon. Even simpler is the perfectly symmetrical "Silence," a single figure, its head and crossed arms bowed between outspread knees (1799-1801). Again the space is undifferentiated, with only a suggestion of a horizontal plane on which the figure sits and of a vertical plane behind it. But much of the picture is extremely dark. Formally the figure is built up of interlocking semi-circles. Here is an emotional reductionism, for in spite of the title, the figure implies only complete and hopeless and helpless dejection, isolation, depression, defeat. In short, the bulk of Fuseli's work is an artistic counterpart to the Terror. It makes the Terror understandable, for the power of Fuseli's ideas (though not their execution) brought into recognition at a high cultural level human capacities not hitherto recognized, or at least presented.

John Flaxman   Exactly the opposite tendency is to be found in
(1755-1826)   the work of a fellow Englishman, John Flaxman.
                       One of the results of interest in the Medieval past
which emerged from the culture of emotional lability of the 1760s
was an interest in the Italian painters before the Renaissance — Giotto,
Orcagna, Duccio — and a similar interest in the primitive art of Greece,
insofar as it was known, and in the previously neglected vase-painting.
There emerged also a rival to Shakespeare — Ossian, a Northern Homer,
the virtual invention of James Macpherson (1736-1796), who claimed
to have translated Ossian's verse from Gaelic or Erse ancient Highland Scottish poetry. The *Fragments* (1760), *Fingal* (1762), *Temora*
(1763) swept through Europe. In these works, it was believed, was

to be found the true primitive, the true natural, the grandeur and nobility of mankind as it was before the overlay of cultural sophistication. A designer for Wedgwood pottery (which made him famous) and a sculptor, Flaxman went to Rome in 1787 for seven years. In the early 1790s he made his famous line-drawings for Homer, published in 1793, followed by similar drawings for Aeschylus (1797). To us, these drawings, particularly in the harder and less flexible engravings made by others, seem academic, but at the time they were seen as exactly the opposite, for "academic" meant the Renaissance-Baroque-Rococo tradition, which not even David had fully transcended. Flaxman himself admired much medieval work, both painting and sculpture, and he also saw in Naples Sir William Hamilton's collection of Greek vases fom Etruscan tombs which were being published in outline drawings by William Tischbein in the very years, 1791-1795, during which Flaxman was illustrating Homer and Aeschylus.

Flaxman's illustrations transported his contemporaries to Homeric Greece, a world of primitive purity, direct emotional expression, and heroic simplicity, and those contemporaries felt that if Homer had been illustrated in his own age, the drawings would have looked exactly like Flaxman's. As in David, the figures are disposed as on a frieze and space is barely defined. Occasionally a couple of lines suggests a shadow on a floor, but the background is pure white, totally undifferentiated; except in an instance in which a god or goddess appears on a cloud, there is no other suggestion of sky. The figures are pure outlines. The only visual information within the figures, aside from hair, consists of simple draperies or faintly delineated muscles. Illusionism survives only in more delicately drawn figures at the back of the scene. Flaxman is interested in presenting emotion only in its purest modality; the figures have no other function. Furniture or armor is given only to fulfill the barest informational requirements.

These illustrations, then, are immediately apprehensible. Hence, no doubt, their popularity for more than a century, as they have been reproduced dozens of times and widely imitated. Indeed, in this century they have been used more than once to illustrate editions of Homer. They are perfect fusions of the natural and the rational, sentiment rationally comprehended, a reductionist ideology exemplified by a severe limitation to the minimally essential. They were as revolutionary in art as the Terror was in politics. Placed against the work of his predecessors, Flaxman's art was as ruthless as Robespierre's politics.

An interpretation of the Enlightenment during the last half of the 18th century which concentrates solely on its sources in the ancient and classic Mediterranean world is mistaken, and it is inadequate to use "neo-classicism" to designate the period, a term as uninformative and misleading as are most period terms in art history. "Neoclassicism" is even more misleading when it is extended to cultural history. The term "classic" used for the style of Haydn and Mozart in conjunction with "neo-classicism" can yield a complete misapprehension of the character of their music. By the 1790s the archaizing factor in painting and architecture had led to a perception of similarity in the origins of Mediterranean classicism and Northern "Gothicism," or, to use another inadequate term, of Northern "Romanticism." The culture of Northern Europe was seen as emerging from a noble barbarian non-Christian background, and the culture of the Mediterranean was interpreted, through an archaizing vision of Homer, in the same way. To preserve the Judeo-Christian tradition, the Old Testament began to be understood in a parallel manner, and the figures of Ossian, Homer, and Moses, the presumed author of the Pentateuch, were grasped as culturally convergent. Thus, in his search for origins for the uncorrupted purity of natural man, the advanced late-Enlightenment culture hero had grasped the equal validity of his Mediterranean and Northern roots. In 19th century architecture, painting, literature, and music (especially opera and program music), Classicism and Medievalism were equally important and equally useful.

Etienne-Louis Boullée   Two architects of the 1790s reveal this
(1728-1799)   cultural fusion, Etienne-Louis Boullée and
                              James Wyatt (1746-1813). Until 1780
Boullée was a practicing architect, designing buildings in an increasingly reductionist and imposing classical style, a style in which the rectan-

gular shapes of solid geometry became steadily more explicit. After 1779, however, he devoted himself entirely to unbuilt paper architecture, buildings on an enormous scale, buildings designed to provide instruction for the people of a rational and egalitarian society — one in which only public and socially stabilizing interaction would be permitted to exist. In his drawings human figures are reduced almost to invisibility. The individual is totally absorbed in masses of humanity. This, Boullée thought, was the natural condition of man, and "nature" evidently meant the perfect sphericity of the earth and the other planets and of the solar system itself. With this ideology he designed in 1784 a cenotaph for Newton, an enormous hollow sphere set in a disk cut away in front to continue the line of the sphere and to expose it, the whole girdled with terraces planted with trees, the natural equivalent of columns. A sun hanging in the exact center of the sphere and surrounded with a model of the solar system was to give forth splendid illumination; or, without that light, holes in the upper surface of the sphere were to reproduce, with natural light, the constellations. Such a fantastic building could not be built even today.

In the 1790s, perhaps, Boullée designed a somewhat similar temple of nature, a semicircular dome. Only the upper part was to be visible from the outside, and it sat in concentric bases of disks mounted with innumerable columns. Within, a similar colonnade was to surround a reproduction of a natural valley sunk below cliffs and climaxed with a cave-like opening to the earth's interior. The rough pyramidal rocks of the cave opening were to be superimposed by a diminutive primitive human construction.

Probably in 1792 he designed a building for the National Assembly. In the center was the circular meeting hall surmounted by a coffered dome, the symbol of cosmic and human unity. But the hall was set in a vast square. At the outer edge were offices. Within these were a corridor and then eight halls for subdivisions (committees) of the Assembly, four square halls at the corners, and four much larger rectangular halls between the squares. On the terraces outside were rigidly and geometrically planted trees; the public spaces within were surrounded by the architectural equivalent to the human, colonnades.

Thus the perfect natural order of the sphere is contained within the rectangular order of human rationality, and the interaction of the two is not only totally reciprocal, but also hierarchically arranged from the order of the cosmos to the subordinate order of the creating and governing individual — a perfection of bureaucratic organization. Boullée's project for a National Assembly thus became the sublime symbol of the social order the radicals of the Revolution were endeavoring to bring into existence. Boullée's architecture, one may say, was a ruthless and overpowering expression of what man and his interaction ought to be. In his projects architecture becomes not a mere symbol of human perfection but an exacting means of so controlling behavior that that perfection might be brought about.

James Wyatt   Boullée's architecture could not possibly
(1746-1813)   have been built, and indeed it was not until
                            Napoleon that the Revolution actually built anything. Then Boullée's ideas were inspirational for buildings designed on a practicable scale. However, in England James Wyatt constructed a fantastically large building not for an ideal humanity but for a single marvelously eccentric and gifted individual, William Beckford (1759-1844). Probably no one in the late 18th century absorbed so completely the Enlightenment culture of the feelings, perhaps because very few were as wealthy, as talented, as cultivated in the arts, and as isolated in their personal lives as Beckford. He of course is the author of that extraordinary oriental romance, *Vathek* (1786). Although he engaged Wyatt to design Fonthill in southwestern England, he himself designed the enormous grounds, a most complete expression of the English style of gardening — a style which had as its aim (and Beckford was one of the few to achieve this objective) so quintessential in intensification of nature that when the garden was mature it seemed to be a natural, not a man-made, production. It was the perfection of the Picturesque. He conceived of Fonthill, which he called an abbey, in the early 1790s and began building in 1795. It was at that time, evidently, that James Wyatt designed his brilliant plan, a vast Greek crucifix, the major axis of which provided an uninterrupted vista of three hundred feet. At the center was a

lofty tower worthy of a cathedral. The building was as much an exaltation of the Picturesque as was the garden.

The Gothic tradition in English building had never been entirely abandoned, nor was Fonthill the first great 18th century house or the first designed by Wyatt. The history of the Gothic Revival from mid-century on was the gradual separation of medieval design — aided by continuing archaeological study — from a superficial decor essentially rococo with Gothic ornament, and from an application of Gothic ornament to classic design and plan. In this innovation Wyatt was instrumental. He had done extensive work on restoring cathedrals, responsible for a great deal of damage to a style that was yet insufficiently understood, and was equally prepared to design in either a classic or a medieval modality. He was, then, among the earliest architects to see the equal validity of Northern and of Mediterranean culture. Like the poet Thomas Gray (1716-1771) and like Herder, he was an inheritor of all of European culture, not just the Mediterranean or, as some enthusiasts were convinced, just the Northern. Although Fonthill could not have been mistaken for a medieval building nor was it supposed to be, the details were of an accuracy scarcely achieved before in the 18th century Gothicizing tradition. Unfortunately, Wyatt was a careless builder and placed great confidence in an artificial stone which could not stand up to the English weather. In 1825 the great tower collapsed. Fonthill rose, contemporaries said, like a dream, and proved as insubstantial.

And that was appropriate, because what Beckford wished was something as visionary as a dream, and something as private. Fuseli's most famous picture was "A Nightmare" (1781), an evocation of the terror of the richly cultivated sensibility. Beckford's Fonthill was an evocation of the beauty achievable by such a sensibility, a dream of the past set in a dream of nature. Fonthill was a strange parallel to Kant's epistemology, so much under the influence of Rousseau, the hero of natural sensibility. Kant's vision of the mind was also a dream of the individual sensibility, and of how that sensibility transforms the world it responds to. And just as Fonthill and its grounds were manifestations of extreme isolation, so Kant could find no path from the individual mind to another mind (even after attempting a relationship by a severe and impossible morality), concluding that man is as essentially asocial as Beckford certainly was. The irrational, which Kant hoped might be eliminated in a distant Utopia, was precisely the quality to which Beckford, served by Wyatt, devoted his intelligence, his taste, and his fortune. If, one can argue for Beckford and his cultural allies, the sensibility, the irrational, the dream, the nightmare (as in *Vathek*) are aspects of the nature of man, is it not rational to grant those aspects a complete realization? The contrast between the visions of Boullée and the visions of Beckford-Wyatt was the contrast between the responsibility of the individual to the social order and his responsibility to his own sensibility. Here in the split between morality and sensibility we find once again the irresolvable Enlightenment split between nature and reason. The great triad of Revolutionary demagoguery was "Liberty, Equality, and Fraternity," but in the 1790s it was becoming evident that the liberty of equality is antithetical to the liberty of fraternity, and that these two liberties can be fused only by violence.

Johann Wolfgang von Goethe   In June, 1776, Johann Wolfgang
(1749-1832)   Goethe was made a member of the
                                Duke of Weimar's cabinet and thus
became a civil servant in a little German principality, one of more than 360. In 1782 he acquired a title and became von Goethe. In later years, long after the French Revolution, he said that he was proud of the fact that he had always allied himself with the nobility. Yet he was always just as proud of the fact that the class of his origin was the ruling bourgeois class of Frankfurt, an imperial city independent of any of the petty German principalities. And this inconsistency gives us a clue into the unique way Goethe dealt with Enlightenment incoherence. In the 1790s Goethe led the way to what has become known as Weimarian Classicism, the effort to establish the universal validity of the Greek and Roman modes of literature and culture. This would not be the archaizing classicism of people like Flaxman, but rather the classicism of fifth-century and fourth-century Greece and of late Republican and Imperial Rome. To a considerable extent he took his literary models from Racine, the

classicism of Louis XIV and his age, the classicism of which Metastasio was one of the late exemplars.

The word that is used over and over again of the mature and aged Goethe is "Olympian," yet he himself said that the only time in his life when he was happy was the period of less than twenty months he spent in Italy (1786-1788). It is not surprising, I would suggest, that from the time of his return from Italy to the end of his life Goethe gives the impression of someone putting on an elaborate public and private performance. His personality, which he himself describes as originally very strange and troubling, something which he could scarcely understand, became a made personality, a constructed personality. And the construction of personality is the theme of *Wilhelm Meister*, the first part of which, though originally drafted in incomplete form probably between 1776 and 1785, appeared in 1795 as *Wilhelm Meisters Lehrjahre*. The second part, *Wilhelm Meisters Wanderjahre*, appeared in 1821 and again, considerably extended, in 1829.

The theme of the novel is how one becomes a master of oneself and a master of life. This becoming is thus presented as a creative act. To construct one's personality from one's endowments is thus not merely *analogous* to the creation of a work of art; it *is* the creation of a work of art, the highest kind of art. Influenced by Herder, whose friend he became and whom he brought to Weimar in 1776 (one of his first important acts as guide and employee of the Duke of Weimar), he conceived of self-creation on the analogy of Herder's conception of culture, or *Bildung*. Just as the history of every culture in the wide or social sense is the history of how that culture created itself from the natural and human resources avalable to it, so the *Bildung* of the individual is the history of the construction of a personality. (The German word *Bild* subsumes almost any type of man-made structure, whether an idea, a symbol, or a plaster cast). And what Goethe meant by *Bildung* is the harmonious realization of a man's potentialities, capacities, natural gifts. The aim of that realization is, however, not a mere analogy with the culture of a society; rather it is the fusion of the culture of the personality with the culture of its society. The titles of the two parts of *Wilhelm Meister* are taken from the old tradition of the successive stages of becoming a member

of a guild, and in Germany the guilds of craftsmen were a more significant part of the social system than anywhere else in Europe, partly
because in the eighteenth century Germany was in many ways still
medieval. The tiny principalities had prevented the development of a
modern state such as France, England, the Low Countries, and even
Spain had achieved. The guilds were powerful and important as one
of the few means of social systematizing across the too frequent
boundaries and frontiers. So Wilhelm must first spend his years as
an apprentice, followed by his wandering years as a journeyman, until
finally he beomes a master, socially absorbed as a doctor — a fusion
signified by his saving the life of his illegitimate son Felix. He is now
truly William the Master.

Goethe's novel was originally called *Wilhelm Meisters Theatralische
Sendung* (*Theatrical Mission*) and was conceived during Goethe's
Sturm-und-Drang period, the German term for what I have named
here the culture of emotional lability, of sensibility, of adaptation
to nature. So from the outset Goethe conceived of mastering life as
a form of acting, or performance, and of performance as a means of
learning what one's potentialities are. Wilhelm, destined to be a merchant, falls in with a troupe of actors and becomes an actor himself.
In the 1795 revision and continuation of the novel, Wilhelm's career
reaches its peak and its conclusion with the preparation of a performing version of *Hamlet*. Wilhelm himself plays the protagonist. Now
to solve a problem faced by a member of the acting company, Wilhelm leaves the theatrical world and enters the world of the nobility.
In so doing he eventually learns that his life had been guided by a
secret society, the Fellowship of the Tower. And at this point the
work develops a strange similarity to *The Magic Flute,* to which, indeed, Goethe once planned and partially sketched a sequel. The Fellowship of the Tower has a remarkable resemblance to the Priesthood
of the Sun, and we see again the notion of a semi-secret lodge devoted
to a rational salvation of gifted individuals to whom the sustaining
and improvement of the social order may be entrusted. Wilhelm is
admitted to the concealed temple of the Fellowship and is initiated
into this quasi-Masonic organization. His initiation takes the form
of revealing to him the real significance of his life to that point and

the imposition upon him of the duties of the organization — the now conscious self-development of true *Bildung,* the harmonious realization of one's potentialities.

Between Wilhelm's departure from the world of the theater and his entry into the world of nobility and the Fellowship, he has the opportunity to read the lengthy "Bekenntnisse einer schönen Seele" ("Confession of a Beautiful Soul"); *schöne Seele* specifically refers to the religious soul, and more specifically to the religion of sentiment, of emotional lability. The tale is of a woman, a friend of Goethe's mother, in fact, who through great personal suffering and profound dissatisfaction with the mundane world in which she lives turns to religion and finds peace and contentment in religious piety. The insertion of an apparent digression at this particular point in *Meister* presents at once a role-model of self-creation and of the kind of contentment with one's life toward which Wilhelm is moving, though he does not yet know it, and at the same time a model that Goethe wishes to transcend by secularization. So the Fellowship of the Tower is a secularization of the church, of religion itself. Both the *schöne Seele* and Wilhelm are discontented and feel misplaced in the lives their social position offers them. The one achieves a mastery of life by coming to understand her innate religious gifts through the *Bildung* of Pietism; the other achives a mastery of life through understanding his innate gifts as an artist, an experience which provides the model for his conception of self-creation, *Bildung,* as the highest form of artistic creation. The one is aided by a social institution, the church, which is, however, not available to the other, who is of a newer generation. Wilhelm is aided by a new social institution, the Fellowship of the Tower, which is, as we have seen, ultimately, through Masonry and the Illuminati, modeled on the organization and practice of the Jesuits.

This secularization of religion and its transformation into culture was made possible by Herder's revelation of religion as a cultural mode, but his attitude towards existence Goethe derived not from Herder but from Spinoza, whom he interpreted in his own manner. What he got from Spinoza was not the Jewish philosopher's rationalism but rather his conception of God and Nature as one. Thus Nature to

Goethe is a vast system of interrelationships which the individual cannot understand, which must seem to him irrational and which, however, he grasps as a system by means of intuition, imagination, poetry, feeling, sensibility. Mastery of life requires the acceptance of the conditions of existence, and the world is itself conceived of as a work of art to be grasped and understood as we grasp and understand a work of art. Nature, Art, and the *Bildung* personality are not only analogous but identical, and thus the creation of the personality as a work of art is not accomplished by reason; it is to be accomplished as Nature is intuitively and imaginatively understood, and as a work of art is intuitively and imaginatively understood — and created. But Wilhelm, after all, had the guidance and aid of the Fellowship of the Tower. One is compelled to ask, What in Goethe's own life during the 1790s was the analogical equivalent of that Fellowship? What was Goethe's guide? What was the fellowship that guided him? The simple answer is that it was the art of Greece and Rome. His fellowship was formed of the artists of classic antiquity, its writers, sculptors, and architects.

Goethe's two works on a grand scale were *Wilhelm Meister* and *Faust,* and the fact that both resisted completion for most of his life indicates that Goethe, for all of his quasi-Spinozistic acceptance of the world, did not achieve that grand harmonization of which classic art served as his supreme emblem. In the long poem *Hermann und Dorothea* (1797) he attempted an extraordinary fusion of the classic and the picturesque. It is the story of how a German innkeeper's son falls in love with and eventually succeeds in marrying a refugee from the French Revolution. The poetic technique Goethe chose was classic, not only in the attempt to write classic hexameters in German but also in the elevated calm which is the poem's narrative mode. It is at once "romantic" in the 18th century sense of that word and "classic" in Goethe's peculiar sense. The classic style is imposed upon the picturesque and realistic material. Here again we find the dichotomy of Reason and Nature, the unresolved problem of situational interpretation which was the very incoherence of the Enlightenment. For all of Goethe's emphasis upon intuition and imagination (terms which must be recognized as among the vaguest and most confusing in the history of European speculation), for all of his rejection of pure reason, he found it necessary to turn, in his classicism, to a shaping and external power equivalent to reason — just as Meister could not achieve his goal without the external and secretly imposed aid of the Fellowship of the Tower. When Goethe was in his beloved Italy he returned once again to the sketches of *Faust,* which he had begun in 1773 and abandoned by 1776. But he could not complete the work and published in 1790 *Faust: Ein Fragment,* which in fact was not carried as far in the story as the original attempt.

Yielding to Schiller's urging, he again took up *Faust* in 1797, publishing *Faust: Eine Tragödie: Erster Teil* (Part I) in 1808. Yet in a way he hated working on it, for it was antithetical to his classicism, and he knew it. *Faust* was a denial of the classicism, of the achievement of the *schöne Seele,* of the goal and eventual achievement of Wilhelm Meister in his fusion of Nature, Society, and Personality. The work opens with Faust's denial of his place in society and culture, just as the *Schöne Seele* and Meister get under way by denying their positions. So Faust's denial is objectified and dramatized in the person of the devil Mephistopheles. Faust is ultimately saved (in Part Two completed in 1831 and published in 1832) because, in spite of Mephistopheles' temptations that he be satisfied, he has eternally striven. This is all very well, but in fact Faust's eternal striving has done a great deal of harm. The presentation of Mephistopheles as the spirit of evil who in spite of himself brings forth good is singularly unconvincing. Goethe himself admitted that the huge work makes little sense and is not informed by a coherence-structuring idea; he predicted, only too successfully, that future scholars and critics would force coherent meaning upon it. Perhaps the real significance of *Faust* lies in Goethe's long struggle with it, just as in that same struggle lies the real cultural significance of *Wilhelm Meister.* These life-long efforts at completion, the results of which are so unconvincing, are revelations that Goethe's Weimarian classicism was no solution to the incoherence of Nature and Reason. Both works are admissions that the harmonious development of the personality in a manner analogous to the development of nature and the quasi-Spinozistic vision of the hidden but real divine system of nature is an impossibility. There are those who have judged Goethe's Olympianism as not only a performance but as a fraudulent performance. It can be said with some justice that Goethe betrayed his genius by his alliance with the aristocracy, an alliance which he regraded with complacency, and by his decision to be a civil servant in a miserable little German duchy. He was a genius, but a genius half-crippled by the incoherence of the Enlightenment. Yet that incoherence forced from him what is his greatest bequest, not triumphantly completed works of art but endless and unresolved self-display.

Friedrich Schiller   Johann Christoph Friedrich Schiller was
1759-1805   envious of Goethe and half hated him be-
                          cause, he thought, of the "natural" ease
with which he believed Goethe produced his works, an ease contrasting markedly with Schiller's own difficulties, his laboriousness, his rationalistic necessity to think through the implications of his dramatic ideas. Schiller was evidently unaware of the years Goethe spent in writing *Egmont* (1775-1787), *Iphigenia auf Tauris* in two versions (1779, 1787), and *Torquato Tasso* (1790), and in 1790 he knew nothing of the long efforts even then expended on *Faust*. And he was of course quite ignorant of the first version of *Meister,* not published until 1911. So he thought of Goethe as the kind of poet Goethe was not. In a sense he was not wrong, for Goethe worked at these major achievements intermittently, more or less as he was inspired to. But Schiller worked continuously and with endless pains and thoughtfulness; he therefore reasoned that his was a divided nature, half poet and half philosopher. After *Don Carlos,* published in 1787 after some years of labor, he turned to philosophy and for a time was completely under Kant's spell.

But it was not long before he rebelled, initially against Kant's uncompromisingly rigorous sense of duty. For Kant the Reason compelled a unity of thought, and in ethics that unity was to be found in Duty, a conclusion which in Kant's system meant that one should always act as if the maxim or principle of one's action were universal, equally binding upon all men. This was the result of Kant's conviction that the structure of the mind was common to everyone, and that rational thought necessarily led to universal conclusions. Now Kant knew perfectly well that in actual practice his ideal of duty was not practicable; yet he thought that if men endeavored to apply reason to ethics his ideal society, his utopia, would eventually emerge, a social condition in which all solutions to ethical problems would in fact be universal. To Schiller this conception of Duty was not only a "monkish asceticism" but also a denial of the validity of poetry and art. His awareness of the contrast between Goethe and himself made him think of natural differences of temperament that would make it impossible for ethical conceptions ever to be universal. And he also saw himself as a man of two temperaments: one a rationalizing aspect and the other a poetic aspect. It is significant that in the 1780s he wrote two historical plays, both placed in the mid-16th century, *Fiesco* (1783) and *Don Carlos* (1783-1787), and also that while during this period he was deep in the study of Kant he wrote a history of the revolt of the Netherlands against Spain (1788), a work which gained him a professorship of history at the University of Jena in the Duchy of Weimar, thus bringing him close to the immediate circle of Goethe. His poetic interests, then, evince an increasing awareness of a familiarity with the philological-historical-cultural tradition, the human equivalent of nature. He was, of course, a reader of Herder's works. He began to understand that the deep conflict between nature, i.e., reality, or history (in other words, the situational aspect of situational thinking) and the rational aspect was not a problem unique to himself but was, in spite of Kant, the true universal condition. And he began to see that Goethe, far from being the naive natural poet he had originally thought, was, though unconsciously, involved in the same conflict, that Goethe's harmonious personality was a *willed construction,* made possible by a quasi-Spinozistic indifference to the ephemeral events of the world — events in which Schiller was intensely interested and to which he could not be indifferent.

The internal conflict in the personality, therefore, was the problem he set out to understand, and in struggling with it he exposed as no one had yet done the incoherence of the Enlightenment. The precipitating event was the Terror, which revealed to Schiller the failure of the claims of Reason to be arbiter of human affairs. He saw man as

torn between the equally valid claims of Nature, which man appre-
hends sensuously, and Reason, which can lead, and in the Terror had
led, to a dead moral absolutism. In a pair of remarkable essays he
worked out his problem and came to a surprising conclusion, a conclusion which almost took him out of the Enlightenment – a conclusion which could hardly be appreciated for nearly a hundred years
(Nietzsche eventually did) and indeed was not fully recognized until
quite recently. The first of these essays was *Über die Aesthetische
Erziehung des Menschen in einer Reihe von Briefen* (*On the Aesthetic
Education of Man in a Series of Letters*), first published in a journal
having only a brief existence edited by Schiller and Goethe, *Die Horen*
(*The Hours*), in January, February, and June of 1795, and republished,
with a little revision, in 1801. The second was *Über das Erhabene*
(*On the Sublime*), first published in 1801 though probably written
in part some time before, except for, in all probability, the last eight
paragraphs, which present his most advanced position.

His first step toward that surprising conclusion was to relabel the
two divergent claims upon men of nature and reason as internal drives.
The source of the first drive, toward the sensuous, toward nature, toward reality, had its origin in man's emergence from nature, or at least
man as a part of nature. The source of the second drive was man's
self-consciousness, which emerged from his awareness of the possibility of responding in more than one way to the same sensory data.
Schiller's original belief that the ultimate source of that self-consciousness was God or the Absolute or some metaphysical reality had been
driven out by Kant, while his separation from Kant removed the
conviction that self-consciousness emerged from the structure of the
mind as a universal.

The only recourse Schiller had, he judged, was to postulate a third
drive, a drive which, astonishingly, he called the drive to play and to
create semblance in place of reality. Here then, lies the source of
man's freedom, for in play man escapes the slavery to Nature and
likewise the slavery to Reason. This third drive, intermediate between
the two, not reconciling them, since they are irreconcilable, playfully
creates a *Schein,* an appearance, a semblance, with the aid of the
imagination. It is an act of creation in which man can use the material

of the world as he pleases and also use the regulatory powers of the Reason as he pleases. Art is not to be identified with the aesthetic but is simply the highest modality of the aesthetic, because in art (and Schiller means only the greatest art) the drive to play and to creating a semblance makes the richest use of the richest variety of the material of reality and at the same time uses the rational powers in such a way as to control that material so that the "form" exhausts the "matter." And by "form" Schiller signifies whatever means of organization man imposes upon a segment of reality — a means not derived or derivable from that reality itself but from the rational and constructive powers of the mind. As an example of form and the semblance which form creates he offers good manners, politeness, elegance of behavior, a semblance or, we may say, a performance which transforms the brutishness of the natural man and the ethical absoluteness of the rational man.

Natural man judges manners to be artificial; rational man judges them immoral and dishonest. But manners are a product of the aesthetic drive, redeeming natural man from his slavery to materiality and rational man from his slavery to the absolute, to unity. Taste is the ability to respond appropriately to the aesthetic, to see it as play and semblance. And Schiller gives up any idea of Utopia, for Utopian ideals always postulate the recovery of an imaginary lost human unity, a unity which is destructive in Kant's duty, in Robespierre's terror, and in Babeuf's equality. For though Schiller does not say so, his concept of the slavery to the rational finds superb exemplification in all three and in Sarastro as well. So the Enlightenment ideal of a society at once natural and rational and made up of men of unified personality is abandoned. Instead, he admits at the end of his treatise that an Aesthetic State can never embrace more than a few men, highly cultivated, highly sophisticated, capable of a true humanity, men who are truly free.

But Schiller goes even further than this. Though the aesthetic drive has no moral or rational or scientific or any other kind of result for the individual, it prepares him to act at a higher level in any modality of human behavior, even though all other modalities are biased either in the direction of reality or of reason, and even though only a few works of art are biased in neither direction. But more than that, it is the aesthetic drive that makes it possible for man to act at all. It is the source of the will and its power, for only in the indifference, the non-commitment of the aesthetic, can a man distance himself sufficiently from both reality and reason in order to think and feel clearly and freely.

Nor is this all. In the final pages of the essay on the sublime, Schiller pushes his position even further. The Enlightenment tradition saw the sublime as awe-inspiring and as emblematic of the grandeur of God and Nature. But Schiller maintains that a higher level of the sublime is the revelation of nature as incomprehensible, and that only the aesthetic can create the distance which makes that incomprehensibility an endurable mode of consciousness. For the highest level of the aesthetic is to see nature itself as semblance. But if one sees nature as semblance one becomes aware that however one perceives it, that perception is an interpretation. In terms of the scheme used in the present book, the notion of the aesthetic makes it possible to grasp the fact that however we see nature it is a situation from which we do not derive that interpretation. But since that interpretation is a creation of the aesthetic drive to play and to create semblance, the materials of that interpretation are derived from the imagination. The Reason is indeed only regulative, for the concepts which it regulates are not its own creation but are given to it by the aesthetic in its process of directing the imagination's fantasies, and this is the case whether those imaginatively constructed concepts are put to use by philosophy, morals, or science. Only in the creation of the work of art and in taste, the adequate response to a work of art, can man know his true humanity and experience his freedom. Only in play and semblance can man transcend both reality and reason and master both, experiencing his divergent and rent personality as a harmony.

With such ideas Schiller arrived at the realization that the Enlightenment had failed, that its incoherence could not be resolved either theoretically or socially. But in a further implication he offered a new possibility. If the source of conventionalized interpretations of the world is the imagination, then those interpretations can be abandoned and transcended. In a series of remarkable historical plays,

Schiller, now certain of the validity of art and his own validity, set out to realize in semblance not the conflicts of the wills of men but the conflict and failures and transcendence of modes of interpreting reality: *Wallenstein* (1797-1799), *Maria Stuart* (1799-1800), *Die Jungfrau von Orleans* (*The Maid of Orleans*) (1800-1801), and *Wilhelm Tell* (1803-1804). One other drama, however, *Die Braut von Messina* (*The Bride of Massina*) 1802-1803, reveals both the source of the power of his late dramas and of his adherence to Weimarian Classicism. It is set in medieval Sicily but modelled on Greek tragedy, complete with choruses and originally with no act divisions. Like *Hermann und Dorothea* it endeavors to unite the picturesque and "romantic" with the classic, and to control the former by the latter. In its unified intensity it is reductionistic and ruthless. But the other plays, though not so ideologically controlled as *Die Braut von Messina,* show the same grandeur of style and power of construction. For a long time they held the stage, though presented now only in historically minded revivals. Their popularity — including the use of three of them for operas — resulted from the unified grandeur, clarity, and reductionism which characterizes them all. Thus Weimarian Classicism is to be understood as the simplification, as we have seen, of all of the arts of the 1790s — a simplification derived from the ideal of natural adaptation, an idea which led to the creation of a domestic architecture still the model for homes today.

Thus Schiller did not transcend the Enlightenment, but he did reveal its incoherence and showed that it had to be transcended. In the detachment, the indifference, the freedom, the non-commitment of the aesthetic — and in its dynamic, the imagination — he pointed out a direction for the transcendence. That direction was to prove inexhaustibly fruitful.

Marquis de Sade
(1740-1814)

Comte (known as Marquis) Donatien-Alphonse-François de Sade presents an odd parallel and complement to Schiller, the one reputed a sexually perverse monster, the other a noble moral idealist. Like Schiller, Sade was faced with an odd personality, one which Enlightenment theories could hardly subsume. The French

Revolution was a revelation to both men, Schiller arriving at understanding slavery to Reason and Sade, in an almost Schillerian way, understanding the slavery to Nature. Sade's oddity, now no longer hidden in pornographic shops and collections but widely known and openly published, was what is usually considered a perverse pleasure in combining sexual excitement and the infliction of extreme pain. Whether he actually engaged in his taste very deeply, or quite moderately, or just a little, or even at all is something of a historical problem. At any rate, he indulged his taste enough, or was reputed to have done so enough, to land him in prison, first in Vincennes and then in the Bastille, from which he was released by the famous attack of July 14, 1789. He became a zealous revolutionary, but in 1801 he offended Napoleon, who in 1803 threw him into the insane asylum of Charenton. There he remained the rest of his life, living eventually with some comfort, companioned by a devoted mistress, and was even helpful to the administration. By all accounts he was, or at least became, a very nice man, as well as a very fat one.

His infamy rests upon a series of pornographic novels, some of which, perhaps, he did not write. Of these the most intellectually interesting are *La philosophie dans le boudoir* (1795) and *Aline et Valcour, ou Le roman philosophique* (1793). The Revolution revealed to Sade that his personal oddity was not very odd at all. On the contrary it was a universal and a natural universal. Reason demands that we follow Nature, and the infliction of pain is Nature's way; in man the infliction of pain brings the knowledge that he has imposed his will, and the infliction of pain in sexual behavior means the expression of his passion in the most natural way imaginable. Further, all the passions of man — murder, theft, robbery, sodomy and all sexual pleasures — are equally natural. If there is to be true liberty, the State has only the right to maintain its existence and to protect itself. It has no right to control the behavior of the passions. The subordination of women, for example, is merely the manifestation of the unjust and immoral ownership of a claim to absolute property right, and love is but the love of property in the interest of unnatural morality. The ideal of equality demands that women be equal to men in expressing and experiencing their passions.

This was Sade's position in *La philosophie dans le boudoir,* a work which like his other pornographic works succeeds in trivializing sexual behavior, and perhaps that was his intention. In *Aline and Valcour,* however, the consequences of his principles are worked out. Theoretically, it should have been written after *La philosophie,* and perhaps it was, but at any rate in the work first published he presents three model societies, each of which ruthlessly reduces Enlightenment principles to what Sade conceives as their postulates and consequences. The first is Utopian, an island in the Pacific called Tamoé. Sade may have known Kant's concept of man as asocial. He certainly accepts it as a fundamental principle of human behavior. But he also realizes that for economic reasons social interaction is unavoidable. So in Tamoé he presents an economic Utopia. Everyone lives alike, and everyone works and is kept busy working, so productivity is high. At this point Sade takes a notion of Rousseau's — the immorality of luxury — and gives it a new twist. Economic surplus brings about luxury which brings about immorality and social disturbance. But to maintain an orderly society productivity must be high, the consequence of keeping everybody working. The ruler of this Utopia solves this dilemma very simply. All economic surplus is given away to primitive and less civilized inhabitants of other Pacific islands. The passions, then, can be controlled only if everyone lives in a modest but comfortable economic equality to maintain which necessitates constant work and no accumulation of economic surplus.

The second Utopia is an African kingdom called Butua. There all inhabitants are entirely at the mercy of the ruler, who is the essence and perfection of asocial man. His subjects are sexually exploited to the utmost limits of sexual ingenuity. They live miserably, but the king lives well, because he absorbs what little economic surplus there is, and also eats as many of his subjects as he can manage. The king lives as every man, Sade implies, would like to. As a Revolutionary did Sade mean Butua to be an emblem or allegory of the real state of European countries, in which a few lived splendidly and the rest, except for those who catered to the pleasures of the few, lived miserably?

Sade sees that neither of these Utopias — the social Utopia and the asocial Utopia — could be helpful to Europe. What is the ideal solution? Here Sade is at his most ingenious and his most impressive. Reason and Nature, he insists, must be satisfied. Therefore an adequate society must always be in a condition of revolution, since Nature and Reason cannot be reconciled and resolved into a unity. The problem, obviously, is to control the permanent revolution so that economic activity and inventiveness are not suppressed and also so that the society is not rent apart and destroyed. The answer is once again to find a way of satisfying man's fundamental need. In each community, then, there is to be a building with appropriate accommodations and arrangements. Every citizen has a right to summon any other citizen (including, if he has the stamina, *every* citizen), and the summoned citizen is completely at the sexual mercy of the summoner. But on another occasion the summoner can be the summoned; there is a condition of absolute egalitarianism in the expression of passions hitherto reserved for the nobility. The effect of this arrangement is that surplus revolutionary energy is drained off, natural needs are satisfied, and society is not committed to static millenialism, but is dynamically maintained.

The wonderful joke of all this is that Sade simply proposed to make legal and public what is in fact in existence but is illegal and private. Criminality and sexual perversity are not aberrations of human behavior but the norms of human behavior, constants at all socio-economic levels, the asociality on which sociality is in fact built — that asociality which is the dynamic force of any society. It follows that every society is always both Natural and Rational. Sade secularizes and legalizes original sin. The complement of Schiller's aesthetic drive is Sade's legalized sexual abandonment and perversion. No one exposed more completely than Sade the incoherence of the Enlightenment. He is the spectre that has haunted and fascinated European thinking about society and morality ever since, and held it spellbound with his outrageous confrontations.

Friedrich von Hardenberg Sometime in the late 1790s Friedrich
(Novalis) von Hardenberg, whose pseudonym was
(1772-1801) Novalis, had an astonishing idea. Language, he decided, is concerned only
with itself, and no one is aware of the fact. Thus it is a great secret
that when one speaks only for the sake of speaking, one utters beautiful and original truths; but when one wishes to speak of definite things
one utters only absurdities. Linguistic systems, then, are like mathematical systems. They are stipulated systems; both are concerned only
with themselves, and thus create a world for themselves. To be sure,
Hardenberg then goes on to say that for this very reason linguistic
systems can mirror in themselves the strange play of relationships
among things, and in doing so he loses the significance and force of

his idea. For the power of this idea about language emerges from the implication that language does not refer to anything except language. But then he shrinks from that conclusion and brings back to language its capacity to refer. In the 1790s it was impossible to grasp the implications of his insight into the peculiarity of language — much less to develop them. Had he been familiar with Herder's extraordinary notion that thought is but covert verbalization he might have grasped the power of his own idea, but Herder's concept was to be neglected for a hundred and fifty years. The cultural tradition that language is the expression of thought was too powerful, and, unfortunately, Hardenberg's brief essay, "Monolog," in which he wrote down his idea, was not be be published until 1846.

Yet we can see in Hardenberg's insight an attempt to transcend the incoherence of the Enlightenment, the incoherence of Reason and Nature. And to this we shall return. But what is to be noticed here is the historical significance of the fact that he had arrived at such a startling notion. The leap to this idea about language could only have come from a cultural shock of the utmost force. To say that when men endeavor to utter certainties about the world they can only utter absurdities is to call into question the whole range of European culture. It denies the validity of philosophy, of religion, of science as these were grasped at the time.

From 1790 to 1792 Hardenberg studied at the univerities of Jena, Leipzig, and Wittenberg; and after pursuing a course of government administration at Tennstedt and while working at his post at the salt mines of Weissenfels, he devoted himself to philosophical studies, particularly the works of Kant and Johann Gottlieb Fichte. He was, then, familiar with the most advanced thinking of his time, and once again it must be remembered that these were the years of the French Revolution, culminating in the Terror of 1794. When Hardenberg began to be published he adopted the pseudonym "Novalis" (the stress is on the first syllable), a Latin word meaning "a field that is ploughed anew or the first time," and laid claim to innovation in a way that scarcely needs underlining.

To grasp what Novalis was responding to it is necessary to consider language from a point of view not available to him. Language — and this has been said over and over — is responsible for the extraordinarily flexible adaptation of man to the world, the result and in part the cause of man's large brain. Such flexibility is not available to smaller-brained animals. And so it is said that man, unlike such animals, is not morphologically committed to an environmental niche. But that is a sentimentality. Man is in fact morphologically committed to language. And if we see, as Novalis says, that language is concerned only with itself, and that the attempt to use language to make specific statements about the world can only result in absurdities, then we can grasp the notion that like all adaptations language too is a maladaptation, an adaptation that limits the adaptive powers of a species. It is language, then, that is responsible not only for man's extraordinary cultural achievements, but it is also language that is responsible for the enormous savagery man has inflicted upon his fellow man and the enormous damage that man has done to the world. And Novalis lived through a period in which the language of the Enlightenment, so sure of its specific truths about the world, truths which he saw clearly as illusions, had effectively guillotined thousands of Frenchmen, and among them some of the best. Interested in science, he could scarcely have been ignorant, for example, of the death in 1794 of the great chemist Lavoisier upon the Revolutionary scaffold.

It is no exaggeration to say that man does not *use* language for the execution of his interests but rather to say that man *is* language. Language constructs a world for us; it controls our behavior in that constructed world; and it constructs explanations and justifications for why we do what we do. And it is successful, as Novalis sees, because language has the power of convincing us of the illusion of reference. But language also contains within itself the power to negate its own constructions. Novalis, perhaps without fully realizing it, used language itself to negate the validity of the linguistic explanations of the world which European culture had forged for its self-control. Thus language has the capacity to create something new, to achieve cultural transcendence, to take the materials of the existent culture and to forge a new culture, or at least a new explanation from which a new culture could be developed. Novalis was one of a few dozen Europeans born in the 1770s who saw their historical task to be the transcendence of traditional European culture.

From the above considerations we can derive clues to certain central obsessions of the Romantics. First was their intense interest in language, for Novalis was not alone in this. If culture is linguistic construction, then cultural transcendence must be achieved by creating new modes of language, new ways of using it, new rhetorics. The mark of the Romantic is not so much his ideas — and we shall see why this should be so — but rather the sharp break or discontinuity of his poetic, rhetorical, and artistic styles from the still culturally dominant styles of the two stylistic traditions of the Enlightenment, the neo-classic and 18th century "Romantic," the tradition of emotional lability. But an idea just mentioned — creating new modes of language — leads to a grasp of another Romantic obsession, creativity. The artist, verbal or non-verbal, as the creator, as the prophet and priest of a new culture, the functional equivalent of religion, is a central figure of Romantic self-definition. And this Romantic obsession gives us a clue as to why the artist, not the philosopher or ruler or scientist, was conceived as the cultural redeemer. Where but in the literature and the arts of the European past does one find significant cultural innovation? Hence, the Romantic interest is a new way of looking at the past, not in terms of the development of stylistic tradition but rather in the emergence of stylistic breaks; and the Romantic saw the artists who made those breaks, those discontinuities, as his models — though he was attempting a greater stylistic break than the past had ever achieved. And from this we can grasp a clue as to why the Romantic artist believed the primary power of the mind to be the imagination.

The 18th century had identified the imagination as the faculty responsible for art. Romantic definitions of the imagination are endless, and none of them is convincing or even means very much. The significant factor, however, is that that imagination was seen as the instrument of cultural transcendence; when the Romantics talk about the imagination they are telling themselves that their task is just that. And from this we can derive a clue as to why they were so intensely concerned with the "self" as distinguished from the personality which adapts itself to the world. If European explanations of the world had collapsed, and with them adequate instructions about what we

should do and how we should act, then it was up to the unique imaginative power of the individual to transcend that collapse and to create
the artistic instruments with which a new culture could be forged.
Again, definitions and explanations of the mysterious "self" are legion
in Romantic speculations. If we recognize that "self" is a pseudo-
entity, then it is possible to grasp why the Romantics were so ob-
sessed with it. Their intense preoccupation with the self was not by
any means a simple narcissism but instead the result of a realization
that explanatory collapse required the individual to create his own
culture unsupported by a traditional culture but of necessity, at least
initially, from the fragmentary ruins of that collapse. Thus the notion
of the self is the very essence of Romantic self-conception.

But here emerges a terrible dilemma. Culture sustains an individual's self-ascription of his own value. That is, the institutions of the
culture confer value or sacredness upon the individual. And without
that self-ascription of value, without that sacredness, without, to use a
more common term, that self-esteem, the individual cannot act. The
Romantic, then, was in the position of having to do the apparently
impossible, to confer sacredness upon himself. And we are back at the
conception of the artist as prophet and priest.

But all these obsessions created immense difficulties. For the initial
efforts at labelling and for several generations afterward the only
appropriate word for the Romantics and their creations — looking
at both from the point of view of their Enlightenment and pre-En-
lightenment contemporaries — is "bizarre." Twenty years after Romanticism began to emerge, Goethe called the Classic healthy and
the Romantic sick. The remark was typical of an uncomprehending
world in which the Romantics found themselves and from which
they were so profoundly alienated. To understand the first generations of the Romantics, it is necessary to call upon a general explanation of the kind of behavior we call deviant; for certainly the immense
majority of their contemporaries regarded the Romantics as deviant,
even when they were judged to be interesting.

The trouble with the notion of deviancy is that it assumes a norm
of behavior, a norm which usually conceals a moral notion of normal-
cy. But in every category of behavior there is in fact a wide range of

behavior, and the norm represents either a model intuitively arrived at, usually normative in character, or what is termed in statistical studies a "figure of greatest frequency." The problem to be explained is not the range but the concentration or accumulation of frequencies, no matter what mode of behavior is examined. This problem can be resolved by the following argument.

As proposed above, language consists of instructions for behavior, but since language is subsumed by culture (in the anthropological sense), what is true of language is also true of the remainder of culture, that is, of non-verbal instructions. Culture, then, is learned behavior, as differentiated from genetically controlled behavior, of which, however, we can know nothing, since any attempt to distinguish genetically controlled behavior must depend upon the subtraction of learned behavior, *such subtraction being itself cultural behavior.* Consequently there is no stability, nor can there be, in determinations of what might be genetically controlled behavior. All that we can observe and endeavor to explain is learned behavior. Two factors, however, interfere with the learning of behavior. The first has already been mentioned, the capacity of language to negate itself and likewise to negate non-verbal instructions. The other factor is even more important. In any learning process there is always some loss of what is to be learned. And in this loss two factors may be distinguished: the competence of the transmitter and the competence of the learner. What this means is that there is always an intrusion of more or less randomness into both kinds of competence. Scientific method, for example, considered as a cultural phenomenon depending upon its transmission, or learning, is designed to eliminate as much intrusion of randomness as possible. But even in scientific method, success in transmission is never complete. From this a general law of culture may be derived. To the degree that cultural transmission is incompetently carried out from generation to generation, there will be a spread of deviance, a spread which I choose to call the Delta effect. In Europeanized culture areas, for example, sexual behavior is very incompetently transmitted; thus in each generation there is a full spread of deviancy from the culturally approved norm.

Furthermore, because of negation and randomness another problem emerges. How is culture channeled: that is, how is a norm maintained? That maintenance involves the period before the transmission (the cultural tradition) and the period after the transmission (ongoing behavior). The answer lies in the phenomenon that transmission is maintained by cultural redundancy, the constant reiteration of the same cultural instructions in various verbal and non-verbal modalities. The legal requirement obtaining over such a long period, and the subsequent widespread practice of church-going after the legal demand has ceased, is one instance. And any classroom reveals the necessity for the continuous reiteration of the same category of cultural instructions. Detailed studies of marriages, to take another example, show that husbands and wives are continuously engaged in repeating to each other and to themselves the same instructions about every element of their interaction, from household economy to sexual behavior. Indeed, quantitatively, the overwhelming factor in human behavior is redundancy.

These considerations give us a valuable clue for comprehending the emergence and subsequent history of Romanticism. By rejecting the two aspects of Enlightenment culture (Nature and Reason) the Romantics also rejected that which Enlightenment culture secularized, the Judeo-Christian tradition. Thus they sundered the chain of ideological tradition, of ultimate ways of explaining the world and the individual's relation to what was not himself, and that amounted to almost everything that was himself. The result was not only cultural alienation. When the works of the opening decades of Romanticism are considered as a body produced by men and women, the salient characteristic is the Delta effect, or a random spread of deviancy. What prevents a full spectacle of randomness from occurring are two things: first, the very small number of individuals involved, a few dozen at the most out of a population in England, France, and Germany of 70,000,000 (or, if we include all of Europe, from Spain to Russia, of 200,000,000); and second, the fact that the cultural transcendence or reconstruction could initially find its materials only in the available materials of the culture. The only thing to do was to reconstitute them. And without a cultural norm, the unique characteristics and assemblage of the personality attributes of each Romantic necessarily played an important role. Hegel was to recognize this phenomenon in his notion of *Aufhebung,* the use of traditional materials to accomplish a cultural innovation. The old materials are both preserved and transformed.

There is an obvious conflict or incoherence between alienation and cultural redundancy. How is alienation to be maintained in intensively redundant social situations? To put it a bit differently, how is alienation to be maintained in circumstances of high interaction, since all interaction is massively redundant? The lives of the Romantics reveal the strategies that emerged. One is social withdrawal, the deliberate entry into a life of low interaction. The other is the little group of the socially alienated. And indeed Romanticism emerges primarily in individuals who rapidly moved into small group interaction.

There were initially two centers. One was in England — William Wordsworth, his sister Dorothy, Samuel Taylor Coleridge, and (a bit removed from the center) Robert Southey and Charles Lamb. In Germany the center was in Jena, the group initially drawn around Schiller and Fichte — the Schlegel brothers, Tieck, Wackenroder, Novalis, Schleiermacher, and Schelling. And before the end of the century Coleridge established intellectual and literary interaction with the German group. In France there was only the isolated figure of Chateaubriand, who actually lived in England from 1793 to 1800, and in Italy there was the even more isolated figure of Ugo Foscolo. Both Chateaubriand and Foscolo had less effect upon subsequent events than did the English and the Germans, simply because neither entered into sustaining small group interaction. The Germans got started before the English did, for they had two advantages. First, in Kant and Herder they had the most advanced thinking of the two strains of Enlightenment culture. Second, the political situation in Germany meant that there was no nationally organized intellectual establishment supported by a single state or government. Thus in Germany a little group assembled sporadically in Jena from all over Germany was the first to recognize the task of what we call — and again, only for convenience — the Romantics, the task of cultural transcendence. Only a few decades before, Germany had been far behind France and England. In fifty years German high culture had not only caught up, had not only through the Illuminati and the

Masons made important contributions to French revolutionary ideology, but now was about to leap ahead of the English, involved more than ever in characteristic English self-complacency, and ahead of the French, caught up in the toils of Revolution and nationalistic self-defense against the rest of Europe. To the philosopher who was not a Romantic yet who can be interpreted as a highway to accomplishing the Romantic purpose we shall now turn — Johann Gottlieb Fichte.

Johann Gottlieb Fichte The Copernican Revolution of Kant,
(1762-1814) as he himself called it, may have, for some at least, fatally compromised the claims of metaphysics to assert the real existence of a realm of being that transcends the world our senses tell us we live in; but it nevertheless gave a tremendous new authority to philosophy. The claims of philosophy to be the queen of the sciences, to have a judgmental and discretionary and regulatory control over all other modes of human activity, received new force from the transcendental philosophy of Kant. "Transcendental" in Kant's sense meant simply that the propositions of philosophical metaphysics looked as if they were making claims to a transcendent (or divine) realm, but in fact did not and could not make such claims. In recent years, moreover, some philosophers have dethroned philosophy from the Kantian ruling status, have insisted that such problems as, for example, the epistemological problem are pseudo-problems and have affirmed that philosophy has come to an end. Herder's insistence that philosophy is not about the mind but about language is increasingly popular, but even so philosophy is mistaken in imagining that it is the queen of language, its most common claim in recent decades.

Observations such as these encourage one to see the course of philosophy as but another manifestation of human culture, as a mode of behavior that is of high rank indeed, but one that, like the arts and the sciences, does not transcend the culture of its time but is subsumed and understood by whatever explanatory control can be managed over the culture of its historical period. Nevertheless, we need a clearer grasp of the place of philosophy in any historical culture and in human culture in general. If we look at philosophy dispassionately and as but one of innumerable cultural modes, what is striking about it is the terrible struggle philosophers have with language. They attempt a precision of definition which in ordinary behavior is not only not necessary but would indeed be a nuisance, unusable, destructive because of its very inflexibility. And they endeavor — or used to endeavor, at any rate — to construct a logic that can control philosophical discourse and be serviceable to and even endeavor to control ordinary language, or at least set up an ideal verbal model. To a dispassionate eye, logic is only an effort to stabilize and control the use of verbal particles — articles, pronouns, prepositions, conjunctions, and even punctuation. The instructive distinguishing feature of this heroic enterprise is that failure is at least as striking as success, a phenomenon admitted by the notion that we need a variety of logics, or that what has been thought of as a unitary logic is in fact a variety of logics. In short, philosophy's effort to stabilize language, even for the most restricted and carefully boundaried technical philosophy, is a failure.

For our purposes here it is not the success or failure that is interesting but the endlessness of the struggle. If we take the biological position proposed above, that language is maladaptive as well as adaptational, that man is morphologically committed to language and cannot transcend that commitment — as philosophy has always tried to do — then we can understand the place of philosophy in cultural history. Every species must struggle against its morphological commitment. Indeed, it would appear that species with the simplest morphological commitments, like bacteria and viruses, have the greatest possibility of survival. If that is the case, man's immensely complex morphological commitment to language does not provide a very encouraging prospect for the human species. It is, therefore, of the utmost importance that in human culture there should be some locus, or cultural space, or mode of behavior in which the maladaptive function of language is directly encountered. As Novalis almost grasped, and as Nietzsche saw clearly in the 1870s, and as more and more people are understanding today, language is truly transcendental. It slips, slides, and slithers on the surface of the world, and that very instability paradoxically improves adaptation (we call it progress)

and at the same time intensifies maladaption, destroying ourselves
and damaging the world, leading us, some think, towards extinction.
Indeed, there is no reason to think that the human race must necessarily exist for another ten minutes, though it probably will, even
though language has given man the capacity to destroy himself completely. Philosophy's struggle to stabilize language, even temporarily,
even for the sake of a relatively brief and highly technical philosophical discourse, is based on a misapprehension. The place of philosophy
in culture is comprehensible if we see it as the centripetally focused
cultural space or locus of culture's universal endeavor to create a
counteradaptation to the maladaptive force of language. Thus the more
a culture becomes aware of its destructive addiction to the ordinary
and mundane modes of verbal behavior, the greater its cultural — and
economic — investment in philosophy, and the higher the status of
philosophy in human culture. That is why the greatest cultures, the
most productive, those with the most striking history of at least temporary success, have all developed philosophies, though it certainly
appears to be the case that even a great and successful culture, such
as China or India, begins to deteriorate if philosophy is stabilized.
The stabilizing situation is made worse if philosophy is allied with
and particularly if it is controlled by religion, a cultural mode which,
from this point of view, stabilizes a vocabulary and a rhetorical mode
by making it sacred, by granting that vocabulary and rhetorical mode
an untouchability. Thus an excellent test for determining whether
or not a culture is in a condition of crisis is the degree of widespread
public attention and importance given to religious rhetoric. The
greater the importance ascribed to a stabilized religious rhetoric,
particularly if it is a rhetoric which the regnant forces in the culture
have once transcended, the greater the intensity of the cultural crisis.

More than one contemporary philosopher has come to the conclusion that what is important and valuable in any individual philosophy
is the broad vision of the problem the philosopher is struggling with,
not the details of his attempts at proof, more properly understood as
the professional rhetoric of the attempt to convince other philosophers,
something no philosopher has ever succeeded in doing. At best he
gains some followers, who, according to other philosophers, are fol-

lowers only because they misunderstand him. Certainly for the purpose of cultural history it is only the *vision* that is worth paying attention to, but to grasp that vision it is always necessary to understand how the philosopher related himself to his predecessors and to
grasp the particular problem he was addressing himself to.

In the case of Fichte neither broad vision nor the details presents
any severe problem. He set out to complete the philosophy of Kant.
His great predecessor, Fichte claimed, had not addressed himself to
the primary task of philosophy: how the mind goes about knowing
the world. Kant had done no more in his critical philosophy than
to analyze the instruments or faculties of the mind. The critical philosophy, great as it was, was no more than a propaedeutic, an introduction to and preparation for engaging with the primary task of
philosophy.

That Fichte was on the right track can be made convincing by
a brief digression to examine Kant's notion of the contemplation of
the beauty of nature and of art, a question which he takes up in the
Critique of Judgment. Not that Kant, living all his life in flat Königsberg, a town noted neither for great buildings nor important collections of painting and sculpture, had ever had much artistic experience. The two principal buildings, the castle and the cathedral, were
both medieval, and Kant gives no indication of having been roused
by the interest in the Gothic emerging in the 1760s. Königsberg
had a musical life of some richness but Kant denied that music has
any meaning whatever and moreover judged that music is an uncivil
art because it bothers the neighbors. As for literature, that he had an
educated man's knowledge of the ancient classics goes without saying.
In spite of this limited knowledge of the arts Kant had no hesitation
in discussing them extensively, but only in order to define the character of the aesthetic experience. And that character, he affirmed,
was disinterestedness. This notion had a deep effect upon the German
Romantics initially and in time on the whole tradition of Romantic
culture. Combined with the immense importance given to art, the
notion of disinterestedness provided a justification and a validation
for the alienation of the artist from the cultural redundancies of his
time.

Yet Kant was clearly wrong, and his wrongness is illuminating. It appears quite obvious that in making a work of art the artist is under the control of an ideology, just as every man always is, no matter what he does. The socio-cultural task of the artist before the emergence of Romanticism was precisely to participate in and to assist in maintaining the redundancy systems of his culture, particularly its religious and aristocratic redundancies. And it is equally obvious that an individual tends to ascribe value to a work of art either because of that ideology or in spite of it, as one admires Dante's great poem but rejects its theology. But such a rejection is not in the service of disinterestedness. Rather, in the service of an opposing ideology. What Kant had done was to confuse the aesthetic experience with the artistic situation. It is the characteristic of the artistic situation, the situation in which one encounters a work of art, that it does not require any action on the part of the observer. Thus a devout Catholic in a church on encountering a painting of the Virgin Mary will pray, though he probably will not if he encounters such a picture in an art museum. Similarly, a non-believer interested in works of art will not pray before a Madonna either in church or an art museum. In the same way a professor of literature preparing a lecture on a literary work will respond to it very differently if he is reading it for amusement and pleasure. The first situation requires him to take action; the second does not.

Now this decision of Kant to define the character of the aesthetic experience is an excellent instance of what Fichte found incomplete in Kant's critical philosophy and illustrates why he felt he had to complete it, and in what direction. In the complicated mode of situational interpretation, which in the Enlightenment had been resolved into the incoherence of nature and reason, Kant had been concerned only with reason, with what the mind brings to the situation. Of the situation itself he merely said it was an unknowable *Ding-an-sich*, a notion which may be effectively thought of as a hypothetical construct the function of which was to maintain reality's presence while Kant went about the business of critically examining our modes of knowing. Fichte was convinced that the first thing to be handled in Kant was that very *Ding-an-sich*, and that what had to be done with it was to get rid of it.

What Fichte clearly saw was that Kant's critical philosophy was indeed concerned only with the mind, and with the correct and justified use of the instruments or faculties of the mind. And what permitted Fichte this interpretation was his perception of the French Revolution as a struggle to apply an inadequate notion of the mind, of reason itself. But this does not mean that his reaction to the Revolution was antipathetic. On the contrary, in common with all the intellectuals of his period, with few exceptions, his primary concern was with freedom, political freedom, and he saw that the Revolution aimed to achieve it. Thus in 1793 he published *Contributions Designed to Correct the Judgment of the Public on the French Revolution.* Eventually his approval of the Revolution was to bring about his dismissal in 1799 from his professorship at Jena, to which he had been appointed in 1794 in spite of his radicalism. The attack on Fichte was carried out under the cover of his alleged atheism.

In 1795 he published his most important work, the foundation of his subsequent philosophizing, *Grundlage der gesammten Wissenschaftslehre (Basis of the Entire Theory of Science,* also translated as simply *Science of Knowledge).* (At the time "science" meant a body of coherent and logically consistent propositions; on the continent it can still mean that, though in Anglo-American usage it is restricted to the natural sciences.) Fichte wrote his masterpiece, then, immediately after having defended the French Revolution. It seems apparent that the French Revolution revealed that philosophy has, or can have, consequences — real political and social consequences. After all, were not the ideologues of the French Revolution universally known as *philosophes*? One of Fichte's major attacks in the *Wissenschaftslehre* is against what he calls dogmatic realism, which is precisely the uncritical fusion of nature and reason, based on the unanalyzed assumption that reason is the product of nature and that one has only to determine what is *truly* natural in order to decide what is *truly* reasonable. It was, then, imperative that the Kantian revolution be completed. If the Revolution was in trouble — and Fichte must have been writing the book during the Terror, which was taking place only 400 miles west of Jena — it was because its ideology was a dogmatic realism, uncorrected by the incomplete critical philosophy. To complete Kant was imperative if the great moral idea of freedom was to be sustained and made a central factor of European life and culture.

The proposition on which Fichte builds his entire structure is that what makes consciousness possible is an act, an act which lies at the base of consciousness and does not enter into consciousness. The mind in knowing itself can only know its faculties. It does nothing but know itself. But if the basic relation of a man to the world is an act, then the mind, or consciousness, must be used by some other force in human nature. And that other force Fichte calls the Ego, or, as it is often translated, the Self. But the Self must not be thought of as a being, an entity, a something, since it is itself an act. It posits itself, that is, it asserts its own existence by an act. It says "I AM." However, when it examines itself it discovers that it includes within itself that which is not itself, a non-Ego, in short, the world. This realization leads Fichte in two directions, towards the world, and also away from it.

In moving towards the world he asserts that his philosophy could be called either real idealism or ideal realism. As he says, his philosophy is not a theoretical philosophy but a practical philosophy; and it seems quite justified to call it a pragmatic philosophy, or at least a philosophy of praxis. The tremendous importance of Fichte lies in the fact that his was the first to attempt to untangle the complexities of situational thinking.

In moving in the other direction, away from the world, Fichte arrives at his notion of the Transcendental Ego. He asserts that the empirical Ego, the Ego or Self we know by observing ourselves, is not unified. We respond to the world, and we respond to our response to the world. But in that latter action we are arrested from action. We take ourselves, as it were, out of gear. But an action can only be performed by a unity, and in this Fichte's thought somewhat resembles Herder's insistence that the whole man acts. So there must be an Ego, a Self, an I AM which is unified and puts us back into gear. That is, the Transcendental Ego is not a thing, or an entity, or a hypostatized word, but an action. And it is always an action towards the world. Furthermore, we can intuit it but we cannot conceptualize it.

But the Transcendental Ego is also an action in response to the world. What gets action going, then, is that the act of self-assertion is both active and passive. The I Am impinges on the world, but the world impinges on the I AM. The World and the Self, then, are contradictions or antitheses. But if action is to be possible (and it is not only possible but occurs) then these antitheses or contradictions must be reconciled and unified and synthesized.

At this point Fichte introduces a very big gun indeed. In its impingement upon the world the Self selects from the world by making use of similarities and differences among the various members of what it determines as the same category. But it is also the case that the world impinges on the Self, forcing the Self to select from the mind's resources as established by Kant. (And here Fichte ingeniously suggests the origin of the various Kantian faculties.) So it would be more accurate to say that the world in its impingement forces the Self to categorize. That impingement upon the world is therefore experienced as an impingement from the world, as a limitation of the action of the Self, the I AM, which is infinite — that is, without limitations except from the world. Such limitation is experienced as feeling. Thus feeling is the dynamic force which keeps the Self going, which elicits the activity which unifies the consequences of the mutual impingements of World and Self, what Fichte calls the interdetermination of Self and World, into a basis of knowledge and action. And that unifying activity is the imagination. At a stroke the imagination is raised from a peripheral place in human behavior to an absolutely central place. The imagination creates the world. The imagination, however, is in itself not accessible to consciousness, which can only experience it; Fichte grants supreme importance to unconscious action; he raises a hundred-year-old idea, the unconscious, to the highest status.

But that creation of the world is easily misunderstood as a static creation. It is necessary to remember that, according to Fichte, any creation of the world by the imagination affords only momentary satisfaction. The reason for the brevity of this halt is that the Transcendental Ego is unlimited, or infinite, simply because it is nothing but an act. Consequently when it recoils from the world upon itself, and when feeling summons the imagination to synthesis, the Ego recoils not from the world but only from a point in its moving outward to the world. That point it experiences not as a terminus but only as a frontier. Since the Transcendental Ego is an act, it is an endless striving towards the unlimited in the world, towards the infinite. What Fichte is saying is that the empirical Ego is unstable, and that its penetration into the world, its impingement upon the world, is unstable, and that the momentarily satisfying constructions of the imagination are necessarily unstable. What this translates into can be put variously as an irresolvable tension between self and not-self, between reason and nature, between man and world, between situation and interpretation.

Fichte never liked the works of the Romantics, even those of the young people at Jena among whom Romanticism emerged. In his devotion to an Enlightenment concept of political freedom and in his insistence upon a moral idealism which he came to identify with God, he never fully emerged from the Enlightenment. Nevertheless, he provided the insurgent German Romantics with a philosophical base and a justification for three crucial ideological factors: the autonomous creativity of the Self, the centrality of the inaccessible imagination in human life (which they were to interpret as establishing the centrality of art for life), and in the instability of the interdetermination of self and world an authority for the possibility of cultural transcendence and the justification for attempting to achieve it. That notion was to include self-transcendence, to be accomplished by what they came to call Romantic irony. Fichte made transcending the Enlightenment possible not by resolving the incoherence of Nature and Reason into a unity, as the French Revolution and Goethe were attempting, but by revealing that incoherence as the dynamism of the human enterprise, its irresolvability as the human opportunity. He removed all the barriers to attacking and disintegrating those cultural redundancies which locked a few insightful individuals into a culture which, they judged, had failed. His *Wissenschaftslehre* authorized cultural vandalism, a disintegrating analytic attack upon tradiional regnant European ideologies.

Ludwig Tieck (1773-1853)
and
Wilhelm Wackenroder (1773-1798)

A novel, *Die Geschichte des Herrn William Lovells* (*The History of Mr. William Lovell*), by Ludwig Tieck ends with precisely the question Fichte had raised. "Who am I? What is that strange *Ich,* that Ego, which engages me in the world and involves me in activities I cannot understand?" Tieck planned his book in 1792 and wrote it from 1792-1796, publishing it in 1795 and 1796. He was a native of Berlin, the son of a master rope-maker, but in the Gymnasium he encountered a group of brilliant young men, the most important of whom was Wilhelm Heinrich Wackenroder. Destined by his father for the clergy, Tieck rebelled and entered into the life of a writer, always a perilous decision — but not for Tieck. He began at once a career of writing successful pot-boilers, sentimental and Gothic novels, the fiction of the culture of emotional lability. And it seems probable that he planned *William Lovell* to be such a work. It begins as a typical 18th century epistolary novel in the tradition of Samuel Richardson, another *Clarissa Harlowe,* perhaps, in which a man is morally seduced into wicked ways just as Clarissa is physically seduced by a wicked man. But while Tieck was writing he had several striking experiences. One was his reading of Fichte's 1794 *Wissenschaftslehre*; the other was a walking tour he made in 1793 with Wackenroder.

That tour in Southern Germany had a profound impact upon both of them. They encountered two cultures unknown to Protestant-Pietistic-Sentimental-Enlightenment Berlin. One was the medieval culture which they found in Nürnberg, an untouched city of the Middle Ages, a great Medieval and early Renaissance cultural center, and the home of Albrecht Dürer, who was to become one of their heroes. Both were to write about him. The other was the culture of Baroque Catholicism — the churches and monasteries of the 17th and 18th centuries, Baroque and Rococo. It was a revelation. Here was an architecture bold, voluptuous, of enormous sensory and emotional power, built in a landscape of extreme beauty. For example, the monastery and pilgrimage church of *Vierzehnheiligen* in Bavaria has an interior like the boudoir of a king's mistress — only far bigger.

Here in southern Germany were two alternative cultures, two modes of beauty and sublimity completely unfamiliar to young men brought up among the cold neo-classic buildings of Frederick the Great and his successors in Berlin, a city build on the flat and sandy wastes of Brandenburg.

But no one is moved by an alternative culture unless he is ready to be moved. The very walking trip Tieck and Wackenroder set out upon, a trip into an unknown world, is an indication of their dissatisfaction with Berlin life and culture. Tieck was a successful writer of Enlightenment pot-boilers simply because he and his Gymnasium friends had already rejected both the rational and sentimental aspects of Enlightenment culture, including Pietism, that sentimental, rationalizing compromise between Protestantism and the Enlightenment. He was successful in what he was doing because his attitude was ironic. More important, however, was that the revelation of alternative cultures came to the two friends in the form of art. The lesson was obvious, though incomplete. Art is the mode of existence and behavior which enables the individual to transcend a culture native to him but unsatisfactory to the point where he neglects it. The problem for Tieck was how to dramatize that cultural failure. And now Fichte came to his aid. The mere sensory impact of the world is not reality. Reality is what the imagination has transformed. But the 18th century had so intensely identified the imagination with the creation of art that the illumination of the failure of a culture could be properly achieved not by philosophy or history but by dramatizing it in literature, in art. That dramatization is the subject of *William Lovell* (1795-1796).

It is a long book, 258 letters written by twenty-five major and minor characters. Lovell begins as a typical product of the culture of emotional lability as it exalts love, friendship, picturesque nature. The time is the 1770s; the book ends while the American Revolution is still going on, or perhaps just getting under way. It is a few years after the 1774 appearance of Goethe's *Werther,* to which in a way it is a reply. Lovell sets out on the grand tour. In Paris he meets Rosa, a fascinating Italian, who persuades Lovell that he is a remarkable man, remarkable because of his qualities of extreme sensibility, his self-conscious sensitivity, and his emotional lability.

His moral duty, then, is to cultivate, to give freedom to that sensibility, so perfectly reflected in Rosa's reaction to him, even though he violates the dull unfeeling morality of ordinary men. Rosa is, in fact, an agent of a Roman named Andrea Cosimo, who is interested in seducing Lovell into his own intellectual and emotional position. From them Lovell learns that all men, except such men as themselves, play roles. Role-playing is an old and obvious metaphor for describing behavior, but Tieck means more than that. It is not merely that "role" is a good metaphor for discussing human activity; rather, behavior is only a role, nothing but a role. Human beings are mere puppets. Only the remarkable man can transcend this. And Lovell proves his remarkableness by violating a large variety of moral decencies. He becomes something very close to a criminal. In Rome Cosimo has organized a secret society of such men, with himself as the leader. This episode comes at the very end of the novel.

It is evident that Tieck was familiar with *Wilhelm Meister* and the Fellowship of the Tower. Lovell is inducted, most impressively, but in the meeting itself nothing whatever happens. In time he meets Cosimo, learns that Cosimo is in fact an Englishman named Waterloo, that he is the great-uncle of Lovell's one time friend Burton, that his manipulative seduction of Lovell is an act of revenge against Lovell's father. He is only what he has made of Lovell, a disappointed sentimentalist; neither of them is remarkable, and the revenge, which consists only of pointless manipulation of others and making puppets of others by persuading them that they are not puppets, is itself only a manifestation of puppethood. Cosimo has merely done to Lovell what he has done to himself.

And now comes the great question Cosimo asks in his farewell letter to Lovell. *Who* has done this? Wilhelm Meister's learning of life is learning the proper role, not acting but something nobler for which he is prepared by the Fellowship. The distinction between Role and Self, or Ego, had not yet appeared. But this distinction emerges from Cosimo's self-revelation. Andrea has laughed at Lovell when Lovell finally managed to see him. And he laughs at him again, and at himself, in a subsequent autobiography. But there is no reconciliation, no resolution of the problem. "And who am *I* then?" Andrea asks. He has no answer but pushes further. He is being sincere at last, but sincerity is nothing, it is useless. "What is that strange *I* that has forced me about . . . that has constrained me to act as I have?" His secret society is pointless. The self-confidence of Catholicism found its most intense expression in the Jesuits, and the self-confidence of the Enlightenment its most intense expression in the Illuminati and the Masons, the imitators of the Jesuits. Goethe's self-confidence in his own personal mode of Enlightenment culture appeared in the Fellowship of the Tower. The emptiness and pointlessness of Cosimo's society reveals the emptiness and pointlessness of all the secret societies of the Enlightenment and of the Enlightenment itself, including Goethe's peculiar and personal mode of it. Cosimo's society reveals the valuelessness of that culture, for the only value of such societies is the manipulation of others. But what is the value of manipulating that which has no value? To think otherwise is to succumb to Cosimo's self-deception, as he eventually realizes.

Here then is dramatized the complete failure of Enlightenment culture and the complete failure of value. The creation of value is the activity of the Self; but if the culture has failed, then the Self too must fail in its value-creating endeavor. Clearly, if the Self is to create value it can do so only in response to a value-laden culture. Would or could the French Revolution do anything more? No, for it was no more than a manifestation of the incoherence of the existing culture, dramatized in Cosimo's purposeless and pointless secret society. The need was for a culture which would not rest upon the manipulation of others, a manipulation which was only self-deceiving manipulation of oneself. In *William Lovell* Tieck presented for the first time the problem and the task of the Romantic.

The immediate problem for Tieck and his friend Wackenroder was to discover a mode of existence in which feeling, as explained by Fichte, might be authentic, not feeling dictated by or merely reacting against a culture of puppets, but feeling emerging from the impingement of the world upon the imagination. But if that impingement was to be experienced and understood, models were necessary.

Tieck and Wackenroder, after their experience of the medieval and
Baroque culture of southern Germany, sought for models in the past.
The culture they had rejected was modern, neo-classical and French.
Southern Germany was the least modern part of Germany, a world
in which the culture of the past had survived. It was not neo-classical; it was not French. And culturally moribund Italy in the late
18th century was even less French, less neo-classical — or so they
thought — and certainly less modern. What they needed was a culture of sufficient power and beauty to justify the repudiation of their
native culture and their alienation from it, a culture uncompromised
by the Enlightenment. That repudiation and alienation were enshrined
in Wackenroder's remarkable book *Herzensergiessungen eines kunst-
liebenden Klosterbruders* (*Heartoutpourings of an Art-loving Monk*),
1797. That was his result of that 1793 walking trip. Tieck's was
Franz Sternbald's Wanderungen (*The Wanderings of Franz Sternbald*),
written from 1795 to 1797, published in 1798, a work planned with
Wackenroder and one to which Wackenroder contributed much.

In this walking trip and in this friendship appear two important
behavioral patterns of Romanticism. First is the wandering itself,
the deliberately randomizing exposure to alien and alternative cultural modes. To be effective, what such randomization requires is an
equally deliberate separation from the redundancies of one's culture.
That is the point of Romantic travelling, the entrance into a social
situation to which one is alien. The other aspect, the friendship, is
equally important. The Tieck-Wackenroder friendship was like the
Coleridge-Wordsworth friendship. Both are the earliest appearances
of the little group, the social institution not secret but separate, not
the condensation and intensification of the redundancies of one's
culture but the creation of an institutionalized opposition culture,
one in which new attitudes, through friendly reciprocation, may
develop and maintain their own emerging redundancies. For this
reason intense friendship is such an important theme in both Romantic life and literature. In earlier periods it was not needed because the individual was sustained by the redundancies of a culture
which he accepted, which his talent or genius condensed and intensified. His task was to purify and make coherent his cultural redun-

dancies. He felt no isolation. Consequently he could work alone, because he was not alone. The Romantics needed the little group because they could not work alone for the reason that they were alone. Wackenroder's was the first consequence of this first Romantic group, the prototype for many such coteries, small-scale and temporary social institutions.

In his short book Wackenroder dramatized his position by assuming the role of an art-loving cloister-brother, or monk, or friar. That device immediately identified him as a Southern, Catholic German. But since he wished to praise not only the Catholic artists of Italy — Raphael, Leonardo, Michelangelo, Piero di Cosimo — but also their great Germany contemporary Albrecht Dürer, he wished also to praise the most powerful German cultural force of the early 16th century, Martin Luther and Protestantism. In particular he praises Luther for the latter's assertion that "music occupies the first place among all the sciences and arts of the human spirit." For Wackenroder this statement gave Luther's authority for granting the highest value to art, and among the arts the highest value to music. It is a theme Wackenroder further explored in his invented musician, Joseph Berglinger, whose story he told and whose writings and letters he quotes. This was the first appearance in the writings of the Romantics of the notion that music is indeed the highest of the arts and the proper model for all the others. It is a theme which would lead to the centrality of music in the Romantic culture of the 19th and much of the 20th centuries.

This praise of music is an important clue to understanding the high value the book places upon religious art and the religious poems included in the work. It is an element in Wackenroder's thinking easily misunderstood, as Goethe did. It is not that the works of Wackenroder's favorite painters, Raphael and Dürer, are important because they present religious subjects. It is just the other way around. Religion is revealed as important by art, and only by art. That is, art is the human creation of the sacred, of value. And art is the product of the imagination, the inaccessible imagination, as Fichte had suggested, a point repeated by Wackenroder in an imaginary letter written by Raphael. Furthermore, as Fichte again had shown, the imagination is activated by feeling. The transformation of sensation into meaning, into significance is accomplished by the transforming power of the Fichtean imagination. That is true of all men, but the artist is unique, first because of the intensity of his feeling and imagination, an intensity which is the mark of the genius, and second because that intensity results in work which can arouse in other human beings — individuals, however, as rare as the artist, as alienated as the artist from Ordinariness — a similar intensity of feeling and imagination. Consequently the test of a work of art is the intensity of emotional response it elicits, but only in those rare individuals capable of such intensity. Thus a theme of great importance in the subsequent history of Romanticism emerges: the response *to* the work of art is as creative an act as the creation *of* a work of art. Furthermore, in an important passage Wackenroder insists that this creative responder need not and must not be limited by what is approved or validated by the artistic judgment of his cultural milieu. Rather, if he is responding properly he is capable of being moved by the art of all cultures, including, significantly enough, not only non-European civilized art but also the art of barbarians and primitives. This point of Wackenroder's was also the position of Tieck, who turned for literary revitalization to folk-tales, despised by sophisticates.

It is necessary to remember that Wackenroder was writing at a time when the most prominent artistic effort in Germany was Goethe's, literally aided by Schiller and paralleled in France and England and Italy, to bring Neo-Classicism to fruition by establishing the principles of Classicism, as determined by the art and architecture and literature of ancient Greece and Rome. (Actually Goethe had already achieved the perfection of *his* Classicism in the 1787 *Iphigenia auf Tauris,* and was never to reach it again). These were, it was claimed, the true models. Wackenroder's affirmation of the superiority, or even the value, of the Renaissance artists — it will be remembered that at the time no distinction was made between the art of the Middle Ages and of the Renaissance — was a direct challenge to the prevailing taste and the authority of Weimar and Berlin, and also the aestheticians and critics of recognized authority, whom he mentioned with distaste and sarcasm.

Wackenroder was not interested in, and indeed contemned, philosophically formalized aesthetics, correct critical judgments, artistic principles; he was interested in feeling. In a very important sense he was not committed to art at all, that is, to a set of objects validated by a culture as something to be admired and acquired. Nor was he concerned with feeling for its own sake, in the manner of the culture of emotional lability. That position found its justification in Nature, but Wackenroder's justification was in the human spirit; that is, it was not derived from Nature nor justified by Nature. Rather he was interested in feeling because it transcended Nature. What he wanted was the capacity of the human spirit to create value. Indeed, for him, value creation, the activity of the transforming imagination, *is* the human spirit. That is why he felt that religion is not the path to art, but that art is the path to valid religion, which is a matter of feeling, not of scripture nor of theology.

Throughout Wackenroder's book the emphasis is constantly upon works of true art as the occasions for the experience and creation of value, and, also, just as important, as evidence of the value-creating power. Hence, the *Herzensergiessungen* is a direct reply to the problem posed at the end of *William Lovell,* the meaninglessness or emptiness or valuelessness of life as life was understood by Enlightenment culture. And this is confirmed by the fact that Wackenroder turns against the art of his time, which he rejects, and to the art of a period in which the subject-matter of art was primarily religious. A culture is not active and vital because it is religious; rather religion is evidence that in the culture the value-creating power is active and vital. That is why European art was most glorious at a time when religion was most vital, a vitality revealed by Martin Luther as well as by the Church of Rome. And for this reason Wackenroder can transfer to works of art and to his artistic heroes the religious epithets "holy" and "divine."

And this transference also determines the life of his cloister-brother, his monk. In the opening paragraphs of Wackenroder's book the monk tells us that he once was worldly, participating fully and successfully in the culture of his time. Yet his devotion to art and to his artistic heroes made him dissatisfied and eventually alienated him from his society and culture. Thus he has chosen to end his days in a monastery, and we must, I believe, think of the marvelous Baroque monasteries of Southern Germany and Austria, not neglected but rich and active. By becoming a monk Wackenroder's spokesman can live in a glorious work of art, and by participating in Catholic ritual he can become an actor in a work of dramatic art. Thus he enters into an alternative culture, a culture which has survived from the past, and sustains the past, a culture in which both religion and art are evidence and means of value creation, and above all a culture in which it is art that sustains religion. Some are converted to a religion for intellectual reasons, philosophical or theological; some are converted from despair, for only in religious exercises can they experience their own value; but Romanticism was to create a new kind of convert, the artistic convert, the aesthetic Christian. Wackenroder enables us to see why and how this new cultural type emerged.

Yet Wackenroder was not himself converted. Just as Tieck helped him with his book, even contributing sections, so Wackenroder helped Tieck in the planning of *Franz Sternbalds Wanderungen.* In the year that book was published, 1798, however, Wackenroder died after a long illness. But before he died he wrote additional material which Tieck published in 1799 in *Phantasien über Kunst, für Freunde der Kunst (Fantasies on Art, for Friends of Art)*, together with essays by Tieck himself. Two of Wackenroder's are worth noting. In an essay on the instrumental music of his day, he pays tribute to the new symphonic art, presumably of Mozart and Haydn, for he interprets those works as portraying not "an individual emotion" but "an entire world, an entire drama of human emotions." Whether or not this interpretation is justified for the symphonies is arguable; but the fact that Wackenroder so interpreted them is properly considered evidence of his capacity for cultural transcendence. Certainly there is some justification for his interpretation, for to portray that "drama of human emotions" is precisely what Beethoven was shortly to set out to do, and it became the primary objective of Romantic composers. What links the music of the late 18th century with Romantic music is precisely that in late Mozart and Haydn the dramatic factor of the culture of emotional lability was beginning to emerge. And it is further evident from Wackenroder's ensuing description of an ideal symphonic movement that what that drama portrayed was the endeavor to create value.

Wackenroder has gone beyond his position in the *Herzensergies-sungen,* which begins with painting and ends with music. The conversion of his monk is in itself a value-seeking drama.

In the essay on St. Peter's in the *Phantasies* what Wackenroder is interested in is the drama of the building of the great church. And in his final essay he seizes upon the source of that drama of human emotions. It is a letter by his musician Joseph Berglinger to the monk himself, and it is an implicit criticism and questioning of the monk's position. For Berglinger presents himself as one shamefully and lustfully attracted to music. Is not music (and all art) a terrible self-indulgence when we contemplate the suffering of men in the real world? How are we morally justified in pursuing and contemplating and responding to works of art? How can we justify the uselessness of art? Berglinger cannot resolve this dilemma. He can only recognize it. But what he does arrive at is the view that in this new cultural situation — this situation without the support of the redundancies of an established culture, this situation in which the individual is alienated and isolated, this situation that has made possible the transforming power of creating value — the experience of value is not and cannot be stabilized. That recognition was to be one of the central themes of Romantic culture and a primary source of its dynamism, of the power of Romanticism to transform *itself.* That instability is the central theme of *Franz Sternbalds Wanderungen.*

Tieck evidently began *Sternbald* in 1795, finishing it in 1797 and publishing it in 1798, the year of Wackenroder's death. Thus the composition of the book overlapped the composition of *William Lovell,* to which, like Wackenroder's *Klosterbruder,* it is a reply, taking up where the earlier book left off, with the question, "Who am I?" It may be considered the first Romantic historical novel. Although *Lovell* takes place perhaps fifteen years before the time at which Tieck began it, there is no effort to tie it into its historical period, except for the undisturbed French monarchy and for the reference to the American wars. *Sternbald,* on the other hand, takes place at a specific time (1520-21): a time determined by the death of Raphael and by Dürer's visit to the Netherlands, the home of the artist Lucas van Leyden. Luther and the Reformation are in the background. There are discussions of the work of Dürer, of Raphael, and of Michelangelo. The descriptions of Nürnberg and Leyden are, in addition, efforts to capture the medieval appearance of those cities in the early 16th century. The book also establishes a distinct feature of the Romantic historical novel, the mingling of imagined characters with historical figures. Two thrusts of Romantic literary enterprise are thus allied from the very beginning, historicism and realism.

These two thrusts may appear to be unconnected, perhaps even to be opposites, but that is not the case. Indeed, the realistic novel as it emerged in the middle decades of the 19th century is best understood as a historical novel about the present, that is, the historically grasped situation of the writer, as the Goncourt brothers were to affirm in the 1850s. On the other hand, if we examine the cultural origins of the great historical scholars of the 19th century — and they were to be found in every European national culture — it is apparent that they emerged from Romantic culture. Further, both realism and historicism are allied in that both are stategies for cultural transcendence. As Tieck and Wackenroder had learned on their 1793 walking trip, when they discovered intact survivals of the past — Medieval, Renaissance, and Baroque — the exploration of history serves to plunge the individual into alternative possibilities. This is the reason for the inclusion of historical figures; they appear not for decoration or mere verisimilitude but because they were in their lifetimes living embodiments or exemplifications of alternative cultural modes. Realism serves the same end. To use Fichte's Imagination for the moment (since it is handy) a culture is the product of the human imagination. It is therefore a transformation by that imagination. Now any transformation, as Fichte was also aware in his notion concerning the effort of the Ego to transcend the boundaries of what the imagination transforms and constructs, necessarily limits the details or attributes of any situation it responds to. What literary realism does (as does "realism" in its most common sense) is to endeavor to overcome or violate the cultural boundaries by exploring those attributes of the transformed situation which the current transformation has ignored and neglected.

The writer of realism, however, must necessarily have some way of limiting his selection of such attributes, even though his primary interest is to overcome and go beyond the culturally defined boundaries of comprehending that situation. His awareness of the limitations of the culture and his exploration of neglected attributes have a reciprocal effect, one might say. His cultural dissatisfaction moves him to focus upon a problem which the cultural redundancies of his situation neglect, or conceal, or ignore. Thus the realistic novel of the Romantic tradition is polemical; it is an attack upon, or violation of, the pieties of his cultural situation, a situation from which he is alienated.

The Romantic historical novelist uses a specific historical past for the same purpose. His method was frequently analogical. Concerned with a factor in his culture which he considers problematic, although his cultural situation does not so consider it, he locates a period in the past in which the problem was also, in his judgment, problematic. Thus he uses a historical period to extract the problem from his own cultural milieu, to isolate it, to separate it from the confusing and compromising milieu in which he finds it. Both historicism and realism in Romantic literature emerge from the same effort to achieve cultural transcendence and from the same dissatisfaction with the regnant cultural norms and redundancies.

To recapitulate briefly, the eighteenth century had developed the intrinsic difficulty in situational thinking into an incoherence between Nature and Reason, the Revolutionary attempt to identify Nature was proving disastrous, and the Romantics responded to this state of emergence not by endeavoring to reconcile Nature and Reason but by demonstrating that their predecessors had by no means adequately explored either. In one direction, the Romantics insisted that whatever Mind (or Spirit) might be, it was far vaster and more powerful than Reason: that whatever the *telos* or end or purpose of man might be, it was not merely to be rational. In the opposite direction, they insisted that the Enlightenment notion of Nature was actually an impediment to the exploration of any situation. Thus, in the distinction between a situation and the interpretation or explanation of that situation imposed upon it, but certainly not derived from it, they found, and were to find, that the distance between situation and interpretation must be made far greater if there was to be any hope of discovering a possible relation or interaction between the two.

The interplay betweeen Wackenroder and Tieck was such that the former had as his primary interest the significance of feeling to thought and mind, while the latter turned to the situation. Their friendship and intellectual partnership show the intimate connection between these two tasks. The problem of both was art. Wackenroder was interested intensely in the significance of art for Spirit; Tieck in the relation of the artist and his art to the situation in which he finds himself. In *Sternbald* Tieck judged the situation of the artist at his time, or himself as artist as analogous to the situation of the artist in the early 16th century. He saw that period as a time when a new artistic grandeur had been accomplished by Raphael, Michelangelo, and Dürer. It was a time of cultural crisis, as the outbreak of Martin Luther — and, above all, his success — clearly indicated. The cultural transcendence of the three great artists was made possible, as well as necessary, by that crisis.

Franz Sternbald, then, is a young artist, a pupil and follower of Dürer, and the novel begins with his departure on the dawn of a summer day from Nürnberg. He has set out on his wanderings, his destination uncertain, to determine for himself what art was being done, what it was accomplishing, and to arrive at a clarified definition and comprehension of himself as an artist and of his artistic task and purpose. He takes up the question of Andrea Cosimo: "Who am I?" Although his aim is to reach Italy, he first wanders north as far as Leyden before turning south, staying at Antwerp a few months; and the part of the novel which is completed (Tieck never finished it) finds him in Rome. He is thus engaged in a randomization of experience, for his adventures are not merely adventures having to do with his art, but also with his erotic life and above all with the natural world.

The novel is filled with rapturous descriptions of nature. The theme of attempting to determine his talents and his character, the theme of

"Who am I" emerges on the first stage of his journey, his return to the village where he was born — he thinks — and the recapitulation in memory of his childhood, particularly his first experience of value. It comes in the form of a brief intrusion into his life by a beautiful girl, still a child, in a clearing in the woods, and that intrusion is repeated when an accident to a carriage brings before him the same girl, again for a short time. Moreover he learns from his father that he is not his father's son, but the father's confession is interrupted and he dies before he can reveal to Franz the truth of his origin. Nor can his mother help him, for she married his "father" after Franz had been taken in. His mysterious origin is a way of indicating that the Romantic has been sundered from his cultural milieu, from his origins, and that he himself has the task of establishing who he is: the task of self-creation.

In his first letter to a fellow apprentice of Dürer, his friend Sebastian, whom he has left in Nürnberg, Franz presents his longing for the unlimited, a condition of existence without boundaries, a condition which he still thinks of as a golden world of perfection for which he pines. What he encounters are not boundaries but the uncertainty of boundaries. This problem is presented in his arguments over the nature and the task of art with various people he encounters during his travels, and poignantly in his wondering whether or not art is useless, the contention of the first stranger he meets and by whom he is helped. In Lucas van Leyden he meets the artist as craftsman, whose aim is technical improvement of the tradition in which he has been trained. To this Franz can only present his admission that the more of the beauty of the world he sees, and the more masterpieces of art he sees, the more enraptured he is, and the more he feels his own inadequacies. Lucas calls him more poet than painter and warns him of the example of Leonardo da Vinci, whose great genius and knowledge of art prevented him from completing very much. On other occasions Franz encounters the question of value in art and the instability of value. Or he meets a man, and paints a portrait of his daughter for him, who is an art-lover but has no real understanding of art: he collects art as one collects precious objects, but objects whose value has been socially defined. Or he meets a sculptor, a worshipper of Michelangelo, who insists that painting as an art cannot compare with sculpture, that Buonarotti is far greater than Raphael. Or he meets a failed painter, a hermit of art, whose paintings are at once attractive and repellent; yet the hermit knows that art and nature are holy, are hieroglyphic revelations of God, of the Divine, that is, incomprehensible except for their revelatory power. And because of his failure to become a great painter the hermit devotes himself entirely to minute, detailed, and loving studies of the natural world, thus transcending his artistic tradition. And Franz meets a countess whose portrait he paints, and in her he perceives the individual whose life is a series of costumes, the personality which turns life into art. Is art nothing but play? And deception? From a portrait he discovers that his lost beloved is the countess' sister, and the countess tells him that she is dead. But she gives him a letter to a noble family in Rome, and in the last chapter he discovers his beloved when he delivers the letter.

In a postscript published in 1843 for a new edition of the novel, Tieck tells us that he planned further adventures for Franz, that Franz would discover his father to be an Italian nobleman and that he would return to Nürnberg after losing his beloved at the 1527 sack of Rome and later regaining her. Many times Tieck planned to continue and to finish the work but, he says, he never could recover the mood. Nor is that surprising, for as it stands the novel is thematically complete. The problem had been explored. The instability of value had been fully set forth, and the explanation for that instability had been presented in the penultimate chapter. An eccentric old man, at whom the art lovers and critics of Rome laugh, has revealed to Franz that the great artist transcends his age. That transcendence is confirmed by the fact that the language of his age can neither understand him nor explain him. He takes Franz to the Sistine Chapel and leaves him there as dusk is falling. Franz "felt inwardly newly changed, newly created, never had art so come to him with lordly power. 'Here you are transfigured, Buonarotti, great self-initiate,' said Franz, 'here soar your terrible riddles, you care not who understand them.'" Or as the old man has asked, "Who understands the words of another?" And so in the final chapter Franz's finding his beloved is the real conclusion to the novel. He is now certain of the transcendent and transcending value of art, of art as the revelation of value. And it is humanized; there is no word of the divine, the holy. He finds his beloved because in human relations love is the revelation of value. Value cannot be seized in words, and explained; it cannot be grasped intellectually; the culture of the 1790s cannot confer it; it can be located only by exploring an alternative culture, a culture in itself a culture of crisis which a few men have transcended; it can be revealed by art to the individual who struggles to go beyond the cultural limits and creates it from himself; it is the Self. Franz Sternbald is Franz Sternbald at last; love is now open to him.

Nevertheless, that love is itself unstable. Franz can stay with his beloved only a short time. He wanders off into the fields and writes a lengthy poem in which nature and love are brought together and the interrelation of the two is symbolized by a sound which recurs throughout the book, the sound of the *Waldhorn,* the French horn, which came to be, as it has been called, the golden heart of the Romantic orchestra. The poem ends on an ecstatic note, and this is the momentary culmination of a recurring theme in the book, the sustained ecstasy and rapture of responding to the natural world, the German forests, a nature from which all other men are absent. But it is not nature that is important here, certainly not the picturesque nature of the culture of emotional lability.

For this new ecstatic note is just the opposite of lability. It is the effort to experience sustained value. It is further evidence that value must be self-created, since the current culture and its institutions can no longer provide a permanently available source of value. Since the experience of value is unstable, it becomes necessary to invent and develop an experience of sustained value, of sustained rapture. Only thus can the individual convince himself that momentary experiences of value are more than brief flashes of what may be a psychological aberration, a perversion of the Spirit, a momentary and delusive escape from the unbearable brutalities of existence. The Romantic abandons not only the picturesque notion of nature, a notion which embraced farms and villages and churches, the successful adaptation of mankind to nature, but he also abandons the notion of nature as

evidence of the beneficence of God or of the bounteousness and perfection for human interests of that secularization of God, the abstraction *Nature*, the God of Enlightenment Deism. This is why the
Romantic's impassioned response to nature is to wild nature, nature
without man. The absence of man — of culture, of civilization, of
interaction, of society — is of greater significance than the presence
of nature, for the natural world is now not evidence of value but only
the occasion for the self-creation of value. Moreover, there is a means
of sustaining value in the ecstatic, rapturous mode which is more
successful than language and even freer from interactional situations
than nature, and that means is music, as suggested by the importance
in *Franz Sternbald* of the *Waldhorn*, which appears in poems scattered throughout the book as well as in the narrative prose. If, as
Franz's old Roman eccentric says, no one understands another's
words, all men can understand music, or, rather, since understanding
is verbal behavior, music can transcend language. Music is the "language" — a term used metaphorically — or the symbol of the emotions; but   since it is separable from other human interests and is
experienced by the individual only as an individual, as a "self," it is,
in the term then in use, the pure language of Spirit. Music becomes
the supreme art and the model art. The Romantic 19th century becomes, as has often been said, the century of music.

Even while Tieck was occupied with the high literary sophistication
of *William Lovell* and *Franz Sternbald*, he turned in a quite contrary
direction, the material of the *Volksbücher*, as they are known in
Germany, of the *Bibliothèque bleu*, the French term, or the Chapbooks, the English equivalent. These were short tales for the most
part derived from medieval romance and printed cheaply in small
format. They were almost the exclusive literature of the uneducated
populace, the small literate portion of the people, members of whom
read them aloud to the illiterate, who repeated them from inexact
memory. They were sold in tremendous numbers, and were of course
regarded with utmost scorn by representatives of high culture, the
educated classes. To use such material for serious literary purposes
was analogous to using today the popular paper-back western for a
serious literary purpose at a high culture level, or analogous to John

Updike's use of the kind of material found only in pornography for *Couples* and *Rabbit Rich*.

Tieck's aims were complex. One factor was his Tieckian, Romantic irony, the absolute inappropriateness of a serious literary artist turning to such material and such style. But his irony was aimed also at the inappropriateness of standardized and redundant judgments of inappropriateness. His purpose, then, is indirectly satirical. Both satire before Romanticism and Romantic satire use the verbal technique of denigration, one of the most powerful instruments of behavioral control, since it attacks the individual's self-ascription of value. Earlier satire, brilliant because it is easy, attacked the failure of the members of a culture to live up to the avowed moral and intellectual values of that culture. It is just shooting fish in a barrel. Its effect depends upon its rhetoric and its wit. Romantic satire, on the other hand, attacks and denigrates the avowed and redundant moral, intellectual and literary shibboleths, or values, themselves. In its ironic form, of which Tieck is the most brilliant early Romantic expositor, it offers nothing in the place of those values. After his first efforts with the ironic use of *Volksbuch* material, Tieck turned to direct Romantic satire.

The second factor in his turning to folk material was what might be called linguistic or rhetorical realism. Assuming that the *Volksbuch* style, both verbally and narrationally, is literary style at its primitive level, to which the material of the sophisticated medieval romances had descended in the mouths of the people, what is the verbal situation from which narrative art emerges? Tieck's effort was analogous to Martha Graham's effort to locate the origins of theater in the fundamental bodily movements of the dance. But such an effort is devastatingly ironic, for it affirms the inadequacy of the whole immense panoply of the literary rhetorics of high culture as they existed in the 1790s. Even before Schiller Tieck had recognized the literary possibilities of play.

In a short novel of 1795, *Peter Leberecht, a History without Adventures*, Tieck had ironically explored the literary possibilities of ordinary, mundane life; and in *Die Beiden merkwürdigsten Tage aus Siegmunds Leben (The Two Most Remarkable Days in Siegmund's*

Life) (1796) he made a first thrust into his exploration of what lies beyond all realistic efforts, the riddle of human experience, its fundamental alogical and irrational character, the position which was to find its culmination in Franz Sternbald's visit to the Sistine Chapel. In 1797 Tieck published two volumes of *Volksmärchen*. A *Märchen* is a folk-tale with a supernatural element. In the traditional *Volksmärchen* that element is both standardized and explicable. It is a mythology, and like all mythology it endeavors to categorize and symbolize those socio-cultural forces which control and limit the lives of human beings, forces to which human beings must accommodate themselves. But in Tieck's work, as in *Der Blonde Eckbart or Der Getreue Eckart* (1799) (*The Trusty Eckart*), the supernatural is inexplicable, riddlesome. Thus he uses the folk-tale to urge his position that the explanations of those forces offered by the regnant culture are inadequate, unsatisfactory, and explain nothing. In *Liebesgeschichte der schönen Magelone and des Grafen Peter von Provence* (*The Love Story of the Fair Magelone and Count Peter of Provence*), published in Volume II of the 1797 *Volksmärchen,* he attempted something quite different. Instead of inventing a folk-tale he used one already in existence, surviving in the *Volksbücher.* The rhetoric is of the simplest, and the narrative style is one of "and then . . . and then . . . and then." Instead of the inexplicable supernatural element, he goes beyond to the accidental, to chance, to the random event. Thus to the extreme simplicity of the rhetoric, the purposely naive, he adds an extreme of intellectual subtlety. Nor is this all. The book is divided into eighteen short sections, and each section includes a poem. The style of these poems is the style of the folk-song. What Tieck appears to be suggesting is that the first step away from the bare, objective, emotionless narrative style was, and is, the poem, the fundamental rhetorical device which makes emotion verbally available. Tieck thus recovers in separable form the foundations of imaginative literature — narrative and feeling.

Another work first published in *Volksmärchen* II was the first of a pair of works even more daring, original, and outrageous than anything he had yet done, and directly satirical. These two works are *Der Gestiefelte Kater* (*Puss-in-Boots*) and *Die Verkehrte Welt*

(*The World Upside Down*) (1799).   In each of these plays there is a
play within a play; in the outer play the characters are the audience.
In *Der Gestiefelte Kater* Tieck satirizes the audience and, through the
audience, the platitudinous and exhausted theater of his time, as well
as the equally platitudinous and thoughtless critical values of the prevailing theatrical and literary culture.   On the one hand the artificial machinery of the theater is exposed, and on the other the dominating practice of criticizing and judging a work of art piecemeal, of
selecting points to made for or against it, instead of responding to
the work as a whole.

In *Die Verkehrte Welt* his satire aims beyond the theater to bourgeois culture in general.   He takes up again the theme of *William
Lovell* and treats it comically; it becomes the *desire* of everyone to
play a role, so that the distinction between the role-playing of the
actor and the role-playing of the audience, the general public, all
members of society, is obliterated.   The plot of the play within the
play, such as it is, is a farcical treatment of the dethronement of Apollo
by Scaramuccio (taken from the Italian *commedia dell'arte* and the
plays of the Venetian Gozzi), who represents bourgeois culture.   This
gives Tieck the chance to make fun of commercialism, sentimentalism, patriotism, war, and, most significantly, revolution itself.   At
the end Apollo defeats Scaramuccio, but the audience will have none
of that.   They insist that Scaramuccio must remain king, thus identi-
fying themselves with the goodness and wisdom of bourgeois culture.
As Apollo points out, they have forgotten that this is nothing but a
play.

In these two works Tieck is playful and comic and amusing, but
his purpose is serious.   What he is attacking is the condition that by
the end of the 18th century the bourgeoisie had inherited from an
earlier high-level culture the rational-sentimental culture of the Enlightenment, and were preserving it in a debased form lacking all
vitality.   It is worth adding that the middle-classes still preserve the
culture which Tieck was mocking.

Above all, these two plays were for Tieck a celebration of the
literary, rhetorical, and linguistic freedom he had achieved.   The next
task he set himself was to invent a new mode of narration, and this

he accomplished in a major work, *Leben und Tod der Heiligen Geno-veva. Ein Trauerspiel* (*The Life and Death of the Holy Genoveva: a Tragedy*), published in 1800. Though it is written in dramatic form and called a tragedy, it was not written for the stage: for one thing it is more than twice as long as the usual play and consists of so many scenes, some of them requiring elaborate sets, that it could not be performed. Nor was it intended to be performed. Rather, Tieck's investigations into the fundamental character of narration led him to invent this new form. The notion of mixing verse and drama he took, of course, from Shakespeare, but the unique use of the sonnet in *Romeo and Juliet* could give no more than a hint of the variety of verse forms he employs — blank verse, rhymed couplets, *terza rima,* stanzaic narration in various forms, including *ottava rima,* taken from Italian verse, and a variety of regular and irregular lyric forms. At one point he abandons the dramatic form entirely and bridges a passage of seven years in a narrative poem of twenty-three eight-line stanzas, though spoken by Saint Boniface, the eighth-century missionary to the Frisians and the organizer of the church in Germany.

Boniface was, in fact, in Germany at the time of the drama, for the tragedy is precipitated by the departure of Siegfried, Count Palatine of Trier and Genoveva's husband, to aid Charles Martel in his defense of Christendom against the Muslim Moors, whom Martel defeated at Tours in 732. Siegfried's return is further delayed by the pursuit of the Moors to Avignon and the siege of that city. His prolonged absence is the condition which makes Golo's love for Genoveva unendurable and uncontrollable. Since she refuses him, he trumps up a story that she has been having an affair with the innocent Drago. Golo, who in spite of his youth has been left in charge of Siegfried's castle, has Drago executed and confines Genoveva in a dungeon, where she gives birth to a child. Golo sends a message to Siegfried that Genoveva has been unfaithful. He then sends Genoveva to the forest to be killed, but the murderers cannot bring themselves to defile a cross which has miraculously appeared and to which Genoveva clings. She is sustained by the wild animals until her son is seven. Siegfried learns the truth; Genoveva is rescued; in spite of her pleas, Golo is executed, and she dies shortly after in the odor of sanctity.

The innovative character of *Genoveva* appears first of all in the fact that though it is written in dramatic form, it is not in any sense a work for the theater. A theater piece is, after all, only a script. It requires speech, gesture, movement, costume, actors, and all the appurtenances available to theater at a given historical period of theatrical history in order to come to life. This is evidenced by the fact that of the countless number of scripts written for the theater, only a handful are readable as works of literature. But this incompleteness of a script is not true of *Genoveva*. Each scene is narrationally and literarily complete and stylistically self-contained. What Tieck was undertaking was a form of narration without the transitions of prose or of poetic narrative. Each scene is like a dot on a graph. It is up to the reader to plot the connective curve, the trajectory of the drama. Thus Tieck put into practice the theory that the reader of a work, the responder to any work of art, is engaged in as creative an act as the artist or writer.

Another innovation in *Genoveva* is its historicism; Tieck set out to create a genuinely historical work, but in a way quite different from the only partially convincing historicism of *Sternbald*. There the historicism is external, and Franz's problems with art and value are only too apparently the problems of the emergent Romantic artist. *Genoveva*, on the other hand, has been admired as a Catholic work, although Tieck was not a Catholic and never became one. Rather his historicism is not a matter of historical events and character but an attempt to recover and present what at the time would have been called, and indeed was called, the spiritual culture of the early Middle Ages, the faith, the beliefs, the miracles, and the surviving magic of paganism. He set out to write *Genoveva* as someone of the medieval world might have written it, insofar as ideology and values are the issue, without any trace of either modern perspective or historical irony.

The importance of *Genoveva* is that with it Romanticism had arrived; Tieck had succeeded in transcending his own immediate culture, had entered into an alternative culture, which he had created from available fragments, and had presented the charm, the freshness, the faith, the magic, the brutality of an early stage of European civilization. For that reason it was recognized as a supremely modern work. The young Romantics, those born like Tieck in the 1770s and those of the next decade, affirmed its creative innovation at once. For some of them it remained a favorite work, but all grasped that here at last was something genuinely new, something truly culturally emergent and transcending. It became a basic text for the development and spread of German Romanticism, generation after generation.

François René de Chateaubriand (1768-1848) While the young German Romantics were putsuing normal lives of young men establishing themselves, Francois René de Chateaubriand experienced a life totally disrupted by the French Revolution. In Paris at the time of the taking of the Bastille in 1789, he found by 1791 that he could accept neither the monarchists nor the revolutionists, even though he was profoundly liberal in his social and political attitudes. In 1791, then, he left Saint-Malo on his famous trip to America, arriving in July and leaving in December. Certainly Chateaubriand later grossly exaggerated how much of America he had seen, but he travelled enough to grasp the beauty of an unspoiled nature and to comprehend the virtues and values of savage Indian life. Returning to France, he decided to join the emigrant Army of the Princes at Trier, and was wounded at the futile siege of Thionville. He left the Army and painfully made his way through Brussels and the Channel Islands to England, arriving there in 1793 and continuing to live there in poverty, exile, and loneliness until 1800, barely maintaining himself by translation and teaching, one of thousands of French exiles in similar plight.

In fact he believed himself to be dying, evidently with good reason; yet during that period he read voraciously and wrote a long book, *Essai historique, politique et moral sur les révolutions anciennes et modernes considérées dans leur rapport avec la revolution françoise* (*Historical Political and Ethical Essay on Revolutions, Ancient and Modern, Considered in their Relation to the French Revolution*). It was finished in 1796 and published in London, and distributed in

Paris in 1797. It is one of Chateaubriand's most neglected works, in part because in the 1827 edition he added footnotes which mocked and repudiated most of what he had said when he was young. Certainly it does not represent the mature and great Chateaubriand who emerged to fame in the next decade. Nevertheless, it is a work of great value for understanding the period: it reveals the impact of the Revolution on an aristocratic liberal, brought up on the ideas of the *philosophes* and *encyclopédistes,* the groups associated with and later derived from Diderot and the preparation of the 18th century French *Encyclopédie,* published 1751-1772 and 1776-1780, the overwhelming monument of the Enlightenment. Chateaubriand was one of those who interpreted the bloody tyranny of the Revolution to mean the failure of the Enlightenment. Yet he had no choice but to attack the *philosophes* with their own weapons, to attack rationalism with rationalism. But his was a rationalism charged with the other factor of situational thinking, the historical. The 1796 *Essay* is the fullest example we have of that intellectual confusion, leading to despair, to *ennui,* to a complete loss of any confidence in European culture and its values, that confusion from which Romanticism was the responding effort at self-extrication.

It is almost always said to be a confused and bad and strangely organized work, but not, I think, by anyone who has taken the trouble to read it. Chateaubriand determined to establish for himself both the cause of the French Revolution and, most important for him, the significance of it for human life and history. His method was analogical; in searching for understanding, he sought to find analogical resemblances between the French Revolution and the revolutions of Athens and other ancient Greek city-states against monarchy, aristocracy, tyranny. This kind of pursuit reveals the depths of his disillusionment with European culture. He was forced to plunge down to the basic element of thought. It has been said often enough that analogy is the poorest kind of logical thinking (more precisely, covert verbal behavior), but the frequency of its failure is a function of the frequency of its use. After all, when we get to the lowest stratum of thought, all we have to think with is analogy; all that we can determine is that two configurations are sufficiently alike so that it is appropriate to respond to both in the same way, or that they are not. For this reason analogical conclusions are easily negated. A determination of analogy depends upon ignoring the attributes of the configurations in question which are actually not identical or sufficiently similar. To undermine an analogy one need only bring forward such attributes. For this reason any conclusion arrived at by a verbal process can never be final, because all such processes are reducible to analogies. Thus, in the 1790s Chateaubriand could be confident in the validity of his analogies, but in later years he could deny that validity whole-heartedly. The explanation for that denial can be found in his later acceptance of the notion of political and even moral progress, an intellectual move made possible and even irresistible for him by his conversion to Christianity combined with his unchanged or at least revived liberalism. That belief in progress is one of the inheritances of the Enlightenment, an inheritance enabled by the realization that progress does not necessarily entail perfectibility.

In the *Essay,* however, Chateaubriand's analogical conclusion is that mankind is doomed to an eternal repetition of the same kinds of historical events, in this case revolution. That was the significance to him of the French Revolution, for the causes of ancient and modern revolutions were identical — the corruptions of morals, the culturally destructive political rationalism of Greek philosophy and of the 18th century *philosophes,* and the belief in human perfectibility common to both, beginning with Lycurgus, the law-giver to Sparta. A few of Chateaubriand's conclusions are worth repeating, for they show the depths of despair to which the incipient Romanticist was reduced. "In love of humanity, it is necessary to protect oneself from observing that vice and virtue often lead to the same results" (Vol. I, Chap. XI). "So true is it that the great words of general justice and phi-lanthropy mean very little. The thirst for liberty and that for tyranny are mingled in the human heart by the hand of nature; independence for one self, slavery for all others, is the motto of the human species" (I, XII). "What ought an Indian think who observes . . . the strange actors of that grand tragi-comic farce which [European] society in-cessantly performs?" (I, XXXIII). (One remembers *William Lovell.*) "Universal republic, fraternity of nations, general peace, brilliant

phantom of a lasting happiness on the earth, adieu!" (I, LXVIII).
"Listen to the voice of conscience. What does it tell us, according
to nature? 'Be free.' According to society? 'Rule.'" (I, LXX). "I
compare the world to a great forest where men lie in wait to slit each
other's throats" (II, II). "The greatest misfortune of mankind is to
have laws and government." (II, LVI). The meaningless retracing of
a circle from which there is no escape — that is the course of human
history in the past and in a future which promises a social dissolution
of which the French Revolution is but the first announcement.

The last chapter is the most beautiful; it marks the emergence of
Chateaubriand as a great Romantic writer, the creator of French
Romantic prose, and poetry. In "Night among the savages in America"
he describes how on his way to Niagara he spent the night in the
forest with a group of Indians on their travels, evidently an extended
family of some sort. His aim is to deny the notion that savages cannot know the joys of civilized happiness. On the contrary, free from
government and laws, they enjoy the happiness of independence and
freedom. But to the despairing European all that is offered is the
grandeur and beauty of American nature. When the Indians and
his guide are asleep, Chateaubriand wanders off from the encamp-
ment to the side of a stream and is enraptured by the forest and meadows flooded by a summer night's moonlight. Once again, as with
Tieck, the determination of nature as a source of value is made possible not so much by the presence of nature as by the absence of man.
This is phenomenal nature, not the abstract metaphysical Nature of
so much of Enlightenment thinking. And the image of the isolated
individual alone before natural grandeur and beauty was to become
one of the pervasive images of Romantic culture — painting, poetry,
and prose — throughout Europe.

Thus the book ends with discovery of its real subject — Chateaubriand himself. He began his introduction with the question, "Who
am I?" But that was not a Romantic question about the self; and as
he continues, it becomes clear that he means, "The reader has a right
to ask, 'By what authority do I speak? What right do I have to ask
to be heard?'" Chateaubriand's answer is: the right of anyone whose
life has been uprooted, ruined, and torn apart by the Revolution.

And not merely such individuals but anyone whose life has been un-alterably affected, any member of European civilization from the pea-sant to monarch. So it is not surprising that the book is marked by numerous inconsistencies; for inconsistency is the indicator of an extreme disorientation. The work is less a coherent intellectual struc-ture than a flailing about, though even so it is far less inconsistent and poorly organized than it is usually said to be. And the depths of Chateaubriand's disillusionment, the extent of the explanatory col-lapse he had experienced, is revealed by one of the few positive posi-tions at which he arrives. The best form of government, he decides, is a hereditary, though constitutional, monarchy. Not only does such a government balance the incoherent demands for freedom and control, immanent in the human heart, but, more important, it in-troduces mystery into politics: it forces upon our awareness and our conscious policy-making the limitations of intellect and emotion, and of our very conceptions of Reason and Nature. Similarly, he praises Christianity not on grounds of religious or of any other kind of truth but for reasons which are pragmatic. In his defense let it be said that a truth-claim is one that makes comprehensible whatever that truth-claim is directed toward; for example, the claim of religious truth is that the world is comprehensible. And insistence upon the ultimate incomprehensibility of the world and of human existence within it is an insistence that the explanatory constructs of European culture and its truth-claims have collapsed. So he denies the validity of metaphysical system-building. In his *Essay* Chateaubriand opens the way to the analytic dismantlement of European culture and to the effort of determining what might be salvaged from its ruins.

Friedrich W. J. von Schelling   Unlike his countrymen Wackenroder
(1775-1854)   and Tieck, Friedrich von Schelling
came from a small town, Leonberg in Württemberg. The son of a Lutheran pastor, he was destined for the ministry. From 1790 to 1792 he studied theology at Tübingen, where he met two young men, both older, Hegel and Hölderlin. Together, the three shared their enthusiasm over the French Revolution and

together they deflected their interest from theology to philosophy. Kant, of course, was the precipitating influence, soon to be followed by Fichte. Schelling started publishing philosophical essays as early as 1793 and continued with one or two publications a year through 1800 and well beyond. Of these essays of the 1790s the most important to emerging Romanticism were the 1797 *Ideen zu einer Philosphie der Natur* (*Ideas towards a Philosophy of Nature*) and the 1800 *System des transcendentalen Idealismus* (*System of Transcendental Idealism*).

The dates are significant. They come after the Terror and the establishment of the Directoire, after the degeneration of the French Revolution. The great idea of the Revolution was freedom, but what had happened fatally compromised the Enlightenment notions of freedom. It turned the relation of freedom to brotherhood into a problem and raised bitter questions about equality. Schelling certainly accepted Fichte's Self-philosophy as a correction to Kant and as a move towards what Kant had admitted that he could not accomplish, a complete and coherent and unified philosophical system. Kant had founded human freedom on the human capacity for moral action, which he thought of as truly transcendent, since it could not be derived directly from Nature. Fichte attempted to improve upon Kant, but Schelling found unsatisfactory and incomplete Fichte's conception of Nature as simply the material or stuff man uses to bring into existence that capacity for moral action. The culture crisis clearly, to Schelling, could not be met or even understood in such terms. For Schelling was familiar not only with the philosophical tradition of Descartes, and Leibniz, Kant, Fichte, and above all Spinoza; he was also familiar with the work of Herder, Kant's great opponent. From Herder Schelling could take two powerful ideas and put them to use: one was Herder's then incomparably rich comprehension and exploration of the natural and human situation in which man finds himself; the other was the notion that man had emerged from nature, that is, that the human mind had emerged from nature. Schelling judged that the epistemological question, the mechanisms of the mind by which it knows the world, had been brought to an acceptable condition by Fichte; so before developing Fichte's Self-philosophy further, he turned directly to the problem of Nature.

He could begin by considering recent developments in science — physics, chemistry, and biology. All three, of course, were by modern standards in a most primitive condition; but it must be remembered that enormous advances had been made during the 18th century. Schelling was less interested in the results of science than in its procedures. It was not enough to say that science puts the question to nature and forces, by experiment, nature to reply. Rather, where did the question come from? Obviously, not from nature itself, but from the human Self. And how was it possible that the scientist could put his questions successfully? The answer to this question Schelling took from Spinoza (1632-1677) and Leibniz (1646-1716): it consists of the idea of a pre-established harmony between the mind and the world. But Schelling could not accept the two philosophers' notion of a harmony between the *reason* and the world. First, science only describes appearance, phenomena; it gives neither knowledge nor an inkling of what lies behind appearance, or, better, what is the ultimate character of matter. Reason can understand matter, but Reason is the creation of the Self. It followed that since we can deal successfully with nature the ultimate character of nature and the ultimate character of the self must be similar. Hence, since the Self is Spirit, Nature must also be Spirit. And so Schelling revived an ancient term, the "World-Soul." But he gave it new meaning, and that act in itself is significant, for what Schelling was after was to determine the *meaning* of the world. Calling upon the ideas of gravity and repulsion and light, he concluded that the meaning of Nature, its ultimate character, is Force — Force which manifests itself in creative activity. Thus the history of nature is evolutionary and the structure of nature is not mechanistic but organic. The world is alive, and its loftiest and noblest evolutionary product is the human spirit.

Although the meaning of nature could be established, it did not follow that man could fully decipher nature, ever. For to do that man would have to be apart from nature, outside of it; but since man has emerged from nature, and since nature is continuously creative, it follows that man can never fully understand nature. Moreover, since his understanding is a product of the creative activity of nature, that understanding must have a history; and since force is infinite and, it follows, the self is infinite, that history can have no final goal, nor can man's understanding. All this, however, meant that man is necessarily what he is. What was crucial, given the crisis brought about by the Revolution, was to found human freedom not on political accident such as the Revolution itself and its aftermath, as Schelling saw each, but on the very meaning of man. The task was to reconcile freedom and necessity. In short, the Enlightenment notion of freedom had to be transcended.

That task Schelling took up in the *System,* written in 1799 and 1800. It has been called the most philosophically accomplished of his works. It certainly made him famous. Yet it has also been called his least original work, simply because it is so Fichtean. But that judgment, common among philosophers, may be questioned. What was original was far more important than what was not, important in the sense of its impact upon the emergence of Romanticism and its subsequent development for many decades. In 1798, at the age of 23, Schelling had been appointed professor of philosophy at the University of Jena, and there he met Fichte, who had arrived in 1796, the year in which August and Friedrich Schlegel also came. In 1799 Tieck arrived, and in that year Novalis occasionally joined the group. Here was the condition of cultural transcendence, the little group or coterie, and Schelling responded profoundly to his interaction with these men, even to the point in 1803 of marrying the former wife of August Schlegel, Caroline, divorced in 1801.

Schelling's first task in the *System* was to move beyond his philosophy of nature by insisting that Transcendental Idealism is also a Realism. The Self emerges only in interaction with a situation. It is the action of a Self upon situations which brings about the emergence of self-consciousness and the gradual restriction of the Self into reason, understanding, and individuality. Thus the aim of the *System* is not so much theoretical as practical. Much of the book is taken up with an elaborate and philosophically technical but also highly dramatic account of how that individuality emerges. Here Schelling proceeded by analogy of the Self with Nature. Just as Nature is an organism and emerges by organistic hierarchy, so does the Self. The last step in the emergence of the Self is the encounter with other Selves, for only in that encounter does self-consciousness become almost complete. But even that stage brings about a realization of a further self-transcendence, a further enrichment of completeness, by the Self's recognition, again by analogy with Nature, that time is a condition of its emergence. Therefore not merely its history but the history of other Selves is also a factor in full self-consciousness, that is, the history of mankind.

But all this involves limitations on the Self. How is its freedom to be preserved and reconciled with necessity? Schelling's answer depended upon Fichte but went further. The reason is simply, he said, that the imagination applies itself to particular situations, and the source of the imagination is the unconscious. Just as, one might say, natural appearances or phenomena are the mere surface of nature, so self-consciousness is the mere surface of the Self. But the Self, as Fichte has shown, is nothing but an act. Therefore, Schelling concluded, when we ask, "What is the Self?" the answer is that the Self is the Will. To put it differently, but not to change the meaning, no matter what accommodations to other selves and to history an individual Self might make, still the foundation of action is the drive of aggression. Self-consciousness emerges, then, from an aggressive action upon and against a reciprocally aggressive Nature.

This notion that the fundamental meaning of human activity is the exercise of the Will was of the highest importance for emerging Romanticism. It provided a rationale and a justification for what the Romantics needed, for several reasons. First, if cultural transcendence was to be achieved it was essential to attack and demolish the ideologies and values of the dominating Christian and Enlightenment cultures. Second, to maintain a position of alienation from a culture, it is necessary for the individual to raise the level of his aggression, to put his self-conscious efforts, in Schellingian terms, into the effort of himself as pure will. Nor is it unlikely that Schelling was moved towards this conclusion by the extraordinarily vital and energetic group in which he was living, a group in which the will shone brightly in every member. And it is even more likely that Schelling was moved to the final step in the System by his membership in that group.

He asked himself what evidence could be found and where it could be found of the adequacy and "truth" of his System. And he found it in a most surprising and very Romantic mode of human behavior; he found it in art. Moving from Kant's notion of art experience as disinterested, he arrived at the conviction that art is the highest of human activities. It is the product of genius, and genius he felt to be characterized by the highest level of self-consciousness and also by the highest manifestation of the unconscious. It uses as its material the appearances of nature, but in its being the purest manifestation of the will, it emerges from the identity of the Force of Nature and the Will of Man. And since both Nature and Self are Spirit, Art is the highest and noblest manifestation of Spirit. Philosophy can only describe the Self and its operations. Art is superior to philosophy because it does what philosophy can only point to. And since the Spirit is infinite, the meanings of a work of art are infinite. And later Schelling was to say that poetry, the least dependent of the arts upon the material of nature, is the highest art because it is the most spiritual — and that the highest mode of poetry is myth.

The importance of this position to Romanticism — although Schelling was not to be the only Romantic who so exalted art — cannot be overemphasized. First of all it assigned to art the highest form of human value. But even more is involved. Since the meanings of a work of art are infinite, and since its power comes from the unconscious, it freed the artist from what had been hitherto his primary social task, the exemplification of the ideologies of his culture. The congruence of this with the position of Tieck in *Franz Sternbald* is obvious, both in the notion of the work of art as a hieroglyph of the meaning of nature and as something that cannot be caught in a net of specific meanings. But from this reasoning it follows that since art is of the highest value, and since it is the highest creative act, it is not dependent upon particular values — that is, moral and ethical judgements and maxims. Rather the creation of art is the creation of value, and the proper response to the work of art is the experience of the value of the Self. The artistic experience becomes an act of communion, in which the value creation of the artist is transsubstantiated into the value experience of the responder. It is thus a redemptive act, but one which is of a new kind of redemption. It is not redemption into divine grace, nor redemption into heaven, nor into a social utopia, but redemption without metaphysical or religious commitment; namely, a redemption *in this world.* The experience of art thus becomes the functional equivalent of the religious experience of the reception of divine grace. Schelling's exaltation of art to the pinnacle of human possibility permits the fullest exploitation of the artistic situation, the fact that it does not require that the observer do anything. And the position gives further support to alienation, for Schelling emphasizes that the genius is exceedingly rare, and that the individual who can receive the benefits of genius's creative act is just as rare. With the publication of Schelling's *System* the religion of art had begun, and the rationale had been provided for the new cultural type already mentioned, the aesthetic Christian. What Schelling's analysis made possible was a complete and full secularization of the sacred, freed from ideological and moral commitments. A product of the necessity of self-consciousness and of the infinite freedom of the Spirit, art, for both Schelling and Romanticism, unified freedom and necessity. Thus the real interest of Schelling was not the philosophy of nature, nor transcendental idealism, nor even freedom (in the Enlightenment or Kantian or Fichtian sense), but the discovery and establishment of a source of value independent of social institutions and uncommitted to any ideology; a source available to the free individual and only to the free individual; a source which when fulfilled in artistic action confirms that freedom.

William Wordsworth   Of that small group of Europeans whom,
(1770-1850)   because of their intense response to the
                               events of the French Revolution, we call
the Romantics, few were as committed to the Revolution and as devastated by what happened in the 1790s as William Wordsworth. At least no one has given so vivid and so searching an account and analysis of the whole process of being swept into revolutionary enthusiasm and then being hurled by the fury of that tornado out into a bleak

wasteland. Born of a good middle-class legal family, orphaned young, and educated at Cambridge, he first entered the ecstatic world of the early years of the Revolution during 1790 on a walking trip across France to Switzerland. Ostensibly to learn French in order to qualify himself as a tutor and guide to some wealthy young nobleman, he returned to France in 1791 for thirteen months. But whatever his motives (and so great was his subsequent rejection of the Revolution that whatever he says must not be accepted without serious doubts and questions) he was soon fully involved, even to the extent of having an affair with a French girl, an affair which resulted in the birth of an illegitimate daughter. He returned to England a convinced Republican and believer in the Rights of Man. But then there followed two events which precipitated him into a moral nihilism, an utter loss of value.

First was England's declaration of war on the French Republic, and the second was the Terror. A passage in *The Prelude,* written at least a decade later, frankly avows his joy at the overthrow and execution of Robespierre. But these two events forced him into an awareness of that incoherence of Reason and Nature which marks the failure of the Enlightenment. In Wordsworth's case Nature was represented by England itself, for not only was England his own country but, far more important, in Enlightenment thought England was the nation which had advanced farthest towards an ideal of freedom and justice and equality. As nations went, England was the most Natural of nations. That England should turn upon the Revolution, even though it was only the English government that did so — the anachronistic monarchy — meant nevertheless that the Enlightenment notion of Nature was false. It was not a matter of Nature betrayed but of Nature as traitor to itself. In the same way the rationalism of the Terror was Reason betraying itself. The effect on Wordsworth was appalling. As he himself was to say, he "yielded up moral questions in despair"; and he further engaged in an activity far more indicative of the loss of any explanatory relation to the world, to mankind, to society, or to history; he devoted himself for months, perhaps as much as a year and a half, almost exclusively to the study of mathematics. Wordsworth's concentration upon mathematics, a semiotic system entirely self-enclosed and with no determinate capacity to subsume anything outside itself, is precisely convergent with Novalis's even more striking insight that language and mathematics are alike in their fundamental non-referentiality.

Like Novalis, Wordsworth's turn for consolation and value to the empty world of mathematics signified a denial of the validity of the European cultural tradition. What Wordsworth had to do was first establish a radically new relation of man to nature. But even that would be, at least initially, too general and too abstract. What he had to do was to establish a bond between himself, William Wordsworth, and the precise natural landscape and situation in which he found himself. As it turned out that need was first satisfied in a few spots in southwestern England. And second, he had also to establish a functional equivalent for failed Reason. That is, it is not the explanations that Reason constructs which are important, but what the construction of explanations does for human life, even though as explanations they turn out to be (as they all do, sooner or later) false and empty. He had to determine the sacred function of Reason, a function quite independent of what constructions Reason might arrive at.

It is fortunate that in recent years the Cornell edition of Wordsworth has uncovered the early Wordsworth, concealed in later years by revisions and suppressions. That new text has revealed Wordsworth's own uncertain apprehension of what was happening to him during those early years; of his recognition that his task was one of cultural transcendence; and of his fumbling transition to it which had to be suppressed so that the complete transcendence might emerge in all its beauty and power. But Wordsworth's manipulations and even perversions of his own work have been doubly unfortunate. Not only have they concealed from us the struggles and remarkable early successes of Wordsworth, different from what we had thought, but they also deprived the next generation of English Romantics — Byron, Shelley, and Keats — of a comprehension of the cultural significance of those years and of Wordsworth himself. Had Wordsworth published not only *The Ruined Cottage* in its original form, but also, and more important, what is now known as *The First Prelude,* published only in 1977, and *Home at Grasmere* (published long after Wordsworth's death as *The Recluse* and almost ignored then and for a long time thereafter) — but especially the first complete *Prelude* of 1805 — the next generations would have understood not only Wordsworth and Coleridge better but would also have grasped far better their own cultural and historical position. Wordsworth was subsequently called by Robert Browning the "lost leader," but he was lost above all for what he did not reveal.

In the poems of the years from early 1797 to autumn, 1800, when Wordsworth sent the second edition of *Lyrical Ballads* to press, there is intertwined a group of themes which appear and disappear and reappear with an extraordinarily intense obsessiveness. They may be called a series as well as a group, for there is a certain emergent sequence to them. The first powerful note is struck in *The Ruined Cottage* (to be published in modified form only in 1814 as the beginning of *The Excursion*). It is the theme of abandonment, of pointless, incomprehensible abandonment, of disappointment. The first English appearance of one of the persistent sign-complexes of the Romantic tradition was in *The Ruined Cottage,* one that was to receive its canonical name only in the 20th century: the Waste Land. (Coleridge was to pick it up almost immediately in strikingly altered imagery in *The Rime of the Ancyent Marinere,* to use the spelling of the first version.) The story is told by a pedlar, and in him appears another Romantic archetype, the detached and uncommitted wandering observer, who exemplifies a second recurring theme, one to become central to Wordsworth's cultural reassessment. The Pedlar is wise, profoundly wise; yet he is a man without education. His wisdom has emerged from an intelligent and sympathetic mind engaged in a random observation of the ordinary poor, weavers and peasants, the bulk of humanity. The tale he tells is of a cottage couple, the husband a weaver. The couple at first did well, but there came a time of general economic depression, one which reduced even some of the rich to poverty. For the poor there was soon nothing. Margaret's husband, Robert, endeavored to keep busy, but his personality (that is, in Wordsworth's realistic portrayal, a complex of behavior patterns) deteriorated, unraveled. Eventually in his desperaation he joined the army, sold himself for a sum which he left at night on the window-sill, unable to say farewell to his wife. She gradually pined away, the child died, and she died, and the cottage and garden, once so carefully tended, fell into neglect and ruin.

In an early poem, written before Wordsworth's cultural crisis, "Salisbury Plain," a somewhat similar disaster is the result of specific social arrangements, of injustice, and of legalized brutality. But in *The Ruined Cottage* the disaster is precipitated by an economic disturbance which Wordsworth blames on no one. At most, the social failure from a war is only a factor, and evidently an incidental one. Ultimately, the tragedy that overcomes Margaret is incomprehensible, and that incomprehensibility was to be intensified in further poems of disappointment, of failure, of abandonment. The first major poetic effort Wordsworth made after his crisis was a tragedy, *The Borderers,* a strange and unsatisfactory work, one easily misunderstood. The villain of the piece has become what he is and has determined to seek revenge only *because* he is aided in desperate circumstances. Wordsworth appears to be saying that ingratitude in return for kindness and goodness is to be expected, *because to help someone is to instruct him that he is incapable of helping himself.* To give aid is the subtlest form of denigration and must arouse a desire for revenge. And this is incomprehensible to any rational morality.

This theme of incomprehensibility is intimately related to the uneducated, uncultivated wisdom of the Pedlar, which Wordsworth presents in the poem as so much more impressive and valuable than his own intellectual and cultural sophistication. *The Ruined Cottage* began that series of poems about the simplest and most ordinary people through which Wordsworth hoped to discover a ground, an origin, perhaps a justification, for the disappointment, abandonment, and cultural emptiness that was the result of his cultural crisis. When he agreed with Coleridge (the great friendship began in the spring of 1797) shortly after the completion of the first *The Ruined Cottage* (the greatness and originality of which Coleridge immediately recognized) to collaborate on a volume of poetry, Wordsworth's contributions were to be poems about ordinary life; so he set about a kind of transforming reductionism which would present his experience in the barest and most direct possible modes.

And in carrying his intentions out his efforts were convergent with those of Tieck: on the one hand pursuing a realism that would push beyond what Enlightenment conventions called Natural Man, and on the other engaging in a linguistic realism, one which would violate and transcend the current conventions of poetic rhetoric, hardly changed from those of the Renaissance. Thus in the blank verse of *The Ruined Cottage* and even in the *Lyrical Ballads* themselves, he violated two of the basic principles of European poetic rhetoric — rhetorical coherence and consistency, as well as decorum, the choice of a rhetoric appropriate to the situation offered in the poem. When he appears to be speaking for himself, his responses, by the standard of decorum, are exaggerated, egotistic, and over-determined.

In these years up to 1800, as we now know, Wordsworth wrote an immense amount of blank verse, a fact that acounts for the extraordinary mastery of that style in "Tintern Abbey" of July, 1798. Thus, to indicate his rejection of cultural tradition, even though he could at first only recombine scattered elements of it, he created a style in which he could move from the most ordinary language, hardly to be differentiated from prose, to an exaltation and a sublimity matched only by Milton. And he could do this in the space of a line or so. But there was a further justification for this to be found in Wordsworth's drive towards a more intense linguistic realism. This, he indicates, is the way the mind actually works, and the way the linguistic process actually unfolds. His poetic style, then, becomes a prime exemplification of all intensified realism, the undermining and denigration and discarding of a cultural tradition and shibboleth. His style made that of his eighteenth century predecessors seem artificial rather than one of a high level of poetic competence.

The themes of abandonment and incomprehensibility, then, appear frequently in the *Lyrical Ballads* of 1798 and in its second edition of 1800, which added a second volume entirely by Wordsworth. In "We Are Seven" the theme is the inability of a child to comprehend death. In "The Thorn" the very misery of the heroine is inexplicable, though surrounded with suspicions, and the poem is Wordsworth's most radical experiment in the most ordinary possible language. "Her Eyes Are

Wild" makes incomprehensible abandonment more incomprehensible by
madness. "The Complaint of a Forsaken Indian Woman" is spoken
by a sick Indian woman left to die alone according to the custom of
her tribe. But of Wordsworth's poems in the 1798 volume the most
remarkable and perhaps the most beautiful is also the most often re-
viled, "The Idiot Boy," to be properly understood only in connection
with "The Tables Turned" with its famous

> One impulse from a vernal wood
> May teach you more of man,
> Of moral evil and of good,
> Than all the sages can.

followed by its adjuration to forswear both the meddling intellect
(which murders to dissect) and the barren leaves of Science and of
Art. That the only joyous creature in these poems, the only one capable
of feeling fully the natural world of owl and moonlight as possibilities
for human value, should be an idiot (actually only what we call today
a retarded child, as evidenced by the fact that in the poem he is sent
on an important errand) is the measure of Wordsworth's cultural shock,
of his abandonment of European culture as in any sense a useful set
of directions for a satisfactory existence. And this rejection is made
all the more powerful and all the more bewildering and successful by
the jauntiness of the tone in which the 1798 poems are uttered.

That jauntiness was intensified in the longest poem he wrote in the
spring of 1798, a poem not published until 1819 — *Peter Bell: A Tale.*
Perhaps had he published it in the 1790s it might have been understood; perhaps not, for the story it tells seems at first glance, and even
at second and third, so inherently absurd that what Wordsworth was
after is easily missed. Briefly, a completely worthless and even vicious
pedlar becomes a decent human being because, quite by chance, he
experiences the faithfulness of a donkey to its drowned master and its
master's family. Wordsworth later explains this conversion as an act
of the Imagination, but it is in fact unexplained, incomprehensible.
Like "The Idiot Boy" and "The Tables Turned" the poem is a denial
of the validity of the European cultural tradition in its moral aspect.

Hence the jauntiness, the air of man freed from a useless cultural burden. *Peter Bell* is the consequence of a severe cultural shock. And that shock is the real theme of the famous "Lines Written above Tintern Abbey," written in July, 1798, and added to the *Lyrical Ballads* after the manuscript of that book had already been delivered to the publisher; that shock is the theme, and the beginnings of recovery.

"Tintern Abbey" is concerned with a revolution in self-perception. Five years prior to 1798 Wordsworth had been on the bank of the Wye River in the course of a walking tour in search of the picturesque. He was then a man of the Enlightenment, and his culture was the culture of emotional lability, and Nature was no more than the occasion for experiencing that lability. But since then the world had become to him unintelligible, a mystery and its burden. Sinking into what he had already defined as a wise passivity, a state of quiet harmony and deep joy, above all thought in the sense of covert verbal behavior, he can "see into the life of things." And that life can only be defined as a presence, a motion, a spirit that moves "all things" and "all thinking things." This extraordinary definition of man as a thinking thing at a stroke subsumes man and nature in the same category, and verbally resolves what Wordsworth had lost, a value-laden relation between himself and the world. But the resolution is only verbal, only a linguistic defense against and escape from "the dreary intercourse of daily life."

It is for this reason that Wordsworth did not yet cease to write poems about incomprehensible abandonment, about random, accidental and meaningless failure. Turning aside for the moment from his astonishing behavior, personal and literary, in Germany, where he went in September, 1798, we find in the second volume of the second edition of *Lyrical Ballads*, dated 1800 but actually published in January, 1801, a group of short poems and three long poems which continued this theme of unaccountable loss. There has been much speculation about the original girl of the entrancing and exquisite Lucy poems, but such speculation is idle. They are like the poems already discussed, a displacement into ordinary life of the death of a culture and the unintelligibility of the world after that loss. But in these poems, by dramatizing a culture failure as the loss of a beloved, Wordsworth cut deeper into his problem, the meaning of the Waste-Land. Since he perceives, in ordinary humble life a beloved is the usual, the almost universal, object of the individual's capacity to ascribe value, cultural failure is increasingly revealed as precisely that, and "the culture of the individual" as the ability to ascribe value to others and to himself. Wordsworth is here taking the first steps towards his comprehension of how to re-sanctify the world and to comprehend the function of the reason in the sanctification (which Wordsworth called "consecration").

And so he continues the theme of betrayed love in three long poems, "Ruth" written in Germany, and "The Brothers" and "Michael" written after his return to England in the spring of 1799 and his settling at Grasmere in his home Lake District in the following December. In "Ruth" a girl is loved by a youth from America who promises her the beauty and freedom of a new life, and then abandons her. There is no explanation for this, except the youth's impulsive and uncommitted style of life, equally unexplained. Ruth becomes a vagrant, a wandering beggar, and we meet one of the great Romantic archetypes, the wanderer as the culturally displaced and alienated. "The Brothers" is even simpler, though told in a subtle dialogue. Two brothers, left orphans, are reared by the good people of their Lake country. One goes away to seek his fortune; the younger and weaker remains. He falls to his death from a high rock, and the older brother returns only to find his grave and to identify it without revealing his own identity for reasons not given. Here the theme of incomprehensibility is presented as meaningless accident. In the greatest of these three poems, one of the finest he ever wrote, "Michael," Wordsworth turns from the love of man and woman and of brothers to the love of father and son. A son is sent off to seek his fortune, falls incomprehensibly into bad company and evil courses, and is forced to flee abroad to hide. Before he left home he and his father had laid the first stone of a sheepfold, which his father continued to work on until he heard of his son's betrayal. After that, in a famous line, he "never lifted up a single stone." In that unfinished sheepfold Wordsworth at last succeeded in creating the connection between love, or value ascription, and culture — what man creates as an emblem and exemplification of that value. The value ascription is what gives the poem its immense pathos, for the link between culture and value is the motive power of action, of Schelling's Will. Michael's sheepfold is Schelling's work of art; and what Wordsworth means by "morality" is the capacity for action.

With "Michael" Wordsworth completed his series of poems on abandonment and meaningless loss, for he had at last found an adequate poetic symbolization of the factors and attributes of the terrible cultural crisis he had undergone. But he could do so only because of what he had been principally engaged on while in Germany, and indeed had already begun before he left England, a long poem most simply described as an autobiographical introduction to a projected long philosophical poem. That commonplace description is not only inadequate; it is wrong. It was Coleridge's idea to go to Germany, in order to master the language and study natural science, and Wordsworth and his sister Dorothy readily joined in the plan for the same purposes. Yet when they got to Germany, late in 1798, they separated. Wordsworth and Dorothy went off to the little city of Goslar and there settled in for the winter. And in Goslar Wordsworth set about writing that vast poem which in time was to become known as *The Prelude.* At first, however, it was nothing of the sort. It was a two-part poem ostensibly about Wordsworth's youth, addressed to Coleridge so that his friend might understand him better. The first part of what is now known as *The First Prelude* was composed in Goslar. Wordsworth wrote the second part in Sockburn-on-Tees after his return to England. The very title is misleading. Wordsworth never gave a title to even the completed and revised *Prelude,* published in 1850. At least the ascribed title is misleading, if it is interpreted in an autobiographical sense, but it is not too misleading if it is understood as the preparation for the great philosophical poem Coleridge had urged him to write. Actually it is an exercise in metaphysical reductionism, or the reductionism of the poems now applied to himself.

First it is to be noticed that it was written in circumstances of extreme social withdrawal, of chosen isolation. Sockburn, the home of family friends the Hutchinsons (Wordsworth was to wed Mary, one of the Hutchinson sisters) also granted the possibility of such withdrawal. And the result of the writing was the retreat to the social isolation and withdrawal from interaction at Grasmere, an isolation to last, more or less, for the rest of his life. The clue or germ of what he had to do was already set forth, as we have seen, in "Tintern Abbey." The task was the resanctification of life, the life of nature, and the sacred or value-laden relation between the two. The task Wordsworth set himself was immensely difficult and absolutely novel. Throughout cultural history, as Wordsworth knew it and as we know it today (though with infinitely greater detail), the experience of the sacred had been accomplished by religion, by philosophy. The sacred was derived from and depended upon, simply, a verbal explanation, whether in the form of the crudest mythology or the most subtle scholasticism. Wordsworth's task was to re-sanctify the world and man without verbal aid, to do so purely on the evidence of experiences of value and of meaning, even moral meaning. His task was, paradoxically, to create an anti-metaphysical metaphysic. To discover, then, "joy whose grounds are true," he turned to the one dependable source and time of life, his own childhood and boyhood, a period before he was caught up in the sophistry of culturally validated metaphysical explanations. And his marvelous poem was built on those spots of time, those moments of value and meaning, which he experienced in those early years.

To be sure, in a sense his enterprise was not fully successful, because he did find it irresistible or even necessary to speak of Powers and Spirits of Nature that fostered him, or that "meanings work like a sea." Twice he even uses the word "God." How seriously he took these words it is difficult to say. The very vagueness of the notions of the unity of being, or of the sentiment of being, or something deeply interfused suggests that these terms are those of a mythology known to be a mythology, that is, a verbal strategy for locating and giving some precision to states of feeling quite consciously both preverbal and anti-verbal. Nor was it only the forms of nature, as it turned out, that were the occasion for the origins of sacralizing, that subjective activity and process which he was to call the poetic power and is what he meant by "imagination." There were also social situations, friendships, games, horseback expeditions. But all of these he traces to the infant's power to claim "kindred with an earthly soul" and "gather passion from his Mother's eye!" Thus he concludes that the source of value and meaning is the inherent, or (as we would say) genetically transmitted power to observe similitudes in objects superficially disparate. Analogical perception is the life of the spirit, of poetry, of imagination. The value of life emerges from man's ability to hold the world together in a condition of feeling enflamed by the analogical imagination.

Thus far he had proceeded with the great poem at Sockburn. In December came the permanent settlement at Grasmere, and in the following spring he wrote the first 457 lines (plus a few others not in sequence) of the poem published in 1888 as *The Recluse* and now known as *Home at Grasmere*. It is perhaps the first appearance of an emergent Romantic artistic mode — the ecstatic. And by that is meant here the objective of the effort to sustain moments of value experience, what Wordsworth has called his "spots of time." A lengthy rational explanation of the world may be justly considered as an effort to sustain verbally the sense of value and the source of meaning and meanings. Such a sustaining process may be reasonably thought of as the object of the construction of any metaphysical or philosophical system.

For a Romantic such as Wordsworth, and even Schelling, who ultimately rests his acceptance of the world on the work of art, the metaphysical systems of the past were no longer available. A metaphysic maintains sanctification. What the ecstatic mode endeavors to do is sustain sanctification by a self manipulation, or more precisely, by taking over from culture the task of giving instructions for behavior, a task to be accomplished by generating those instructions from the individual's unique resources. For Wordsworth this can be done and must be done verbally, since he had already concluded that poetry is identical with the creation of value. He thus has the task of bringing about a non-verbal state of being by verbal means. His device is to convert the vale of Grasmere, where his new home was nestled, into a hallowed place, into a sacred place, a temple consecrated to the Romantic Self, the power of the alienated and isolated individual to achieve his own purely secular redemption; into a holy of holies where nature and the mind of man are unified by the mind's creative powers and by nature's. Shortly, within most probably a year or two, in the passage that came to be known as the "Prospectus to the Recluse" and first published in the preface to *The Excursion,* he calls it a great consummation, a wedding. Thus he succeeds at last in what, given the logic of his cultural situation and its crisis, had to be accomplished. The sexual metaphor embodies the anti-verbal, anti-explanatory, anti-metaphysical coming into being and sustaining of the human power to create value. This at last was Reason in its most exalted mood, the discovery and identification of the ecstatic, sacralizing function of the imaginative reason.

Samuel Taylor Coleridge   Like Wordsworth, Coleridge was at
(1772-1834)   first sympathetic with the French Re-
                                volution, but in 1796 he began to alter
his attitude. The son of a clergyman, educated in London's Christ's Hospital School (1782-1791) and then at Cambridge (1791-1794), in 1795 after various youthful adventures more than customarily silly even for Enlightenment youth, he found himself in Bristol. There he began a life of a general man of letters, at first giving lectures on religion and politics, then in 1796 undertaking his own journal, the *Watchman,* which lasted only a few months, trying his hand, like Wordsworth, at a tragedy, *Osorio,* publishing his poems, joining with Wordsworth in *Lyrical Ballads,* and contributing frequently brilliant editorials on politics to the anti-Administration paper, the *Morning Post.* After his return from Germany (he was back by July, 1799, after less than a year) he soon went to London to write for the *Morning Post* on full salary, and after a little more than a year living near Wordsworth in the Lake district and a return to London in January, 1801, he once again became fully employed at the *Morning Post* in September of that year. But unfortunately by that time he had already begun to be deeply dependent upon laudanum. He had become, bluntly, an opium junky. What followed were years of disaster, of physical agony, of lying, of plagiarism, of promises unkept, and of elaborate descriptions of manuscripts as ready for the press of which

not a word had been written. Almost everything of the next two decades which once contributed to his fame we now know was simply stolen from various German Romantics — Fichte, Schelling, and the Schlegel brothers, primarily, but also from Kant and from philosophical compendia. This is all the more heart-breaking because during a period of less than a year (1797-1798) he wrote some of the most wonderful poems in English, poetry in which he leapt from quite ordinary 18th century verse to Romantic poetry of almost incomprehensible originality.

There really is no question that his friendship with Wordsworth was responsible for this brief blooming, but it was by no means a matter of influence. Rather, he recognized in Wordsworth one who like himself had entered the wasteland and had found the imagery to symbolize it. Already in April, 1796, in Number VIII of the *Watchman*, he had begun to realize that the French Revolution was moving in a direction that undermined the validity of everything it had undertaken to accomplish. From playing the redeemer of mankind, France was becoming trapped, sunken, degraded into an imperialistic nationalism. Coleridge withdrew further into his odd Christian radicalism, a combination that was to recur frequently in the course of the 19th and 20th centuries in various forms. Nor need it seem surprising, for Enlightenment radicalism was only a secularization of doctrines central to Christianity. He continued therefore, like Wordsworth, his anti-governmental position; and like Wordsworth he was in a political limbo, increasingly alienated both from a reactionary government and from a failing revolutionary France. In March, 1798, France decreed the Helvetic Republic, and this attack upon a traditional center of political liberty, even though that tradition was more than a little sentimental, forced Coleridge, or so he felt, into a position that denied the validity or even the possibility of the political and social establishment of Liberty, which now became the personal achievement of the individual human being. The possibility and the foundation for that true liberty was the "one life within us and abroad," Schelling's *anima mundi* and Wordsworth's "something deeply interfused" with nature and the human mind. Indeed, Wordsworth may have picked the notion up from Coleridge, since certainly Coleridge held it before meeting Wordsworth. Yet Wordsworth certainly held it in a mode different from that of Coleridge, whose position was less radically distant from an Enlightenment Christianity. On the other hand it is possible that Coleridge's position would have been more metaphysical had it not been for the influence of Wordsworth, already moving toward that radical metaphysical reductionism which was so strikingly central a tendency in his thinking and in his poetry.

But the real point is that when Coleridge and Wordsworth met, perhaps for the second time, at Racedown in the spring of 1797, Coleridge, as we have seen, recognized the remarkable quality of *The Ruined Cottage* and above all realized that in Wordsworth was a man with whom he could be in the profoundest sympathy, for both were moving in the same cultural direction. Coleridge's claim in "France: An Ode," his response to the aggression of France towards Switzerland. that liberty could not be achieved by social instrumentalities meant that like Wordsworth he was engaged in rejecting his cultural tradition and in becoming increasingly alienated from the dominating traditions of European culture. And that is the theme of his greatest achievement, *The Rime of the Ancyent Marinere.*

The foundational trope or metaphor of the poem came from the great sixteenth and seventeenth century voyage and travel compilations of Richard Hakluyt of 1589 (enlarged 1598-1600) and those of his assistant and successor, Samuel Purchas, in 1625: a voyage of discovery the culmination of which was the voyage around the world from England around Cape Horn to the Pacific and thence back to England. To tell the story of the poem would be otiose, for everyone educated in England or the United States knows it. But the poem's interpretation in another matter. For in fact it was a new kind of poetry. In an allegorical narrative the most important proper names, and sometimes all of them, belong to an explanatory system of which the poem itself is an exemplification. In this poem there is nothing of the sort, at least in the poem's original form. Indeed, we are justified in seeking to explain the poem, to consider it as a kind of allegory in which the proper names do not belong to any explanatory system, only because the lines "And she is far liker Death than he; / Her flesh makes the still air cold" are changed in the final version

(1817) to "The Night-mare LIFE-IN-DEATH was she / Who thicks man's blood with cold." The clearly allegorical proper name, capitalized by Coleridge, provides a strong instruction that the whole poem is properly considered an exemplification of some kind of explanatory system — although at first glance indeterminable — whether religious, political, metaphysical, or psychological.

With this hint it is possible to discern a pattern to the whole, and that pattern is best understood as concerned with the relation of the individual to his culture. The first step is to realize that the Mariner commits the same kind of action twice — first when he shoots the albatross which had played with the sailors and shared their food; and second when he interrupts the wedding and holds the wedding guest back from a celebration of social solidarity. Both actions are violations of community and as such are typical Romantic cultural vandalisms. This redundancy is extended when the priest to whom the Mariner confesses goes mad. Confession does not, as it should, restore the Mariner to solidarity with a community. And by a further extension of this redundancy the Mariner is condemned to eternal wandering and telling his story without receiving absolution or membership in any community.

Coleridge does not provide explanations for any of these actions and events. He is interested only in the nature of the act and its consequences. This is why the ship set out from England with no stated purpose either of exploration or of economic enterprise. Coleridge thus abstracts society, or community, from the matrix of interactions, without considering the possible purpose or goal of social relationships and patterns of interaction. So the Mariner's act is incomprehensible; Coleridge appears to be looking at Wordsworth's incomprehensible abandonments from the point of view of the abandoner, the violator. And it might even be said that the Mariner's crime (as Coleridge calls it in his 1817 gloss) is a manifestation of an alienation symbolized most traditionally by the antarctic cold, which is subsequently identified with Life-in-Death. But this cold is followed by the entrance into a new world, one into which no human had ever penetrated. The Mariner finds himself in an absolutely novel cultural condition, one in which his primary feeling is guilt as indicated by the heat, by the albatross hung around his neck instead of the cross, the emblem of Christian community, and by the death of his shipmates. He is now completely alone in a terrifyingly hideous and repulsive world. But again incomprehensibly he blesses the horrifying monsters of the world, and blesses them unconsciously. "Unaware" is Coleridge's word. Here is a parallel to the subsequent creation of Liberty by the culturally unaided individual in "France: An Ode." The albatross drops into the sea; the Mariner is freed from a culturally assigned and determined guilt. Beneath the notion of liberty in "France" lies the profound notion of the ascription of value; the Mariner's hideous world suddenly changes into a world of great beauty. Moreover it is done unconsciously, Coleridge's way of indicating with the utmost commitment that the creation of value is not a social act but one which arises from an individual's resources — resources which he does not know he has and which he cannot consciously control.

And now it rains; and the dead shipmates work the ship, a way of indicating that the Mariner is now entirely separate from and alienated from community. Moreover the Spirit of the Pole, the representative here of the one life within us and abroad, or of the *Anima mundi*, propels the ship And so the Mariner returns home to face a new disaster. The Hermit cannot shrive him; he can find relief from his agony of alienation only by telling his story, but that is only a temporary relief. He becomes the Romantic wanderer, condemned to repeat his story, condemned to interrupt or violate rituals of community such as weddings, condemned only to spread to others a cultural infection that makes them sadder if wiser. And the famous moral, "He prayeth best who loveth best, / All things both great and small" undermines traditional religious modes by asserting that they depend on, are only a manifestation of, something far deeper: the capacity to create value from the unique resources of an individual, without the support of culture. And the concomitant cultural infection that makes men sadder and wiser is that the cultural forms of the European tradition are no longer capable of releasing that capacity.

It is quite possible that when Coleridge wrote *The Rime of the Ancyent Marinere* he had no notion of what he meant by it, what cultural pattern he was realizing and exposing, and that only afterwards did he understand what he had been investigating by means of that astonishing poem. But if that is the case he shortly knew, for in concluding "France: An Ode," published in the *Morning Post* for April 16, 1798 (written after but published before the *Mariner*) he states what he had done. Before nature, winds and waves, on a sea-cliff, his only companions the pines, in the presence of nature but in the absence of man, he "shot my being through earth sea and air, / Possessing all things with intensest love, / O Liberty! my spirit felt thee there." And he states it again in even more mysterious form, again in a form which he himself might not have understood, in the astonishing "Kubla Khan." When it was written we cannot be certain, but it is enough that it was written or at least sketched during these miraculous months of association with Wordsworth, in 1797 or 1798. Again we must look for the overall pattern, and assuming that it was written, like the *Marinere* and "France," after a severe cultural crisis, that pattern is not difficult to discern.

The world of culture, the garden of the great Khan, cannot exclude or redeem the terror of life which underlies it, the caves of ice, the measureless caverns, the sunless sea, the demon-haunted chasm with its endless surging of energy from the depths and the darkness, the "ancestral voices prophesying war," the tumult of the appearance and the disappearance of the sacred river. And the poet goes on to insist that could he re-create that vision of sublimity and terror, of beauty and destruction inextricably intermingled, other men would be terrified by him, would regard him as a kind of sacred monster; for *his* paradisiacal vision would be one of ascribing value to that ineluctable unity of sun and ice, of beauty and violence, without the false consolations of religion and metaphysics. "Kubla Khan" is a vandalizing attack upon a culture that has failed. The conditional character of that vision must be always kept in the foreground in understanding the poem. The "if" is the recognition of an utter and perilous need for cultural transcendence, and in those days at least, as the *Mariner* and "Kubla Khan" make quite clear, Coleridge recognized the peril and the price, the heavy cost to the individual, of a significant cultural transcendence. That heavy cost was to be discovered and paid again and again in the course of the Romantic tradition. Was Coleridge's addiction to opium the consequence of the fact that he could not indeed pay that price? Was his addiction a failure of nerve?

August Wilhelm (1767-1845)   The Schlegel brothers, born in
and   Hanover, came from a literary
Friedrich von Schlegel (1772-1829)   family; their father wrote hymns
and didactic poetry and their short-lived uncle wrote numerous plays and superior criticism. Both went to the Göttingen University and the younger, Friedrich, also attended Leipzig. In 1795 August arrived in Jena, where he was followed by Friedrich in 1796. The younger brother had the more original and brilliant mind, but the older was adept at systematizing and popularizing many of Friedrich's more important ideas. Together they gave new meaning to the already rather worn word, *Romantic,* equating it with the modern, both in the usual sense of post-Classical and also in the sense of post-French Revolutionary. They recognized more sharply than anyone that a new cultural epoch had begun in Europe, and had to begin, an awareness still to arrive in England and France.

In particular they were responsible for the common identification of German Romanticism as the yearning or longing for the infinite. But what they meant by the infinite is by no means easy to grasp. And in fact they meant a number of things. One notion meant that unlike Classical art, Romantic art would be formally without established limits or rules, limits and rules maintained by culture and the power of political, religious, and cultural institutions. Thus the notion that literary and any artistic genres had rational or natural foundations could no longer be tolerated. On the contrary the new literature would be characterized by a mixture of genres; the boundaries of genres would be overrun, and the boundaries between the arts would no longer be of any significance or force. At times, however, they meant by the infinite the transcendent, the divine, noumenal reality, the realm of the sacred. This notion of the infinite, however, is particularly vague because it is only a negative notion. That is, it negates the culturally existent conceptions and artistic and philosophical realizations of the sacred. Thus the Romantic infinite is not merely indefinable; it is incomprehensible. In this latter attribute, the incomprehensibility of existence itself, its absolute resistance to rational understanding, Schlegelian Romanticism has much in common with the contemporaneous notions of Wordsworth. Indeed, the function of this use of "infinite" is not to say anything at all in particular, not to commit the user of the term to any position, but rather to identify the cultural task as emergent, as absolutely novel. Thus the "Self" and the "infinite" are often made identical, or else made to subsume each other, become attributes to each other.

That same cultural emergence appears strikingly (and perhaps, for the future, most valuably) in Schlegelian theoretical criticism concerned with the formal character of literary works of art. It was the Schlegels who, picking up a late Enlightenment metaphor for the world, urged the notion of organic form or, in its most common occurrence, organic unity. Coleridge appropriated this notion and gave it popularity in England and subsequently in the United States, where it experienced a remarkable and depressing renaissance beginning in the 1930s. It is a term of powerful appeal, principally because it is very nearly meaningless. A literary work is obviously not an organism, either plant or animal. Nor is the notion of "unity" much more useful, since any perceptual or semantic field is unified if one's criteria are sufficiently loose, and none is if the criteria are sufficiently stringent. Nevertheless, the Schlegels were trying to get at *something* when they invented the term, and an understanding of what they were attempting to locate and confine can contribute significantly to an understanding of Romantic art up to the present and probably into the future.

The first thing they were trying to determine was normative; a work of art is not properly judged by whether or not it is constructed according to the demands of the protocols of a genre. (Their notion of the infinite had already disposed of that.) That position led to the next step, that the interactions of the various parts or factors or themes or forces within a work of art were not to be determined by already existing cultural demands and protocols but were to be imaginatively discovered by the artist in the process of creating the work of art.

This was a notion of the highest importance for the development of Romantic art and it led to the most striking characteristic of that art — its intricate and complex organization. For more than a hundred and fifty years it has been said that Romantic art is formless. Nothing could be further from the truth. Rather, the art of the preceding periods is by contrast formless. A work of literature — and the longer it is the truer this is — of the medieval and Renaissance periods (and by Renaissance is meant here, and only here, the cultural period through the Enlightenment) is more than anything else a package: the organizational principle is primarily additive. In the late Enlightenment the artist could achieve something like perceptual unity only by an extreme perceptual simplification, as we have already seen. All this can be most easily observed in such works as Pope's *Essay on Man*, a particularly pure example of the grab-bag principle of literary organization.

As a description of artistic organization the Schlegels' notion of organic unity is almost meaningless, but as a demand upon the artist it was of the highest importance. What it meant was that it is the task of the artist to organize his work according to unique principles, principles derived as far as possible from the semantic character of the literary work, and that that organization should be as intricately complex and tightly interwoven both thematically and formally, as he could make it. The Schlegels demanded that the artist encompass in the work of art both the chaotic incomprehensibility of the world and the organizing power of the transcendent human artistic will imposed upon that chaos. It was not for nothing that they were friends of Schelling, considering his exaltation both of art and of the will. Thus the culturally transcendent task of the artist became the creation of a work unique and emergent both in meaning and in structure. Only in such a work, only in such art, could the Romantic self be realized, be concretized. And in the successful accomplishment of that artistic task, the sacred in human existence becomes visible and accessible. Art is the sacramental, and it confers its sacredness on artist and art-responder alike.

For Friedrich Schlegel, however, art was not the only nor indeed the highest and noblest manifestation and realization of the sacred.

In publishing in 1799 his unfinished novel *Lucinde* he originated a tradition that was to persist to the present in the history of Romantic culture: the highest mode of the sacred is the erotic. When it was published, *Lucinde* aroused considerable opposition and even shock; it was thought to be pornographic, though by today's standards the sexual factors were not only veiled but often enough rather difficult to discern. Nevertheless they are there, no matter how delicately and wittily introduced. In *Lucinda* the "erotic" means something quite specific — the assertion that sexual interaction is the highest and noblest mode of love. Enlightenment sentimentality had sharply separated and polarized lust and love, but Schlegel unites them. To be sure, he is sufficiently morally orthodox to see the fullest erotic consequence in marriage and children, but he also insists that friendship between men is also a mode of love; and he certainly appears to hint, though with the utmost delicacy, that such friendship can and indeed should reach its fullest experience in a sexual relation.

What Schlegel is doing is akin to the reductionism of Wordsworth, and even in Wordsworth, who has been accused of prudishness, the possibility of creating and experiencing value through sexuality is certainly strongly hinted at in the exquisite Lucy poems. Nor is it irrelevant that the recently discovered letters of Wordsworth to his wife Mary are intensely passionate. The erotic, then, is for Schlegel that aspect of nature most conducive to and susceptible to transformation by the imagination into the sacred, not into the source but into an occasion for experiencing value. Thus he calls Lucinde a priestess of the night, one who achieves the union of the sacred and the sexual at the traditional time of sexual intercourse. In the same way he praises the noble frankness and beauty with which the classic artists of Greeece and Rome portrayed in both literary and visual art the sexual act. Now in support of Schlegel it may be said that sex is a stage on which any human interest can be acted out. What he discovered is that the sacred, the experience of disinterested ascription of value, can be experienced during coitus. It may seem absurd, but this discovery was exactly analogous to Wordsworth's response to a field of daffodils or to his conversion of the value of Grasmere into a holy place, imbued with the sacred — pure disinterested value.

Schlegel also presents yet another theme of importance, akin to Wordsworthian reductionist thinking: in seeking an explanation for the sacredness of the erotic, he concludes that the function of that experience in human existence is the creation of individuality and the confirmation of selfhood. Moreover, he finds the fullest confirmation of that selfhood in one's confirmation of the selfhood of the sexual-erotic partner, or one's mistress, or, better still, one's wife, or even one's friend of the same sex. Thus the sacred, the ascription of value, the confirmation of the Romantic Self are all to be accomplished not only apart from and independent of existent social institutions (for the erotic justifies marriage, not the other way around), but even by means of a conscious vandalization of traditional and normal moalities.

The powerful innovation, the exalting cultural transcendence of the semantic aspect of *Lucinde* is paralleled by the very way it is put together; it is so different from what is ordinarily thought of as a novel that it scarcely seems a novel at all. The subtitle is *Confessions of a Blunderer,* an ironic instruction to the reader that his expectations for an ordinary novel are certainly going to be disappointed. It is indeed what Schlegelian criticism called for, a mixture of genres, for it includes letters, meditations, narratives, essays. But it is by no means a grab-bag or package kind of 18th century literary organization, although at first reading, it seems so disorganized as to hardly deserve the name of any kind of structure. But subsequent readings reveal something quite different. What one discovers is that every sentence contributes, no matter how obliquely, to the dominant theme of the work, and to what one might call the local modality of that theme in the section or sub-section in which the sentence appears. And this is clearly what Schlegel wished to achieve — prose rhetorics with the kind of intricate completely internalized literary organization hitherto found only in usually brief lyric poems. Earlier literature quite easily submits to extracts of "beauties," but with *Lucinde,* as with Wordsworth's long blank verse poems, we have already arrived at the structural characteristic of Romantic art, soon to appear in music and painting and architecture. The Romantic arts, to the degree they are fully Romantic, can neither be easily subsumed by traditional literary genres nor do they gracefully submit to dissection into self-subsistent extracts. Thorough organization, what in music is known as *durchkomponiert*, has become the emergent stylistic attribute of Romantic art.

Novalis 2   In 1808 Friedrich Schlegel became a Roman
(1772-1801)   Catholic; and it seems more than likely that the in-
tense religious concern of the Jena Romantics was one of the stimuli which led to his decision. That concern was at its highest level in 1799 and 1800 and its center was the work of Novalis, even though he was not living in Jena but in Weissenfels, only forty miles to the northeast, between Jena and Dresden. (Novalis had been born on his father's estate forty miles northwest of Dresden, and his family had moved to Weissenfels in 1784). He is a particularly pure example of how the breakdown of the Enlightenment produced in individuals who experienced that breakdown a wide range of seemingly unconnected interests, interests which they made a heroic effort to bring together and even to unify. Thus Hardenberg, of noble origin, was and wanted to be a good civil servant, studying mining at Freiberg, after the more usual kind of classical education at Jena and Leipzig and law at Wittenberg, and becoming in 1799 a member of the directorate of the Saxon salt mines. Thus he was involved in the emerging chemical industry of the 19th century. But as "Novalis" Hardenberg was quite different. His attitude towards nature was not scientific; it was a metaphysical attempt to unite science, poetry, and philosophy, particularly by reviving and continuing one of the least scientific and least rational traditions of the previous three or four hundred years. It goes by various names: mysticism, hermeticism, the perennial philosophy, neo-Platonism. For Novalis, Jakob Böhme (1575-1624) and the Dutch philosopher Franz Hemsterhuis (1721-1790) were especially important.

It is one of the curious and instructive results of the development of what has been called here situational thinking that this occult tradition (as I shall call it) should have experienced a powerful revival in the 16th and ensuing centuries. Its appeal needs to be under-

stood if its appearance in the Romantic tradition is to be comprehended. Very possibly, in its most respectable intellectual or at least philosophical (they are not quite the same thing) mode it is to be found in
Leibniz's notion of a pre-established harmony between mind and
world, between reason and nature. We have already encountered a
simple form of the problem in the history of painting. How is it
that a mathematical system of perspective gives what certainly appears to be a better control over the purely visual aspect of nature
than a system of simple copying of appearance? To be sure, no visual
art is a matter of simple copying but is always culturally established
convention; but that fact makes the problem even more perplexing.
As was pointed out in the beginning of this chapter, Novalis grasped
the independence of language from the world, but he relied upon a
notion of pre-established harmony between mind and world to account for the power language has over the world, even in its lowest
power — that of "representation." In short, as Kant was fully aware,
the steadily growing success of science and, he could have added, of
incipient industrialism, made what is known as the epistemological
problem not less puzzling but more so.

For certain personalities this problem is unendurable. Perhaps it
is only the rare individual to whom it is not; even the unsophisticated,
even the illiterate, are convinced that there must be an explanation
for everything, so deeply has language engraved in them the habit of
explanatory expectation. It may indeed be the case that the intracta-
bility, indeed the insolubility, of the epistemological problem may be
a simple result of the fact that it is a pseudo-problem, and currently
a few philosophers have actually begun to think so. The epistemological problem appears only when language is thought of as passive
or inert, or having a mirror relation to the world. But if language is
thought of as coordinating, or, better still, as controlling human behavior, then the epistemological problem disappears. However, from
the early 15th century on, the more successful rationalism was in
demolishing pre-scientific and even traditional religious explanations
of reality, the more enticing the occult tradition became, since both
mind and language were thought of as inert mirrors. (And it is hardly
necessary to add that occultism is still leading a very vigorous life.)

We have seen how Schelling, Coleridge, and Wordsworth all revived and for a time toyed with the notion of the *anima mundi,* a thread in the occult tradition. What happened was that as rationalism and skepticism about religious and theological explanations of the world became more powerful and effective, there developed an explanatory vacuum. As the rational and scientific comprehension of the world became more effective, the world became increasingly meaningless, not to use "meaning" in the sense of comprehensibility but in the sense of any human value, and of any value to humans.

In "Die Christenheit oder Europa" ("Christendom or Europe") written in October and early November, 1799, destined for the Schlegels' journal *Athenäum,* but not published until 1826, Novalis wrote:

> Still further, the hatred of religion extended itself quite naturally and consistently to all objects of enthusiasm. It made imagination and emotion heretical, as well as morality and the love of art, the future and the past. With some difficulty it placed man first in order of created things, and reduced the infinite creative music of the universe to the monotonous clatter of a monstrous mill, which driven by the stream of chance and floating thereon, was supposed to be mill in the abstract, without Builder or Miller, in fact an actual perpetuum mobile, a mill that milled of itself. (Trans. by Charles E. Passage)

What had happened was the famous appearance of the distinction between fact and value. However, what this really meant in terms of the language in which man organizes his relation to the world and directs and controls his response to it was that explanation and justi- fication and validation were differentiated. But in actuality this dif- ference, like the difference between fact and value, is not difference of meaning but a mere difference of function or use. That is, any statement can be used for the purposes of explanation or justification or validation, or, in different terms, for the assertion of either fact or value.

Hence the Leibnizian pre-established harmony provided a pseudo-solution to only part of a pseudo-problem, the epistemological part. But even as far as it went it was unsatisfactory, for it failed to account for error, and in particular moral error. And of course it quite failed to provide justification and validation. It provided only explanation, and did so only by relying upon a religious tradition which its own rationalism was undermining. What the occult tradition offered was a mythical explanation for the increasing sense of separation from nature, and that myth had an element in it which fit perfectly into the French Revolution's attempt to unify nature and reason by means of social institutions. For in the occult tradition there was also a form of the myth of natural man born free but everywhere in chains, as Rousseau had so strikingly put it. Between mind and nature there was once a paradisiacal unity, but that unity became disrupted, the condition in which we now exist. Hence our suffering and our feeling not at home in the world. Novalis' aim was to be once again at home. That is, by the union of poetry, philosophy, and science (possible because the basic ideas of science are arrived at, he said and rightly, by intuition) primary unity would be restored. But instead of the restoration being accomplished by a political act, an impossibility, it must be accomplished by the imagination — by, it follows, poets, who would thus become the redeemers of mankind.

This redemption, this re-sanctification of the world, would not come about according to the traditional Christian model. On the contrary the new paradisiacal state would be at a higher spiritual level than the original state And the explanation for the transcendence lay in the fact that the occult tradition did not see the intermediate state of disunity as a state of evil. The condition of disunity was not a polarized antithesis to either the old unity or the new but a necessary path to the new. Thus, for example, Novalis could say in Chapter VIII of *Heinrich von Ofterdingen* (to which we shall return) *"Das Chaos muss in jeder Dichtung durch den regelmässingen Flor der Ordnung Schimmern"* ("In every poem chaos must shimmer through the regular veil of orderliness"). Chaos is the instrument for the creation of the higher unity of a world of peace and love. This explains why in this revolutionary transition to a new world a reborn and new-born unity of man and world, man and the infinite, science is as important as philosophy and poetry; for science, inspired by the imagination, bit by bit builds up an understanding of nature (if only a practical understanding, as in mining or chemistry), and imagination in the form of poetry is the activating force of every man at every moment. What Novalis did, then, was to pick up the occult tradition, particularly from Böhme and Hemsterhuis, and use it, it seems most probable, as a mythology or, as he called it, a fable, in order to indicate the necessity for the creation of a new cultural epoch — the task of the Romantics.

His first effort was *Die Lehrlinge von Sais* (*The Novices of Sais*) begun early in 1798 but abandoned by May, 1799. He took the notion of the Temple of Nature at Sais in Egypt from a poem by Schiller, "Das verschleierte Bild zu Sais" ("The Veiled Image at Sais"). Schiller warns that the veil of the image must not be lifted, but Novalis is concerned precisely with lifting it, with transgressing the limits set by tradition. Man must penetrate the secrets of nature, but he cannot do so either by purely rationalistic means nor by purely moral ones. Nature must be approached and her mysteries penetrated with love. The comprehension of nature must be an act of poetry, imagination, and worship. It is reasonably clear what Novalis is attempting. In an interpolated fable he tells the story of how Hyazinth, a youth estranged from his beloved Rosenblütchen, sets out to comprehend the world, and in a dream lifts the veil of the goddess Nature and is reunited with Rosenblütchen. Thus the comprehension of fact must also be a comprehension of value, competence in dealing with the natural world must be founded in love for that world, and the discovery of the true inwardness of nature must be the discovery of the self — the "ego of the ego," as he puts it. What this amounts to, first, is Novalis' realization that the nature philosophy of Goethe and Schelling is premature; the reunion of man and nature into a paradisiacal unity lies distantly in a mythical future. And second, that the currently available attempts to combine reason and nature, the efforts of the Enlightenment, are failures. Though *Die Lehrlinge von Sais* is incomplete (hardly more than a 25 or 30 page fragment), Novalis is endeavoring not to solve the secrets of nature, but to show that all human resources, from the most sensual to the most intellectual, must be employed to achieve that perhaps unachievable goal. It boils down to the position that the true knowledge of nature and self cannot be achieved without the union of the two and the sanctification of that new unity.

His next important intellectual effort was "Christenheit oder Europa", inspired by Friedrich Scheiermacher's (1768-1834) *Über die Religion; Reden an die Gebildeten unter ihren Verächtern (On Religion: Speeches to its Cultured Despisers)*, published in 1799. For Novalis the most important point Schleiermacher made was that institutionalized religions, such as Christianity itself, though the best available, are but *manifestations* of religion; for religion is the inmost kernel of the self, or at least religion emerges from the self in the longing to establish a union of the finite with the infinite. So Novalis shows first a purely imaginary middle ages of Catholic unity (though he may not have realized how imaginary it was), followed by the Protestant revolution, and the emergence of rationalism — the conception of the world as a meaningless and valueless mill. What the French Revolution really shows, then, is that that old world is dying, and that a new world is coming to birth through struggle and warfare. Neither the old Catholicism of the Papacy nor Protestantism will be able to meet what the new world requires. A rejuvenated and new kind of Christianity must be the unifying and binding force of a new Europe of peace and joy. Not surprisingly, Friedrich Schlegel refused to publish this in his *Athenäum;* and, when appealed to as arbiter, Goethe also rejected it.

In the ensuing *Hymnen an die Nacht (Hymns to the Night)* Novalis attempted to make his vision and his cultural demand clearer. (Evidently he finished them in December, 1799, and they were published in the *Athenäum* in the issue of the following August.) In this mixture of a new form of poems in prose with a traditional form of poems in verse, Novalis in the very rhetorical structure, both in language and in the mixture of prose and verse, attempted a cultural transcendence by proposing a stylistic metamorphosis. Nor was that the only stylistic innovation, for the thematic material of the hymns is a mixture of sexuality, eroticism, and Dionysianism, but with traditional and almost commonplace worship of Christ and Mary — except that even these figures are seen as creations not of the day of reason and sun but of the night, which is identified with death, itself a realm distinct from life and equally distinct from the traditional immortality of the soul or life after death. It is conceived, rather, as an other or altered state of being, and a state which is the true source of creativity, religion, and worship of nature and value. Again, the hymns are most appropriately interpreted, particularly in light of Schleiermacher's denial of anything but the mythical significance of finite and historical religions, as a demand for cultural transcendence, to be achieved by establishing, as in *Lucinde,* a new union of finite and infinite, of eroticism and the transcendent. In short, the realm of night is the true realm of freedom in every possible meaning of the word. And that is indicated by what is common in Romantic culture, the reversal of traditional value symbols from negative to positive. Just as in Novalis night becomes good, so in Coleridge and Shelley, the traditionally evil snake becomes the symbol of goodness; and more than half a century later Wagner reversed the values of day and night in *Tristan und Isolde.* These reversals signify the Romantics' awareness of the task of creating a new ground for human culture, their realization that the old ground had failed.

Almost immediately after completing the *Hymns* Novalis turned in the first months of 1800 to his major fictional and cultural effort, *Heinrich von Ofterdingen,* destined, because of his long sickness and early death in March, 1801, to remain a fragment. In that winter and spring, he wrote Part I, and in the summer part of Part II; and except for a few notes and sketches, that was all. Yet the book was to become the primary text for German Romanticism. Or rather, one image in it was to become the primary symbol. And that symbol was the blue flower, which the book's hero, Heinrich, a poet of the early 13th century, sees in a dream. The work was written as an antithesis to, even an attack upon, Goethe's *Wilhelm Meister.* Even while writing *Die Lehrlinge von Sais,* also modelled to a certain extent, and in admiration, upon Goethe's novel, Novalis had thought *Wilhelm Meister's Lehrjahre,* as did Friedrich Schlegel, one of the most important phenomena of the age. But by 1800 he had come to think it commonplace, bourgeois, reactionary, narrow, pinched, an effort to maintain the status quo, just as Weimarian classicism was equally an attempt to maintain that same status quo, and Goethe's activity as a civil servant (always, he was to boast, he had sided with the aristocracy) as a political effort of the same kind.

Heinrich, like Novalis, is half poet, half scientist, and above all a spiritual seeker. In an interpolated fairy tale Novalis presented the fullest form in his writings of what has been called here the occult tradition — the fall from unity into a creative suffering and the emergence into a higher unity, in which, for example, the traditional distinction between love and sexual coitus is obviated. Love and sex are one. And in Part II of *Heinrich Ofterdingen* Novalis explains what he means by fable, the symbolic revelation of the meaning of the world and of history, a revelation made possible by individual conscience, which is the individual's freedom. It is fable because even the poet cannot say what has happened or what will happen. He can only indicate in mythic terms the possibility, the necessity for a cultural transcendence, for new patterns of relation of man to nature, relations which must be created by the conscience of the individual Self. That is the true meaning of conscience, and the blue flower is the symbolic manifestation of the moral capacity of man to create a new and higher condition of existence, a new world. It is thus Novalis' most notable achievement to have converted the occult tradition, which up to then was believed to be a scientific-religious truth, into poetic fable, into symbol, into myth — to reveal at once its unreality and its importance. Novalis thus created incipient Romanticism with the most powerful and attractive symbol of the task of the Romantics, the creation of a new culture, out of and on the ruins of the culture of the preceding 2500 years of European cultural life, at the very least. Thus the first Romantics had discovered that the French Revolution meant the emergence of a new world only in the sense that it proved the failure of the old.

Ludwig van Beethoven
(1770-1827)

Beethoven is the most striking and most important of those artists who were successful, even triumphantly successful, in the styles of the late Enlightenment, but who in spite of that success transformed their art completely and powerfully in the opening years of the new century. In the case of Beethoven that emerging style has been known traditionally as the second of his three periods, divisions inadequate yet irresistible and lasting. It has long been maintained that Beethoven was never a Romantic composer. but in recent years the Beethoven of the second period and after has been called Romantic with increasing frequency. There are good reasons to do so. In 1801 Beethoven told Carl Czerny that he was quite dissatisfied with what he had composed so far. It is difficult to believe that that dissatisfaction could have been purely technical or musical, or that it arose from some self-determination of incompetence. His mastery of the Viennese classical style, as brought to fulfillment by Mozart and especially Haydn in the 1790s, as sketched out in Chapter I, was consummate, and was widely acknowledged by the music loving and musically sophisticated aristocratic and bourgeois public of Vienna. Indeed, from the time of his arrival in Vienna in 1792 his progress had been rapid, and after a few years of further study, principally with Haydn, though that seemed to have been relatively unrewarding, and with the pedantic but thorough Albrechtsberger, his success in Vienna and on extensive tours was soon established, even to the point, as he boasted in a letter, that he was making a good deal of money.

His dissatisfaction, then, was not merely with himself, but rather with himself as master of a style established by composers greater than he himself yet was. His dissatisfaction was with a style and — since his subsequent transformation and transcendence of that style was to be such a radical one — with the culture that that style exemplified. It must not be imagined that Beethoven was an uncultivated man, in spite of his weak spelling and weaker arithmetic, for he read and admired Schiller's *Don Carlos* and Goethe's *Wilhelm Meister,* and more important, he was an assiduous reader of August Schlegel's translations of Shakespeare, which began to appear in 1798. The story is well-known of his remark that to understand his Sonata No. 17 (Opus 13, No. 2), composed in 1802, one should read Shakespeare's *The Tempest.* If he read the critical works of the Schlegel brothers, particularly their writings on Shakespeare, we can scarcely know, yet there is sufficient evidence that Beethoven knew the important literary works of his contemporary culture. To comprehend the civilized, the cultivated Beethoven, it is useful to look back to his early years in Bonn.

He was the third generation of his family to be a court musician for the Elector of Cologne; from the age of thirteen he had played in the opera orchestra. His social status as the son of a musician and as a promising and obviously gifted musician was anything but high. Nor was his social position improved by his alcoholic father. Nevertheless by his late teens he had been taken up into a cultivated group of the aristocracy and higher bourgeoisie. Nor was such an experience exceptional at the time. It must be remembered that, except for a few cities such as London and Paris, the social life at the end of the 18th century and well into the 19th was conducted on a scale so small that it is very difficult today even to imagine. The best examples today are to be found in certain remote towns of Italy, such a Aquila or Lecce, small cities of 60 to 70 thousand which maintain a rich and sophisticated intellectual and cultural life. In cities of that size, talent, wherever it appears, is noticed, particularly at a time when the upper classes considered it a moral obligation to discover, foster, encourage, and patronize talented youths from the lower social orders. Today that responsibility has been relegated to educational institutions, and it is quite possible that the system of discovering talent and genius is today considerably less effective.

Beethoven's experience was by no means uncommon. The result was that, to judge from the scant evidence of his early letters, and from such sources as the text of his *Cantata on the Death of Joseph II* (1790), he became fully acquainted with and imbued by late Enlightenment ideology. That he was very much in sympathy with the French Revolution, at least in the early 1790s, seems irrefutable, and that he resented the socially privileged status of the aristocracy throughout his life seems equally the case. In a letter of 1793 in which he quotes Schiller's *Don Carlos,* he asserts his precepts. "To do good whenever one can, to love liberty above all else, never to deny the truth, even though it be before the throne." These are the sentiments of any intelligent and passionate and modern young man of the 1790s. But Beethoven's interest in the French Revolution is further indicated by his subsequent great interest in its music, particularly that written for political occasions, and his selection of an opera libretto from France, a story supposedly based upon an incident of the Revolution itself, the deliverance of an unjustly imprisoned man.

Thus it seems reasonable to say that Beethoven was not only a master of the Viennese classical style but that he was also fully aware of the relation of that style to the culture and the social circumstances from which it emerged and for the delectation of which it was created.

To reject that style was to reject a culture, and this was more than a political act. Beethoven's determination to create a new style was the typical Romantic conversion of late Enlightenment political liberty into cultural liberty.

The first strong indication of his restlessness is to be found in the Septet, Opus 20, composed in 1799 and 1800. The contemporary critic Charles Rosen has penetratingly called the style of this work not classic but classicizing. It was enormously popular, but Beethoven came to detest it, and for very good reason. Unlike the Opus 18 quartets or the first ten or eleven piano sonatas (through Opus 22) it appears to be written without conviction, to be almost parodic. It is easy to agree with Beethoven's later judgment and to find it one of the most irritating pieces of music ever written by a great composer. The Septet is indeed a strange revival of an already outmoded type of composition, a divertimento, not in the three or four movement form which had become standard for the sonata, even traditional, but in no less than six. It sounds very much as if Beethoven were offering to members of a culture for which he had become contemptuous a triviality of the sort which would amuse them, written at a time when he was just interested in writing serious music, but in compositions which would be serious all the way through.

Already in the six quartets of Opus 18 that desire had begun to emerge (1798-1800). In the opening movement of the first quartet appears a mode of composition which he was to push to extraordinary lengths, the domination of a movement by a single short motive. The most famous example, of course, was to be the first movement of the Fifth Symphony; but already it is worth considering the significance of this device, or significances, for there are several. First, it is an instance of that reductionism which we have already encountered in Wordsworth. Music is now reduced to an essence, to a single phrase of meaning, and the meaning of that phrase is exhausted. It is not a matter of obsession, as has been suggested by various critics, but rather a matter of the imposition of the will of the composer on every phrase of a musical movement. Such insistence is a raising of the level of aggression, a deliberate drawing attention to a generalized aggressive mastery. It is, in a sense, a deliberate breach of manners, in 18th century terminology, of decorum. That desire for a thorough-going seriousness was also to be found in another emergent element in these quartets, one which it is enough merely to mention here, for its significance needs to be explored more thoroughly in the music of the next eight or nine years: the greater weight is given to the last movements, a violation of the 18th century principle that the final movements should be pure entertainment, a principle only rarely challenged even by Mozart and even more rarely by Haydn.

This restlessness of Beethoven emerges in the new century with three closely related piano sonatas, each of which changes the sonata pattern and experiments with new possibilities. The first of these is Opus 26, Sonata No 12, in A flat (1800-1801). The first movement is a theme and variations. Beethoven had already written a number of theme and variations sets, charming but of no great interest or serious-ness, and all but the most recent (WoO [Work without opus number] 77) taking the theme from melodies in popular operas. To none of them had he assigned an opus number, and with only a few and surprising exceptions did he ever vary his practice of assigning opus numbers only to compositions which he regarded as important. To begin a sonata with a theme and variations of a style far better suited to a second movement was unprecedented. He had suddenly taken a musical pattern hitherto used for essentially trivial musical purposes and promoted it to a position of importance, the first movement of a sonata. Within a few years Beethoven was to subject the variation set to extraordinarily novel transformations, reaching an astonishing height of seriousness and passion in the variations of the last movement of the Third Symphony, the *Eroica*.

The significance of this development is dual. First, the variation set gave him the opportunity to explore what is usually known as the development of a musical idea. But to use that term is to be confused by an evolutionary metaphor. A more accurate term is the transforma-tion of an idea. No composer has written such elaborate sets of varia-tions, has so thoroughly explored the possibility of the device, as has Beethoven; and it is instructive to remember that the last movement of his last sonata, Opus 111, 1821-1822, consists of a theme and varia-tions. In this first serious set of variations already appears what Beethoven was to do with the form. It is not a musical idea that is being transformed, but a condition of the personality, of the self, a condition of an individual's relation to the world. Consequently in the middle of this set in Opus 26 there is a variation in the minor, an interruption to the progressive mastery of a relation to the world which is the subject of Beethoven's sets of variations. For the second significance of Beethoven's fascination, almost obsession, with the variation form is precisely the opportunity it offers to exert one's will upon a melody which, now that it has been written, is a portion of the world the relation to which is to be transformed.

This first movement ends with the presentation of a new theme, quiet, descending in pitch, and dying away. It is withdrawal. But the second movement, a scherzo, is a new summons to action, a re-iteration of an upward thrust of three notes, a determination once again to encounter the world. But what does that world offer in the next movement? A "funeral march on the death of a hero," a further example of reductionism, for the theme is hardly more than a reiterated rhythm, interrupted by drum rolls and trumpet calls in the minor, upward leaps that dramatize the hero's defeat. And so the fourth movement is even more surprising, for it is a kind of toccata or perpetuum mobile, a charming but unserious movement that, most surprisingly, dies away into nothing, as did the first movement. The first three movements are culturally emergent because they present a drama, and a drama made more significant by the fact that in the last movement Beethoven turns his back on it with an air of insouciance and indifference, of a willed withdrawal from that which has preceded, but a withdrawal without issue, one that ends in good-humored negation.

The next two sonatas, written in 1800 and 1801, Beethoven published as a pair, Opus 27, Nos. 1 and 2, both labeled "*Quasi una fantasia.*" They are, he is saying, sonatas, but sonatas transformed by the fantasia idea. The effect in No. 1 in E flat major is almost of a work not in separate movements. The first movement begins quietly, moving alternately up and down, presenting a condition of perfect calm and poise, suddenly interrupted by a rude, almost tempestuous passage, thematically quite unrelated, and certainly not a second sonata theme, and followed just as suddenly by a repetition of the opening. The effect is that of two quite unrelated subjective conditions or personality states, or related only by polarization. A brief scherzo follows, attempting a resolution of this polarization in action, and successfully, for it in turn is followed by a slow movement of a significance not encountered in Beethoven's music before this, nor indeed in anyone else's. It is his first attempt at the ecstatic, and the significance of reaching and maintaining that condition of, as we have seen, the apprehension of pure value is what ensues — the longest, the most dramatic, the most energetic, even explosively energetic, section of the work. And the importance of the ecstatic to that wonderful release of aggressive energy is driven into us at the end of the work by a brief return to the ecstatic, followed by a sudden and even briefer triumphant explosion of aggressive energy. So the drama of the sonata is the invasion of a condition of poise and perfection and the resolution of the problem that invasion entails.

Opus 27 No. 2 in c sharp minor is the most popular of Beethoven's piano sonatas. It is the "Moonlight Sonata," a title given it long after Beethoven's death. It is less of a fantasia than No 1 in this Opus, for in fact it is a quite regular four-movement sonata from which the first movement has been omitted. So it begins with a slow movement that is in itself an extraordinary musical invention, and has always been recognized as such. First the unbroken reiteration of triplets, almost always in the minor, indicates a state of being under repressive control; there are only a couple of momentary and illusory gleams of relief. And then the theme itself is the dotted rhythm found in the funeral march of Opus 26, but abstracted and isolated from the context of a march. It is just the opposite of the ecstasy in the preceding sonata, and perhaps the two works really should be performed in immediate sequence. The movement presents an imprisonment in a condition of static depression, an inability to move out of it. The one effort is failure. The second movement seems unrelated, but in relation to the last movement it is a deliberate turning aside from repression and melancholy, and it is unsuccessful. For the last movement is the most violent music Beethoven had yet written, and perhaps anyone had yet written, an abandoned sundering of the bounds of decorum.

The momentary surcease of grief in the second movement is taken advantage of to unleash a storming of the ramparts of the emotional prison which is the theme of this sonata. Towards the end there is an upward run that promises escape, but it fails; and the movement thus stands as a powerful assertion of the failure of the aggressive effort to transcend the limitations of a situation. In this work Beethoven discovers the tragic failure in the human enterprise (and perhaps *of* it). And that discovery is of the utmost importance, for now the really great Beethoven begins to emerge, the Beethoven of Romantic cultural transcendence.

The omission of the first movement in Opus 27 No. 2 is a powerful indication of Beethoven's determination to shift the weight of the sonata pattern or plan to the last movement, a more or less tentative effort in Opus 27 No. 1, but unquestionably assertive in No. 2. But why should he want to make this change? The question is important, for it is a pattern further developed not only by Beethoven but by all composers in the rest of the century in sonatas and symphonies. The first level of explanation is obvious. The shift marked an almost violent, and almost brutal, negation of the traditional pattern of Viennese classicism. It was Beethoven's rejection and denial of his masters, Mozart and Haydn, his declaration of independence. It is an early instance of the Romantic artist's need to assert the uniqueness of his self by negating the stylistic practices of his masters.

But this is not the only explanation appropriate to this problem. In negating the style of concluding a sonata, Beethoven negated the meaning of the traditional conclusion. If, once again, we define culture as instructions for performance, or directions that transform behavior into actions and performances, then the traditional conclusion was an instruction to the audience (and the composer himself as a member of his own audience) to accept his culture, to regard culture as guidance. In reversing and negating this pattern Beethoven was instructing his audience (and himself) to deny the validity of the instructions of their common culture. His aim, and the aim of his successors, was not to leave the audience in a condition of satisfaction, one brought about in the 18th century by the final two movements, which are fundamentally dances, but in a condition of excitement, either the excitement of exaltation or the excitement of despair (as in Opus 27, No. 2). In either case the aim is to excite and arouse the audience so that the individual members are prepared to transform their self-conceptions and their conceptions of existence. It was, in a famous twentieth-century line by Auden, to bring about "new styles of architecture, a change of heart." Briefly, the new aim of the Romantic artist was to incite the listener, or the reader, or the observer of painting or sculpture or architecture, to a self-transformation, the necessary precondition for transcending of the individual's culture.

Somewhat similar to the efforts of the two sonatas of Opus 27 is a string quintet, Opus 29, composed in 1800 and 1801. The first two movements could have been written five years earlier, but the last two are strikingly different. The scherzo obsessively reiterates a one-measure theme, and the finale is the most dramatic and most complex he had yet composed. The first two movements are fashionably suave and lovely, but the last two are insistent, dramatic, and urgent. The next piano sonata, No. 15, Opus 28 (known, rather pointlessly, as the "Pastoral"), composed in 1801, is one of the most extended he had yet written. Here Beethoven is exploring the possibilities of a work in which all the movements are of equal weight and importance. including even the short scherzo, which offers in intensity and abruptness what it lacks in length. What is most remarkable about the work is the steadiness of the rhythm throughout, so that it has an almost *ostinato* effect. It is a work of clear and virtually uninterrupted outpouring of energy — a work that is designed to radiate an extraordinary self-assurance and confidence.

In the very next year, 1802, Beethoven develops that confidence in an amazingly innovating series of works, the three piano sonatas of Opus 31, completed early in the year, the three violin-piano sonatas of Opus 30, completed late in the year, and in between the two remarkable sets of piano variations, Opus 34 and Opus 35. In the same year he also composed his second symphony, Opus 36, and it is instructive that this work intended for public performance and a large audience reverts to the Classical Viennese style of the 1790s. Beethoven's stylistic transformations were still private, for small and sympathetic audiences. No. 1 of Opus 31 is an exploration of the possibilities of the rapid run and of the trill, for all three movements are designed to explore and exploit the expressive possibilities of these two devices. In the first movement the runs appear in both the major and the minor. The first presents an unhindered raising of the level of aggression when it moves upward. When it moves downward, and in a major key as well, it expresses a maintaining of a high level of aggression in circumstances of the acceptance, and the intensification of that acceptance, of cultural control as guidance. Thus, the downward movement or lowering of the aggression while the speed and volume maintain the aggression, means that the behavior is in the service of a more powerful force. The second movement explores the possibilities of the trill, which in its ambiguity of direction is like the coiling of a spring, the summoning of aggressive energy. The last movement returns to the possibilities of the run and explores it thoroughly; but the conclusion or coda is highly innovative. Suddenly the steady, confident, and balanced movement forward is interrupted. Efforts are made to get it going again. These efforts fail, and the movement ends with a witty and quiet equivalent of a shrug of the shoulders.

The second sonata in this series picks up precisely that problem of hindered and baffled activity. It can be reasonably asserted that this sonata is not only the greatest sonata Beethoven had yet written but his greatest work in any form. The first movement is an exploration of the expressive possibilities of the broken chord or arpeggio. It opens with a tentative and hesitant, barely assertive, upward-moving minor arpeggio, immediately and brutally cut off and hurled back by a rapid downward thrust. The effort is repeated, with the same result, but this time the rapid figure is itself converted into an upward movement, though still in the minor. It is sufficient, however, to get the main action of the movement under way. It consists of a powerful thrust upwards from the base on the minor chord, followed at once by a treble figure of effort and failure. This sets the dramatic struggle of the movement, and of the sonata. The second movement again opens with an upward arpeggio movement, in the major, but the movement as a whole is one of extraordinary hesitation, tentativeness, repeated efforts to get going, occasional successes, and final failure. The last movement is built almost entirely on a single phrase, an upward leap and an immediate falling back, but a falling back so far that a further effort is abrogated. Not even the last movement of Opus 27 No. 2 is so passionate, and this movement of Opus 31, No. 2, is longer and more developed. It concludes with a final supreme effort to break out of the prison of hindrance and frustration, and the failure of that effort. The movement moves downward into failure and emptiness. It is easy to say that what inspired this work was Beethoven's awareness of his growing deafness, but if we consider the larger stylistic implications for the musical culture and its social and cultural setting, it seems more justifiable to assert that what this work is about is Beethoven's alienation from that cultural situation. It is a work providing a powerful argument and support for those who would claim that in these opening years of the century Beethoven was moving into the culture of Romanticism.

The third sonata in this Opus 31 set returns to the major mode, and has been called "happy," a term only barely adequate, if at all. It begins with a strange tentativeness, and the first movement is a struggle between hesitation and its transformation into an exuberant release of energy. The second movement, atypically not a slow movement (nor is there any in this sonata) preserves the achievement of the first movement by a driving *ostinato* in a moderate tempo. It is relentless in its steady outpouring of aggression. The third movement is a minuet, but so unlike the 18th century minuet that it is almost a scherzo. The fourth movement is a consummation. It is a tarantella, not quite a rondo and not quite a sonata-allegro, but approaching violence, restrained by a steady though rapid rhythm, ending with powerful and assertive upward-leaping chords. It seems to be Beethoven's purpose that the opening of the sonata emerge from the emotional despair and alienation of No. 2, and that the work be consummated in a release from the emotional blockage and imprisonment of its predecessor.

The two piano works that follow are also a departure. They are sets of variations, for the first time on original themes, not popular tunes from operas, and as independent works instead of parts of sonatas. They are, then, celebrations of the composer's powers to transform his own creations. Opus 34 consists of a theme and six variations. It rises to a climax of violence in the fifth variation and then a sequence of fanfares introduces the final variation. It begins in an almost dance-like and quasi-trivial manner, but is gradually transformed and exalted into a rapturous abandon maintained by trills and runs. It terminates in powerful aggressive chords, but then all this is smilingly withdrawn in a partial repetition of the theme in a quiet and gently subdued manner. This is the first instance of a set of variations which is dramatically constructed. Splendid as it is, however, it is only a prelude, a warming up, for Opus 35, "Fifteen Variations and a Fugue on an Original Theme." But the theme was not new. Beethoven had already used it for his ballet *Die Geschöpfe des Prometheus* (*The Creatures of Prometheus*), written in 1800 and 1801 and first presented, with great success and numerous repetitions, at the Burgtheater in Vienna on March 28, 1801.

Moreover, he was to use it again, in another set of themes and variations, for the last movement of the Third Symphony. Opus 35, however, is even longer than that movement, and in fact is the longest single composition that Beethoven had yet composed. It can be accounted, moreover, as the first grandiose virtuoso piano piece of a century which was to see so many of them. And it is doubly virtuosic, both as a composition and in the demands made upon the performer. A work of symphonic proportions, it is best understood as a symphony for piano, for it contains a variety of musical effects that are ordinarily to be heard only in a symphony, and a 19th century symphony at that. It is of note, too, that frequently a variation leads directly into the next one without pause and by means of a carefully constructed bridge passage. Of all his compositions up to this point, it is the most obvious and direct precursor of the revolutionary Third Symphony. In it can be heard all the discoveries that Beethoven had made, all the advances and stylistic transformations he had accomplished, combined in a work the first half of which is characterized by a passionate and often wild and even brutal exuberance. But that immense release of aggression accomplished, it then subsides into a quieter and calmer variation, followed by a largo which becomes increasingly rapturous and ecstatic. But still dissatisfied, he moves directly into a fugue.

It is the first of Beethoven's instrumental fugues, and of great importance as indicating what so many Romantic artists experimented with — a return to the Baroque. The reason for this revival can be seen by observing, in all the arts, the general stylistic development of the 18th century. Baroque art is characterized by a high level of perceptual discontinuity, but the steady tendency of the arts in the 18th century was to reduce that discontinuity. Emotionally, no form of western music is so expressive of disturbance and conflict and polarization as the fugue. This was precisely the emotional character that the Romantics desired intensely to bring back into art. The drama in Opus 35 is that the fugue appears between two rapturous sections, the largo and the final variation on the theme. What Beethoven appears to be saying is that the ecstatic rapture of the largo must be earned by an even more profound exposure to the complexities of existence and an even higher level of aggression than that yet accomplished. Only then is the rapture justified and can the theme be truly transfigured. The drama of the Third Symphony is thus adumbrated.

The third piano concerto, Opus 37, however, is evidence that Beethoven was not yet ready to face the large public with his drastic shift of the weight of a three or four movement work from the first movement to the last, or even to the practice of making the three principal movements approximately equal in weight (1803). What is significant about this concerto is the fierceness of the opening minor theme, and indeed of the whole opening tutti. Its upward thrust is a powerful raising of the level of aggression and then an encounter with an even more powerful hindrance. So the theme falls back, and falls into an initially fruitless repetition of a two-note upward thrust, while the second phrase consists of an even more powerful aggressive thrust — concluded by a reversal of the two-note final motive so that it moves down instead of up. The effort to overcome this fruitlessness is the drama of the movement. The second and third movements, however, could almost have been written in the 1790s. This concerto may have been composed as early as 1800, but probably was completed, at any rate, in 1802, even perhaps in 1803, since the first performance was on April 5 of that year.

The year 1802 also saw the composition of three violin-piano sonatas, Opus 30. They are complementary to the three piano sonatas of
Opus 31, even to the extent that in both sets the first and third sonatas
are in the major and the second in the minor. What Beethoven had accomplished for the piano sonata he now achieved for the violin-piano
sonata, the movement, that is, toward a more complex instrumenta-
tion.   Consequently the climax of his rich experimentation with
and development of the one or two instrument sonatas of the opening
years of the century reaches a climax with violin-piano sonata Opus
45 known as the "Kreutzer," one of Beethoven's most famous works.
This is a complement, in a way, to the Opus 35 variations, for it is
equally a virtuoso work, dedicated to one of the most famous violin
virtuosi of the day, Rodolphe Kreutzer.   With it Beethoven moved
the violin sonata from the private drawing room to the public concert
hall.   The great tradition of the Romantic instrumental virtuoso is
begun in its full significance.   For the meaning of such works and
such performers and performances is that it lies within the power
of the individual to overcome cultural limitations, especially those
established by the conventions of 18th century aristocratic decorum.

The first climax of this virtuoso tradition and the climax of Beethoven's development in the first years of the new century was of
course Symphony No. 3, Opus 55, the *Eroica*.   Of this work, which
everybody who knows music at all knows well, there is little to be
said.   The pattern of meaning is perfectly clear: the initial struggle
of the heroic individual, the funeral lament over his failure, his rebirth in the intoxicating third movement, and his triumph in the
fourth.   However, the greatest musical weight of the work is still
in the first movement, though it is almost equalled by the other movements.   The most significant stylistic transformations achieved here
are: first, the unprecedented length; second, the unprecedented musical
complexity; third, the display of compositional virtuosity, not only
in the complexity but in the ability to keep such a long piece of music
perfectly proportioned by classical standards and at the same time
continuously moving forward, continuously exciting and arousing.

It is Beethoven's grandest and most uncompromising effort so
far to bring about in the audience a re-orientation toward the world

and their cultural situation. In the dual aspect of culture as both *directions* for behavior and as *model* for behavior, it made upon the audience a new kind of demand, a kind subsequently called "difficult" (as it was at the time) and *avant garde*. In that sense, like so many Romantic works, it was an act of aggression towards the audience, but at the same time for those who could understand it, Beethoven offered a model for raising the level of aggression to the point at which an outmoded culture can be transcended. One can quite easily show the continuity of Beethoven, even in this work, with his predecessors Haydn and Mozart, and thus maintain that Beethoven was not really a Romantic composer. Nevertheless it is obvious that in the opening years of the century Beethoven accomplished more than a mere stylistic development; he had created a new kind of music, a kind which, though built upon Viennese classicism, was nevertheless a cultural emergent. That fact was recognized at the time. And ever since, it has been recognized that in these years Beethoven began a new musical epoch, that is, a new *cultural* epoch.

Friedrich Hölderlin   Between Beethoven and Hölderlin there is a
(1770-1843)   remarkable similarity. Born in the same year
(Hölderlin in March and Beethoven in December) both wrote works of the fullest competence in the style of the late 18th century; and both, at very nearly the same time, around 1800-1801, rejected that style and created a new one recognizably a style of an emergent cultural epoch. Although Hölderlin lived until nearly the middle of the 19th century, longer than Beethoven, his poetic life effectively came to an end in 1805. By then his mental condition, that is, his behavior, had begun to deteriorate so badly that by 1807 he had been placed in the care of a carpenter in Tübingen. For the rest of his life he lived in a tower on the river Neckar. The intellectual tension which he was endeavoring to resolve proved irresolvable. The resulting incoherence and loss of confidence in both his own value and his sources of value became so intense that he erupted in outbursts of rage. Neither he nor his friends could tolerate his behavior, and the external constraint under which he was

placed was so strangely acceptable to him that he placed himself under an equivalent internal or psychological constraint. The source of his disturbance was that tension of the 1790s, that endeavor to resolve Reason and Nature which we have already encountered. But for Hölderlin the difficulty was far greater than it was for most of his contemporaries, and more impossible to resolve.

From 1788 to 1793 he studied at the Theological Foundation in Tübingen, in southwest Germany, forty miles south of his birthplace at Lauffen, north of Stuttgart. He was at Tübingen when the French Revolution erupted, and, along with his friends and contemporaries at the Tübingen Stift (or Foundation), Schelling and Hegel, he was intoxicated with enthusiasm at the prospect of an ideal society. Very soon he was inspired by Herder with the idea of the poet as the source of community and the heart and essence of that community's religion, as, in short, the mediator between the divine and mankind. It was by no means an uncommon notion, but for Hölderlin it took a particularly dangerous mode. His Utopia was not precisely in the future, but rather in what the future promised, he thought, a restoration of and return to an ideal society and culture of the past, a time when man, nature, and the gods were welded into a perfect unity. And that time was ancient Greece.

It was, of course, a purely fanciful, imaginary, and unreal notion of what classical Greece was actually like, and this vision of unity placed Hölderlin in an impossible intellectual, poetic, and religious position. Those who originally placed in the future the ideal society which they expected to emerge from the Revolution could either displace it into an even more remote future, as often happened in the course of the 19th century and indeed still happens — thus protecting themselves from complete disillusionment — or they could come to the Romantic realization that Utopia is a mere intellectual or more properly a verbal construct. Such a displacement was impossible for Hölderlin, for his idea of ancient Greece was, as so often happened in the Enlightenment, a secularization of pre-lapsarian innocence, of the Judeo-Christian vision of man before the Fall. It is not surprising that he was eventually to attempt a synthesis of Greek and Christian mythology. The immediate result was to poeticize the ideal of that promised world in a style derived from the idealistic Enlightenment poetry of Schiller. But by the end of the decade his style had profoundly changed, and a style began to emerge which was not fully and adequately understood and prized until the 20th century, when for the first time his poetry had a deep influence on other poets, particularly Stefan George and Georg Trakl.

The key to Hölderlin's stylistic transcendence is to be found in his novel *Hyperion, oder der Eremit aus Griechenland (The Hermit from Greece)*. Various sections were first published in Schiller's journal *Die neue Thalia* in 1794; the complete first part appeared in 1797; but the second not until 1799. By then, his concept of the work had changed. Hölderlin places the story in 1770, when there was an abortive effort by the Greeks to throw off Turkish possession and control. Actually, what Hölderlin presents is a transparent allegory of his own relation to the French Revolution. The novel includes, for example, a band or secret society such as we have met before. It turns out to be sinister and corrupting. The brief success of Hyperion and his friend Alabanda against the Turks is followed by the selfishness, the opportunism, and the corruption of the rebels. Hyperion first seeks death in a sea battle, and that failing, and his beloved Diotima having died, he goes to Germany. The novel is written in the form of letters to Bellarmin, a friend Hyperion makes in Germany. And the work concludes with a diatribe against German society and culture, for Hölderlin has come to see Germans as half-men, incapable of moving towards an ideal society — towards a community at once divine and natural and human — and equally incapable of grasping their own petty inadequacy. Thus Hölderlin was alienated not only from the French Revolution but also from his own country and countrymen.

So he was left with the impossible task of writing poetry which would mediate between the divine and a mankind which had no interest in such mediation, which was incapable of grasping, let alone sharing, Hölderlin's vision. This burden was imposed upon a life which in itself was socially and economically unsuccessful, for he was unable to establish the journal he planned and was reduced to what he had been doing ever since he had left Tübingen in 1793, private tutor-

ing in wealthy families. That had already led to his tragic and un-
fulfilled love for the wife of one of his employers, Susette Gontard,
his own Diotima, whom he saw for the last time in 1799 and who
died in 1802. The importance of this love to him was that he distorted
it into an assurance that his ambition of poetic access to divinity
was realizable. Thus it is apparent that his conception of the divine
was far less anthropomorphic than symbolic of the human capacity
to create value. Though he never spelled it out in such terms, his
poetic presentation of gods, such as Äther, and demi-gods, such as the
Rhine, indicates that the divine, if not a human creation, is nevertheless apprehensible by the poetic power, by human effort rather than
divine revelation.

This comprehension of the divine and man's relation to it led Hölderlin to his new style, a style that transcended that of Schiller and indeed previous European poetry, which even in fantastic narrative had
always been didactic. It always exemplified some moral or religious
or philosophical or psychological proposition. So in the 17th century
Sir William Davenant, inspired by the philosopher Thomas Hobbes,
spelled out that poetic function of poetry — to exemplify and thus
sustain the social virtues, particularly those of the upper class of the
society for which and in service to which the poet writes. To exemplify the virtues of an ideal or Utopist society is not to change that
conception of poetic function, even though the ideal society did
not yet exist. In the last couple of years of the 18th century Hölderlin began to write poems from which the didactic, the exemplary, had
disappeared. His poems had a fundamental similarity to and convergence with Coleridge's *Ancient Mariner,* in which the individual's
creation of value independently of community forever sunders him
from community. John Constable, the painter, recognized this new
character of poetry, a character which can only be called a Romantic
and Modern character. He said that Coleridge's poem was like music,
a quality that Coleridge himself recognized when he asserted that his
poem contained too much of a moral, leaned too strongly towards
the exemplary and didactic.

Hölderlin's greatest poems are guilty of no such flaw, and for that
reason were as puzzling at the time as, for example, *The Waste Land*

was to be 120 years later. Indeed, it was only after that poem's appearance that Coleridge's poem began to be understood, just as Hölderlin's poetry had to wait nearly a hundred years. Furthermore, the similarity to or convergence with Beethoven's style after 1801 is also striking. In Beethoven's earlier work, that of the 1790s, the concluding movement (or movements), as in the work of Haydn and Mozart, is equivalent to the exemplary moral in traditional European poetry. They are assertions that all is well, that the virtues and values of the socio-cultural situation are not to be questioned. To change that conclusion, as Beethoven did, was to assume a critical attitude towards those virtues and values — towards that socio-cultural situation.

In the world of Hölderlin and Coleridge Romantic poetry was born, the kind of poetry that has been called symbolic rather than didactic. Symbolic is not a very illuminating term, other than suggesting that the real subject of the poem is not the ostensible or surface subject. The individual who is alienated from his culture, as Hölderlin came to be alienated, is faced with the problem, as Coleridge had grasped in *The Ancient Mariner,* of creating value in the absence of and in isolation from a community. But that means also the traditions of that community. The anguish and ultimate madness of Hölderlin, comparable perhaps to the drug addiction of Coleridge, exhibits with extraordinary intensity how terrible and devastating that problem of creating value can be, even in spite of the poetic success which Hölderlin unquestionably achieved. In such great poems as "Bread and Wine," "The Archipelago", and even more in the great hymns of 1800 to 1803 (such as "Der Rhein" or "Patmos" of "Celebration of Peace") Hölderlin speaks in an entirely personal manner. The struggle he presents is his own struggle, unsustained by anything but the memory of ancient Greece. His difficulty, his tragedy, was that that memory was not enough, could not accomplish what he needed. As time went on, that memory is revealed gradually as only a memory insufficient for the burden placed upon it.

For the individual who has become alienated from the value sources of his culture, primarily religious but by no means confined to religion; primarily sacred, but by no means confined to the officially sacred, there is only one possible subject for poetry, indeed for all art: the dramatization of the struggle to create value from what are conceived as the individual's unique resources, from the very irreducible surd of individuality. Thus, Hölderlin's late poetry is scarcely rivaled in early Romantic art by the profundity of its exploration into the meaning of selfhood. That is why his divine and semi-divine beings, including even Christ, are not revelations of an already socio-culturally existent and defined divinity, but are instead projections or symbols of the source of sacredness from the depths of what is conceived of as the self. Thus in one of his greatest hymns, "Patmos," Hölderlin seeks the island where St. John the Apostle experienced and wrote his apocalypse. Hölderlin's purpose, it appears, was to perform for the cultural crisis of the early 19th century what the Apostle had achieved for the crisis of the emergence of Christianity. But in the subsequent "Mnemosyne" all that vision of ancient Greece and of the fusion temporarily achieved, of Greek and Christian mythology, had been reduced to a mere memory, and that was insufficient for the cultural crisis he was struggling with.

As poignantly and profoundly as he had revealed the Romantic cultural task, Hölderlin did not fully transcend traditional European culture. The language of that culture betrayed him, for that language demanded that a revelation of value be verbalized, that is, made final and absolute. The realization that he had only memory and that memory is not enough meant to Hölderlin that his task of mediator of the divine was not, for him, possible. He did not quite grasp the Romantic perception that it is not possible at all, for anybody, that the inherent instability of the experience of value is the ineluctable condition of being human, whether there is or is not a divine, a supernatural, a transcendent reality. Hence, once again, the importance of Beethoven not merely for the music of the ensuing 19th century, but for all Romantic culture. Because of his musical dramatization of the struggle towards value, a dramatization not committted to verbalization, and therefore not committed to some formulation and finalization of the absolute, music was to become the model art, the central art, of the Romantic tradition and of Romantic culture. Hölderlin achieved in his late poetry a cultural transcendence comparable to Beethoven's of the same years, of the new century, and convergent with it, but that transcendence was a stylistic achievement, not paralleled by an ideological achievement. He failed to understand that in changing the style he had changed the problem, that the tension between human and divine is not something to be resolved, that it never has been resolved, the claims of religions and philosophies to the contrary; that the tension between the human and the divine is irresolvable; that experience of value is inherently unstable; and that the only resolution to that tension is non-existence. And non-existence of a sort is precisely what descended upon Hölderlin, and what he endured, for forty years.

Chateaubriand 2   The failure of the Revolution was already ad-
1768-1848   mitted in 1799, when on November 9 Napoleon, back only a month from Egypt, overthrew the Directoire and established the Consulate, in appearance still a republican government but in fact a dictatorship by Napoleon. On May 18, 1804, that fact was made official when the First Consul became the Emperor Napoleon. The establishment of the Consulate meant above all that public order take precedence over revolutionary freedom. This was so obvious that shortly the emigreés, those who had fled the Revolution, begain to return. Among them was Chateaubriand, who by means of a pseudonym and a Swiss passport, provided by the London representatives of the Prussian government, returned to France on May 6, 1800, carrying with him proofs of the opening chapters of *La Génie du Christianisme* (*The Genius of Christianity*) and two sections of his vast uncompleted romance, *Les Natchez*. One section, *Atala,* he published separately on April 3, 1801, and published again with the second section, *René*, as Chapters in *La Génie* on April 14, 1802. *Atala* made him famous at once. It was extraordinarily successful, and separately *René* and *La Génie* were equally sensational in the impact they made on the cultural life of the time. To be sure, it was a matter of luck for Chateaubriand that on April 8, 1802, Napoleon signed the Concordat with the Papacy, re-establishing Catholicism as the official religion of France.

Chateaubriand explains in his splendid autobiography, perhaps

his greatest work, *Mémoires d'Outre-Tombe,* published after his death
from 1848 to 1850, that his return to Christianity was inspired by the
death of his mother in 1798, and her dying message that he become a
Christian. About all this there has been vast discussion, of little significance. As we have seen, even in the *Essay on Revolutions* he was
already praising Christianity on pragmatic grounds, and perhaps his
conversion was equally pragmatic. The French have been heatedly
arguing ever since about the sincerity of Chateaubriand's return to
Christianity, but the problem, aside from being insolvable, is irrelevant.
Not only was his return probably pragmatic, and thus the question
of his sincerity becomes inappropriate, but more important, *La Génie
du Christianisme* is not primarily concerned with Christianity at all.

The clue to Chateaubriand's primary concern is to be found in
the *Essay on Revolutions* and in the *Mémoires.* The former affirmed
the failure of the Revolution and the latter asserted the consequences
of that failure. "What are the troubles of 1648, compared to that
Revolution, which devoured the former world, of which perhaps it
died, leaving after it neither an old nor a new society?" (Part II, Book
XIII, Chapter I). And that position was affirmed by the state of
France as he observed it when he returned to it in 1800. Poverty,
decay, dirt were everywhere, even in Paris. The effect of social disorder — a disorder close to collapse — was evident in the absence of
men working in the field. All this was the more striking after the
cleanliness and prosperity of England, in which he had been living
for eight years. The only consolation, one that outweighed everything else, was the conversation, and the intelligence, of Parisian life.
As for the Napoleonic regime itself, that was only a gimcrack and
tasteless imitation of the true grandeur of the world of Louis XIV,
of *le grand siécle.* The effect of his return to France on Chateaubriand
was that he set to work to revise and complete *La Génie du Christianisme,* for the French situation revealed to him all the more saliently
the true theme of that work: What is civilization? Chateaubriand,
then, saw with greater clarity than anyone else the necessity of the
times, a cultural transcendence which involved a fresh establishment
of the grounds of civilization.

Yet this is not to say that he succeeded in doing so, except in a most odd and unexpected way.   In spite of his protestations and his feeble attempted proof at the end of the book that Christianity is and must necessarily be a revealed religion   what he really demonstrates is not that since Christianity is true it is the proper foundation for civilization, but rather that since Christianity has proved itself as a proper foundation for civilization it must therefore be true, but "true" in a pragmatic or functional sense.   The briefest summary of the work can show the drift of his thinking, for the terms "argument" or "demonstration" which I have used above are too powerful for what he accomplishes.   The book is divided into four parts, "Dogmas and Tenets," "The Poetic of Christianity," "The Fine Arts and Literature," and "Worship," spread over 22 books, and 177 chapters.   In a recent French edition that division produced less than four pages per chapter. Such statistics are of interest, for they show how little sustained argument Chateaubriand actually offers.

In Part I he is concerned to show how Christianity can sustain an individual from despair, how the Christian virtue of charity provided a new moral and emotional foundation for civilization, how the doctrine of original sin is the only possible explanation of human behavior, how the wonders of nature demonstrate the existence of a creative and sustaining deity, and how the moral law and the feelings "prove" the doctrine of immortality. In the second part he sets out to demonstrate that the poetry of Christianity is superior in moral tone and delicacy and profundity of feelings to the poetry of the classic world, concluding with a demonstration that the sublime of the Bible is loftier than the sublime of Homer.   In Part III he turns to the fine arts, to philosophy, to history, eloquence, descriptions of nature, and ruins — attempting to show that in all of these areas of endeavor the works of Christianity are superior to the noblest and most beautiful works of ancient Greece and Rome.   In Part IV he writes of the beauty of churches, ceremonies, prayers, vestments, funerals, tombs, the imitation of Christ carried out by the secular and the regular clergy, the unique effort of Christianity in its missionary work (and here, he thinks, is his most powerful demonstration of the civilizing power of Christianity), the achievements of the military orders, and the immense benefits to mankind rendered by

Christianity: hospitals, schools, colleges, universities, and the papacy as the radiating center and power of Christian civilization; and the salutary effect of Christianity on arts, manufacturing, commerce, laws, politics, and government. Now it is obvious from this rundown that Chateaubriand cannot possibly say much about each of the many topics he touches on. And in truth the book is intellectually feeble and philosophically trivial and dull. Yet it produced a profound effect and roused both intense antagonism and equally passionate defence. Chateaubriand himself published in 1803 a *Défense du "Génie du Christianisme"*. Some of this excitement is easy to understand. The antagonists saw as attacked and threatened the whole secularized structure of Enlightenment thought, the foundation of what the Revolution had accomplished, the overthrow of the exhausted, corrupted, and debased old order, so completely allied with the Church, so dependent upon Christianity and the Church for its ideological justification. An attack upon Chateaubriand's work was a covert attack on Napoleon's Concordat with the Papacy. One class of defenders, predictably, saw their religion praised, sustained, justified intellectually and culturally. Certainly one effect of the Revolution was a religious revival which interpreted its excesses, its horrors, its destructiveness, as God's punishment upon a society in which secularization had led to moral deterioration.

But neither of these can provide an adequate explanation for the immense popularity of the work and the lasting effect it had upon French Romanticism and French 19th century literature in general. It is often said, for example, that the book was responsible for the revival of Gothic architecture and the taste for it, but though Chateaubriand does discuss it, he does so only briefly, so superficially and so platitudinously that it is difficult to believe that he could have had anything more than a trifling effect on the Gothic revival. To come to a somewhat better understanding of the work's success and impact it is useful first to consider the two *nouvelles* which Chateaubriand included, *Atala* and *René*.

Atala tells the story of a Natchez warrior, Chactas. His tribe having been defeated in battle, Chactas, then a youth, was swept by the refugees to St. Augustine. There he was taken in and cared for by an old Spaniard named Lopez. In time, however, he longed for his home and his Indian way of life and set out for his home on the Mississippi. As Lopez had warned, he was captured by tribal enemies and would have been sacrificed had he not been rescued by Atala, an Indian girl, half Spanish and a Christian. It turns out, in fact, that she is the daughter of Lopez. Escaping together, for Chactas refused to leave without her, they are saved by a French missionary, Father Aubry; Chactas looks forward now to marrying Atala, but she takes poison, having vowed to her mother to honor her mother's vow to dedicate her daughter's virginity to the Queen of the Angels. Unaware that such oaths can be lifted by the church, she determines to die rather than to live without Chactas. The story concludes with the beautiful description of her burial, the subject of a famous picture by Girodet (Louvre, 1808), only one instance of innumerable paintings, plays, and souvenir jugs and spoons inspired by *Atala*. This story is told by the aged Chactas to René, the Frenchman who had fled in despair to America to live with the Indians. The story is designed to exemplify how Christianity brings to the savage world a superior sensibility and a superior morality.

The Christian lesson of *René*, however, is simply tacked onto the end, and the power of the *nouvelle* is quite independent of it. For René was to become the primary French exemplification of Romantic alienation. Brought up in a remote part of France, preferring solitude from an early age, and in love with his sister Amelia, René becomes a typical Romantic wanderer, roaming about Europe from Sicily to Scotland. His sister, for reasons he does not comprehend, takes the veil and eventually dies within the convent. René flees from Europe to America and enters the Indian life, even taking an Indian wife. The occasion of the story is in his telling to Chactas, a second Indian, and a Christian missionary the events of his life and his reason for coming to the Natchez in the hope of experiencing some happiness. He presents his problem with the utmost succinctness. It is the Romantic problem: "I am only in search of some unknown good, whose intuition pursues me relentlessly."

Was that unknown good his incestuous love for his sister, of which she is aware and which she returns — hence her taking the veil — but which he cannot face? It is possible, but if so the Romantic dilemma is merely given another twist. The desire for the forbidden and in the course of the 19th century the exploration of the forbidden are important and frequently dominating Romantic themes. To enter into the forbidden serves first the function of violating the culture from which the individual is alienated and is thus a superb symbolization of that alienation. At the same time it denies the validity of the values of that culture, of its sanctions as well as its taboos. And further, and perhaps more important, it raises the level of aggression and in doing so confirms the sense of a selfhood not dependent upon the sanctions of an existent culture. All these interests are at work in *René*, and thus it provided a model for those younger individuals who were disenchanted both with the Revolution and the Napoleonic dictatorship.

What made these two works so popular, however, and to a certain extent also *La Génie*, was the extreme stylistic beauty of Chateaubriand's prose and of his descriptions of nature, both in Europe and in the extraordinarily new setting of America. Chateaubriand offered a rapturousness, and an ecstatic suspension of feeling, in his descriptions of nature — and above all of a nature untouched, unsubdued by European culture, power, and society — that was utterly novel and original. This gives us some insight into the extraordinary success and impact of these works. French culture had long been extremely self-conscious about style, not only style in the arts but also style in living, in the performance of various socially validated roles. In *Atala* and *René* and in certain descriptive passages in *La Génie* Chateaubriand created, most self-consciously (for he revised these works, particularly the two *nouvelles,* over and over again) new stylistic possibilities for French prose. He created a prose which, because of the nature of the syllabic and scarcely stressed French verse, was almost poetry, which often, indeed, could be scanned and even printed as poetry. A new genre emerged, that of the prose poem, a genre in which works of extraordinary interest and beauty were to be created in the course of the 19th century. This recognition of a stylistic transcendence in his work offers a clue to the astonishing success and historical importance of *La Génie*.

The Christianity Chateaubriand offered was not a theology; it was not even a morality or a set of emotions. What he offered was a style of life. And this provides an explanation for the intellectual super-ficiality of the work, and for the brevity with which he considers each facet of Christianity brought to the reader's attention. In each instance it is just enough to exhibit the topic's interest, its charm, even its elegance. It is not his argument but the accumulation of dozens and dozens of tints of belief and behavior touched by belief. The result is a masterly and almost irresistibly expressed sense of a way of life, of a life style, of a cultural style, of a style of civilization. The great-ness and importance of Chateaubriand's work to Romanticism is not merely that he offered a stylistic transcendence, but also that he offered a sense of, an apprehension of, a realization of style itself. The importance of this lies in the fact that all behavior is styled, and that style is a mode of apprehending behavior and of behaving which can accommodate endless incoherences and inconsistencies. When we consider human life as a stylistic mode, then the coherence that ide-ology demands can be ignored, can be flouted, even rejected. Style is ideologically non-committed, ideologically free. To conceive one's way of life in terms of style is to have that freedom which Chateau-briand demanded of life.

The Revolution, he saw, gave political liberty, but political liberty is not the same as cultural freedom, for political liberty is a matter of, and is maintained by, ideological considerations. The subtle power of *La Génie du Christianisme* and its strange and persistent influence upon French Romanticism — it has never gone out of print — its cultural importance even today, lay in its covert revelation that re-ligious belief — and any ideological commitment — is a matter of style; and that self-conscious stylization of one's life is the way to human freedom.

Etienne Pivert de Senancour
(1770-1846)

Two years after *René* first appeared another work was published which analyzed René's cultural situation with a richness and subtlety greater than Chateaubriand had achieved.

Obermann by Etienne Pivert de Senancour was published in 1804. Completely overshadowed by Chateaubriand's far more sensational work, *Obermann* was neglected until the 1820s, when French Romanticism emerged as a recognized school of literature. Sainte-Beuve, the dominating critic of French Romanticism, saw to the republication of the work in 1833 and wrote a preface for it. Only seven years later George Sand wrote the preface for a third edition, and after that the work was kept in print in a long series of reprintings of her edition. Senancour was at last recognized as one of the first French Romantics. He himself had led a rather unsatisfactory life as a general man of letters, inhabitant of a French counterpart to London's Grub Street, but in time was rewarded by a government pension.

Obermann was a new kind of work, a combination of two established genres, the epistolary novel and the essay in the manner of Montaigne. The story it tells is simple enough. Obermann visits Switzerland, particularly the country on the north of Lake Geneva and in the valley of the Rhone, which flows into the southeast corner of Lake Geneva. He is about to settle down there, at least for a time, when financial difficulties recall him to Paris. He is threatened with losing his fortune (perhaps an indirect recognition of the disturbances caused by the Revolution), and while he awaits the outcome he flees Paris and wanders in the forest of Fontainebleau. In time his affairs are settled; much is saved from what had promised to be total ruin. After some time in Lyons he turns to Switzerland and buys a property near Vesey, on the north shore of Lake Geneva. There he settles down with a friend, who has also experienced the disillusionment of the times. The letters in *Obermann* are to a less disillusioned friend, written to justify his behavior, and are written over a period of nine years (ten, if we include a few added in the edition of 1833). Since a first version of the work was published as *Aldomen* in 1795, we can assume that the period covered runs from 1793 or 1794 to 1802 or 1803, the period that saw the failure of the hopes of the Revolution, the corruption of the Directoire, and the dictatorship of Napoleon's Consulate. These events are not mentioned; yet it was widely recognized, by Matthew Arnold, for example, in his two poems about *Obermann* (1849, 1867), that the bleakness of Obermann's vision was a result of the failure of the Enlightenment in the fury of the Revolution.

Senancour begins his project with two Enlightenment notions, both of which he subjects to drastic revision, just as he subjects the epistolary novel to considerable transformation. The first was the idea of the man of feeling, an exemplar of the culture of emotional lability. But Senancour wanted a new model of that figure, a conception that included not the mere expression of feeling but the peculiar melancholy and *ennui* that emerges from a deliberate restraint or repression of feeling, a repression that has emerged from the failure of a culture that ought to guide and release feelings. That, it is evident, is his new conception of the place of feeling in human life. What this amounts to is the recognition that the 18th century man of feeling was a sentimentality, since it does not recognize the human necessity for self-imposed control, and Senancour is one of the first, as well as one of the most accurate, to reject 18th century sentimentality as a feeling state unjustified by the human condition. For the culture of lability or emotional fluidity assumed a fundamental unity in human affairs, a vision Senancour denies, seeing man as caught in an eternal duality, a perpetual oscillation, and as the victim of some invisible power which governs the human world by a toss of the dice, which manipulates men as if they were numbers.

This is but the first of Senancour's efforts so to analyze man as to remove him from any special or unique place in nature, to see him, to be sure, as a product of nature, but a product of no greater intrinsic value than that of any other natural product. For that duality in human affairs, that oscillation, is the condition for the second Enlightenment notion which he places in new circumstances, the notion that the human destiny in a world of delight and sadness is to augment the sense of joy, to struggle against the degradation and humiliation of experience. Thus the human destiny can never be fulfilled.

From this sense that man is a product of nature in which he can never be at home, can never feel that he truly belongs, can never find fulfillment, Senancour arrives at what was to be one of the great themes of the ensuing cultural life of Europe, *ennui,* boredom, aimless restlessness, total disillusionment. Thus he insists that what the world calls the social edifice is only a randomly assembled, miscellaneous conglomeration of wretchedness and delusions. Philosophically, he turns to the skeptical tradition, so powerful in France, the tradition which had found one of its earliest and grandest homes in Montaigne's "Apology for Raymond Sebond" in Book II of the *Essais* (1575-1576, 1578-1580), particularly the section "Man has no knowledge," a position with which Senancour thoroughly agrees. What is new in *Obermann* is Senancour's joining together of that skeptical tradition with the post-Enlightenment *ennui,* and what makes the book so interesting is the subtle exploration of that restless boredom, the effort, always vain or at best only temporarily successful, to achieve some sense of joy, some sense of value. For he has touched directly the most sensitive nerve of the cultivated man since the middle of the 1790s: the only irreparable loss is the loss of desire. *Ennui,* then, emerges from the exhausting effort to recreate, to re-evoke, to re-experience — desire.

The problem emerges from the very situation that was responsible for the loss of desire. What Senancour presents is another instance of the fearful demand put on the Romantic individual to create desire from his own resources, since the normal sources of desire, cultural instructions, had failed with the failure of the culture. This he recognizes with one of his most telling and cutting conclusions: the great misfortune is to be driven to act freely. What Senancour has grasped is that desire is not given by nature but is, as it were, a cultural artifact. Hence the wandering throughout western Switzerland and in the forest of Fontainebleau.

Here is one of the earliest examples of an important theme, only adumbrated in *René* but fully developed in *Obermann,* the theme of wandering or randomization of behavior, and also a penetrating explanation of that theme. The wanderer's desire is the re-awakening of desire. The oscillation of which Senancour speaks is revealed in the momentarily effective re-awakening of desire before some beautiful bit of the natural world, and the fact that it is only momentary, only transient. And that transience of feeling becomes, therefore, one of the primary and most interesting revelations of *Obermann.* Any desire, it becomes clear, any interest, any experience of value or beauty must necessarily be transient if it is not supported by a culture and by the redundancies of behavioral instructions of that culture. The question thus arises, Why is it that a human being can be interested in anything, can be capable of desire?

Senancour's answer emerges in spite of his insistence that any general theory of human nature and of the laws of the world is only a random guess. For he sees that there are not just two basic human attributional tendencies, the tendency to self-preservation and the tendency to the preservation of the species, but three; and the third is the tendency to order. But we must also necessarily conclude that of all our dreams (and we live in a world of dreams) the dream of a perfect order may be the furthest from reality. If reason is a dream, a delusion, if we can know nothing about nature, and if the individual is nothing more than "the accidental expression of a transient combination," then the Enlightenment ideal (fundamentally Christian) of a union of reason, nature, and man, is one of the worst of illusions. Nevertheless this tendency to order is the only human tendency on which it is possible to build desire, interest, value.

And at this point Senancour makes one of the most important Romantic discoveries. What Obermann is saying leads one to the conclusion that an interest, or order, or desire for the individual alienated from his culture, for the individual reduced to wandering, is to find a place of repose, a situation of stability — always in isolation. Only isolation can give us even hope of success to both use and escape from freedom. Only in isolation is the grip of use and wont relaxed, are the cultural redundancies avoided and escaped from. Only a drastic and nearly total reduction of the rate of one's interaction with other human beings is the condition for creating an interest from one's unique experience. One must escape both the ordinary and what the culture defines as extraordinary. Both must be transcended. and the isolation that Obermann achieves is the primary condition for that success. Yet it is not a total isolation, for Obermann has made his Swiss home in company with a friend, Fonsalbe, a man as disillusioned and *ennui*-ridden as himself. He has done so for he realizes that desire, an escape from *ennui*, from meaninglessness, begins with love, but not with love of others. That comes later, after the primary love a man must have, one that is forever indispensable —

a love of himself. Only a love for oneself — a self-ascription of value — can provide a basis not merely for love of others but for action itself, for life itself. Hence only in isolation can that love blossom and become a source for faith in the value of life, for success in desiring.

Ugo Foscolo   On the south side of the Alps from Obermann's
(1778-1827)   wanderings there had already appeared a short work
                     culturally convergent with de Senancour's *Ober-*
mann. It was the novel *Ultime Lettere di Iacopo Ortis* (*Last Letters of Jacopo Ortis*). It was first published in incomplete form in 1798 and created such a sensation that a sequel was published in 1799 by Angelo Sassoli, a sequel now thought to have been to a certain extent under the control of Foscolo himself. Whether infuriated or not by this fabrication, he set to work and published a complete version in 1802. The work was again revised and published in London in 1814 and in a final and definitive edition of 1817, also in London, to which Foscolo had exiled himself in 1815, refusing to have anything to do with the Austrians who occupied Milano, where he was residing, after the fall of Napoleon. Of the various works derived from Goethe's *Werther* of 1774 none is so closely modelled on that novel as *Ortis.*

Yet there is a great difference, even though the plot of *Ortis* is superficially about a disappointment in love and a subsequent suicide. Foscolo differs from Goethe, however, in the social, political, and cultural significance both of the love and of the suicide, for the story is precipitated by the Treaty of Campo Formio (now Camp Formido, a town some fifty-five miles northeast of Venice, near Udine).

But to understand the political and ideological import of *Ortis* it is necessary to have some knowledge of the Revolutionary French in Italy, and particularly of the role of Napoleon in that new French invasion of the valley of the Po. The French attack on Italy was unavoidably brought about by the fact that Vittorio Amadeo III, King of Sardinia and ruler of Savoy, joined the first coalition of European Powers against Revolutionary France. That was in 1792. In short order the French occupied the provinces of Savoy and Nice on the

French side of the Alps, failed in an attack in Sardinia, but managed in December, 1793, to recapture Toulon, which they had lost in the preceding August. The siege of Toulon was of immense importance for one reason only. It established Napoleon's reputation and elevated him to the rank of brigadier general.

But the war languished during 1794 and 1795. In January, 1796, however, Napoleon proposed a plan to conquer Italy and in March arrived at Nice and shortly began an invasion of the Po valley. The aim of the Directoire in ordering this campaign was not merely the defeat of the Austrians, who then possessed the Duchy of Milano. It was above all booty, loot, the confiscation of the liquid wealth of Italy, particularly of the Italian aristocracy, and the artistic wealth as well. Rome, for example, was eventually subjected to a looting more thorough, it appears, than the famous Sack of Rome by the Imperialist troops in 1527. In a series of brilliant battles Napoleon forced his way against the Austrians the full length of the Po valley, utterly defeating the Austrian armies at the siege of Mantova and pursuing them by way of Gorizia on the extreme eastern border of Italy into Austria itself, heading for Vienna. However, his position was insecure. He made peace at Leoben, southwest of Vienna, on April 18, 1797, and then returned to Milano to begin the consolidation of his conquests.

His impact and the impact of the revolutionary armies had been enormous. It is summed up in young Foscolo's ode of 1797, "Napoleon the Liberator." Already Foscolo had fled Venice (though not born there he was of a Venetian family) because of his liberal, even revolutionary ideas. But in May, 1797, the Venetian oligarchy abandoned their duties in panic, the Doge abdicated and the ancient and once glorious Venetian Republic came to an end. The territories of the Republic, which extended as far west as Bergamo, almost within sight of Milano, began to disintegrate into mostly republican and quasi-revolutionary self-rule. Napoleon reorganized the Duchy of Milano, the old Venetian territories west of Verona, and the papal possessions south of the Po into the Cisalpine Republic, but the full significance of his plans for north Italy had not yet been unveiled. That was to come with the treaty of Camp Formio, signed on October 17.

During the summer Napoleon had seemed to the Italians to be ind-
deed the great liberator of Italy from foreign domination. It had not
yet become irresistibly obvious that the Cisalpine Republic, subsequently called the Italian Republic, and the various other divisions
of Italy established by the French were to be mere instruments of
French domination, more destructive economically and artistically
than any foreign domination of Italy had ever been. All that was
yet to come, but the treaty of Campo Formio pointed the way. For
that treaty was, in the eyes of many Italians and all Venetians, a supreme Napoleonic betrayal. In return for the Austrian Netherlands
(now Belgium) France granted to Austria the possessions of the entire
old Venetian Republic east of the Adige and north of it where, south of
Verona, it turns East and parallels the Po. Napoleon had expelled the
Austrians from Italy only to readmit them, even granting them Istria
and Dalmatia, ancient possessions of Venice. Foscolo, who had returned to Venice after the fall of the oligarchy, once again had to
flee from his home city before the Austrian occupation and repression
of patriots, liberals, and revolutionaries. Within a few months Napoleon, who had extended the French control over Italy as far as
Rome, returned to France, saw that the invasion of England was
impossible, and in May, 1798, set out for Egypt, from which he
did not return until August, 1799.

During his absence from Italy the Austrians in the alliance of the
Second Coalition, together with the Russians, set out to drive the
French from Italy. By the autumn of 1799 they had virtually succeeded. But then Napoleon, having landed in France and established
the Consulate, which, as we have seen, made him virtually dictator
of France and of the Revolution, prepared for the reconquest of
Italy. He attacked through the St. Gotthard pass, memorialized in
the famous painting by David, retook Milano and restored the Cisalpine Republic. By the treaty of Lunéville of February 9, 1801, the
former condition of Italian arrangements was re-established, Austria
retaining Venice and its share of the Veneto. The March 27, 1802,
treaty of Amiens between France and Great Britain resulted in the
general pacification of Europe and the consolidation of the French
conquests. In August Napoleon became consul for life and, among

other titles, President of the Italian Republic, which succeeded and slightly enlarged the Cisalpine Republic. Nevertheless Foscolo continued fighting with the Italian armies under French control, since he still hoped that the Revolutionary ideologies spread by French occupation and above all by the French troops would lead to the emerging idea of a united and republican Italy, an ambition not to be fulfilled until after the Second World War. It has been suggested that the suicide of the fictional Jacopo Ortis made the continued life of Ugo Foscolo possible. Be that as it may, Ortis's suicide takes place on March 27, 1799, the day that the grand duke of Tuscany was driven out and the French occupied Florence, but also the day the Archduke Charles of Austria defeated the French army of the upper Rhine at Stockach. It was a day of triumph for a tyranny of oppression and for a tyranny of liberation. There was no way out for Ortis. Was there a way out for Italy?

To answer that question we must first look more closely at Ortis's responses to his situation. At the beginning of the work (the first letter is dated 11 October, 1797, before the actual signing of the Campo Formio but when its provisions had become known) he writes to his friend Lorenzo Alderani, the subsequent editor of the letters, from a family property in the Euganean Hills, southwest of Padova, to which he had fled: "The sacrifice of our country is complete." He knows that his name is on the Austrian list of the proscribed, and he has fled at the urging of his mother. In true Enlightenment fashion he is consoling himself with the lives of Plutarch, but he has arrived, and is one of the first to do so, at the Romantic function of history: "The imagination loves to rove among past ages and possess another universe." His taking the past as an alternative possibility rather than as a moral or political model indicates the alienation of the Romantic. And shortly that alienation is confirmed by his discovery of the universality of theft. Ours is a race of thieves. Soon a visitor, Signor T———, a refugee from the political disturbances of Padova, calls upon him. He returns the call and meets T———'s daughter, Teresa. Shortly he falls in love, and he comes to know why after he has examined further his situation and his understanding of it. Nature has become incomprehensible to him; he sees society as the enemy of the individual, and individuals as enemies of each other; metaphysically, like Obermann, he has entered into a full pyrrhonism. And so, "in an exacerbated soul, in which the other passions are desperate, love becomes ominipotent" (March 17). The beloved becomes the sole source of value. And in that same letter he says that the French "make the God-given theory of public freedom seem execrable." And in the next sentence he expresses his contempt for Napoleon — base and cruel. And he mocks those who think that because Napoleon was born an Italian he is interested in Italy. No, Napoleon is interested only in himself. And, finally, "Not to know men is a dangerous thing, but to know them without having the courage to deceive them is fatal!" But in spite of his misanthropy and his skepticism he feels a "patriotic furor growing stronger in my blood."

And that furor is given new impetus by a new message and warning from his mother. He is not safe in the Euganean hills. He must leave Venetian (now Austrian) territory at once. So by way of Rovigo and Ferrara and Bologna he journeys first to Florence. His life as a political exile and Romantic wanderer has begun. In Florence history overtakes him — Michelangelo, Machiavelli, Galileo. The memory of these great men, however, also warns him that they were persecuted. "Persecution of the living, honor to the dead: both document the malign ambition which gnaws at the human herd." (27 August), His next stop is Milano, where he becomes a friend of Giuseppe Parini (1719-1799), the greatest Italian poet of the later 18th century, notable for his defense of Italian culture and his attacks on the aristocracy for their trivial imitation of French manners and customs and costumes. His exposure of the irresponsiblity of that aristocracy places him in the Enlightenment. To Ortis he is the noblest living representative of Italian tradition, both literary and moral. This friendship and further meditation raises his patriotic furor to new heights, as well as his patriotic despair, coupled with his despair over mankind. And he decides in February, 1799, to leave Italy and go to Nice, to France and perhaps beyond.

Yet this plan, really an aimlessness, is not fulfilled. At Ventimiglia, on the coastal road to Nice, now just inside the Italian border, then part of the French-established Ligurian Republic, the former Republic of Genova, at the very edge of Italy, he reaches the nadir of his depression, though no solution of his problem — he arrives at a foundation for morality. Nature is the enemy of man, and man is the enemy of society. Therefore there is only one basis for morality and for action — compassion. So, though he does get as far as Nice, he turns back at once, irresistibly drawn, in spite of plans to go to Rome, to his native country, to the Euganean hills. In a few days he makes a rapid, secret, and dangerous trip to Venice to see his mother for the last time, and then returns to his Euganean villa by foot. He writes his last thoughts — "we are all enemies" — and his last letter to Teresa. He has reached a complete emptiness, "On every side I see nothing but infinities which absorb me like an atom." (March 20, 1799). On March 25 he stabs himself, and dies the next morning.

Yet from this debacle emerge the seeds of a new Italian culture, marked more than in any other country by a convergence, almost a fusion, of patriotism and Romanticism. This relationship is particularly and forcefully presented in *Ortis* by Jacopo's inability to leave Italy. The place of his problem must be the place of his solution. And his suicide is only an anticipation of what probably would have happened to him under Austrian domination; at the very least he would have been imprisoned. The clue to this convergence is the emphasis upon Italian culture and Italian history. Ortis's remark about history as presenting an alternative world indicates that what Foscolo was aiming at was a cultural transcendence, to be achieved, however, by the study of Italian history and above all by the study of the history of Italian culture, as his vision in Florence reveals.

So it was less nationalism — an Enlightenment idea — than cultural patriotism that became the informing idea of Foscolo's subsequent work and the works of his Italian Romantic followers — for he was the first. The difference between Foscolo's proposal to use the past to create a future and Hölderlin's was that the latter's vision was of a past that never existed, while Foscolo insisted upon the transcending power of a past that not only had existed but in fact continued to exist in the endless wealth of glorious works of art scattered throughout Italy with an inexhaustible and almost unbelievable prodigality.

One further point of interest in *Iacop Ortis* remains to be mentioned. Foscolo's style in this work was a complete break with traditional Italian rhetoric, which had become extremely elaborate, neoclassical, artificial, and elegant. Foscolo wrote his book in realistic language, convergent with the style of Wordsworth. Instead of the high rhetorical tradition, he wrote in a language close to the spoken language, at least the spoken language of educated people and the style in which they wrote their letters. Part of the shock of the book, and one source of its popularity, was precisely in this undermining of rhetoric and its exhausted culture by a recasting of literary language. This above all was Foscolo's allegiance to the realism of Romanticism.

Ortis died because in March, 1799, there seemed to be nothing in any direction but betrayal of Italian interests. Foscolo lived to fight in the various Italian armies, even though they were under French control, even after Napoleon declared himself Emperor in 1804 and in 1805 King of the Kingdom of Italy, which superseded the Italian Republic, the 1802 successor to the Cisalpine Republic. When Foscolo published the complete version of *Ortis* he was still only 24 years old, and only four years later he wrote his greatest completed poem, "Dei Sepolcri" ("On Tombs"), written in Milan and published in April, 1807, in Brescia.

The occasion of the poem was the French Edict of St. Cloud, promulgated June 12, 1804, and extended to Italy on September 5, 1806. Burials could no longer be made in churches; they must be made outside of inhabited places; all graves must be marked with stones identical in size and shape; they could bear only inscriptions officially approved. It was a strange law, Foscolo thought, and correctly, for it was a new kind of law, a creation of a new or modern bureaucracy, itself one of the most notable creations of the Napoleonic regime. And it was strange because it not only denied the living their age-old mode of establishing their relation to the dead, but it also denied the dead their share in the living. In short, seen from the perspective of *Ortis,* "Dei Sepolcri" is concerned with the transmission of culture and the means human beings have created to keep their cultures alive.

So Foscolo, alluding perhaps to a letter in *Ortis,* speaks of the tombs of great Italians. First he laments that Parini has no tomb, for tombs are the prime symbol of what he had come to see as the only redeeming human virtue, compassion. And he admits, too, that the law has some justification and rationale, for the churches have become crowded with dead bodies and the stench of the dead, mingled with incense that fails in its masking purpose; and the cities are filled with images of death. So he turns to the ideal tombs of the past, and also to British graveyards, for the poem is addressed to Ippolito Pindemonte (1753-1829), who had written so beautifully of English estates and places. And then he remembers his own responses to the tombs of Machiavelli, Michelangelo, and Galileo, tombs which Vittorio Alfieri (1749-1803), the 18th century Italian poet of powerful classical tragedies, had also visited when he lived in Florence as a young man and to which he returned after his escape in 1792 from the Paris of the Revolution. And this memory of heroism draws Foscolo's mind back to ancient Greece and finally to the Troad, the source of the Julian race which founded Rome and European civilization. The tombs there are memorials of that civilization which it is the task of the present to renew. And the last image is that of Hector, forever honored because he shed his blood and sacrificed his life for his fatherland.

Thus Foscolo establishes even more firmly than in *Iacopo Ortis* the unique Italian association of history, patriotism, and cultural renewal. Italy had been so dishonored for centuries, and had been so economically damaged for as long, that the task of creating a new Italy was enormous, of creating a united Italy even more intimidating. Yet it was done, through immense suffering, suffering that continues, but it was achieved, though not completely, even today, because through Foscolo the immense force of Romantic cultural transcendence was channelled into activity bound to have — and by intention — a political result. The aggressive force that Ortis could direct only against himself, Foscolo directed outward, against a tyrannous occupier, in "*Dei Sepolcri.*"

Philipp Otto Runge   Foscolo was the youngest Romantic we have
(1777-1810)   yet encountered, and yet he was, culturally,
          a first-generation Romantic in that his move-
ment into Romanticism was entirely self-generated, quite ignorant of
and independent of what had already been achieved by the Germans
and the English. The painter Philipp Otto Runge, a year older, however, is a second-generation Romantic, in the sense that he was inspired
by certain of his German predecessors, Fichte, above all by Tieck,
by Wackenroder, by Schelling's philosophy as it had developed up to
1801, and even by the Schlegels. He was born on July 23, 1777, in
Wolgast in what was then Swedish (i.e., West) Pomerania, which became part of Prussia only in 1815. In 1795 he joined his older brother
Daniel in Hamburg — and to his great advantage, for his brother, a
merchant in a city of merchants, was intimate with the most cultivated social group in Hamburg. Thus, through working in his brother's
firm, he became acquainted with the artists and writers of the city,
and, of greatest importance, was inspired, inflamed by *Franz Sternbald.*

Although he had started his artistic education late, it soon became
apparent that he was talented, and his wonderfully generous brother
sent him off to what was then the principal place to study art in
northern Germany, Copenhagen. He studied there in the Academy
from October, 1799, to early 1801. There again he became acquainted
with highly cultivated individuals, particularly those in the circle
of the poetess Friederike Brun. He had been preceded in the Copenhagen Academy by Caspar David Friedrich, like himself one of the
founders of German Romantic painting, born in Greifswald, only less
than twenty miles west of Wolgast. When Runge left Copenhagen
for further study in Dresden in 1801 he went to see Friedrich in Greifswald, for both had a common friend in another student, C. C. A.
Böhndel. In 1802 Friedrich followed Runge to Dresden and remained
there when the latter left Dresden in 1803, soon to settle for the rest
of his short life in Hamburg. While in Dresden it is of great cultural
weight that he became acquainted with Ludwig Tieck and also, evidently, with the Schlegel brothers.

The most important event of 1800, however, was his decision in

Philipp Otto Runge
Die Hülsenbeckschen Kinder
reproduced by permission of the Hamburger Kunsthalle

January to participate in the Weimar competition, an affair established by Goethe and his associate H. H. Meyer to make classicism (actually neo-classicism) the dominant and indeed permanent model for German art. Of the two themes proposed in the *Propyläen,* their journal founded to propagate this position (though it ceased publication in 1800), Runge chose the second, "Achilles and Skamandros." His entry, submitted in August, 1800, did not win the competition. The result was that Runge, inspired by his growing familiarity with the principles of the first German Romantics, decided that classicism was no longer a viable style, and that the task was to create a new German style of art, founded on the principles of the Romantics with which he had become familiar and whose works he was coming to know with increasing intimacy and mastery. This completely self-conscious decision to achieve an artistic cultural transcendence was the first appearance of Romanticism in the visual arts.

That effort took two directions, antithetical, yet parallel and complementary. One direction was the kind of realism we have already encountered. In Runge's work it is to be found above all in portraits — of himself, of his brother, of his wife, of his parents and their grandchildren, and of his own children, and of his friends. The most notable achievements were "The Hülsenbeck Children" of 1805 and "The Parents of the Artist" of 1806. Hülsenbeck was one of his brother's business partners. The picture shows the two older children, the older girl and the younger boy, pulling a third child, still a baby, in a four-wheeled cart. Runge eliminates every traditional trace of charm, of cuteness, of helplessness, of fragility, traditional in portraits of children, at least those of the 18th century. These are vigorous figures, filled with volition and aggression. The boy looks directly at the spectator and brandishes a whip. His older sister, though at first glance less self-assertive, is actually leading the little procession and at the same time assuming a protective attitude towards her brother. The child in the cart is already a personality, self-assertive and determined. It grasps a leaf of a giant sunflower at the left, and the gestures of its feet and particularly toes echo the striding forward of its two siblings.

But this purposefulness is not confined to the children. The great sunflower, a symbol in Runge's thinking of divine energy in the world, is highly anthropomorphic, repeating in plant form the energy, the aggressive thrust of the children.   Runge, in short, has caught the power and even violence of children without at all making them little adults.   That power and violence though only hinted at is truly an attribute of the child.   And this true childish attribute is further under-lined by the quite deliberate use of colors which in themselves and in combination are unattractive.   Even the landscape in the back-ground, of Hamburg outskirts, is quite commonplace, as are the fence and the house at the right edge, deeply recessed at the end of the fence which turns at right angles and runs back towards the house. Thus the confining effect of the fence is reversed, and the children are seen as moving toward an unlimited, undefined, free space, as if toward an unknown adulthood.

That motion from left to right is repeated in the portrait of his two parents with two of their grandchildren, but with entirely dif-ferent symbolism.   The parents, dressed in dark clothes, are presented against the background of their house, which occupies three-quarters of the picture.   The dominating colors are the black and deep brown of their clothes and the dark green of the wall of the house, relieved only by a line of closed shutters at the left.   In all probability these shutters are a symbol of the closure of the parents' life.   Old as they are, however, the assertiveness and determination of the father is proposed in the stick and hat carried in his left hand and extending beyond the edge of the house into the airy but brooding landscape at the right, which occupies almost exactly one-eighth of the picture — in the upper right-hand corner, separated from the children be-neath by a pointed fence.   The landscape is a bit of the Peene, the channel separating Wolgast from an off-shore island on which is the town of Peenemünde, to become famous in World War II.   One of the children is in pink, the other, mostly concealed by a lily stalk, in grey. In Runge's iconography the lily stands for light, life, rebirth, the dawn, the resurrection.   The older child, looking towards its grand-parents is grasping a lily, the younger is pointing to another lily blos-som.   Thus Runge asserts the continuity of generations and the firm participation of his aged parents in the activities of life.

And all this, like the "Hülsenbeck Children", is painted in an uncompromising realism. One device, then, that Runge used to undermine classicism was precisely that literalism which classicism cannot tolerate. But indeed "literalism" and "realism" are terms not strong enough to indicate sufficiently the character of these paintings, particularly of the faces. Such terms cannot express the harsh exposure, almost brutal, of the cragginess, the downright ugliness, of human flesh when it is observed without illusion or consolation. Yet in spite of that it cannot be said that these faces are dehumanized, or, better, subhumanized. There blows through these uncompromising masks a transcendent human value.

The second direction is also suggested in the portrait of Runge's parents in the symbolism of the lily. For Runge in his determination to create a new art also set out to create a new iconography. And this was the driving interest in the series of works for which he became famous and for which he planned a destiny brought to almost nothing by his early death. This series is "Die Zeiten," four drawings created between Christmas, 1802, and July, 1803; four copper engravings not finally finished in their first edition until spring, 1805, and in their second edition something like a year later. (On April 16, 1806, Runge sent the four sheets to Goethe.) By this time, evidently, he had determined to recreate the series in four paintings. First came what has been subsequently known as "Der Kleine Morgen" ("The Small Morning"). After many and very beautiful preliminary drawings the painting was completed by October, 1808, having been the work of the preceding summer. He then determined to execute the scheme of the four panels on a very large scale, to be housed in a Gothic building designed for them, and to be experienced to the accompaniment of choral music written for this purpose alone. When he died in 1810 "Der grosse Morgen" was unfinished, although numerous extraordinary preparatory drawings had been executed. He gave instructions that it was to be dismembered, but that was not done until the 1890s; the various segments were brought together and mounted against a neutral background in 1927 and 1928.

"Die Zeiten" meant to Runge not merely the times of the day, but also the times of the year and the times of the cycles of human existence, the cycles of eternal birth, maturity, fading, extinction, re-birth, the eternally rotating complementarity of day and night, dawn and evening, life and death, sacrifice and resurrection – and above all the transcendence of the human spirit over its fleshly limitations – the emergence of light from darkness and darkness from light; in short, all the metaphorical possibilities of light and darkness, day and night.   And his task, as he conceived it, was the primary task of the Romantic, the re-sanctification of the earth and of human life, the re-establishment of value.   The rejection of classicism, or Weimar-ian neo-classicism, was the rejection of a failed culture.

Few Romantic works offer so deliberate an instance of planned cul-tural transcendence as Runge's "Die Zeiten."   First, the style of the works is derived from John Flaxman, but is utterly transformed. Runge retains the abstractionism of Flaxman's severe outlines, but contradicts it, negates it, and transcends it with the most exquisitely observed draughtsmanship of plants and flowers, of an almost botanical accuracy.   Hence there arises in the drawings a powerful tension be-tween the idealism of the outlines and the naturalism of the details. Furthermore, to increase that tension, he engages in an idealism far surpassing that of Flaxman, which was, after all, an abstraction not from the world but from the tradition of Renaissance art, aided by ancient Greek vases.

Runge's idealism comes out first of all in the severe symmetry of each drawing, so complete that any asymmetry, such as the placing of the fallen roses in the engraving of "Morning," is all the more power-ful and hence naturalistic.   But that idealism also comes out in the extreme freedom with which Runge treats proportions.   In "Morn-ing," the lily of the dawn, a lily on which six naked children sit, and above whom three naked children stand upon the lily's pistils, is quite out of proportion with the size of the roses; and both are immensely out of proportion with the segment of the sphere of the earth, which is inscribed across the bottom of the interior picture.   "Interior," because each scene is surrounded with a frame, the general import of which is always the movement from death to life, from earth to heaven, from root to flower, from crucifixion to the lamb of God, from owls to the sacred dove.   Again, in "Morning" four lily stems are bent over, in perfect semicircles, with blossoms already closed at the end of each, and on each bent stem sits a child musician, child, rather than cherub, for they are far different from the usual cherubs, even though evidently derived from the child angels in Raphael's Sistine Madonna, which had an immense influence on Runge and which, of course, he knew in Dresden, its home.

In "Day" the lily is at the top of the inner picture, its pistils fully extended and its petals already curling downward. The lower four blossoms have already closed up, that is, become seed pods, and the plant is surrounded with a corona, or halo, a great circle in smaller proportions of sunflower blossoms. In "Evening" the lily of light, again crowned with six embracing children on the petals and three on the stamens, above whom floats the evening star, instead of the morning star, has now sunk below the round of the earth, so that only the upper part of each petal is visible. In "Night" it is entirely gone, but a sunflower, abstract rather than botanical, although surrounded by botanically accurate flowers, has taken its place, but sunk into darkness. Rather, the upper part of the picture is occupied with a great curve of poppies, each surmounted by an angelic child with a star above.

These poppies first appeared in the preceding picture, "Evening," in which the sinking day lily is flanked and arched over by enormous roses, Runge's emblem for maturity. In the preceding picture, "Day," a sharp difference is made in his depiction of male and female children. On the right the males are crowned by a stalk of wheat, on the left the females by a stalk of flax. In the middle the female personification of day embraces the children. It is the time of ripeness, of fruits of the earth. She sits in a symmetrical half-dome bower made up of radiating different kinds of leaves. Before her is a fountain into which water flows from a fish's head, and in front of that is, foreshortened, a perfect circle or half of flowers. In "Night" this bower is repeated, but this time as two bowers, half visible at each side of the picture at the lower corners, and in each bower lie a male and female child, embracing in sleep. But all this is but a list of a few of the more obvious symbolisms of Runge's original iconography, which, Goethe said, amazed him, delighted him, and maddened him because it contains so many delightful puzzles, puzzles which together propose a sanctification of life and human effort.

When Runge decided to repeat these drawings in four paintings, in typical Rungean fashion he rethought his whole iconographical design. The originals contained an inconsistency. The last three panels are each dominated by a clothed female figure, goddesses of fruitfulness, of maturity, and of quiescence and rest before the rebirth. He concluded that a similar goddess would be necessary for "Morning," the only design executed as a small painting and then partially carried into a large one. Thus the "Small Morning" preserves from the engraved "Morning" only the blossom of the lily with six angelic children. In place of the stem is the goddess Aurora, nude and partly wound about with her own golden hair, glowing in the light of the sun just on the verge of rising above the sea over which she floats. Below the sea is a vast landscape, and in the center, at the bottom of the picture, that is, nearest to the observer, is a new-born baby, iconographically related to the Christ Child. The lily blossom is the keystone of an arch of four angels, and below, two more pairs are symmetrically placed, two children at the edge of the sea, two at the front with hands stretched out toward the babe. The frame for the interior picture is dominated on either side by the root, the bulb, the leaves, and the blossom of an amaryllis, the iconography of the whole moving from the sphere of the earth eclipsing the sun at the bottom to a glory of innumerable cherubim at the top, the iconography moving from the earth through blossoms to the heavens and the angelic choirs.

The whole ensemble is an iconographically rich exploration and exposition of the notions of birth and revival and resurrection. Nor is it surprising that Runge chose this scene as the first of four projected paintings to be undertaken, for it expresses with great precision and beauty exactly what he was attempting to do, to bring art itself, culture itself, to a radiant and transcendent new birth. Hence, instead of completing the sequence of four small "Die Zeiten" he went on with hardly any delay to the planning and execution of the huge "Large Morning." Its nine surviving fragments now pieced together differ little from the "Small Morning," except in the figure of Aurora, who is much more richly developed, particularly the glory of her radiant hair winding about her. And the time of day is a little earlier, closer to dawn than, as in the preceding "Morning," to sunrise itself. Happily, we also possess for this final effort of Runge a series of wonderfully beautiful preparatory drawings.

Runge died in 1810 of the white plague, tuberculosis, but in his "Zeiten" and above all in the two painting versions of "Morning" he bequeathed radiant symbols of a newborn culture, of a religion Christian, pantheistic, and occultist, of nature penetrated and suffused with beauty and value. His ideas of a new art and something of his practice inspired the other Pomeranian artist, an artist even greater than himself, Caspar David Friedrich, an artist who lived long enough to carry his ideas triumphantly to climax and conclusion.

Caspar David Friedrich   Like Runge, Friedrich also studied at the
1774-1840   Copenhagen Academy, from 1794 to 1798, and like Runge he too was trained in its rather rigid neo-classicism, training consisting mostly in drawing from plaster casts of the antique. In May, 1798, he left Copenhagen and, stopping on the way at his birthplace, Greifswald, and at Berlin, went to Dresden, the other important art center of northern Europe, where Friedrich could hope to find an audience and a market. Dresden, often called the Florence of Germany, was then a city of great beauty, now only partially restored after the terrible devastations of World War II. But its buildings and its painting collections were not the most important aspect of the city for Friedrich's art. Stretching east was the valley of the Elbe, and on the border of Bohemia were the Riesengebirge, a mountain landscape of great beauty, called affectionately the Saxon Alps. Bohemia itself was not far away and Friedrich made innumerable wandering excursions through the area, constantly searching for new landscape ideas and images. And in addition he often returned, particularly in his early years in Dresden, to the area of his home, especially the town of Neubrandenburg and above all the island of Rügen, famous for its spectacular chalk cliffs

and its neolithic dolmens, known as Hünengraben. Near Greifswald were also the Gothic ruins of the Cistercian Abbey Eldena. These were subjects which appeared again and again in Friedrich's work.

His first years in Dresden were spent in learning the art of landscape and in developing his unique landscape iconography. His first step was to master the technique of drawing in sepia and in establishing his own style, which was a cultural emergent of striking character. His sepia drawings made his reputation and in 1807, incidentally, he began to paint in oil. At once he emerged as the most important artist in Dresden. In 1810 he was elected to the Berlin Academy and in 1816 to the Dresden Academy, where he also acted as instructor in landscape painting. His crucial years were 1807 to 1809, for in these years he established his unique landscape art.

The exact relations between Runge and Friedrich are in some doubt, but there is no question that they knew each other, and little doubt that the younger man had a decisive effect on the older. Runge's 1801 declaration that the future of art was landscape seemed to have been decisive for Friedrich. So in 1803 he too undertook a series of four drawings of the times of day, the times of year, and the life cycle. These drawings were destroyed in 1945, together with several of his most famous and beautiful paintings. (A few years later he repeated the series, but this set has also long since disappeared. They may have been in oil but more probably were sepia drawings.) By 1804 or 1805 he had clearly begun to establish his style.

The numerous drawings that survive from his early Dresden years show that first of all he was interested, as was Runge, in the precise artistic description of the real world — pine trees, rocks, mountains, the ruins of Eldena and several other similar places, dying and dead oak trees, dolmens, plants. These were the elements that went into his peculiar iconography, and the organization of his paintings was dictated by iconographic requirements. In the typical Friedrich picture a foreground is abruptly presented; that is, without any access for the observer, and a background appears without a middle ground, without transition from the foreground to the back. Thus for many of his paintings the observer has a sense of the remoteness, even inaccessibility, of the landscape before him. So the distinction between ordinary landscape experience, whether in reality or in pictures, and the strangeness, the extraordinary character of what Friedrich is concerned with is established and emphasized. For what his iconography is concerned with, is the distinction between this world and the other, the beyond, *"jenseits,"* as the Germans call it, sometimes mysterious and strange, sometimes offered as a paradise. Hence between the observer and that distant other world there are two abysses, that between the observer and the foreground, and that between the foreground and the background. This obliges Friedrich to organize the painting in parallel planes. The device in itself lends a certain degree of abstraction, and that degree is greatly intensified by the emergence in Friedrich's work of these years on an increasing symmetry of things and figures in the foreground and the placement of the mountains in the background, except in those pictures in which the background is made up of only sea and sky, or sometimes mist. Here we see, though less rigorously, the Rungean symmetry.

The greater the symmetry in a painting the greater the awareness of the human structural and organizational power — the will, one might as well call it — that went into the composition and is imposed upon the subject matter, especially if the subject matter is landscape or anything natural or man-made ordinarily perceived in asymmetrical fashion. This pictorial structure is entirely in accord with Friedrich's insistence that his landscapes were projections or materializations of his feelings. Though derived from the 18th century culture of emotional lability, this position of Friedrich's is really quite different, for the abstraction of the results emphasizes not emotional lability but emotional stasis. It was to lead in his later paintings to extraordinary efforts to capture in a painting the experience of the ecstatic.

The elements and meanings of Friedrich's iconographical schemes can be briefly enumerated, for he used them again and again throughout his lifetime. A stone in the foreground signifies faith in Christianity; ivy, resurrection; distant mountains, God; ships, the transition from this world to the other; blue sky, promise of immortality and resurrection; dolmens, pagan religion; dead or dying oak-trees, the persistence of pagan religious feeling in its successor, Christianity; Gothic ruins, the failure of institutionalized religion; graves, death;

the cross, Christianity. Thus Friedrich is a transitional figure. The meaning of his paintings is traditional, except for the significance of the ruins, and they provide the clue for his creation of a new kind of allegorized landscape. What he insists upon in his paintings is that the traditional modes of religious feelings are moribund or dead or exhausted, and that he is creating in his landscapes not only an objectification of his own feelings but an objectification that would inspire the observer to a similar renewal, free of institutionalization. But this iconographical system also requires that each configuration be painted with a kind of hyper-realism as a way of indicating its semantic intensity. The result is again an expression of the will of the painter, an aggressive intensification of feeling.

What are evidently the first two oil paintings by Friedrich, at least the first two to have survived, were done in 1807, "Seashore with Fisher" and "Fog." His mature style has already appeared, and with such success that his elaborate pietistic iconography is not denied but made irrelevant. His new conception of landscape painting has universalized the precise signification of his iconography. In the first a sharply painted foreground, with fisher's nets and a rack for drying hay, both with pietistic significance, are separated by a brook leading (by implication) to the water's edge, another Friedrichian sign, the path of life. Beyond is the sea, half obscured by mist and with a barely visible boat and sail; at the top of the canvas the clouds thin out to reveal patches of blue sky. In the other painting a rocky shore with a buoy opens, with more traditional transition, on a mist-covered sea, in which a small boat is moving towards (probably) a larger ship. In the first painting the equivalent of the small boat is the figure of the fisher, looking out towards the sea. It is the first of Friedrich's many pictures in which a figure, eventually to become far larger, at times almost vertically filling the canvas, looks out toward a different world. And this has been interpreted as the longing for death and another world.

These allegorical meanings, however, have been proposed only recently. There is no particular reason to question them, and yet they strike one as inappropriate. The reason is that Friedrich has made these images both so attractive and so haunting that the contrast between the sharp foreground and the misty background reveals the religious allegory as only a special case of the universal longing for a different mode of existence — a mode at once longed for and yet recognized as of vague and indeterminable character. It is the longing not for the infinite but for the as yet indefinable but nonetheless of real possibility of attainment.

The next two paintings are quite possibly a pair, both probably painted in 1807, for increasingly Friedrich painted pairs of companion and related pictures. In both the movement towards symmetrical organization is intensified. In the first, a dolmen such as those to be found on Rügen is placed on a snow-covered hilltop and surrounded by three oak trees; the tops of two of them have been broken off or perhaps blasted off by lightning; and both are covered with the stumps of sawn-off branches, signifying death. But the tree in the background, immediately above the dolmen, is intact, and perhaps still living, and the top seems to be reaching out towards the background. Here Friedrich is concerned with the continuing vitality of the religion that created the dolmen. In the companion picture, "Ausblick in das Elbtal" (View into the valley of the Elbe") the scene is summer. In the foreground is a mountaintop crowned with an immense rock and surmounted by tall fir trees. In the back is the misty paradise-like valley of the Elbe with the river winding through it. Again there is further movement towards a symmetrical organization, and the pietistic rock and fir tree are subsumed by a more general or universal feeling of vitality and aspiration, of this life as value-laden as the life beyond.

The next pair of pictures is derived from the earlier "Times of the Year." "Summer" is so much a repetition of the sepia drawing that it is regressive, but "Winter," or "Monk in the Snow," is the original "Winter" rethought and intensified. In the center is a broken tree stump, an emblem of death; to the left is an oak tree with most of its branches broken or sawed off; to the right the ruins of a Gothic church. Somewhat to the right of center a monk, leaning on a staff, is approaching the ruins, which arise from below the snow-covered foreground. The painting is at once an emblem of the end of life and an emblem of the death of the old institutionalized religion.

The next painting is far different from this pair derived from "Times of the Year." "Morgennebel in Gebirge" ("Morning Mist in the Mountains") is seen either from a mountain top or as if the observer were floating in space.   It shows an almost symmetrical and pyramidal mountain peak, the lower slopes of which are covered with trees, mostly firs, and mist; the upper part is a rock outcropping on the very apex of which is a tiny cross surrounded by a halo-like break in the clouds.   These clouds or mist are moving diagonally across the painting and are thus in counterpoint with the almost perfectly symmetrical mountain peak.   There is thus a striking contrast between the immense upward thrust of the peak — given an almost living energy by the floating mists, as well as by its very upwardly thrusting power, forcing itself, as it were, through the mists — and the tiny cross. Here again is a kind of universalization or subsumption of Christian pietism by a more inclusive affirmation of value.

The next painting, executed in 1807-1808, is the famous "Das Kreuz in Gebirge" ("The Cross in the Mountains"), an altarpiece painted for the castle of Tetschen in Bohemia, commissioned by Count Franz Anton von Thun-Hohenstein at the suggestion and request of his wife. The idea of a landscape for an altarpiece was probably suggested by Kosengarten, who commissioned Runge for a landscape altarpiece for a chapel on Rügen, the unfinished "Rest on the Flight to Egypt."   Friedrich's painting is still in the frame he designed. It shows the eye of God in a triangle surrounded by a glory, at the bottom, between a sheaf of wheat and a branch of grapes, symbols, of course, of the Eucharist. From Gothic columns on either side spring palm branches with five cherub heads and at the top a star. The picture itself shows a steep rocky peak, once again pyramidal and seen from an undefined and undefinable position. The peak is clothed with fir-trees, and from its crest a tall crucifix rises, facing away from the spectator towards the setting sun.

Friedrich himself explained the picture. The setting sun is God the father who has disappeared from the world when Christ entered it. "This sun sank and the earth was not able to grasp the departing light any longer. There shines forth in the gold of the evening light the purest, noblest metal of the Savior's figure on the cross, which thus

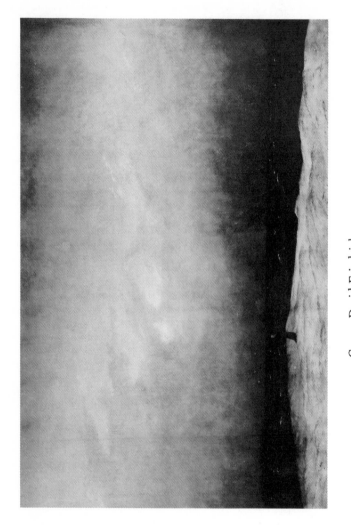

Caspar David Friedrich
Der Mönch am Meer
reproduced by permission of the Nationalgalerie
Staatliche Museen Preussischer Kulturbesitz, Berlin (West)

reflects on earth in a softened glow. The cross stands erect on a rock, unshakably firm like our faith in Jesus Christ. The firs stand around the evergreen [i.e., the ivy on the cross], enduring through all ages, like the hopes of man in Him, the crucified." And yet the painting is as equivocal as it is beautiful, and as beautiful as it is original. In fact it caused a considerable disturbance when it was first exhibited in Friedrich's studio at Christmas time in 1808. The Romantics were entirely on Friedrich's side in the quarrel and quite rightly. For as in the view of the Elbe Valley, and in the "Morgennebel in Gebirge" the most powerful image is precisely the smallness of the crucifix. If the rock from which it rises is faith, then it is not Christ who supports faith but faith that supports Christ. There is a hint here of Christianity as a mythology, not a revealed religious truth, and the notion that God is no longer available suggests rather that the naive belief in God is no longer available. Once again the pietistic allegory appears to be subsumed by more universal feelings of affirmation of the value of existence. The explanation is that as soon as Christian doctrines and dogmas and beliefs are separated from their traditional symbolizations, the arbitrary nature of the belief and the symbol is revealed, and thus the arbitrary nature of the belief is uncovered and revealed as itself a symbol of something else.

This hint is strengthened by the next pair of pictures, both the work of 1809, though the first, "The Monk on the Seashore," was not finished until Friedrich repainted the sky a second time in 1810. This is not only Friedrich's most striking image but one of the most striking pictorial ideas of the 19th century. It shows a monk, almost certainly a self-portrait, gazing out across the sea to a dark bank of clouds beyond. Only at the top of the picture does the cloud bank end to reveal pale blue sky, though even above that there is another bank of dark clouds. The picture thus consists almost entirely of horizontals, against which the tiny figure of the monk appears, his head below the horizon of the sea. It is doubtful if any artist has painted a more powerful image of loneliness, alienation, and the questioning of the mysterious and incomprehensible world, with only a partially consoling evidence of value in the strip of blue sky, itself partly covered with clouds and mists. The costume of a monk, a member of a religious order, indicates clearly the failure of institutionalized religion. The companion picture emphasizes this failure. Both pictures were exhibited at the salon of the Berlin Academy in 1810, and were purchased for the Crown Prince of Prussia, Friedrich Wilhelm. The second picture is known either as "An Abbey in an Oak Wood" or as "Burial of a Monk in an Oak Grove." The suggestion is strong that the burial is of the monk in the preceding picture, as current Friedrich scholarship believes, and thus by implication the death of Friedrich as an institutionalized Christian. All that is left of the abbey is a door with a tall gothic window above it in a ruined narrow wall. A cross is in front of the gate, and a short procession of monks is carrying a coffin into what is left of the abbey. Grave markers are scattered about on either side, and the ruin is set in a grove of dead oak trees, all with broken branches and most with broken off tops. The lower third of the picture is enveloped in deep shadow, the upper third in a pale evening sky, a post-sunset sky, with a crescent moon, which might signify resurrection.

This picture offers the most complete pictorial symmetry Friedrich had yet attempted, and even more than its companion picture is organized in extreme horizontal planes. Can this pictorial structure mean other than "Let the dead bury the dead"? The association of these dead oak trees with the pagan dolmens in previous works certainly seems to suggest that institutionalized Christianity is as dead as paganism. And what Friedrich as a Romantic was attempting to do, or rather what he was attempting to do that makes him a Romantic, is literally the re-creation of Christian feeling free of institutions and even of specific dogma and doctrine. Inspired perhaps by Schelling, Friedrich used ancient Christian symbolism in new situations to reveal both the necessity as well as the possibility of recreating Christian belief through natural forms. This was not a religion of nature but the use of nature to reveal religious feelings for a transcendent mode of existence, if not of reality itself. As Heinrich von Kleist said of Friedrich's pictures, "It is as though one's eyelids had been cut away." Friedrich's aim in his pictures was to drive the observer into a realization of an emergent kind of spiritual need. Almost no artist of the early 19th century made so complete a break with the tradition of

European painting. Here we find the beginning of that extraordinary path of painting which led in the 20th century to what we still call Modern Art.

Jean-Auguste-Dominique Ingres   Unlike Runge and Friedrich, Ingres
(1780-1867)   was born into an artistic atmosphere.
His father was the principal artist of the city of Montauban in south-west France, having come there from Toulouse in 1775. Still but a child, the young Ingres studied drawing with his father, and as early as 1791 he went to Toulouse and studied in its Academy of Art until 1797. His father had also taught him to sing and play the violin, so that when he was only fourteen he was playing in the orchestra of the Théatre du Capitole. His gifts were recognized early, and in 1797 he received the first prize of L'Ecole Centrale, the new designation, after August, 1793, of the Academy of Toulouse. Nor was the prize itself enough, for it was also affirmed by his mentors that he would "one day honor his fatherland by the superiority of his talents." So when he went to Paris in August, 1797, to study with David he had spent most of his seventeen years in the world of art and music, of high culture generally, a culture of old and rich tradition even in Montauban and Toulouse and far more so in Paris, where he became at once associated with the man widely recognized as the greatest painter of the day. Yet in spite of the difference between his background and the remote, provincial, and in youth almost anti-artistic environments of Friedrich and Runge, there is a remarkable cultural convergence between the Frenchman and the two Germans.

Certainly at first Ingres was more than an obedient student of David; he was perfect. From this period remain five male nudes, painted in 1800 and 1801, which show his absolute mastery of everything that David could do in the way of drawing and modeling. If anything they are better than what David could do, better in the sense of Ingres' more acute and exacting realism. In 1800, however, he received only the second place in the competition for the Prix de Rome, the governmental grant to study at Rome for five years.

The painting he submitted was a typical bit of Davidian historicism and Enlightenment antique nobility; it was destroyed in a fire in 1871. But in the next year with a scene from the Iliad he received first place in that competition. Like the previous year's work it was designed to show his mastery of the male nude, of drapery, of chiaroscuro — of the whole panoply of academic Davidian values and requirements. Even so, John Flaxman, then passing through Paris, declared the painting superior to all others of the French school which he had seen.

Because of financial difficulties in the state itself, the award for winning the prize had to be postponed for five years, during which, however, Ingres received a pension and a studio. And these years were crucial, for during them Ingres created his own style, forged his independence from David, and arrived at that plateau of perfection from which he never departed and hardly even changed. This leap, this cultural emergence, was possible because the conquests of Napoleon had made avaiable to Ingres a possibility other than that offered by David's version of the French tradition. What had happened was that from his sack of Italy Napoleon had assembled in Paris, beginning in July, 1797, glorious examples of Italian painting, especially of the fifteenth and sixteenth centuries. And these Ingres examined, studied, and used as means of freeing himself from his tradition. This use of the past, this historicism, to achieve a cultural escape and transcendence is, as we have seen, a highly typical, even a central Romantic strategy.

The first result of his Prix de Rome was his first important commission, a full-length portrait of Napoleon which the then first consul ordered as a gift to the city of Liège. In subsequent years, indeed for most of the century and even into the twentieth, Ingres was to be set up as the Classic master as opposed to Delacroix, the Romantic. Ingres, it was reiterated wearisomely, was the master of line; Delacroix of color. Only in 1967 when the great exhibition of Ingres was held in Paris on the hundredth anniversary of his death did French critics begin to realize, or at least to admit, that Ingres was a Romantic artist. This first important commission certainly hints at it. First of all, the color is almost violent. Napoleon is dressed in bright red velvet, and Ingres has increased the area of red by draping one of the tails of the consular uniform on the majestic (and Napoleonically vulgar) chair. Almost everything else in the picture — the carpet, the wall, the draperies at the window — is green, except for the dullish blue of the velvet upholstery on the chair and the covering on the table, with its deep fringe of gold. All these colors thrust the picture at the observer, and that aggressive visual attack is made all the more powerful by the steeply raked floor in the manner of the 15th century or of 20th century Matisse.

Nor is this mention of Matisse beside the point. Not only is Matisse the 20th century heir of Ingres, but Ingres already shows some of the devices which are considered so absolutely the marks of Matisse's style. Indeed one can almost say that Ingres is at his greatest when he reveals affinities with modern art, and least successful when he endeavors to be a traditional French history painter. Even though Delacroix and others were to master history painting, that was not the direction in which 19th century painting and the Romantic tradition were to move. What makes the modernity of Ingres at first hard to grasp is that modern painting emerged from the landscape tradition, but Ingres' greatest works are portraits.

In the same year in which he painted the Liège Napoleon, 1804, he painted a self-portrait. What we have now is not what he originally painted, for he reworked it as late, perhaps, as 1850. The original showed him erasing with his left hand a chalk drawing of a portrait he was then working at. In the repainting the easel and canvas are turned away from the observer. Only the lower right hand corner of the canvas is visible, and the left hand has been moved to the breast. This expunging of an act of expunging is indeed curious. Did the aged Ingres wish to conceal the fact that as a young man of twenty-four he had celebrated his own power to wipe out the way he had been taught to paint? For that is what he did in his first series of commissioned portraits, his first masterpieces, the portraits of the Rivière family, father, mother, and daughter. begun in 1804 and finished in 1805. In these he declares his independence from David. Inspired by the 15th century Italians, he omits from the portraits nearly all chiaroscuro, beginning with Monsieur Rivière. The effect is to turn areas of the same color — the coat, the trousers, the red table-cover, the dull greenish background (still Davidesque) — into patterns, and this patterned effect is further exploited by the sharpness and undulations of the bordering lines.

These tendencies are further developed in the portrait of Madame Rivière, who is half enveloped in a magnificent shawl. The picture is not a rectangle but an oval, and that oddity further emphasizes the patterning and the line, the last being brought out by the painted decoration of the sofa on which Madame Rivière is reclining against huge blue velvet pillows. The effect is that of a marvelous arabesque, a tension between real surface and fictitious depth, a movement towards the late 19th century realization that a picture is a flat surface covered with areas of paint. In the portrait of Mademoiselle Rivière this tendency towards a flat arabesque, in spite of increased chiaroscuro, goes even further, for the picture is an assemblage of curves, all derived, evidently, from the perfectly curving eyebrows and smooth hair outlining the perfectly curved head of the subject. The face thus has a strange, unreal, hieratic look. The work is less a portrait than it is a picture, a work of art exhibiting the mastery and will of the artist.

The next picture of importance is even more astonishing: Napoleon again, but this time in his imperial robes, seated upon the imperial throne (1806). It is a huge picture, of overwhelming power, but significantly the power does not lie in the figure of the Emperor. Napoleon is pale, almost ghastly, while the imperial robes are of an unbelievable richness and complexity — amounting to vulgarity. The picture is so hieratic that it verges on parody. What Ingres has done is to place Napoleon's head in a concentric series of explicit and implicit circles, so that imperial force seems to be radiating from the too consciously imperial and majestic face. These circles are enclosed between two sceptres so placed as to imply and almost form explicitly a great triangle, its apex at a point below the cushion on which rests the extravagantly embroidered imperial left boot, the right one concealed by the robes. And the robe forms an immense arabesque of patterns. The effect is to emphasize, as in the Rivière portraits, the fact that this is a picture, not a portrait.

Jean-Auguste Dominique Ingres
Marie-Françoise Beauregard Rivière
reproduced by permission of the Musée *du Louvre*

Ingres himself said that his object in painting was a perfect reproduction of what the eye sees — and then something more. And that
something more is the affirmation of the selfhood of the Romantic
artist, the something more which he contributes and which is the
source of the painting's value. It is Ingres' denial of and transcendence
of the traditional idea of art as imitation; a work of art is made object; it expresses not nature but the artist's creative capacity and
power. Ingres' turning a painting towards a flat arabesque was his
way of asserting the cultural independence of the artistic imagination. In this second portrait of Napoleon is the demonstration of
the superiority of the artistic imagination to political power. For
this picture shows imperial majesty no longer as vice-regent of divine
power, of the emperor as the earthly representative and almost avatar
of God himself, but as play-acting; the imperium is no more than
the vulgar propaganda of a splendor designed to impose itself (with
what uneasiness!) upon a population already exposed to democracy.

Indeed, one wonders why Ingres was not punished, even executed
for this extraordinary portrait. On the contrary. The state was at
last able to put once more into practice the *Prix de Rome,* and in
August, 1806, Ingres left Paris for Italy — and did not return for
years, not, in fact, until 1824, self-exiled and alienated from his natural
home and tradition. Of his works in Rome by the end of the decade
one needs to be mentioned, the "Woman at the Bath," also known as
"The Large Bather" and "The Bather of Valpinçon." Ingres painted it
in 1808, and it reveals in magic perfection everything that he had
been endeavoring to accomplish. The woman is seated on a linen-
covered couch, but her back is towards us. Of her face only a bit of
eyebrow and the tip of her nose are visible. She is thus depersonalized,
turned into an object to be painted, and she is so placed that Ingres
can turn the outline of her body into a continuous melody of curving
lines. And once again, the draperies hanging at the left, the drapery
in which her hair is bound, the drapery around her left arm and flowing
beyond her left leg down to the floor, the folded draperies of her
couch, the patterned edge of that cover and its fringe, the colored
trim to the drapery hanging at the left, the curved cone of the only
couch-foot showing — all these are synthesized into a wondrous arabesque of pattern and of line.

The notion that Ingres was a man of line rather than of color was, of course, wrong, but the recognition of the importance of line in his work was a response to that arabesque of line which flattens his paintings and makes of them such an enchantment that the equivalent can be found only in music. Late in the century Walter Pater was to make the famous remark that all art tends to the condition of music. What he was feeling his way towards was that music, not being an imitative art, is the model art, for it expresses in its purest form the creative will — the selfhood — of the artist. That music is indeed the model art became a widely held aesthetic conviction by the 20th century and lay behind much of the cultural emergence of the early twentieth century, of what we still call modern art. In "The Woman at the Bath" Ingres had already arrived at a painting which is pure visual music. In spite of his exquisite realism he added, as he said, something more, and that something more, that tendency towards abstraction and arabesque, not only allied him with Runge and Frie-drich but made an even more powerful move than they did towards what, in a hundred years, was to become of the art of painting.

Heinrich von Kleist   Like Ingres, Kleist has often, even tradi-
(1777-1811)   tionally, been denied classification as a
                             Romantic writer because he is so different
from writers such as Tieck or Wackenroder or Schelling or such later
Romantics as Brentano and Fouqué. Yet it has also been impossible to
classify him as anything else, and so he has been taken somehow
as a unique case, though one with extraordinary parallels to and implication for the literature and culture of the 20th century. Actually,
however, his development is almost a perfect exemplification of Romanticism in the larger sense, the sense at work in this investigation.

He was born in Frankfurt-an-der-Oder, some forty miles east of
Berlin, now at the very edge of the German Democratic Republic
but then in the heart of the Margravate of Brandenburg, ruled by the
King of Prussia, then and until 1786, Frederick the Great. Kleist
was of an old military family, for generations serving in the armies
of Brandenburg and Prussia, and he too was destined for a military

life. In 1793, when he was not yet sixteen, he was in the army as
an ensign. Posted to Frankfurt-am-Main in March of that year, he
served in the Prussian army of the First Coalition against the armies
of the French Revolution. But by 1795 Friedrich Wilhelm II of Prussia, weary of the struggle, economically depleted, and more interested
in his territorial gains from the partitioning of Poland, withdrew from
the Coalition and made peace with the French, confirming them in
their conquests on the left bank of the Rhine. As a result, Kleist
returned to Prussia and went into barracks in Potsdam. In March,
1797, not yet twenty, he was promoted to second lieutenant.

He was, nevertheless, becoming increasingly dissatisfied with army
life. In Potsdam he filled his leisure time with study and reading and
music, and it is clear that he became possessed by what were already
outmoded ideas and ideals of the Enlightenment; nor is it conceivable
that he was unaffected by the victories of the Revolutionary armies,
which by now, of course, had seen even greater triumphs, including
Napoleon's conquest of northern Italy and the threat to Vienna itself. An essay by Kleist on the certain way to achieve happiness was
written in 1798, and that certain way, in good Enlightenment fashion,
was of course the way of virtue. The outcome was that by 1799 he
had come to see the army as a form of tyranny and the condition of
the ordinary soldier as that of slavery. He requested permission to
resign his commission, a request the King granted in April, 1799, with
the prospect that Kleist would enter the civil service. Quite the contrary: having arrived at a typical Enlightenment egocentrism, Kleist
departed for Switzerland in order, he hoped, to establish himself
there into a Rousseauistic farm life. But the French control of Switzerland shortly made that dream impossible, and, furthermore, in the
spring of 1802 he suddenly began to write his extraordinary series of
plays, soon to be accompanied by an equally extraordinary series of
stories. He set out not only to be a writer but to be a profoundly
original writer, a writer of first importance.

This transformation of a soldier into an author was something
that his military family could hardly accept, and indeed never did
accept. It is possible that their disapproval, together with the failure
of his literary ambitions, may have had something to do with his

suicide in November, 1811. His plays were mostly either unproduced or unpublished or both; the two journals he started failed. By 1811 all of Europe was under the control of Napoleon and his family; Prussia had lost half of its territory; and Kleist had become a devoted patriot. Or perhaps it would be more precise to say that he had become an enemy of France, of Napoleon, that is, of the Enlightenment which France and Napoleon had come to emblemize. That rejection of the Enlightenment had already begun, it is more than likely, in 1800, the year in which he began his wandering. For aimless wandering, as we have already seen in several figures and will see again and again, both real and literary, is an acute symptom of that dissatisfaction with the Enlightenment, that awareness of the collapse of Enlightenment modes of explaining the world, which led to the cultural emergence of Romanticism.

In 1800 Kleist experienced what has long been known in criticism and scholarship as his "Kant crisis." Exactly what of Kant Kleist actually read, or whether or not he indeed read anything by him at all, or if he read certain Kantians, such as Fichte, or if even what he knew of Kant he had gleaned and gained only by hearsay, by accounts from individuals (and there were several candidates among his friends) who had read Kant and whom he trusted — all this is really unknown. So it is not surprising that scholarly accounts of what Kleist actually got from Kant and why Kant had such a devastating impact upon him are as many and various as there are accounts. Just as there is now little agreement on what Kant actually said and accomplished, there is just as little agreement on what effect he had upon Kleist. Nevertheless, as we read through Kleist it is not difficult to guess why Kant had such a devastating impact, moreover, one that was responsible for Kleist's abandonment first of his plan to enter the civil service and second for his plan to settle into Rousseaustic farming.

The word "plan" is used here with good reason, for in his letters of the time Kleist spoke of the necessity for a *Lebensplan,* a plan of life — a plan that would be uniquely satisfactory to his unique needs. So he seems first to have grasped what few have grasped in Kant. Kleist refused to accept Kant's attempt to get out of the dual problem posed by the following notion: if the human mind can know the world only in terms of human interests, then an individual mind can know the world only in terms of its individual interests; and by the consequent difficulty that it is therefore impossible for one mind to know another mind. Kant fell back upon an impossible and pragmatically useless notion of duty in order to provide a foundation for moral action. Kleist's notion is that the individual's duty is to construct a plan of life derived from and expressive of an individual's unique interests and aptitudes and, above all, his sources of self-satisfaction.

Kleist's next step seems to have been to assert that it is impossible for the individual to know the difference between truth and error, and also that if an individual is vicious he will know the world and find his satisfaction in terms of his viciousness. But to Kleist it also followed from this that it is often wise (and perhaps always, at least for some individuals) to conceal one's interests. From this position he arrived, perhaps with the aid of a minor Romantic philosopher, Gotthilf Heinrich von Schubert (1780-1860), at the conclusion that one can know one's interests only from what one does, and that one's real interests are inaccessible because they are unconscious. (The notion of the "unconscious mind" had been around for a century and, as we shall see, it was to play a central role in the thinking and poetry of Wordsworth.) Thus not only is the world incomprehensible but the individual is fundamentally incomprehensible to himself. In fact, if there is a central theme or problem to the work of Kleist, it is that of conscious and unconscious deception and self-deception. In short, the world — and this is a notion we have already encountered — is incomprehensible, and since human beings, including ourselves, are part of the world, they too are incomprehensible. To understand human beings, therefore, we must search out as best we can their interests, and those interests, again following Kant, are bound ultimately to be asocial.

Kleist's first effort to write a play was *Robert Guiscard,* and his avowed aim was to create a mode of tragedy that would synthesize and transcend into a new tragic mode the tragedies of Greece, of Shakespeare, of Goethe, and of Schiller. Profoundly dissatisfied with this first attempt, he destroyed the manuscript; but he rewrote and published some years later in his abortive journal *Phöbus* the opening scenes, hoping to interest a publisher in the completion of the work (1808). This effort also failed. The setting is the Norman camp before Constantinople, under siege by the Norman Duke Robert Guiscard. Guiscard's people are suffering terribly from the plague and beg Robert to lead them home. But he conceals from them both his plan to become Byzantine Emperor and also the fact that he himself is plague-stricken. At this point the fragment breaks off, but what we have is magnificent. Kleist reveals himself here as one who has grasped the very nature of drama, of the dramatic, of the truly theatrical as, for example, Schiller never quite did. For if one accepts Kant's notion that man is fundamentally asocial and can know the world only in terms of his own interests, then two consequences follow.

First, the world is necessarily inimical to human interests in its incomprehensibility and in its independence *from* human interests. But to the individual other individuals are part of the world. Therefore for any individual both the world and other individuals are a hindrance to the fulfillment and establishment of his individual interests. Hence, deception is the necessary means for manipulating others. Second, social relationships, those modes of interaction which make egoistic action possible, are thus only a superficial covering and concealment of the fundamental incoherence and inimicality of man's relation to man. And what we call the dramatic arises precisely in those situations in which individuals recognize the persons and the non-personal situation (with whom social arrangements require that they interact) as necessarily a hindrance, as necessarily inimical, to their asocial self-assertion. To put it in terms common to the period, drama emerges when the will encounters what it must interpret as an inimical will, whether of man or of nature.

Kleist's next play was *Die Familie Schroffenstein,* which he wrote in two and possibly three full versions, and which was published in Bern early in 1803 after he had left Switzerland in October, 1802. The dramatic situation is that two branches of the same family have divided the family possessions, but there is an agreement that if one branch should die out the heir of the other branch would inherit.

The child of one branch is accidentally drowned, but this death is misinterpreted as having been engineered by the other branch, which in turn suspects the first branch to be responsible for the death of one of *its* members. The resulting confusions and misapprehensions are responsible for the murder of a go-between, a member of a minor branch of the family, and eventually the murder of their own children, a youth and a maiden in love, by the heads of both families; and the realization of what they have done is responsible for their reconciliation. The story goes that when Kleist read this tragedy to his friends they all burst into laughter, led by Kleist himself. (In spite of its absurdity the work was performed at the National Theater in Graz early in 1804.) But Kleist's point was serious enough, and he was seriously engaged in a search for a basis for morality and sociality, which become possible when deceptions are revealed for what they are.

So he next tried his hand at comedy, first in an original work and then in one modified from Molière. The original work was *Der Zerbrochene Krug* (*The Broken Jug*), one of the best of German comedies, on which Kleist worked from 1803 to at least 1805 and perhaps 1807, years during which his wanderings continued as far west as Boulogne and as far east as Königsberg. In 1807 he sent the play to Goethe who in 1808 had it presented at Weimar, but divided into three acts, a theatrical barbarism. The play was finally published in 1811. Here again the theme is deception, both on the part of Adam, a village judge in Holland, and Eva, a girl whom he has placed in a compromising position. Both desire to conceal the truth from Ruprecht, Eva's fiancé, but a supervising judge, investigating the honesty and competence of village judges, is responsible for finally clearing up the matter, disgracing Adam and vindicating Eva, whose quarrel with Ruprecht is resolved. And even Adam, though removed from his judgeship, is, it is hoped, at least innocent of falsifying his accounts.

In *Amphitryon,* however, written in 1806 in Königsberg and published the following year in Dresden (though not presented on the stage until 1899), Kleist develops his theme more subtly. This is the old story of how Jupiter took Amphitryon's place and impregnated his wife, Alkmene, with Hercules. Kleist, once again dealing with deception, in this case Jupiter's deception, remodeled Molière's light comedy into something deeper and richer than comedy by the effect of Jupiter's deception of Alkmene. At the end, the reconciliation of the three protagonists is only superficial, for Alkmene experiences the terrible wound of distrust, not merely of another, but far more deeply the distrust of herself, because of her failure to penetrate Jupiter's disguise and the consequent self-deception. Now Kleist plunges deeper into the problem of deception and is ready to explore its significance in all of human life. One such significance is the pathetic, almost tragic, isolation of Alkmene at the end, her awareness, it would seem, of the asociality of human intercourse. The play is also notable for a stylistic transformation in Kleist's writing — a vastly extended vocabulary and the development of a syntactical style of increasing intricacy, a complexity that involves the reader in the risk of deceiving himself into understanding what he is reading.

These tendencies are intensified in *Penthesilea,* begun in Königsberg, continued in the French prisons in which Kleist was confined after being arrested under suspicion of espionage by the French in Berlin in January, 1807. He was not released until the following July. He finished the play in the fall of 1807 in Dresden, published a fragment of it in the journal he founded in Dresden, *Phöbus*, and published it as a book in the same year. The first attempt to present it on the stage took place only in 1876. Kleist sent the manuscript to Goethe in the hopes that he would produce it in Weimar, but Goethe at once recognized the work as a challenge to the Weimarian ideals of the classical antique, for Kleist used a classical theme to reveal violence and the irrational; and this was long before these factors were recognized as fundamental to the culture of ancient Greece.

In *Penthesilea* Kleist reverses the legend that Achilles killed the Amazon queen, Penthesilea, at the siege of Troy and has Penthesilea kill Achilles. In their first encounter Achilles defeats Penthesilea. She is unconscious and he accompanies her back to her camp, where initially he lets her believe that she has defeated him. They fall in love. In the end, however, he tells her the truth and insists that she accompany him to his home, rather than to hers, to which as an Amazon she must take her captives. They are separated in the struggle between Greeks and Amazons. She is enraged at the deception practiced upon her and above all, it is apparent, at the way Achilles has manipulated her. He now sends her a challenge. He intends to try to fight unarmed, to surrender to her, and to go with her to her home, enjoy her and leave her when he is ready and if she refuses to return with him, thus planning further deceptions and manipulations. Penthesilea, however, is so aroused that she summons dogs and elephants and takes the great bow of the Amazons. She meets him, shoots him through the throat, and while he is still alive sets her dogs on him and herself rends his breast with her teeth. All this she does unconsciously, and although she has Achilles' body brought back with her she has no memory of what has happened. When she does discover what she has done, she kills herself.

Goethe was not alone in being horrified at this version of the story of the Amazon Queen. Many have been horrified since. Yet it is entirely consistent with what Kleist had written so far, except that it goes even more profoundly into human interests, into deception for the purposes of manipulation, and into the superficiality of civilized behavior, including the conventions of warfare. Penthesilea's rage and madness, her unconscious destruction of Achilles, her savagery seem hopelessly inexplicable until we remember that what Kleist is concerned with here is the individual's inability to comprehend his unconscious interests and the superficiality of civilized behavior; beneath which lies the profound asociality of human beings, their capacity to conceive of anything as a hindrance to their self-assertion, and their corresponding capacity to use their utmost power to destroy what is perceived as such a hindrance. The most stunning remark in the play, moreover, is made when Penthesilea recognizes the dead body as that of Achilles and realizes what she has done. She intended, she says, to kiss him, not kill him, and she asks, "What is the difference between a kiss and a bite?" There is none, for ultimately, slaying and loving are acts of asocial aggression, expressive of the will of the individual to impose his fulfillment upon an inimical and resisting reality. By ordinary means of accounting for human behavior, by normal notions of what we call motivation, Penthesilea's violence is inexplicable. But that is precisely Kleist's point — the incomprehensibility of human behavior, as incomprehensible as the world in which man finds himself.

Kleist's next play, *Das Käthchen von Heilbronn,* written in 1807 and 1808, presented in Vienna in March 1810, and published the same year, need not detain us. It is an effort to achieve some kind of popular success of already somewhat worn Tieckian medievalizing Romanticism. But another play, *Die Hermannsschlacht (The Battle of Arminius)*, though not of the same quality as *Penthesilea,* is central to Kleist's thinking. Written in 1808 in Dresden, it was published (by Tieck) only in 1821, and produced only in 1839. Kleist had hoped that it would be widely performed and be an incentive to the not yet active movement against the hegemony of Napoleon. The Wars of Liberation were not to begin until 1813, after Kleist's suicide. His notion was that Germany would see the parallel between its present situation and Arminius' rebellion against the Romans and his defeat of Varus in the 9 A.D. battle of the Teutoberg Wood. Kleist's mode of inciting patriotism, however, was strange, for he reversed the situation of *Penthesilea* and used deceit and bitter hatred to achieve a morally desirable end, the expulsion of an invading foreigner. Thus he establishes deceit and manipulation as necessities for controlling an incomprehensible reality.

Kleist began his last and greatest play, *Prinz Friedrich von Homburg,* in 1809 and finished it in the summer of 1811, probably, though perhaps as early, at least in more or less completed form, as March, 1810, after he had settled down in Berlin at the conclusion of nearly a year of wandering. The play is based on an incident of the 17th century wars of the Elector Friedrich Wilhelm of Brandenburg. In Kleist's drama the young Prince, overeager in battle, disobeys orders and attacks the Swedes before he should have, the third time he has ignored battle orders. A victory is won, but the Elector has the Prince court-martialled for disobedience and condemned to death.

At first the Prince is sure that the Elector is only playing an elaborate charade in order to conform with military protocol, but he is disabused, and pleads for his life to the Electress in the most abject way, terrified and crushed by the sight of the grave that has been dug for him. His beloved, Natalie, Princess of Orange, goes to the Elector and persuades him to grant the Prince his life. The Elector consents on the conditions that the Prince deny that he has been justly con-

demned and disapprove the judgment of the court martial. The Prince
refuses to do so and affirms the justice of his sentence. In the final
brief scene he is blindfolded and led into the garden of the Elector's
palace (the garden in which the play opened) to the sound of the
dead march, convinced that he is to be shot. His blindfold is removed;
the Elector gives the wreath of Victory to Natalie, who places it on
the Prince's head. He faints, is revived, is hailed as the victor of Fehr-
bellin, and asks, "Is it a dream?" The play ends with shouts to renew
the war with the Swedes: "Into the dust with all the enemies of Brandenburg!"

Interpretations of the play have been argued endlessly, but in the
terms proposed here what it suggests is clear enough. In the opening
scene, the Elector plays a trick upon the day-dreaming Prince, so
lost in his fantasies of future love and glory that he is unaware of
what is in fact going on around him. It is clear that the Elector does
not comprehend the imaginative fantasy-loving personality of the
Prince. Yet he must use him. And that he can do only by manipulating
him, and tricking him, and deceiving him. His method is to drive the
Prince into an experience of deepest humiliation, begging for his life
from the Electress. The Elector is at first confused when Natalie tells
him of the Prince's abject collapse, but he sees at once how he can
use it. The Prince can live only if he affirms that the sentence was unjust, for the Elector is sure that the Prince in order to regain his self-
respect will submit to and approve the judgment of the court-martial.
Thus he is required to condemn himself to death, and since he does
so, the Elector frees him. The play is not about how the Prince is
educated into being a responsible officer. His final remark, "Is it a
dream?" certainly suggests otherwise. Like *Die Hermannsschlacht*
the work is concerned with the fact not that deceit and trickery and
humiliation are justifed in social management by responsible power
but rather that they are the only tools responsible power has, since
from the nature of things it cannot understand the personalities with
which it has to deal and which it must use. Manipulation and exploitation are the necessary conditions of social institutions.

In September, 1810, and August, 1811, Kleist published two
volumes of stories, as astonishing as his plays. "Michael Kohlhaas"

was begun as early as 1804 and partly published in *Phöbus* in 1808. "Die Marquise von O. . ." was finished in 1807 and first published in 1808. "The Earthquake in Chile" was written and published in 1807. These were in the 1810 volume. The 1811 volume contained two stories written and published in 1810 "The Beggarwoman of Locarno" and "St. Cecilia, or The Power of Music," and three written in 1811 to fill out the volume: "The Engagement in Santo Domingo," "The Foundling," and "The Duel."

The finest are the first two in the 1810 volume but all the others are of great interest. In the opening sentence of the first story, Kleist defines Michael Kohlhaas as "one of the most upright and at the same time one of the most terrible men of his day." Kohlhaas is infamously and unjustly treated by the servitors of a petty noble; he sets out to rectify the situation, to achieve an absolute justice. And he does so by increasingly violent means. Eventually he reaches his goal; his horses are restored to him in the condition in which he was forced to abandon them, but he himself, because of his crimes, including the burning of cities, is executed. Kleist's concern, of course, is to comprehend how the upright and the terrible can be combined in one man. That they can be combined is no mystery, for personality is as incoherent and incomprehensible as the world itself. Rather, the question is what turned uprightness into terror. And the answer is that Kohlhaas demands of the social world precisely that absolute reason which is the source of the idea of pure justice. Kohlhaas is thus the antithesis of the Elector of Brandenburg and of Arminius (in *Prinz Friedrich von Homburg* and *Die Hermannsschlacht*); and Kleist's point is that the only alternative in social management to deceit, trickery, and manipulation is brute force. And hence Kohlhaas's uprightness is converted into an intense desire, a violent will, to wound that which has been a hindrance to his determination to establish the absolute. Kleist is making a point similar to Hegel's insistence that absolute liberty can be achieved only by absolute violence. It is not stretching interpretation too far, I think, to affirm that in this story Kleist is analyzing the failure of the French Revolution to realize its aims, noble and sublime as they were.

"Die Marquise von O. . .," an Italian noblewoman, is saved from being raped by a group of Russian soldiers, and her savior is a Russian officer, who, then, while the Marquise is not only asleep but unconscious from her terrifying experiences, rapes her himself. Thus later she discovers herself to be pregnant with absolutely no knowledge of how it could have happened. The officer finds her and tries to persuade her to marry him — before she can learn of her condition. She gives a tentative consent, but the Count is ordered to go to Naples. While he is away she realizes that she is pregnant. Rejected by her family she advertises in a newspaper that the father reveal himself. To her horror it turns out, of course, to be the Count. But in the end she marries him and forgives him. What she must do is accept the fact, as he puts it, that the Count is both angel and devil. Her happiness, then, is a condition of her acceptance of the incomprehensibility of human behavior, for no explanation is ever offered by anyone of how the Count, an upright and indeed moral and even noble young man, could have been so criminal. Certainly he is determined to make up for his fault by marrying an attractive and independently wealthy young widow, and had he not gone to Naples on official army business he would have resolved the Marquise's problem by an immediate marriage and thus a successful deception. But he also uses the necessity of the Naples mission to manipulate the Marquise into accepting him, at least tentatively. On the other hand it is equally inexplicable that the Marquise, who is initially presented as a woman of extraordinary refinement and moral sensibility, should, after an initial and not very long-lasting revulsion, have happily married a man who raped her and have fathered by him a whole series of what Kleist calls "little Russians." The story, presented with deep seriousness, suddenly ends in a nearly frivolous manner.

In "The Earthquake in Chile" two youthful lovers are condemned to death for carnal knowledge and the birth of an illegitimate child. An earthquake saves them from execution, but only temporarily; for the reorganization of the people of the city into a social institution, specifically by means of a religious rite, results in their death at the hands of the mob, their accuser being the girl's father. Through a mistake their child is saved, but the child of the man who had befriended them, mistakenly thought to be their child, has its brains dashed out. But this furious action of the mob is entirely the result of the fact of a priest's having persuaded the mob that the earthquake was the punishment of God for the sin of the young lovers. Here, Kleist turns aside from his theme of deceit and manipulation to the significance in human affairs of pseudo-explanations, the self-deceit that rises from the refusal to accept the incomprehensibility of the world. The story is thus a companion piece to "The Marquise of O. . .", the antithesis of that story.

Of the stories in the 1811 volume "The Beggarwoman of Locarno" and "St. Cecilia" are explorations of the impact of the supernatural, the ghostly and the miraculous. In the first, faced with inexplicable and ghostly manifestations, the protagonist commits suicide by setting fire to his own castle — because, Kleist tells us, of sheer weariness of life. In the second, four brothers are driven into insanity by the miraculous appearance at the performance of a sung mass of St. Cecilia herself. In another story, "The Engagement in Santo Domingo," a man kills the girl who loves him, and who is trying to save his life, because he misunderstands her beneficent deception. Discovering his error, he kills himself. In "The Foundling" a decent and upright man turns into a murderer on discovering that the foundling he has taken in is thoroughly vicious. Indeed, he refuses absolution so that he can pursue his enemy in hell. The theme is that of the "Marquise of O. . ." — the inherent contradiction and incoherence of personality.

And finally in "The Duel" a murderer reveals his crime because his alibi was the result of a trick played upon him. And yet, in spite of the fact that the narrator calls him a black-hearted villain, on his deathbed he reveals the truth and saves the lives of two innocent people. The theme is the same as that of "The Foundling," but reversed, so that instead of a good man inexplicably becoming bad, a bad man inexplicably becomes good. To the end of his life, then, Kleist continued to explore the possibilities of what he had broached in *Penthesilea,* the inexplicability of human behavior. There is every reason to believe — and it is scarcely surprising — that Kleist, like the protagonist of "The Beggarwoman of Locarno," committed suicide on November 21, 1811, from sheer weariness with life.

The greatness of Kleist lies in the fact that he begins that ruthless analysis of human behavior which was to become one of the most important and indeed dominating strands of the Romantic tradition during the next hundred years, and beyond. His work is a true realism, for his aim is to undermine the sentimentalities, the consolations, the rationalizations, the pseudo-explanations with which men and women conceal from themselves the true character of their interactions. And yet from that very deceit and self-deceit, manipulation, and self-manipulation can emerge decent and civilized behavior. With his terrible eye for the facts of the matter Kleist cannot even grant himself the consolation of condemning humanity. Perhaps that was what killed him.

Wordsworth — 2   During the first decade of the new century Wordsworth's poetic career moved in a direction to a considerable degree unsatisfactory to him and certainly surprising to us. Coleridge had persuaded him that his great task was to write a vast philosophic poem, but this proposal indicated that both men had not yet by any means fully transcended a now irrelevant culture. The notion that the mark of a great poet was the creation of a long poem, an epic work or a grand philosophical work on the model of Lucretius, is obviously a traditional one, but there was the likelihood which neither Coleridge nor Wordsworth seemed to be able to see, that such a work was no longer appropriate under the new cultural conditions of Romanticism, and perhaps not even possible. And indeed the event itself was to reveal that it was not possible. A long philosophical work depends upon the existence of an explanatory mode unquestioned by the poet and fully sustained by his culture. Furthermore, it traditionally required the capacity to maintain a stylistic continuity over immensely long and uninterrupted poetic spans. Such a style requires a powerful tradition. Neither of these conditions still existed. The function of the kind of explanatory mode required for a long poem is to provide an objectification and simultaneously a source for an unquestionable sense of value, a reified redemptionism. But that was precisely what Romanticism had come to question, indeed, had seen destroyed. Hence the most typical Romantic work is cyclical or episodic; moreover it is not stylistically continuous as, for example, were *Paradise Lost* or Pope's *Essay on Man.*

Already in 1799, if not earlier, Wordsworth had arrived at his notion of "spots of time," as he called them, moments of pure value, although it was to be some years before he arrived at what was to him a satisfactory explanation of what he was talking about. Then, in 1805, he was able to write of

> those passages of life in which
> We have had deepest feeling that mind
> Is lord and master, and that outward sense
> Is but the obedient servant of her will.
>
> (*Prelude*, 1805, XI, 279-273).

Such moments of value are unpredictable; even though we may feel that outward sense is the servant of the mind, they cannot be summoned by willing. It is reasonably clear that Wordsworth is endeavoring to find a substitute for the traditional idea of grace, and above all a substitute that would be purely naturalistic. He is interested in an analytical and psychological explanation of these moments, as is indicated particularly in the way he interprets them as moments of relief from depression. For it is apparent that depression, which he had already referred to as the weary weight of this unintelligible world, is his most frequent emotional experience. What it comes down to is that the immense hopes, the immense confidence in his future as a poet of the highest calling (the subject of "Home at Grasmere") was already, in 1800, failing him. The cultural conditions for a long poem, both its content and its style, were utterly incoherent with the notion of spots of time, with the notion of the moment of illumination, the impermanent and fleeting moment, as opposed to the traditional belief in the permanency of value.

In short, Wordsworth was faced both with the problem of what to write about and the problem of how to write about it. The poem in two parts that he had written in 1798 and 1799, known today as *The First Prelude,* had opened in an odd way. "Was it for this" that

Derwent River sang to him when he was a babe and was a "playmate" when he was older? But there is no antecedent for "this." That antecedent was not to be supplied until early 1801, or more probably not until January to February, 1804, and when it did appear it turned out that what he was referring to was his failure to pursue his vocation as a poet — a failure revealed in the failure of traditional subjects for narrative poetry to interest him and arouse his poetic power: some medieval tale of Britain, some chivalric tale, something perhaps from classic history, or the settlement of the Americas, or from Swedish or Scottish history, or some tale of his own invention. And the other possible theme, a "philosophic Song," he shrank from in the feeling that he was still too immature, too inexperienced in human thought and life. Thus either the theme is unsatisfactory, or else something is wanting in himself. So all the fostering experiences he described in that untitled poem of 1798 and 1799 have come, after all, to nothing beyond the vocation to be a poet but no comprehension of how to bring into existence that high destiny.

For years he was to be faced with demands from Coleridge that he write *The Recluse,* the grand philosophical poem, and it is also evident that his immediate family, his sister Dorothy and his wife too, it seems likely, and perhaps as well his sister-in-law, Sara Hutchinson, kept urging him to do so, or at least kept making it evident that they expected it of him. And it is true that he made an effort in the second decade of the century, composing *The Excursion* as the central of the grand poem's proposed three parts; but beyond that he could not proceed, though he was only forty-four when *The Excursion* was published. Evidently he came to be oppressed, if not tortured, by a sense of his own failure, of his own inadequacy. The almost universal judgment that Wordsworth ceased to be a great poet as early as 1810, or even 1807, is extremely common, even though he did some excellent work long after, even late in life. But there was not much after 1810, and most of it was pedestrian. Others than his family felt that he was frittering away his powers in writing short poems. Thus we must imagine Wordsworth as deprived of the cultural support of even the little group which has ever since the 1790s been the Romantic's substitute for general cultural support. Wordsworth had the little group in 1797 and 1798 in Dorothy and Coleridge, with the occasional addition of Lamb and the partial support of Southey. But by the early 1800s he had it no longer, in spite of the fact that it was perfectly evident that he was not frittering away his time and talent in short poems but instead was writing some of the most successful short lyrics and sonnets of the 19th century, enough to fill two volumes in 1807.

To understand Wordsworth during this decade and probably long after, we must think of a man alienated from his immediate familiars, but alienated in a way neither he nor those familiars understood. This comes out in four sonnets untitled in the 1807 *Poems in Two Volumes* but in subsequent editions called "Personal Talk." It is enough to point out that in these poems he affirms his preference for silence in his own home and family circle, his preference for the company of books, and his willingness to die could he be sure of being numbered among the poets men value — and this after having written (he must have known it) some of the most beautiful poems in the language, though not, to be sure, very many of them. So in 1801 he accomplished very little, except, most illuminatingly, that he both took up once again the so-called *First Prelude,* writing some of what was to become Book III of that poem, and dropped it again.

In 1802, however, he once more began to write short poems. Two of them are particularly instructive, for they are representative of a whole group of poems of these years, in one way or another representative of almost all the poems in the 1807 edition. These are "Resolution and Independence" and "Alice Fell," and they are important because they reveal, though Wordsworth seems not to have grasped it, that the whole tendency of that mode of cultural transcendence known as Romanticism, is analytic, not synthetic. Yet his conception of the long poem, as dictated to him by Coleridge, was synthetic.

In these two poems he is concerned with a most interesting problem. How do individuals whose lives are of the utmost deprivation — one a very old man, endeavoring to gain a livelihood by gathering leeches from a steadily decreasing supply, the other a child, an orphan girl weeping over the loss of her ragged cloak — how do such individuals maintain their sense of the value of existence and therefore of themselves? How do they keep going? And in the first of this pair, it is clear that Wordsworth himself finds it extremely difficult to keep going at all, in spite of the beauty of a morning, so that he cannot but think on "mighty poets in their misery dead." The leech-gatherer evidently keeps going by maintaining his financial independence; the orphan girl by her attachment to a cloak, her equivalent of a spot of time.

In other poems of these years Wordsworth is intensely involved with pursuing this theme, and with finding examples of attachment to life not only in other human beings, such as a Highland girl singing to herself while working alone in the fields, or even such moments in the lives of kittens and dogs and in the most humble of flowers. Some of his most successful moments and poems come when he himself feels such attachments, such illuminative moments, and the poems are not merely celebrations but are more significantly analyses of the conditions in which such moments occur. Yet as early as 1804 he begins to write his celebrated "Ode" to which later he adds the subtitle "Intimations of Immortality from Recollections of Early Childhood." Here he is concerned with his increasing inability to experience moments of value, an inability which he (mistakenly, I believe) universalizes. And again we are faced with the problem of not knowing how seriously we are to take his suggestion (it is hardly more than that) that such moments are evidence of a prior existence. Probably not very seriously. It is more reasonable to believe that he is creating a myth of the transcendence of the mind, and also of how the conditions of human life tend to obscure and perhaps destroy that will of which the pure unhindered expression is responsible for the moments of absolute value.

These various analyses of the conditions of value appear to have been responsible for his rediscovery of the possibilities of the sonnet, a verse pattern which though used by William Lisle Bowles and by Coleridge in his imitative and uninspired youthful poetry had scarcely been used for a serious or "heroic" purpose since Milton. It was exactly what Wordsworth needed, a poetic pattern short enough to make possible a stylistic continuity. His revival was an example of the frequent Romantic turning to forms and artistic modes of the

distant past as a strategy for evading and denying the dominant modes
of the surrounding culture. Furthermore he rediscovered or reinvented
the sonnet cycle, and the cyclical form was to be one of the most
important vehicles of 19th century art — to be found in music, in
the song-cycle, in the cycle of operas, in the cycle of novels; in the
increasing use of recurrent themes in both opera and symphony;
and eventually in cycles of painting. Thus, in the 1807 volume slightly more than half of the separate poems are sonnets, and the second
part of that section of the first volume forms a cycle of twenty-six
"Sonnets dedicated to Liberty," actually his responses to the various
events of the Napoleonic wars.

What the cyclical mode of organizing a work recognizes is that the
creation of meaning is not unique to the artist or philosopher but
in fact is a norm of human behavior. Thus, in the "Ode," Wordsworth can call the child "best Philosopher" because it is creative
of meaning from infancy, a creativity uncorrupted by cultural platitudes. The cyclical form at once admits such creativity is a matter
of moments of illumination and at the same time offers the reader
the opportunity to exercise *his* creativity by building a structure of
meaning from the records of illuminated moments. And this he can
do by analyzing the implied connections among those moments.
And that kind of analysis is exactly what Wordsworth himself accomplished in the *Prelude,* the untitled work he finished in 1805 —
the analysis of the conditions in which moments of illumination occurred and the analytic discovery of the significance of those moments as a sequence.

Either late in 1803 or early 1804 Wordsworth turned again to the
poem he had abandoned in 1801, at first with the idea of writing a
poem in five books and then, as he got into his subject and began to
understand what he was doing, a poem in 13 books (14 in his final
revision, published after his death in 1850). Paradoxically this long
poem is about why Wordsworth cannot write a long poem. Or to
put it a little differently, Wordsworth can engage in an extensive
expression of the poetic imagination only when his subject is the
poetic imagination. Beginning, as we have seen, with the problem
that he cannot engage in a major effort, he turns to the fact that

after his despair over the failure of the French Revolution, in which he had so heavily invested, he was able to recover from that despair and enter upon that period of creativity which lasted from early in 1797 through 1800 and the publication of the second edition of *Lyrical Ballads.* If he could understand how that recovery came about, then he could arrive at what he thought — mistakenly, it would seem — he needed to do, construct a great philosophical poem.

Now the most curious aspect of this ability to write a long poem, though not the poem he wanted to write and fancied he was destined to write, fancied he *ought* to write, is that he did it in the absence of Coleridge, just as the *First Prelude* was written in Germany and Sockburn in the absence of Coleridge. He was able to start again, picking up from where he had left off in 1801, when he knew that Coleridge was leaving England to go to Malta in search of health (a fruitless journey, of course, since his bad health was a direct result of his opium addiction). In January, 1804, Coleridge, who had been with or near Wordsworth much of the time for the past four years, left the Lake country for London and shortly set sail for Malta. He was not to return until August, 1806. In the meantime Wordsworth finished *The Prelude,* probably in May, 1804, and in December, 1806, at Coleorton, the residence in the Midlands of Sir George Beaumont, the patron of both poets, read it to Coleridge. Ostensibly it was written for Coleridge and to explain Wordsworth to Coleridge. But one can be permitted to believe that that was but an excuse to satisfy demands that he get to work on the long philosophic poem. For it is quite apparent that Wordsworth wrote the poem in order to explain himself to himself. The work is the consequence of the collapse of Enlightenment modes of explaining the world, of explaining the individual, and of explaining the relation between the two.

And that is the story *The Prelude* has to tell, the story that has already been presented in the previous chapter. As a narrative, it culminates in Wordsworth's experiences in France and his subsequent despair in the French Revolution and collapse. And so in Books XI and XII the title, the same for both, gives the subject of the poem, "Imagination, how Impaired and Restored." Yet that title is misleading, for in fact Wordsworth cannot tell us how that impairment and restoration occur. The reason is that he conceives of it as an unconscious process, comparing the imaginative life to a river that goes underground and subsequently emerges into light and air. Thus he moves the spots of time passage from its original position in Book I to Book XI, directly after his assertion that he had once again come to stand in Nature's presence, as in boyhood, "A sensitive, and a creative Soul."

And thus he reveals the true character of the poem. First, it is not, as it has often been taken to be, an autobiography. Rather it is an analysis of the conditions of those experiences in which the mind's will is lord and master of the senses. The spots of time are moments of operant imagination. And on the other hand the poem is an analysis of those modes of behavior the indulgence in which have a deteriorating effect on that power and which, as he indicates in his metaphor of the river, drive it underground. What it comes down to, psychologically, is that the memory of those spots of times makes it impossible for the power to experience the reawakening of such illuminative moments. Second, the "spots of time" passage shows how the poem is constructed, what kind of poem it is. Because of these moments it is primarily an episodic poem, so much so that one wonders if it would be a far greater poem had Wordsworth made it a truly cyclical poem, consisting only of those moments of illumination without the connective passages — sometimes of narration, sometimes of a kind of philosophical speculation — together with passages which negate those moments, periods of despair, valuelessness, emptiness, blankness. That he did not do so, that it was to be some time before he consciously wrote cyclical poems in *The River Dudden* and *Ecclesiastical Sonnets,* is but an indication of what we should expect: the fact that the new culture, although he announces its possibility at the end of Book XII, had not yet fully disengaged itself from the old.

But though he cannot really tell us how the imagination is impaired and restored, he does endeavor to offer an explanation of why both of these experiences can happen. Thus, the rest of the poem is devoted to the kind of philosophical speculation which Coleridge wanted him to devote his great work to. And oddly enough, it is an explanation remarkably like one we have already encountered, in Schelling. Indeed, it is so like Schelling's explanation that one wonders if Coleridge had not gained some knowledge of Schelling's *System of Transcendental Idealism,* published in Germany in 1800, and transmitted it to Wordsworth. Perhaps it is not at all probable, yet it was not to be too long before Coleridge became acquainted with Schelling, and it is always necessary to remember that surviving documents give us only a very incomplete notion of what actually happened in the past. Still, it is safer, if not more reasonable, to fall back upon the concept of cultural convergence in order to explain the resemblance.

Regardless, Wordsworth presents us with the notion of both Nature and Man as Spirit, and of Nature imposing itself upon the human spirit in the modes of beauty and of fear. For both Nature and Man are from God. The active imagination, the true source of poetry, brings about an ennobling interchange, and we are reminded of the conclusion to *The Recluse,* perhaps written at this time but most probably between 1801 and 1802, in which, as we have seen, Wordsworth conceives of the relation between Man and Nature in a sexual metaphor, so that both are manifest in an active Will. In Book XIII, "Conclusion," Wordsworth tells of his ascent of Mt. Snowdon in Wales, and of his climbing above the clouds at night into a vast landscape of mountaintops and mist, illuminated by the moon. And from a rent in those clouds arises the sound of waters. The whole scene is to him a metaphor or emblem of the Mind of Nature, and the sound of the waters is emblematic of its unconscious power, balancing the unconscious will of the human apirit. But, and thus he ends the poem: beautiful as nature is, the mind of man transcends it, for it becomes conscious of its own beauty, and thus a thousand times more beautiful than the earth on which man dwells; divine as Nature is, Man is more divine, for he can be conscious of his divinity and of Nature's. And thus Wordsworth still maintains his hope that man may be redeemed into a life of happiness. For it is evident that man's capacity for pleasure, for happiness, and for that intenser happiness Wordsworth calls joy, is proof of man's divinity.

Having finished *The Prelude,* for which he had neither title nor sub-title but simply called *Poem Addressed to S. T. Coleridge,* Words-

worth tried once more to write *The Recluse*. He had the fragment
written in 1800, "Home at Grasmere," to which he had added what
has become known as "The Prospectus for *The Recluse*," published in
1814 in the Preface to *The Excursion*. That passage not only held the
sexual metaphor of the relation of the human mind to nature; it also
defined specifically Wordsworth's theme, "the mind of Man, / My
haunt and the main region of my song." And that is enough, almost,
to explain why he could not write the great philosophical poem; he had
already in *The Prelude* composed his great psychological poem. That
is, when we use the word "mind" we can be concerned either with
what we subsume under "philosophy" or what we subsume under
"psychology." Wordsworth's basic difficulty was in a sense a semantic
one, since the distinction between these two uses of "mind" had not
been established. Misled by Coleridge into thinking he ought to write
a philosophic poem, he was unable to realize that not philosophy
but psychology was his proper subject. The lengthy addition he now
made (completing it some time in 1806) to "Home at Grasmere"
— linking what he had written to "The Prospectus" — is a perfect
instance of his proper subject. It is almost entirely concerned with a
further exercise of his poetic imagination on the Vale of Grasmere,
its further sanctification. In the new section, however, he turns from
the Vale as Nature to the Vale as Human Home, as an emblem of
that community which, as a man alienated from his culture and society,
he so desired. What he is actually doing in this section is endeavoring
through poetic composition to repeat the effect upon him of his
spots of time, to reawaken his mind's will as he had so recently defined
it. This endeavor is intensely interesting as a Romantic strategy, for it
is an instance of that therapeutic self-manipulation of which many
modes are invented by the Romantics to function as substitutes for
prayers uttered under the control of an organized and socially established religion.

Romanticism has been inaccurately and inadequately called "spilt
religion," but that is not the case at all. Rather, for the Romantics —
that tiny segment of the European population — religion and the Enlightenment secularized mode of it had gotten spilt, and it was the
task of the individual Romantic to create a substitute for it. Hence,

Wordsworth quite deliberately and consciously sees his poetic function as priestly in its most significant task, the sanctification of existence. And this makes it easier to understand the divergence between Wordsworth and Coleridge on *The Recluse* and why Coleridge had an unfortunate, even baleful, effect on Wordsworth. For Coleridge wished Wordsworth to write a synthetic poem on the metaphysics of value, a task for which Wordsworth had neither the talent nor the training nor the inclination. What Wordsworth wanted to write was an analytic poem on the psychology of value. The difficulty really lay in the fact that psychology had not yet spun itself off from philosophy and set about establishing itself as a scientific rather than speculative discipline, an ambition by no means adequately fulfilled even today. Indeed, a better label for what Wordsworth was attempting to do than "psychology" is "cultural anthropology," an intellectual discipline and modality then undreamed of. One of the categories of that discipline is indeed that of the "sacred," the study of how all cultures establish and maintain and re-establish after crisis the value of the culture and of the individual members of that culture. It is both a measure of Wordsworth's originality and of the demands that the cultural transcendence of Romanticism placed upon the individual that in *The Prelude* and in "Home at Grasmere" he succeeded in exploring and illuminating the culture of value, the psychology and anthropology of the sacred, to a degree and with an illumination unprecedented in European culture.

Joseph Mallord William Turner (1775-1851)   In the very years Wordsworth was finishing *The Prelude,* publishing *Poems in Two Volumes,* and completing "Home at Grasmere" Turner was deeply involved in the Thames Valley in a new kind of sketching, a breakthrough in his art that was to result in the gradual emergence of his extraordinary style of the mid-19th century, a style to be understood only a century later. His native talent for painting was unlimited and had been manifest from an early age. Indeed he has been called not only the greatest English painter (a judgment it is impossible to dispute) but even the greatest of all European painters. That latter evaluation is at least arguable, for surely no other painter has ever developed Turner's sheer technical mastery of watercolor and oil, or has been able to do with the application of a brush to a paper or a canvas what Turner could. This can be put in an obviously simple-minded and even naive way by asserting that Turner could think of more things to do with a brush loaded with color than any other painter has ever been able to.

Certainly it would have been impossible to guess from his early work the direction his development would take or the greatness of his achievement, except for one powerful indicator: his early and rapid mastery of the available late 18th century styles, first of watercolor and then, in the late 1790s, of oil. That mastery was soon recognized; his genius was soon asserted; and in a few years he became, to judge by the measurement of the income he could earn and the prices for his paintings he could command, amazingly successful. He was even proposed as a full member of the Royal Academy a year earlier than rules of the Academy permitted. And though he was not elected then, he was as soon as he reached the proper age.

He began as a topographical watercolorist, in part earning a living by painting watercolors of gentlemen's estates. Thus from the outset his primary interest was in landscape, and this fact was part of his good fortune, for landscape painting was to become not only more than the equal of the once hierarchically superior history painting, but also the path to the art of the 20th century. So by pursuing the possibilities of landscape, Turner was to arrive in the 1840s at a kind of painting that would have been incomprehensible to his contemporaries had he not known better than to exhibit such paintings publicly. Instead, he did something quite extraordinary. He not only willed them to the nation but he included in the Turner Bequest (not to be fully catalogued or even examined for more than a hundred years) all his sketchbooks, endless watercolors, and hundreds of oils; many of the latter he had bought back from their original purchasers or from their estates. And this extraordinary action gives us the first clue to Turner's self-conception. He realized that his individual paintings, beautiful as they were, derived their full meaning only from their relation to the rest of his work. He conceived his life work, then, as a vast entity consisting of thousands of discrete elements, separate but not truly separable. Thus the thought of that work as a great cyclical unity, each painting being, to use Wordsworth's illuminating phrase, a spot of time — of the artist's time — rather than a mimesis of a place. The analogy between the Turner Bequest and *The Prelude,* finally published only a year before the Bequest was effected by Turner's death, is instructive. And the first indication of what he was about came even before the Thames Valley sketches.

But it is necessary to go back a little closer to Turner's beginnings, and to consider what he accomplished in his first exhibited paintings. Turner's first step was to master those styles of landscape dominant in the admiration of English connoisseurs, the styles of Richard Wilson (1714-1782), the first purely English landscapist, and Joseph Wright of Derby (1734-1797), whose specialty was night scenes. To these should be added the landscapes of Thomas Gainsborough (1727-1788), though these were less important to Turner than those of Wright and Wilson, especially the latter. In addition, there was the whole long tradition of sea pieces by English artists, which, however, were little more than imitations of the Dutch sea-piece painters of the 17th century, vastly admired and widely collected in England. Now what Turner set out to do was not merely to learn from his predecessors, or to imitate them, but rather to rival them, to become their equals in their own styles, and then to surpass them. And this, in the judgment of various of his contemporaries, he succeeded in doing. From 1798 to 1800 he exhibited a whole series of pictures in the style of Wilson, plus several he did not exhibit. In these he showed himself to be Wilson's equal and in some ways his superior. Most significant in his departure from Wilson's style was his addition to that style of a complexity and richness in detail which was different from the typical neo-classicism of Wilson, with its devotion to a formal simplification. In the same years he exhibited a series of sea-pieces which were received with great enthusiasm, recognized at once as surpassing anything of the sort hitherto achieved by an Englishman. And also he showed in the same years two night pieces, demonstrating that he could do whatever Joseph Wright could do.

But that was not enough for him. In English taste the great landscapists were four 17th century artists: Nicolas Poussin (1593/4-1665); Claude Gellée, le Lorrain, known in England as Claude Lorraine (1600-1682); Gaspard Dughet (who took the name of Poussin from his brother-in-law, Nicolas) (1615-1675); and Salvator Rosa (1615-1673). Turner now set out to equal these great artists and to surpass them in spite of the admiration for them by cultivators of the taste for the picturesque. In 1800 he exhibited the carelessly titled "The Fifth Plague of Egypt" (the subject was really taken from the seventh plague), achieving what some critics of the time recognized as equalling or even surpassing Poussin. It was immediately bought by one of Turner's early patrons, William Beckford of Fonthill, whom we encountered in Chapter I. (He was forced to sell it, such were the expenses of Fonthill, in 1807). The explanation for the judgment that it surpassed Poussin lies in the fact that it appealed even more than the work of Poussin to the popular taste and rage for the Picturesque, the culture of emotional lability. Turner met the demands of that culture because he was gifted with an eye for the detail of nature, for minute discriminations, for example, of color or of mountain configurations, and with a prodigious memory for what he saw. His source in the culture of the Picturesque is further indicated by the fact that in 1798, the first year such a practice was permitted, he included in the catalogue of the annual exhibit of the Royal Academy a quotation from Milton to accompany his Wilsonian "Morning amongst the Coniston Fells, Cumberland," and thereafter for some years quotations from James Thomson's *The Seasons,* the first part of which was published in 1726 and which, together with the landscape descriptions in *Paradise Lost,* was the chief literary source of Picturesque culture.

The next important forward step for Turner was made possible by the Peace of Amiens. So in 1802, after having been elected in February to full membership in the Royal Academy, he set out in July on the first of many trips to the continent. This journey gave him his first experience with the mountain scenery of Switzerland and just as important (as it was at the same time to Ingres) on his return through Paris his opportunity to see, to examine, and to study intensely the great collection of Italian old masters which Napoleon

Joseph Mallord William Turner
Falls of the Rhine at Schaffhausen
reproduced courtesy, Museum of Fine Arts, Boston. Purchased with bequest of
Allice Marian Curtis and from Special Picture Fund

had stolen from Italy and assembled in the Louvre. Titian particularly interested him, and especially Titian's technique and his color-
ing. There were as yet in England no great public collections and
museums of art, only private collections, such as Beckford's purchase
of a group of "Altieri" Claudes, which Turner was able to see. Hence
the importance of his Paris experience. But even before that, in Switzerland, he had moved in watercolor to a new freedom of brushwork,
but this work was in his sketch books and remained there, unknown,
until after Turner's death Ruskin took apart the large Swiss sketch
books and exhibited them.

The combination of these two experiences meant an important
new step towards transcending the limitations of the late neo-classical style in which he was still enmeshed. The first public assertion
of that freedom came, it would appear, in "Calais Pier, with French
Poissards Preparing for Sea: An English Packet Arriving," exhibited
in the Royal Academy in 1803. For the first time we find in contemporary criticism complaints about "want of finish," a complaint
that was greatly intensified on the exhibition at the Royal Academy
show of 1806 of "Fall of the Rhine at Schaffhausen." Indeed several
critics thought, evidently quite seriously, that Turner was mad. He
had, indeed, violated two closely related neo-classical shibboleths.
First, he had transferred from his Swiss watercolors that freedom
of revealing the brush-stroke. That is what is meant by "lack of
finish," and that charge was to be made over and over throughout the
century against those artists who escaped the painterly platitudes
of the time. It is both amusing and instructive that John Ruskin,
who was to praise it so in Turner, was quite unable to tolerate it in
the work of Whistler. And second, Turner had violated the Enlightenment and by then platitudinous modes of representing nature. He
painted the falling water of Schaffhausen exactly as he saw it, a blur
of spray, instead of in an idealistic mode of what it might look like
if it were motionless.

Even though the Schaffhausen picture was painted three or four
years after he had seen the falls in 1802, it revealed already some of
the results of his intensive work in the Thames Valley, beginning in
1806 and extending through 1808. Some of that work was in water-

color, but the most important consisted of oil sketches, a large series on canvas in his usual size of about three feet by four, and a small series, painted on mahogany veneer. In these, or at least in most of them, Turner departed from his usual custom and painted out-of-doors. And the results are quite evident, for in these works, even more than in the Swiss watercolors, he accomplished what he was clearly aiming at, the escape from the commonplaces of his tradition and a determination to govern his painting by observation of the natural world. To be sure, so pictorial was his imagination that he could not help composing a picture, but that fact does not detract from the freshness of these works. Furthermore, though the watercolors seem certainly to have faded, the oils have not, and they are in a higher key, more brilliant, than anything he had done or that had been accomplished by other artists in the tradition which formed him and from which he was now escaping.

Here, then, was a prime example of that cultural transcendence which is the mark of the Romantic, that determination, as in the nature poetry of Wordsworth, to paint the natural world as if it had never been painted before. One of the results of his new convictions and perceptions was "Sun Rising through Vapor; Fishermen Cleaning and Selling Fish" (exhibited 1807). In 1831, writing his second will, Turner bequeathed this painting to the National Gallery with the proviso that it hang next to pictures by Claude Lorraine. It is clear that he believed that he had in fact surpassed Claude. The painting is but an early example of how the work in the Thames Valley was responsible for the striking alteration and development of his style in the last years of the decade. Not only did he paint in a much higher key, but also the freshness of his observation continued, his transcendence of the conventions of picturesque and neo-classical landscape painting. This is particularly noticeable in his skies. In earlier years the clouds were the clouds of convention, convincing enough if one did not examine them with any care. In his new paintings, however, the skies were completely innovative. When one studies these skies and then looks at actual skies, one realizes that one has never really seen skies. That is, it is not only true that painters transform the world according to conventions, but moreover that we actually see the world in terms of conventions — abstractions or visual categorizations which are the norms of anyone's perceptions. That is why we so readily accept the conventions of painters. Visually we live in a world of platitudes as much as we do verbally. Turner's first great achievement was the realization that every one of his paintings, whether the merest sketch or elaborately finished paintings for the Academy and the art market, required an innovative perception of the world.

That continuous innovation requiring a continuous self-transformation had its beginning with his "lack of finish," with the revelation of the brush-stroke; for the brush-stroke is the assertion of the Romantic self, the assertion that the painting is not a mimesis but an expression of the creative artist. Hence the shock of such works to established critics and connoisseurs, the contempt, hatred, and enmity of such a man as Sir George Beaumont, for such responses amounted to a recognition that their pictorial culture had been attacked and vandalized, and that the traditional notions of the Sublime, the Beautiful, and the Picturesque had been dismissed: that they themselves had been dismissed.

Further, the combination of the brush-stroke and the new skies was given further power and new significance by the fact that in these late pictures of the decade Turner lowered the horizon line, with the effect of course that more of the painting was devoted to the sky, often enough at least two-thirds. And such skies! The inexhaustible inventiveness of Turner's skies, the endless subtleties of color, the ever-varied disposition of layers of different kinds of clouds, the infinite variability of cloud shapes make Turner's skies unique in the history of painting. Yet to understand these skies fully it is useful, even necessary, to consider them from a cultural and artistic position of a hundred and fifty years later, the school of painting known as abstract expressionism. Nor is this inappropriate, for abstract expressionism was the outcome of a process in the history of painting *begun* by Turner, a process which may be usefully regarded as the analytic abstraction of color from object and its investigation as a semiotic system in its own right. Without committing oneself to ascribing specific meanings to specific colors, it is enough to point out

that about the time abstract expressionism was emerging, it was discovered that the recovery of patients in hospitals could be retarded
or hastened by the color with which their rooms were painted. Color
can be connected to behavior by thinking of it as subduing, controlling,
and releasing behavioral energies.

Aside from the greatness of Turner as a painter, his cultural importance lies in the fact that he was a landscape artist, thus necessarily conceiving, as he began to realize fully the implications of his
releasing the force of color, that color is a mode of light. Hence one
of his revolutionary techniques was his beginning to paint landscapes
on a white ground, so that light was reflected through the layers of
colored paint. The resulting brilliance was his aggressive assertion
that landscape is not a hierarchically lesser mode of painting, lesser
than historical, genre, or portrait painting, but that it was potentially
and theoretically not only equal to those modes but even superior
to them. The explanation lies in the freedom the landscape artist
has in disposing of color and light for expressive purposes, "expressive" in the sense of symbolizing behavioral energies. Turner's discovery of this significance of color was to be repeated often in the
course of the 19th century by one landscape school after another.
The other modes of painting limit the artist's disposition of light
and color by the demands of the subject, involving figures and locations, usually interiors and exteriors of buildings. But landscape
imposes no such limitations. The color and the light are entirely
at the disposal of the artist. This is why when the breakthrough into
modern art took place in the first decade of the twentieth century,
that breakthrough emerged from the landscape tradition. And that
is why Turner himself in his very latest seascapes, paintings he never
exhibited for he knew that no one could possibly understand them,
actually had by then so analyzed the expressive function of color
that before his death he had arrived at abstract expressionism.

John Constable   On August 1, 1809, John Constable placed that
(1776-1837)   date on the back of a painting that can be said
          with some justification to be the first painting

John Constable
Malvern Hall in Warwickshire
reproduced by permission of the Tate Gallery

in Constable's mature and personal style. It is "Malvern Hall in Warwickshire" (Tate, London), and it represents as much of a stylistic
leap as that which Turner had accomplished in the preceding three
years. The difference is that Constable, who got a much later start
in becoming a professional painter than Turner and had started studying at the Royal Academy only in 1799, had up to that time done
virtually nothing of any great interest. What he had painted was
hardly more than student's work, even though in 1802 he had a painting accepted for the annual Royal Academy exhibition.

The first movement in the direction of new landscape style occurred in the spring of 1808, when he returned from London to his
home village at East Bergholt, Suffolk, between Colchester and Ipswich. His father, a prosperous merchant who owned several mills
in the vicinity, had built there a handsome house, and a few yards
away Constable had purchased an old building and converted it into
a studio. That was in 1802, a year in which he began laborious studies
of nature, for he had arrived at the realization that painting of an
acute and accurate natural realism had never been done. Yet these
studies, which continued for some years, show little of the mature
Constable. On the other hand the oil sketches of the spring of 1808
and of 1809 were of an entirely novel quality and character. Because
they were not painful and laborious, they have a freshness, a spon-
taneity, a naturalness, a convincingness, in spite of the apparent rough-
ness and even, at first glance, carelessness of brushwork. They give
one the impression of having grasped an aspect, a momentary appearance, of the natural world which his early carefully mimetic studies
had nothing of. And it is also quite obvious that they must have been
painted on the spot, in the open air, just like the Thames Valley sketches of the preceding couple of years.

These sketches, then, and the first large-scale effort to apply what
he had learned from them, "Malvern Hall in Warwickshire" (1809),
evince the typical Romantic transition from a conception of a painting
as a mimesis to a conception of it as an expression. And years later
Constable was to compare painting with poetry and music, to emphasize in typical Romantic fashion the role of "imagination," and,
we may add, though he did not, the role of the will − the imaginative

will. An examination of various documents pertaining to Constable suggests very strongly where he got that idea — from Wordsworth and most likely, surprising as it may seem, from *The Prelude,* Wordsworth's great unpublished poem. Nor, as we shall see, is it necessary to exclude the possibility that he was also inspired by the work that Turner had been doing for several years before the spring of 1808.

The Wordsworthian connection emerges from the pages of the diary of Joseph Farington (1747-1821), a very minor painter but one known as the "Dictator of the Royal Academy." Farington's diary is full of information about the London art world from 1793 to 1821. In 1799 he notes his first meeting with the young Constable, but for the present purposes his annotations in the ensuing years of his conversations with Sir George and Lady Beaumont when they called at his studio or when he dined at their London residence are of the greatest importance. For Constable had been introduced to Sir George as early as 1795 at the home of Beaumont's mother in Dedham, only a short walk from East Bergholt, where Constable's father owned a mill, one that Constable in subsequent years often painted. Beaumont recognized Constable's talent, became a patron of the young man, and saw him often. Making allowance for their difference in social station, it is fair to say that in time they became friends.

Now Beaumont was not only a patron of artists, a collector of old masters, and something of an amateur painter himself; he was also intensely interested in literature and in the first decade of the century became patron and friend of both Wordsworth and Coleridge. As we have seen, it was at Coleorton, Beaumont's home in the Midlands, that Coleridge and Wordsworth met after Coleridge's return from Malta. For some years Wordsworth had kept Beaumont informed about the progress of *The Prelude*; but more important, Beaumont, and no doubt Lady Beaumont as well, read it in 1806. They were the only ones aside from Coleridge and Wordsworth's immediate family who knew the poem so early. They were immensely taken by it, enthusiastic to the highest degree. And the importance of Farington's diary is that it preserves the evidence that in November, 1806, Beaumont told Farington about *The Prelude,* and that the Beaumonts were constantly praising both Wordsworth and Coleridge and particularly the Preface to *Lyrical Ballads*. Constable, very likely prompted by Beaumont, whom he often saw when the latter was in London in these years, himself met Wordsworth on a sketching trip to the Lake Country in the summer of 1806. The Beaumonts urged everyone, according to Farington, to read the *Lyrical Ballads,* recently republished in 1805, and the *Poems in Two Volumes* of 1807.

From Wordsworth Constable could have learned three ideas of such importance that together they can account for the sudden transcending stylistic leap he made in the spring of 1808. First is the notion that not the mimesis of nature is important but the *response* to nature. This could easily have come from Wordsworth's "Tintern Abbey" with its contrast between the passive and the active perception of the natural world. Second, from the Preface to the *Lyrical Ballads* Constable could have grasped the significance of the famous description of the origin of poetry as "emotion recollected in tranquility." This is, obviously, an expressive theory of art, utterly different from the mimetic theory of nature poetry as practiced by James Thomson and such followers as William Cowper. And third, perhaps most important, was the synthesis and transcendence of both of these notions in Wordsworth's theory of "spots of time," spots not of natural space, but of the artist's creative perception. And Beaumont could have described to Constable exactly how Wordsworth used these spots of time as the primary building blocks of *The Prelude,* the passages which make that work the masterpiece that it is — which, as suggested above, all by themselves, without connecting tissue, could have made a great poem. And there is a further notion that Constable could have derived from Wordsworth by way of Beaumont, both directly and by way of Wordsworth's poems: the notion of "natural piety," that feeling state which creates a continuity of selfhood, which uses memory for the purposes of sanctification. And in Constable's subsequent work we find him returning again and again to the same scenes in Constable country — the valley of the Stour, the area in which he was born, in which he grew up, and to which he returned again and again. And the result is that the scenes of dozens of his paintings can be exactly located, even to the spot where Constable was standing when he did at least the preliminary oil sketches, just as in the Lake country one can visit even today the exact spots of so many of Wordsworth's poems and passages in his longer works. It is thus probable that Constable learned from Wordsworth the very notion of sanctifying the natural landscape through the creative activity of the artist's imagination.

And yet it is quite possible that Constable could not have learned how to apply what he gained from Wordsworth without the example of Turner. It is notable that he proceeded in the path of "lack of finish" which his patron, Beaumont, had so bitterly and contemptuously condemned in Turner. Turner could have provided the catalytic example because in 1804 he added on to his house in London his own Gallery. There he exhibited pictures shown at the Royal Academy but not yet sold, and, more important, pictures which he did not exhibit at the Academy — pictures which in the crucial years before the spring of 1808 were evidence of his new style, the style worked out in those sketches of the Thames Valley. And indeed some of the large pictures most probably exhibited in the Turner Gallery were of Thames Valley scenes. Given the fame of Turner and the difficulty for young artists of seeing pictures by great masters, it is probable that Constable availed himself of the opportunity. There is some indication that he did so and that what Turner had done had a truly catalytic effect on him; for the sky of "Malvern Hall in Warwickshire" is not like the skies that Constable had painted before, the skies of the pictorial tradition, but it is a sky of England, a sky such as before this only Turner had ever painted.

Walter Scott   That particularity of place and time to which Con-
(1771-1832)   stable devoted his life as a painter, which Turner
                    also, at least in his Thames Valley sketches, was
intensely devoted to, which is to be found in Wordsworth, at least the as yet unpublished Wordsworth, is also a mark and attribute of the poetry in the first decade of the century of Walter Scott, to be found also in his later novels of Scotland. Fully to enjoy the works of Scott, poetry and prose, with a Scottish setting, one needs good

maps, for every movement of the characters can be located most precisely. Nor is that enough, for that particularity was so vivid that it inspired a new business enterprise — that of touring the Lady of the Lake Country north of Glasgow, a tourism still active. Scott's writings inspire one with a longing to see their settings. Moreover in his work is to be found a further particularity, a particularity of behavior or, more precisely, of learned behavior, that is, of culture in the anthropological sense.

In many particulars of his own personality and beliefs Scott was always a product of the Enlightenment, especially of the wonderful Scottish Enlightenment, which in the second half of the 18th century and the early decades of the 19th earned Edinburgh, deservedly, the title of Athens of the North; and his political position, a rational Toryism, was typical of the conservative Enlightenment, having much in common with the anti-Revolutionary position of Edmund Burke. Nevertheless, Scott experienced that cultural dislocation which is the mark and stimulus of the Romantic artist, and he experienced it very early in his life.

When still a child he was lamed, evidently by infantile paralysis, and sent to live in the country with relatives, some thirty miles southeast of Edinburgh — in the 18th century a respectable distance. There he gradually regained his health and, though he was lame the rest of his life, became immensely vigorous and strong; nor did he let his lameness ever interfere in the ensuing decades with his exploration of the Border country, that once turbulent and bloody area of Scotland that bordered on England. The Border warfare having ended, the year 1775, for example — when Scott began to be fully aware of his surroundings in both country and city — was only thirty years distant from the '45, the final effort of Prince Charles Edward, the Young Pretender, and of Scotland to gain the English throne and an equality with England, if not independence. That as a child he met and talked with veterans of the '45 hardly needs to be said. Of greater importance to Scott was his gradual penetration into the life and culture of the Border, into a world as yet virtually unaffected by either the beliefs or the manners of the urban 18th century; a world in which the culture of the past still existed and which, as Scott grew older,

he saw disappear under the impact of modern roads and increasing
ease of access to remote regions – though even today there are large
patches of the Cheviot Hills which lie on the border, stretching northeast from Carlisle, which are virtually roadless and as wild as the Highlands, the depopulation of which had already begun.

Scott was educated to enter the law, and he did so. Thus it was
many years before he began to realize his gifts as a writer. An encounter in the 1790s with the literature of the German *Sturm und
Drang* had an almost intoxicating effect upon him, and he translated
ballads by Bürger and plays by Schiller and others, though his German
was a bit approximate and his translations were filled with mistakes,
even howlers. Nor did he translate these, even though some of his
ballad translations were published, with any sense of entering the
world of professional authorship. That he did so was almost an accident. The effect of the encounter with German literature was to
make him aware of a different culture, a culture which was at once
modern and yet had certain affinities with the popular literary culture
of the border. And of course he had a model much closer to home
in the sophisticated poetry derived from popular origins of Robert
Burns, born in 1759 and dead in 1796, an artist whom Scott always
felt to be infinitely superior to himself.

But then Scott never fully grasped the greatness of his own literary
genius. That originally Scott's ideological interest in popular literature was an example of Enlightenment sentimental primitivism is
unquestionable, but at the same time his work had from the beginning
a vividness and an authenticity quite different from the work of his
English model, Bishop Thomas Percy's *Reliques of Ancient English
Poetry,* published in 1765, reissued with additions in 1775 and 1794.
The contents of this work were quite miscellaneous, extending over
several centuries, but what interested Scott most were the equivalents
and occasionally other versions of the ballads he was collecting while
still a youth from the farmers and shepherds and old wives of the
Border country. Percy found his ballads in the Percy Folio, now in
the British Library, the most important source of ballad literature.
But Scott found his alive in the mouths of living people, one of whom
even complained, quite accurately as it turned out, that to write down

the ballads and publish them would be to destroy the tradition, for they were living oral literature, not written and thus embalmed.

Inspired by his own discoveries, by the German ballads, and especially by Percy, whom he admired profoundly and in time corresponded with, he set out to publish his collection, conflating various different versions of his ballads into a single version and occasionally filling out the metrical pattern with words of his own. For this he has been condemned by modern scholars. Even at the time that kind of emendation of traditional texts was heatedly condemned by such scholars as Joseph Ritson (1752-1803), as well as the great subsequent editor of the *English and Scottish Popular Ballads*, the American Francis James Child (1825-1896). Scott can be defended easily enough by pointing out that such emendations and conflations are typical of the transmission of any oral literature, and scarcely to be avoided. Thus Scott was merely doing to the ballads what had always been done. But this defense is of little importance compared with the fact that in his own way Scott identified himself with the singers of the ballads, that he entered into that tradition, that he absorbed a culture alien to his immediate urban, legal (his father was in the legal profession), and Enlightenment cultural environment. How he did this is of great interest and importance, for it is a striking example of the Romantic capacity to transcend one's immediate culture — so striking indeed that Scott became the first popular Romantic writer in any country, and in time became the best-known Romantic author of Europe, at least in the early decades of the 19th century.

When Scott published his *Minstrelsy of the Scottish Border* (the first two volumes in 1802, a third volume of modern ballads, of which few but Scott's still have any interest, in 1803) handsomely printed and originally issued in Kelso, itself a Scots Border town, it did not consist merely of his version of the ballads he had collected. There was a lengthy introduction giving the history of the Border and of the great families of the Border, and an account of the life and the customs of the region. Part One of the work consisted of "Historical Ballads," and for each of these there was a full explanation of the historical circumstances from which the ballad arose and to which it refers, together with voluminous notes. Part II, "Romantic Ballads," has similar introductions and commentary, though not so lengthy.

Now this kind of research was known at the time as antiquarianism, and later Scott was to write a novel called *The Antiquary,* in which he gives a kind of amused and half parodic portrait of himself as antiquary. Modern theoreticians of historiography make a sharp and usually invidious distinction between the mere antiquary and the true historian, and in his portrait of Jonathan Oldbuck of *The Antiquary* Scott himself seems to accede to that distinction. But if so he was unfair to himself and to the antiquarians of the time and subsequently. For the true descendant of the antiquarian is not the historian at all; it is on the contrary the figure for whom in Scott's time the proper term did not yet exist. And that term is "cultural anthropologist." To read the prose of Scott's *Minstrelsy* is to follow Scott penetrating through history to the culture of the world from which the Border Ballads emerged. That was what made it possible for Scott, even before the publication of Volume III of the *Minstrelsy,* to begin writing that series of narrative poems which became the most successful poems ever published in England up to that time — and considering the size then of the literate and well-to-do public, certainly no more than four or five hundred thousand at the very most, the most successful poems in the history of English literature.

The first three of these long verse narratives are the work of the first decade of the century. *The Lay of the Last Minstrel,* begun in 1803 and published in 1805, *Marmion,* begun in 1807, and published in 1808, and *The Lady of the Lake,* begun in 1809 and published in 1810. In the Preface to the first of these he is perfectly frank about what interested him: "The Poem . . . is intended to illustrate the customs and manners which anciently prevailed on the Borders of England and Scotland . . . . As the description of scenery and manners was more the object of the Author than a combined and regular narrative, the plan of the Ancient Metrical Romance was adopted." Such a romance Scott had already edited and published in 1804, *Sir Tristrem.* But the prosodic model was not taken from such works but from his friend John Stoddart's repetition from memory of what he had heard Coleridge recite of his own poem, *Christabel,* not to be published until 1817. The proper prosody for narrative or long poems then current was either the heroic couplet, still being used by George Crabbe, or the somewhat more modern blank verse in the tradition of James Thomson.

Thus Scott abandoned both the contemporary and medieval models for something having the freedom and lack of specific rules of the most modern and innovative verse. Yet the poems are transitional. As he frankly indicated, Scott was not very interested in plot, in telling a convincing story. Hence, many of the ingredients of the first two poems are derived from the Gothic novel, that late Enlightenment product of the culture of emotional lability, devoted to the possibilities of the categories of the sublime, the beautiful, and the picturesque. Thus in the first poem, *The Lay of the Last Minstrel,* there are supernatural elements, and in *Marmion* Scott does not scruple to use such already outworn devices as walling up alive a nun who has violated her vows. Those are but typical examples of Scott's splendid literary carelessness. And indeed very little of these poems is devoted to narrative at all. Life, customs, scenery, historical situation are his concern. And the importance of history to him is indicated particularly in the extensive notes which accompanied the poems from their first appearance. Indeed, so extensive and so interesting are the notes that one is almost inclined to think that Scott wrote the poems for the sake of writing and publishing the notes. So when he came to writing his Waverley Novels in the next decade he simply included the notes in the body of the narrative itself. And indeed *The Lady of the Lake* is the finest of these works or the poems that followed, for it has almost nothing of the Gothic ingredients in the story, and the narrative itself is, except for the denouement, completely convincing and believable.

Why this was so deserves some consideration. In the first place one of the odd factors in the notes to all three poems is Scott's careful distinction between which characters have a historical origin and which do not, even though by name and behavior they may appear to be historical. Thus Scott clearly makes a distinction between the historical and the fictitious, and in doing so violates the tradition of verisimilitude, that is, of pretending that the fictitious is historical.

Like Friedrich Schlegel in *Lucinde* Scott, in these works, has an analytical attitude towards fiction. He writes fiction not to write to
fiction's ends, but to use fiction as a tool for exploring and establishing an alternative culture. That attitude was not only to have a profound effect on his novels but was indeed to be the reason for those
novels. Scott violates the basic age-old assumption of fiction — the
pretense that it really happend.

This innovative attitude towards fiction makes possible a new attitude towards the writing of history. In *The Lady of the Lake* the
Gothic elements have disappeared. The story could have happened,
and much of it did. By melting together the fictitious and the historical, and by providing notes that make the distinction between
the two, Scott reveals history itself as a construct, as an invention;
that is, any piece of historical writing is temporary, valid only until
further research has invalidated it, as it necessarily must. In this poem
Scott created the first truly modern historical fiction. Historical
fiction, which appears to be and is often said to be paradoxical and
realistically impossible, is possible because the conjunction of fiction
and history analytically implies the fictiveness of historical constructions.

Scott is a Romantic artist because he reveals the artist as willing
the past into existence, but an existence, of course, that is purely
verbal. It is precisely that consciousness of himself as a product of
a historical situation and of several incompatible and unrelated and
genetically differing cultural traditions gives Scott his modern, that is,
his post-Enlightenment and Romantic character. And this first fully
emerges in *The Lady of the Lake* because in that poem he turns away
from the Border history and culture which had formed him and given
him independence from his urban Enlightenment culture. It is his
first work set completely in the Highlands, and a theme is the conflict
between the Lowlands and the Highlands, beginning in the latter
and ending in the former. It is the first work in which his central
theme emerges, that cultural conflict the awareness of which is responsible for Scott's cultural transcendence, for his new insight into
both fiction and history. The fictiveness of both can be sustained only
by Scott's particuarity of time and place. Exact location of both

time and place and exact particularity of behavior, or culture, is what
sustains and supports the fictive character of both imagined and historical construction in Scott's invented historical narratives. In Scott's
fictional world both history and plot are equally justified as excuses
and tools for the particular examination of men and women in a
given place and time. To penetrate through history into culture is
to reveal what we call historical events important enough to be recorded as mere froth on the steady flow of human culture, and of
personality as the revelation of that culture. And at the same time
in Germany things were happening which reveal what Scott was doing
even better than can be revealed by Scott himself and by an examination of Scott.

Des knaben Wunderhorn   In 1805 and 1808 two young Germans,
Clemens Brentano (1778-1842) and Achim
von Arnim (1781-1831), published an anthology of poems written
by various authors during the preceding three or four hundred years.
Like Scott, they were inspired by Percy's *Reliques* and also by Herder's
collections of folksongs published in 1774 and 1778, and Arnim
was familiar with Scott's *Minstrelsy,* the lesson of which he had understood. For *Des knaben Wunderhorn* (*The Boys' Magic Horn*),
like the *Minstrelsy,* is more than and different from the Enlightenment primitivism of these 18th century collections. Brentano and
Arnim were excited by the work of the first German Romantics, particularly Tieck and Wackenroder and Novalis and the Schlegels, with
whom Tieck became acquainted in Jena in the last years of the century.
In 1802 in Göttingen Brentano and Arnim met and in that year went
on a famous Rhine journey in which they first encountered folksong
and folk poetry. In 1804 they decided to publish what they had collected; the first volume appeared in the next year, the second and
third volumes in 1808.

It is a huge anthology, with hundreds and hundreds of poems from
all kinds of sources — old chronicles, folksong fly sheets, popular poems
from the 16th and 17th centuries, and poems by such German poets
as Pitz (1597-1639), Spee (1591-1635), and Gerhardt (1607-1676),

poems that had become popular with the uneducated populace. Nor did they hesitate to change, emend, and improve the texts they selected and to add many poems of their own. This last indicates that their attitude was like Scott's. Their work had made it possible for them, in their own perceptions, to enter into the tradition which they were recording. And it was more than a literary tradition that they were interested in. Like Scott, and partly inspired by him, they wished to bring into life a buried and forgotten world, not a mere literature but a culture. Though only a few years younger than their immediate and inspiring predecessors, they were of a new generation in the sense that they felt the impact of what had been accomplished in the 1790s, and that shock was to isolate them from the culture of the Enlightenment, while at the same time the achievements of the 1790s were not in themselves sufficient or sufficiently realized to provide a complete cultural sustainment or support.

The intricate confusions and almost painful and certainly literary disruptive self-consciousness of Brentano's first important novel, *Godwi* (1801), is a powerful indicator of the disorientation and sense of cultural loss and meaninglessness that Arnim also felt and which he made the theme of his novel *Armut, Reichtum, Schuld und Busse der Gräfin Dolores,* begun in 1808 and published in 1810. Eventually, Brentano was to enter into Catholicism and devote himself for years to a visionary nun, while Arnim was to withdraw to his estates. Their work on *Des knaben Wunderhorn,* then, did not resolve their cultural problem, nor did anything else; but their original work does reveal why they undertook it and what they hoped to accomplish.

What they were endeavoring to discover, to reveal, and to establish was a usable past. What they realized was that the high culture of the middle ages had been superseded at that level by the educated culture of the Renaissance, but that the medieval culture had survived in the poetry of the uneducated, the ordinary, people. Theirs was a work of cultural archaeology. At the conclusion of his introduction to the work Arnim speaks of the past, the present, and the future of *Geist,* a word often said to be untranslatable — and which certainly is not translated successfully by the English "spirit," unless we recognize that "spirit" is also concerned with the capacity of man to give value to his experience, that is, to sanctify it. The poems in *Des knaben Wunderhorn*, no matter what cultural level or sophistication or lack of it they evince, are, then, examples of how human beings are natively, instinctively, as it were, artists and poets. The collection exhibits the unbroken tradition and capacity of the people, without aid or benefit of high or educated culture, to carry out that essential task of man, that task which makes everything else possible — the essential task which to Arnim and Brentano is the task of art, the task of renewing and continuous recreating the capacity of people to make sense of their experience, to organize it, to clarify it, and to ascribe value to it.

The work can be thought of as an effort to prove the validity and truth of Schelling's conception of art as the highest of human activities, and it did so by showing that the artistic impulse exists at all levels of culture and education and social organization. It shows that high art is not sustained by wealth or social power or political or religious alliances or even education or what we ordinarily mean by cultivation, but rather that it is held up and supported by the ubiquity, the universality, of art. And that is the importance in German Romanticism of *Des knaben Wunderhorn*; it showed that the individual innovative artist — condemned to innovation by the failure of tradition, by the Revolution which called that tradition into question, and then by its failure through calling itself into question — nevertheless could achieve a cultural transcendence by founding his efforts on the conviction that as an artist he was engaged in the spiritual essence of humanity, that he could be free of tradition because humanity supported him. *Des knaben Wunderhorn* was a witness to the self-renewing spiritualization of mankind. And it appeared while the great theory of the spirit, of, more properly, *Geist,* was being written and published, Hegel's *Phänomenolgie des Geistes* (*Phenomenology of the Spirit*).

Georg Wilhelm Friedrich Hegel   Like so many of his contempo-
(1770-1831)   raries, Hegel was initially enthusi-
                                        astic about the French Revolution;

but unlike so many of them and in spite of the fact that he rejected the Revolutionary ideals he recognized its tremendous importance for the realization of human freedom, and that it was a "necessary" step in that realization. Yet is is also true that in discussing historical events he does not use "necessary" in a philosophically rigorous way but in the looser sense of ordinary speech. He recognized the failure of the Revolution, but he saw in that failure a far more important success in that the Revolution destroyed so many social forms and institutions that had outlived their usefulness and had become thoroughly decrepit. The explanation for that emptiness of the forms of the Ancien Régime is like his explanation of the value of the Terror: the ideal of Absolute Freedom, he saw, necessarily brings into existence Absolute Tyranny. Thus, the concept to be rescued from the Terror and the conversion of the Revolution in a military despotism is the destructiveness of relying upon pure abstractions. And this is curious, for Hegel has the reputation of having been the most abstract of philosophers, the furthest removed from the empirical world. But in fact exactly the opposite is the real character of Hegel. He is a Romantic philosopher precisely because he saw that the failure of the Revolution was the failure of the Enlightenment. Thus the abstract character of Enlightenment thinking was revealed and its incoherence or, to use a Hegelian term, its diremption or splitting into the abstractions of Nature and Reason with no way of bringing the two together.

In this revelation of the failure of abstraction Hegel saw that world history had entered a new stage, or more precisely that *Geist* had done so. The great problem in Hegel is what he means by *Geist,* just as an equally puzzling and equally important problem is why a man who had written extensively in a style of lucidity and elegance and wit should have written his first book, *Phänomenologie des Geistes,* in what has been called the worst style of any philosopher, so utterly the opposite of lucid that there are passages which professed and professional students of that book judge to be incomprehensible — a book which is at once one of the great works of Western philosophy yet which contains passages that competent philosophical scholars call silly.

Hegel was born in Stuttgart on August 27, 1770, the same year as Beethoven, Hölderlin, and Wordsworth, and just under a year following Napoleon's birth. In 1788 he graduated from the Stuttgart Gymnasium and entered Tübingen Stift. There he became friends with Schelling and with Hölderlin, who was the closer friend and from whom, perhaps, he gained his devotion to the culture of ancient Greece. Hegel was desolated at Hölderlin's fate. In 1793 he passed his final theological examination; his first job was that of a tutor in Bern, which he left in 1796 and, on the recommendation of Hölderlin, who was tutoring in Frankfurt, took a tutoring job there, remaining until 1801. During these years as a tutor he wrote a series of theological essays, not published until 1907. In these he reveals a very typical radical Enlightenment attitude towards Christianity, and it is instructive that instead of the usual Enlightenment favorable attitude towards Jesus he developed a relatively harsh position, seeing not only Christianity in its historical development but also Christ himself as enemies of intellectual freedom. His humanistic ideal was strongly influenced by Goethe, by Schiller, and by Kant's anti-Christian writings of the 1790s. But he objected also to Kant's concept of morality as imposed and moreover as one impossible of being practiced. So sympathetic was he to the Enlightenment and to the Revolutionary ideals that the influence from Goethe and Schiller was untouched by the writings of the early German Romantics, including those of his friend Schelling, though he did not feel himself yet in a position to refute or attack Fichte and Schelling.

With the assistance of Schelling, still his friend, in 1801 he moved to Jena and qualified as a *Privatdozent* at the University, the center of the first group of German Romantics. With Schelling he established a philosophical journal and wrote a number of essays and reviews. When Schelling left Jena in 1803 the journal ceased publication, for Schelling founded a new journal in Würzburg. Hegel continued his lecture courses at the University and soon began to write his system of philosophy. His initial efforts were unsuccessful; into them suddenly burst — it seems the best term — the *Phänomenolgie des Geistes*, sometimes translated as *Phenomenology of Mind* and sometimes as *of Spirit*. As we shall see, both terms are unsatisfactory. The first mention of the work is dated in September, 1806. His publisher was in Bamberg, and he soon sent him the first half of the book; but the publisher was so fearful that Hegel would not finish the work at the specified time (the contract originally stipulated that the completed manuscript be delivered in April, 1806) that he required a bond. Hegel was unable to put up the money, but an old friend, Friedrich Niethammer, did so. Consequently, Hegel had to finish the work in a hurry and wrote the last half of the book in two weeks, finishing on the eve of the Battle of Jena, October 13, 1806, the great battle that marked the end of the Holy Roman Empire. In January, 1807, he read the proofs and sent the famous Preface to his publisher, the last part of the book to be written, and in the opinion of many, the best. Finished copies of the work were ready in April, but the front matter was not identical in all copies, and half of the edition of 750 was unbound. (In the meantime Hegel had had an illegitimate son, Ludwig.) It was two years before the first reviews appeared. By then the disastrous political and military situation had dispersed the faculty of the University of Jena, and in February, 1807, Hegel had to take a job in Bamberg as the editor of a newspaper. He was stuck there until the fall of 1808, when he became rector of the Gymnasium at Nürnberg, where he remained until 1816.

One of the best clues to understanding the *Phenomenology* is Hegel's remark that the ancient Greeks could begin their philosophical speculations with Nature itself and develop their abstractions from that foundation, but that contemporary man had those abstractions ready made and hence his great task must be to find his way back to Nature. He perceived that Kant's famous inability of man to know the thing-in-itself was no more than an exemplification of that devoted and un-reasoning, uncritical, and unanalyzed dependence upon abstractions of which the hollowness was revealed by the Revolutionary Terror and by the inability of the French to realize the abstract ideas professed in the early stage of the Revolution: liberty, equality, and fraternity. Moreover, the depth of Hegel's penetration into European culture is revealed by his realization that this living in terms of abstractions was by no means confined to the elite, educated, cultivated classes, but had penetrated, principally through the impact of Christianity, into the depths of the population.

One of his most brilliant and lucid essays provides a superb clue to the character of his thinking. He did not publish it, nor do we know when he wrote it, perhaps in the 1820s but with almost equal likelihood in 1807 or 1808. It is "Who Thinks Abstractly?"(A translation is to be found in Walter Kaufmann's *Hegel,* New York, 1965). And Hegel's answer is that it is the common man who thinks abstractly, and that only the highly cultivated and intellectually sophisticated and self-conscious philosophically trained man can think concretely. So, when he calls in the Preface for a new relation to the world, he is self-consciously calling for a cultural transcendence marked by the return from abstraction back to the concrete. That this position is convergent with the many other movements towards "realism" or "particularity" which we have seen in figure after figure hardly needs pointing out. And here the term "self-consciously" is of the utmost importance in yielding up the structure of his thinking. Hence it will be necessary to try to understand what he meant by that term.

To begin with, his call for a new and self-conscious relation of the Reason to the Concrete or Nature at once raises several questions. First, what was that immediate relation of the mind to the world with which the Greeks, he thought, could have begun? That is, why did it *necessarily* lead to the high and destructive abstractions which are the intellectual tools of modern man? But at this point arose the most perpexing problem of all. The language, vocabulary and syntax, which Hegel had at his disposal had been developed gradually in order to solve various philosophical problems, the result of those solutions being simply a higher level of abstraction. That language was not designed, therefore, to solve the problem which it itself posed.

The terrible struggle and incomprehensibility and confusion — and, just as frequently, the brilliance and the profundity which the *Phenomenology* exhibits, that Romantic stylistic emergence — was, then, simply the result of using the available philosophical language to solve a problem it was, as it were, designed to avoid and even conceal. Hegel's task was to make that language do exactly the opposite of what it was designed to do. Moreover from this arose the need for a system. Human thinking was already systematic, but it was abstract. To negate that system required a system equally rich and powerful. That lay in the future, since he had already failed to create it. And in that failure arose the whirlwind which burst upon him in the form of the *Phenomenology*. In order to create the system he must first fully comprehend and explain why the system was required. The system itself would require both a return to the concrete and, at the same time, not require the abandonment of the abstract but the preservation of the advantages that abstraction gives mankind — but without that unself-conscious dependence upon abstractions which makes them so destructive. The history of human thought must be saved as well as transcended. Indeed, the transcendence would be possible only if what mankind had already accomplished was saved. One of the great failures of the past was, indeed, the abandonment in each stage of human development of the previous stage.

Hence the *Phenomenology* unfolds in two movements, or tendencies, or purposes, or waves. One is the movement from simple perception to self-conscious spirit as we now — in the first decade of the nineteenth century and in Europe — experience it and can comprehend it self-consciously. The other is the movement of thought from the earliest emergence of civilization in archaic Greece (and also, in Egypt, India, China) to that first decade, that is, to the Hegelian enterprise, the effort to understand what has happened and what needs to be done. Roughly the first part of the book is concerned with the first movement, and the second part with the second; but the two movements intertwine, overlap, support, and undermine each other in what is frequently the most confusing manner imaginable. They come together only in the final pages of the book.

In unfolding the first movement Hegel begins with the simple act of basic perception, which recognizes the mere existence of reality, or, better, Nature, but does nothing to instruct us as to what to do about it. In the clumsy metaphysical language available to him, Hegel asserts the emptiness of the category of Being, a category with neither attributes nor content. What makes action possible is that man brings something to nature from himself. (And indeed contemporary neurophysiology now confirms this.) The most vital fact is that man recognizes that nature is not himself and that something of himself must be put into nature if he is to act. This is the heart of Hegel's departure from Kant, for he saw Kant's system as lifeless and therefore unhistorical. Kant missed the dynamic of Hegel's thinking, which has already been suggested above — negation, contradiction, conflict, struggle, incoherence, resolution at best temporary. Thus, as in absolute freedom leading to absolute tyranny, the full development of any idea, since it is an abstraction from the concrete, necessarily summons into existence its opposite, its negation, its contradiction. This can be clarified if we think of abstraction as an extraction from the concrete, an action which forces the extractor to recognize what has been left behind, unsubsumed and unaccounted for. Thus emerges a negation of the original abstraction.

From these struggles within the mind at a low level of abstraction emerges first Consciousness, the conflict-ridden and gradual realization that the individual can change his behavior without reference to or dependence upon the concrete, upon Nature. Thus he reaches the level of Understanding. But now comes a self-conscious alienation from himself, for he begins to comprehend the fact that if he can change his behavior, that is, his relation to the world, then his behavior was originally formed and established by something other than himself. Thus he negates himself, and now he must negate that negation, which he does by recognizing in others that same alienating self-consciousness he has experienced in himself. (Again and again, the Romantic locates the roots of the ethical in empathy.) Thus, he comes to recognize that the original *creation* of behavior has the same source as the *change* or *modification* of behavior, in "*interpersonal self-consciousness.*" And this recognition leads him to the next stage, the emergence of *Geist,* which is more than, and different from, both "mind" and "spirit."

When Hegel asserts that the category of Being is empty he is taking up the problem that Plato first brought sharply to the fore: the "ideas" with which we organize our perceptions of the world are not derived from the world. The best that Plato could do was to say that they had a divine origin, since he too, having reached the stage of alienating self-consciousness, grasped the truth that the ideas do not emerge from the individual mind. Nor had Kant done much better; hence his attempt to resolve the problem by imposing a conception of duty, that is, by bringing the interpersonal into existence by fiat. Hegel saw clearly the untenability of Kant's solution and the impossibility of his "morality." As the basis for ethical behavior he proposed instead "Sittlichkeit," obedience to the customs of one's culture, and he was fascinated by Sophocles' *Antigone* because it showed two customary traditions of the same culture in powerful and irresolvable conflict or negation. Such are the conflicts of *Geist*. So we are now in a position to propose a series of definitions of that word which will bring out some of the richness with which Hegel invests it.

First, Hegel means by "phenomenology" the description of the spirit, that is (given his mode of going about this problem), the successive modifications of the spirit, without offering a systematic explanation of, for example, a causal character for their being what they are. So "phenomenology of spirit" first can be translated as the "phenomenology of meaning," that is, how man adds to and modifies the concrete in order to be able to respond to it in a way satisfactory to himself, for whatever reason. But this is not enough. A proper extension is the "phenomenology of the emergence of meaning." Even closer to what Hegel is getting at is "the phenomenology of the human creation of meaning." And then, "the phenomenology of the human creation of meaning as a collective enterprise." Finally, "phenomenology of the history of the human creation of meaning as a collective enterprise." Further, the character of this history is not, as previous philosophers had thought, orderly, regular, and unhistorical, or transcending history, but, as Hegel so tellingly and profoundly says, that history is a Bacchanalian revel. Thus he brought into play as no philosopher had ever done, both the eroticization of the human enterprise and the element of randomness.

Now, the source of that randomness is to be found in what might be called the dual character of Hegelian dialectic. One side is, as we have seen, the dynamics of negation, but the other — and this is a point of the utmost importance for Hegel and for the future of European culture — is the encounter between *Geist* and the concrete. Thus, in a famous passage which was later to mean so much to the young Karl Marx, Hegel points out that the establishment of slavery meant that in time the slaves must throw off the control of their masters, since their masters will have sunk back into a self-indulgent enjoyment of abstractions, while the slave is required in his labor to test those abstractions against the world and, to use a modern term, by "feedback" to reveal their inadequacy. And this process reveals the human exercise of the will and the introduction of the unpredicted and the random into the human enterprise. So if we wish to substitute a modern term for Hegel's *Geist,* it is not at all difficult: all that we need is the term "culture" in its anthropological sense — or even more simply, learned behavior.

In the second part of the *Phenomenology* Hegel turns to what he had touched upon both briefly and extensively in the first part, the history of *Geist,* the second of what I have called the two movements or waves of the work. And the bulk of this second part is devoted to the achievements and the ultimate inadequacy and failure of the Enlightenment. What he objected to in Kant, for example, is that Kant made room for faith. But Hegel sees religion, or the various human religions, as no more than moments in the emergence of the spirit. Philosophy, or at least Hegel's philosophy, thus transcends and subsumes religion. And so finally he can say that the Absolute, a fancy name in Kant and Fichte and Schelling for the term "God," is not in some other realm of being but is in fact identical with the development of *Geist,* to its present stage. And that present stage is the recognition that the individual is the creation both of his sensibility (that is, of his senses), and of history — and that the fact that the Absolute is a historical reality means that the new stage in the development of *Geist,* or the Absolute, is the realization of precisely that: history is both the human opportunity and the human Golgotha, or Calvary, where man is both crucified and redeemed.

But that redemption means only that now, with the emergence of Hegelian phenomenology, which is indeed but one of many contemporary similar realizations, man can be fully self-conscious of his self-creation; that his redemption lies in the return to the concrete. Yet given his history he must in that return to the concrete subsume his history, self-consciously, and return not in his original naiveté but with a full systematic resourcefulness of his culture. Having arrived at the Absolute, all he can do is to return to Being and start all over again, only this time knowing what he is doing.

And this is Hegel's final implication. The cultural transcendence which was necessitated by the French Revolution's revelation of the hollowness of its own abstractions — and thus the hollowness of all the abstractions of history (while history itself alone is not hollow) — is that man can and must start again, but now with a cultural freedom (as distinguished from mere political freedom) that he has never known before.

Beethoven — 2   And Beethoven had already arrived at precisely
(1770-1827)   that cultural freedom.   Like the painters of the
decade, Runge, Friedrich, Turner, and Constable,
and by the end of 1803, a few years before any of his cultural companions and equivalents, he had accomplished that cultural transcendence which Hegel with immense struggle and only by forcing his philosophical rhetoric into new directions was about to grasp "intellectually," that is, by verbal manipulation.   The important lesson of this precedence of Beethoven over Hegel (and the similar cultural leaps of the painters) is that what we call "thinking," even of a highly abstract and sophisticated character, can be accomplished in non-verbal sign systems — music and painting — and, as with Wordsworth, in non-discursive language.   One can respond, then, to a cultural situation by manipulating non-verbal signs and thus generate cultural instructions.

It is not surprising, therefore, that Beethoven celebrated the achievement of the Third Symphony with a work of jubilation. He began the "Waldstein" Sonata, Opus 53, in 1803 and completed it during the first half of 1804.   The opening movement begins with an extraordinary theme; nothing in the history of music was like it.   The theme starts with a repetition of chords at a high rate of speed.   It is like a trill, in that it moves neither up nor down, neither increases nor decreases the level of aggression.   And it begins softly, it is a summoning of energy.   And then suddenly it hurls itself upward, and is almost immediately cut short by a descending motif of but a few notes.   A pause, and then another attempt is made. In a few bars Beethoven epitomizes and condenses a summoning of energy, like a horse pawing the ground, a release of that energy towards the world, and the encounter with a hindrance as brutal and rapid as a knife-cut, or rather, to make his point sharper, in spite of that cut the initial thrust continues for a few notes and is then terminated by a second downward blow or cut. The rest of the movement, longer than any previous sonata movement (just as the Third Symphony was longer than any previous symphony), continues this struggle in increasingly dramatic and powerful fashion, until at the end the initial assertion is consummated in a series of powerful chords.

The second movement is a surprise, and the fact that Beethoven discarded the original second movement (subsequently separately published and known as the "Andante Favori" WoO 57) shows both that he was still finding his way towards a new music and also that the work was dramatically, perhaps verbally, conceived. For the second movment is absolutely original. It is built entirely on a single motif, a chord, a hesitant upward thrust in two notes and third higher note, followed by three repeated chords that are like a plateau at which the upward yearning thrust has temporarily arrived. It is a questioning, a wondering of "What next?", a dramatization of the myterious openness of possibility that is the result of a cultural transcendence.

This brief second movement is followed by an answer of great length and pianistic virtuosity, again built almost entirely on a single melody, marvelously varied. It too begins with a repeated note and — after a series of downs and ups lower than the opening note, and indicating a balance of aggression and restraint of aggression within a mood of acceptance of guidance — returns to those opening notes and repeats them frequently, ending inconclusively, then followed by an outburst of scale passages, a freedom of activity. The rest of the movement is then celebratory of that freedom, synthesized with an exquisitely tempered control. Towards the end the speed of the main melody is suddenly doubled, a further indication of energy release; there is a return to the original tempo, and the sonata concludes with an ecstatic affirmation, at first accompanied by trills and then with triumphant chords.

A more powerful and certain affirmation of the joy at arriving at a new mode of being can hardly be imagined, and Beethoven himself was never again to do anything precisely the equivalent. And for good reason. Once the Romantic has arrived at a new cultural plateau he is committed to a life of continuous self-transformation. Not content with a superb and artistically efficient style, he must develop that style to its utmost and then go beyond it. And this Beethoven was shortly to do.

Sonata No. 22, Opus 54, is a kind of concentration or distillation of the Waldstein into a more lyric and subtle form. But the next sonata, Opus 57, No. 23, known as the "Appassionata" (not Beethoven's title), is at once a complement to the Waldstein and a going beyond it. In one significant way the opening of both works is similar — the presentation of the theme, a pause of silence, and then another attempt to get going. The forces unleashed in Opus 57 are, however, far more powerful than those of the Opus 53. The opening phrase moves immediately downwards. It is a withdrawal, but (it is almost at once apparent) a withdrawal in order to summon forces of energy. The movement is now upward, but as in the Opus 53, it is soon blocked; and another attempt is made. But shortly after there is an explosion of violence, a thundering of chords from the bottom of the keyboard to the top. The struggle is now fully under way; and the drama that follows, a drama of release of energy and violent hindrance of the action of that energy, is developed with seemingly endless technical resources. Yet all this struggle ends in failure, and the movement dies away into near nothingness, a few notes repeated in exhaustion. The second movement is a different kind of withdrawal, a turning away from the struggle to a briefly lasting paradise, a stillness, initially music almost without motion and only gradually awakening to gentle and lyrical life. And then, as in Opus 53, the third and final movement breaks into this logical beauty. It begins with a downward plunge, a plunge which is repeated over and over, which becomes as obsession and from which the one apparent escape is not an escape but a momentary and illusory surcease of the continuously reiterated defeat.

And the work ends with a wild plunge into the bass. A tremendous energy has been released and has been defeated. There is, moreover, in this work an anticipation, or first use, of a motive which is to become a universal symbol of an irresistible and opposing power, the opening phrase of the Fifth Symphony, which Beethoven himself, in words which have become outworn but which still must be paid serious attention, called Fate knocking at the door. It appears in the first movement of the Appassionata and is a clear indication that the work is concerned with the encounter with a destructive and inimical force. Beethoven began the work in 1804 and finished it in August, 1805. What it says is that the exultant celebration of a heroic transcendence of one's culture, the subject of the Waldstein, and its consolidation in the next sonata, can only be a temporary victory. The struggle must be renewed at a higher level.

Although Beethoven started work on the Waldstein before he began to compose his opera, *Fidelio,* the composition of that sonata and of the next two, Opus 54 and Opus 57, was simultaneous with the composition of the opera, which was finished in the summer or perhaps the early autumn of 1805. The first performance was on November 20, 1805. The original libretto was written by J. N. Bouilly for Pierre Gaveaux and presented in Paris on February 19, 1798. Bouilly based his story of unjust and tyrannous imprisonment and of rescue by a devoted wife on an incident of the French Revolution which took place in Tours and in which Bouilly himself played the role of official liberator, Don Fernando in the opera, which he set in Spain. Two years later Bouilly wrote the libretto for Cherubini's *Les Deux Journeés*, which Beethoven called the best of opera libretti; perhaps his attention was drawn to *Leonore ou L'amour conujugal* by Ferdinand Paer (1771-1839), an Italian composer and from 1801 to 1806 Kapellmeister at Dresden. In 1803 Paer was in Vienna. Certainly he knew of Gaveaux' opera, for on October 3, 1804, he presented his own *Leonore* at the Dresden Court Theater. There is some reason to think that Beethoven knew Paer's work before composing his own version; later he owned a copy of the score.

To be sure, the re-use of old and frequently used libretti was, as we saw in Chapter One, a commonplace in opera composition, one which was to last well into the 19th century. But there is no doubt that

Beethoven's opera is infinitely superior to Paer's. Not only, of course, was he by far the greater composer — Paer is almost forgotten, though famous in his day — but the story had for him a peculiar personal significance. Florestan is the victim of a cruel fate; he is abandoned in the depths of a dungeon; no one knows who he is; nor do his wife and friends know where he is. He is isolated in despair. His wife Leonore, however, is capable of hope, even where there is no justification for it, and through her own efforts is victorious over the destructive forces. One might say that she is the Waldstein sonata, and Florestan is the Appassionata. The opera ends, of course, in jubilation. Nevertheless much of it is regressive, a reversion to an 18th century musical style. The full musical encompassing of the Hegelian diremption into despair and hope could not be countered and overcome by an Enlightenment situation. Indeed, Beethoven could accomplish that only in music abstracted from any dramatic situation, that is, on the grandest scale, in the symphony, or in something very like a dramatic situation, the concerto, and to that form Beethoven turned in 1805 and 1806 in the Fourth Piano Concerto, Opus 58. In the second movement, in particular, Beethoven created a kind of abstraction from operatic situation, in the great dialogue between piano and orchestra. Here the Romantic self is exposed in its full nakedness and in its effort to achieve an assertion of value not dependent upon existing socio-cultural conditions.

Also in 1805 and 1806 Beethoven wrote the three quartets, Opus 59, which as a sequence move from struggle and despair to an almost jocund affirmation. They are written on a symphonic scale and are further explorations of the three possibilities for music with which Beethoven was now almost exclusively concerned: negation, the judgment of the world as totally oppressive and hindering; an exploration of the possibilities of overcoming such a judgment; and a triumphant affirmation of that overcoming. Thus in Opus 59, No. 1, the slow movement explores new depths of exhaustion, of an enfeeblement of the will, and in the last movement of Opus 59 No. 3, there is a joyous abandonment to vigorous affirmation beyond anything he had yet achieved.

Evidently the next important work, one to which he strangely did not assign an opus number (he usually used an opus number only for works he thought of as important as opposed to pot-boilers and, to use a later term, salon music) was "32 Variations on an Original Theme in C Minor" (WoO 80). This is again a stylistic emergent, one of the most original works Beethoven had yet composed. For the thirty-two variations take hardly more than ten minutes to perform, and each flows into the next without cadence or, frequently, any sharp indication that a new variation has begun. The boundaries of the variations are uncertain, though once under way each variation is clearly a variation of the original theme. The result is a work of extraordinary and even extreme concentration, in which everything Beethoven had learned about expressing a vision of reality as one entirely frustrating to the will is epitomized.

But this exploration meant that the opposite direction could also develop in new ways, ways that went beyond triumphant affirmation into attitudes of purest glowing ease, of transcending beauty. The Fourth Symphony, Opus 60 (1806), attempted something of this sort, not very successfully; in some ways it was regressive to the 18th century symphony. However, in the next work of importance, the Violin Concerto, Opus 61 (1806), Beethoven did accomplish this new vision. Here at last is world of purest value, clear even of the struggle towards triumph. Yet there was still something to be said about that struggle. Early in 1807 he wrote an overture to Collin's play, *Coriolan* (opus 62), the theme being one of tragic struggle and defeat. This work and the "Leonore Overture No. 3,"which he wrote for the 1806 revival of *Fidelio,* are significant in originating what was to become one of the most important 19th century forms, the orchestral tone-poem, the overt admission of a verbally conceived program, that is, a set of instructions determining the emotional course the music is to take. And "overt" is probably the correct word; there are numerous hints that Beethoven covertly controlled his musical invention and judgment by just such verbalizations.

The most famous has already been mentioned, the so-called Fate motive of the Fifth Symphony, Opus 67, conceived as early as 1804. The principal period of composition was 1807, and the work was finished in the early months of 1808, the first performance being on

December 22, 1808. Description of the Fifth Symphony is hardly necessary, but a few points need to be made. The first movement, of course, is completely dominated by the hammer-blows of the opening theme, which had already appeared in the Appassionata Sonata. Reality is conceived of as pure hindrance which forces a lowering of the level of aggression, a subduing of the will. At the end of the movement, however, the theme is reversed in the last measures. The leap is not down but up, and it is an upward leaping fourth, not a downward leaping minor third. The struggle has had a promising outcome, promising enough, at least, for the rest, the breathing space, the paradisaical beauty of the second movement. In the third the rhythm of the opening theme is repeated, but this time without change of pitch, a summoning of energy without commitment to either attack or retreat. After various emotional explorations of the consequences the return of that theme leads without a break (as do a number of works of this period) directly into the enormously scaled and triumphant fourth movement.

Nothing like it, of course, had ever been written. It is the consummation of the process of musical exploration of (let us use a Hegelian term) the *Geist* begun in 1801. And it establishes the pattern for the 19th century symphony. The last movement is the weightiest, the longest, the most important. It is the one that makes the most demands upon the audience — not, like the 18th century last movement, a reward to the audience for briefly exposing itself to trouble. And the final powerful chords, which seem never to come to an end, affirm a readiness to endure any eventuality, and an openness to new and unanticipated experiences.   It is a pure affirmation of the self conceived of as will.

It has been said often enough that this heroic struggle of Beethoven during the first decade of the 19th century, a struggle that yielded such new possibilities for music that Beethoven has long since been called the man who freed music, was the consequence of his deafness and his struggle to overcome the despair into which such an affliction must necessarily cast a musician. But this may be doubted, or at least doubted as the sole factor. Rather, the deafness may be thought of as an aid to what he set out to accomplish in 1801, the creation of a new kind of music. That determination was cultural, not personal; yet the deafness perhaps aided him in his ambition by providing a personal analogy or symbol of the cultural conditions which oppressed him and which he saw brought into question not only by the Revolution but above all by what had become of it. Hence, the famous incident of Beethoven's destroying the original dedication of the Third Symphony to Napoleon because he had made himself Emperor may be thought of as considerably more revelatory of his deepest concerns than was the deafness itself. As we have seen, Beethoven was not an intellectual boor, as he is so often presented, but a genuinely cultivated man, one who read widely in literature and philosophy. It seems unlikely that he read Hegel's *Phenomenology,* but he was one of the few men in Europe who could have understood fully what Hegel was trying to accomplish. For Beethoven was trying to accomplish the same thing.

In 1801. because of existing socio-cultural conditions, Beethoven set out to create a new music. And by 1808 he had succeeded. Thereafter the terrible struggle ebbed away from his music, and from the fury of the past emerged a radiant transcendence. Now he could write the Pastoral Symphony, No. 6, Opus 68, the work of 1807 and 1808. Now he could create a complement and conclusion to the Fifth Symphony. He could forge a musical world of beauty, pleasure, and happiness. His cultural alienation and isolation had truly freed him.

Chapter IV

Romanticism Confirmed
1810-1815

By 1810 the general contours of Romanticism had emerged and had moved towards a dynamic stability. And that stability was dynamic because Romanticism was not only directed to achieve a transcendence of European culture but, more than that, its very principles directed it towards a transcendence of itself, and, moreover, a continuous self-transcendence. The paradox of the Romantic tradition was already emerging — a cultural stability, or, as Hegel would say, a stability of *Geist,* marked by a radical instability. Such a notion, such an ambition, was something new in human history. Certainly instability and even cultural transcendence had occurred again and again in the past, but as a consequence of various social and above all economic forces or factors. It was, in Romantic parlance, unconscious. Now cultural transcendence became conscious and, to use a common Romantic word, willed. And in that willing, Romanticism broke from the European past, even the human past.

Yet it must never be forgotten how few individuals were engaged in this extraordinary enterprise. We have examined the writings, the paintings, the music of twenty-four individuals in England, France, Italy, and Germany. And there are hardly any others to be considered — others, at least, who were originators in this radical development of the European spirit. Yet there were others of importance of whom we know almost nothing. They were the men and women who read the philosophy, the poetry, the fiction, the essays these few produced, and listened to their music and responded to their paintings; and in doing so, they not only responded in a way that must be judged creative (and by Romantic principles *is* creative), but also established these figures by their receptivity and comprehension. Or at least, even if, as we must assume by analogy with the uncomprehending affirmation of radically innovative twentieth-century artists, comprehension was lacking, what was not absent was a recognition that something new had emerged and that that something, whatever it was, was a response of the utmost importance to socio-cultural conditions of a unique, revolutionary, and endlessly urgent character. It is only reasonable to conclude that there were many individuals in Europe who responded to the times as the Romantic artists and philoosphers did, but who themselves were incapable of generating verbal and non-verbal transformations of their response into painting and music and poetry and fiction and philosophy.

We can imagine an ideal figure among this group, perhaps a figure who did exist, an individual of supreme sensitivity and intelligence and knowledge of what was going on in the innovative modes of art and thought. Such a figure by 1810 could have recognized the configurations of the new culture as they had already emerged. It is reasonable to hazard the notion that he would have identified the central thrust and preoccupation of the new culture in its various forms — the creation of value from the individual's own resources, made necessary by the failure of political, social, religious, and cultural systems to provide that value, that affirmation of life which was at the same time an affirmation of the affirming self. If religion is recognized (as so many of the Romantics did recognize it) as the traditional human mode by which the value of existence and of the individual was affirmed — the mode that affirmed the divinity of man — then the central Romantic thrust was not in the ordinary sense religious but was instead an endeavor to identify the function of religion in human life and to ascertain and create an alternative to religion. And that alternative, the Romantics concluded, was art itself, for in the act of the creation of the work of art the artist, they were convinced, echoed and exemplified and fulfilled the creative power of nature, of reality itself, of the universe, even, as the more daring proposed, of a creating Deity. Put simply, the French Revolution and its consequences had destroyed, they were convinced, the traditional paths by which the sacred had always entered human life, the traditional modes of sanctifying existence. It was to be the task of the artist to discover in the act of artistic creation the path by which once more the sacred might enter human life. And that task was made the more difficult by the revelation that the French Revolution had given a new depth to an old belief, Original Sin — vicious behavior in a vicious cause. But now there stood out powerfully an unveiled murderous violence among men, not only released in a just and even admirable cause, but enthusiastically gloried in and rationally defended, though defended probably is too weak a term.

So it is not surprising that certain themes appear and recur which were transformations of that sense of desanctification, the themes of the incomprehensibility of the world, of abandonment, of the waste land. Wordsworth, for example, may never have completely recovered. That possibility is supported by a narrative poem he wrote in 1805 but did not publish until 1819, *The Waggoner,* a tale of how a highly competent man, proud of his job as a carrier of freight in the days before railroads, proud of his equipment and above all of his horses, got drunk one night, not far from Wordsworth's home, and lost his job. The point of the tale is the sheer pointlessness of what happened, an event, an instance, one suspects, among so many events which it is impossible to interpret in any significant or valuable way, a position which Wordsworth dealt with by the jauntiness of his style. And at the same time Wordsworth wrote various narrative lyrics which show an effort to make sense out of triviality, to explain especially trivial transgressions. This failure of meaningfulness the Romantics had to wrestle with, and one result was the central Romantic epistemological theme of the irresolvable tension between subject and object, between mind and world, between man and nature.

But already in these first years of Romanticism there was emerging what was to become the resolution of that tension, a resolution that maintained, as it had to, the irresolvability. So that it was less a resolution than a way of dealing with irresolvability and exploiting it. That way or method had not yet received its name but it was already in existence — pragmatism (or instrumentalism or operationalism), a solution that was to transcend idealism and realism and empiricism and skepticism. Hence, the Romantic re-interpretation of religion was at heart a pragmatic or functional interpretation.

That acceptance of an irresolvable tension between man and his environment meant that old ideologies and beliefs and metaphysics that purported to resolve that tension had to be abandoned, escaped from, vandalized, destroyed. This necessity was transformed and realized in images of wandering, of alienation, of social withdrawal and a concomitant low rate of interaction. Two strategies were of particular importance and power in escaping from the existent dominating, exploiting, and manipulative culture. One was realism, both a rhetorical realism and a realism of imagery in literature and painting. The other was historicism, which provided on the one hand an escape from the existent culture into a model of an alternative culture, and on the other hand a way of abstracting problems from the existent social situation and examining them under different circumstances. Moreover, historicism was also effective in undermining ideologies and beliefs by revealing that they were neither revealed truths nor philosophically·and logically necessary truths but the consequence of identifiable historical forces. Thus realism and historicism went hand in hand, or were opposite sides of the same coin, and in all the arts historical realism became a dominating style. And closely related to that notion is the so frequently found assertion that music is the ideal art or even, at times, that music is the greatest of the arts — though that claim is found less frequently, since the exaltation of art had the effect of subverting the old hierarchy of the arts and placing all of the arts on the same plane of value.

The importance of music arose from the fact that music is non-verbal, for any verbalization necessarily implies, though as weakly as may be, a metaphysical position — one of ideologies and beliefs. Music, therefore, is free of belief, of the kind of assertion possible only to verbal behavior. Music becomes a transformation of the Romantic composer's response to the cultural crisis at the beginning of the 19th century. As Robert Schumann was to say around 1830, "I react to everything that happens in the world; politics, literature, people — whatever it is, I think in my own way about anything that may want to find an escape, an expression in music. That is why so many of my compositions are so difficult to grasp, because they are related to remote interests, interests, incidentally, which are often significant, since anything remarkable in our age seizes hold of me so that I have to give it musical expression." No composer in the Romantic tradition has stated so concisely, so clearly, and so tellingly how the Romantic composer conceived of the task and the poten-tiality of music. Romanticism is at its very roots an anti-metaphysical position. That is why it developed from itself pragmatism, and why music became its most successful mode, successful in the sense that of all the 19th century arts music has survived best in its 20th century conditions.

Chateaubriand — 3   Yet, though looking back we can see the con-
(1768-1848)   tours of emerging Romanticism with some clar-
                   ity, at the time few could do so, and individual
writers and artists were still struggling to discover and to understand what in fact they were doing. So it is not surprising that, particularly in the period from 1810 to the close of the Revolutionary-Napoleonic period in 1815, various individuals fused, or at least put side by side, both Enlightenment and Romantic notions and ideologies. This in-coherence was particularly true of writers; for, as we have seen, it is

much easier to achieve a cultural transcendence in the non-verbal arts than in the verbal ones, and easiest of all in music. Verbal Romanticism requires a far greater self-consciousness and intellectual sophistication in order to separate from each other verbalizations derived from different ideological and cultural sources. Why this should be so is worth exploring, for it is a phenomenon frequently to be encountered in the course of the 19th century and still today. Marx's mixture of Enlightenment and Romantic notions is one of the most striking.

The history of highly abstract (or ideological) verbal constructs reveals two characteristics: first, the author of such a construct is not aware of incoherence; and second, the critic can always discover incoherence. This has become especially obvious in the 20th century, in which the Romantic tradition has developed such powerful analytic or, to use a currently fashionable term, deconstructive capabilities that any supposedly coherent verbal construct can be revealed as incoherent. The process by which this is accomplished is to change slightly the meaning of central terms in the work under critical examination. Such a tactic is possible because meanings are not immanent in words, because the meaning of any utterance or word is the response to that utterance or word, and because the appropriate response is a matter of cultural convention which must be learned with great precision. Furthermore, even in an extensive verbal construct, such as a lengthy philosophical treatise, it is virtually impossible to stabilize the meanings of central terms. Nor, indeed, is such stabilization even desirable, for the development of an argument depends in great part upon exploiting the potentialities of "developing" (that is, changing) the meanings of crucial terminology. Thus, and only thus, can an argument get richness and flexibility.

It is hardly necessary to point out that the author is convinced of the coherence of these changes, since he sees them as developments. The critic has only to see them as changes, rather than as developments, in order to demonstrate internal incoherence in the author's argument. Thus in the period we are concerned with, the term "freedom" can at once depend upon an Enlightenment notion of political rights and a Romantic notion of cultural disjuncture. And such a fusion can be judged to be either intellectual richness or intellectual confusion. A particularly telling example of what we can now see as incoherence can be found in a work finished in 1810. Chateaubriand's *Les Martyrs ou le Triomphe de la Religion Chrétienne* (*The Martyrs, or The Triumph of the Christian Religion*).

In 1802 Chateaubriand set out to write a work which would demonstrate and prove the thesis of *Le Génie du Christianisme,* that Christian art is as capable of beauty as Pagan art, and, moreover, since it possesses moral and religious beauty, is necessarily superior. Now the great literary form of pagan literature was the epic as created by Homer and continued by others, of whom Virgil was the greatest. So Chateaubriand must write an epic. And there was precedent for Christian epics: Dante, Tasso, Milton, Voltaire (in *La Henriade,* 1723). To demonstrate his position adequately, he needed a period in which the Christian and the Pagan were simultaneously present in the culture, and a story in which the conflict between the two might be embodied in two characters, one of whom converts from Paganism to Christianity, while the other falls away from Christianity into Paganism and returns. He needed a story, furthermore, in which the highest devotion to Christianity as superior to Paganism could be presented, that of martyrdom. But he also needed a denouement in which the martyrdom culminated in the triumph of Christianity. He chose, therefore, the persecutions of the Christians under Diocletian and Galerius from 303 A.D. to 306 A.D. (to 313 A.D. in the East). Constantine, having defeated Maxentius in the battle of the Milvian Bridge on the edge of Rome, October, 28, 312, soon after became a Christian and established Christianity as the religion of the Empire. This was the triumph of Christianity which Chateaubriand needed.

Eager as he was to create an epic and to prove that Christianity and the highest form of literature are compatible, Chateaubriand did not attempt a poetic epic but with, he believed, the sanction of Aristotle he set out to write his epic in prose. And to maintain the epic tradition he included epic machinery, God, angels, devils. In addition, the principles of the epic tradition demanded that the writer of the epic be learned, but not in the sense that Chateaubriand set out to be learned. He proposed to achieve a historical accuracy and a topographical accuracy. His historicism itself was innovative, for previous epic writers had not concerned themselves with that mode of learning. Epic learning was rather ideological or theological or philosophical and literary. In setting out to use historical scholarship Chateaubriand was participating in the Romantic drive to realism. And the same drive was to be found in his second endeavor, topographical accuracy. That could be achieved only at first hand.

In 1806 he journeyed to Greece, the Holy Land, and Egypt, terminating his travels in Spain in 1807. (He published an account of these travels in *Itinéraire de Paris à Jérusalem et de Jérusalem à Paris* in 1811). Here again is that interest in realism which, as we have seen, has as its aim the undermining of accepted notions, ideologies, and beliefs. Historical and geographical and social and cultural realism, then, can all be included under the general rubric of Romantic skepticism — not a skepticism about the power of the human mind but rather a skepticism about what the human mind had so far accomplished. But it was precisely this skepticism which undermined Chateaubriand's literary achievement in *Les Martyrs*. His historical and topographical scholarship works against the epic tradition. Thus, though Chateaubriand insists that he is writing an epic and not a *roman,* that is, a novel, the most readable parts are precisely those that have every touch of the novel, and particularly of the historical novel, such as the hero Eudore's battles in Batavia against the Francs and his experiences with the Druids in Brittany. It was these chapters, in fact, that were to inspire the great historian Michelet (1798-1874) to become a historian. It was the evocations of landscape and of times past rather than either the epic machinery or even the love story that gave *Les Martyrs* its interest and made it a successful work. And it was more than temporarily successful, for it gave birth, evidently, to that genre in fiction, opera, and film which takes as its theme the triumph of Christianity over paganism; and in so doing preserves precisely that incoherent fusion, perceived as coherent, of Christianity and historical realism.

And that fusion is indeed incoherent, for in the last two centuries historical and archaeological scholarship has made increasingly untenable the legends of the early years of Christianity. Thus Chateau-briand combined in a single work incompatible factors, one of which was destined to undermine the other. Nor need this surprise us, since, as we have seen, Chateaubriand's belief in Christianity was funda-mentally pragmatic or operational or functional. But in terms of the history of culture the incoherence of *Les Martyrs* is revealed in the fact that the genre of literary fiction was to displace the epic — so that when subsequent writers wished to write on an epic scale, they chose instead the extended cycle of realistic fiction. The first example in France was to be Balzac's *La Comédie Humaine,* but the first example anywhere of the cycle of interacting and interrelated novels was the Waverley Novels of Walter Scott.

Chateaubriand published *Les Martyrs* in 1809, but the work was not complete until 1810, when, in the third edition, he added an "Examen," a defense of both his religious and his literary positions. But more important than this defense was his addition to the text of extensive notes, amounting to, in number of pages, 45% of the text itself, though in number of words perhaps 25% to 30%. And these notes are often more interesting than the text itself. But of greater significance, they denied the self-subsistent validity of that text. An epic, written in poetry or prose, is a work that requires no justifica-tion for itself or its contents other than its existence. To add notes is to propose a justification for its historical accuracy and thus to assert that its value lies in that historical accuracy, not in its theology, its morality or its literary invention. For an author to become his own annotator is to assert that his claims for acceptance rest upon his historical scholarship and topographical reliability. Such authorial behavior is an admission that the epic form and tradition are no longer valid. It proposes to meet on its own ground both the literary and the historical skepticism which the author, unconvinced by his own ambitions, assumes will be the response of the reader, a reader whom he can only imagine in his own image. The annotations, the "Remarks" on the twenty-four traditional books of the epic, reveal Chateaubriand's failure to be convinced by his own precepts, his awareness that he was making a literary effort no longer appropriate to a new cultural epoch. The annotations are the ultimate admission and revelation

of the incoherence of *Les Martyrs* and of its own partial and unsatisfactory appropriateness to a new age.

Mme de Staël   Anne-Louise-Germaine Necker, Baroness de Staël-
1766-1817   Holstein (a title and name she took from the Swed-
                          ish ambassador to France, whom she married in
1785) was Swiss by birth and French by culture and inclination. She
believed Paris the only place in the world worth living in, but was
condemned to spend much of her later years, having contracted the
enmity of Napoleon, in her chateau of Coppet in Switzerland and
sometimes in flight in places as far apart as St. Petersburg and London.
As a child she had grown up in the salon of her mother, once the
beloved of Gibbon, and in the company of the brilliant group that she
assembled around her famous husband, the Swiss banker, who was
called several times to save the finances of the French monarchy and
who ultimately failed in a task in which probably no one could have
succeeded. Mme de Staël was a convinced liberal, the central position
of the Enlightenment — somewhere between Enlightenment Toryism,
such as that of the English Edmund Burke, and Enlightenment radicalism, such as that of Robespierre. Her position on the place of literature
in society, which she published in 1800 as *De la literature considerée
dans ses rapports avec les institutions sociales* was that literature does
and should have its justification in maintaining morality and contributing to social progress.

Her two novels, *Delphine* (1802) and *Corinne* (1807), are manifestations of late 18th century sentimentality, exemplifications of
the culture of emotional lability, given a somewhat more contemporaneous interest by their infection with Enlightenment feminism. Delphine commits suicide when her beloved falls victim to the Revolution.
Corinne dies of grief when her beloved yields to convention and marries according to his family's wishes. Both are destroyed by their
conviction of the possibility of a secular redemption accomplished
by the perfect happiness of erotic fulfillment. It was something Mme
de Staël sought all her life, and only rarely and momentarily found.
Yet the two novels are in no sense critical of the desire that destroys

their heroines. Just as Mme de Staël never wavered in her political liberalism, so she never abandoned the parallel notion of emotional liberalism. She was, in short, unaffected by Romanticism, although she was intimately associated with several individuals who clearly belonged to the new culture, particularly August Wilhelm Schlegel.

It is all the more surprising, then, that Mme de Staël wrote a book which was to become something of a Romantic bible, and that she herself came to be known as the "mother of the Romantics." *De l'Allemagne (On Germany)* was almost ready for publication in October, 1810. Two volumes had passed the censors, with a few changes which she accepted willingly enough, and the third volume was in the process of typesetting when on the personal orders of Napoleon the type was seized and broken up and the entire sizable edition was pulped. Mme de Staël was ordered to leave France within twenty-four hours, although in fact she was given a little more time than that. Enough of proofs and manuscripts was saved so that it could finally be published in England by the famous publisher John Murray in 1813, an English translation appearing in 1814. The explanation for Napoleon's arbitrary action was that Mme de Staël had been annoying him for years, and the implication of the book was that the freedom of thought enjoyed in Germany had been the cause of a cultural creativity in direct contrast with the current sterility of France itself. The explanation lay in German division into numerous states and the absence of centralized authority, even after Napoleon had reduced drastically the number of independent principalities; and all of Germany, and much of Poland as well, was either ruled by members of Napoleon's family or was dependent upon the Napoleonic empire. Further, the emphasis of the book was not on what was currently being accomplished in Germany but what had been accomplished in the past. The cultural life of Austria, particularly in music, was exaggerated by Mme de Staël in order to make the greatest possible contrast with the stultifying Napoleonic control. Napoleon was enraged when he examined the book because its clear lesson was that his régime was opposed to and destructive of the values of civilization, and indeed was inimical to everything the Enlightenment had achieved, including the ideals of the Revolution.

This anti-Napoleonism does something to explain the importance of *De l'Allemagne* to the emergence of Romanticism. In itself it had little to say that was directly pertinent, for, in accordance with Mme de Staël's untouched Enlightenment liberalism, most of the book was about the achievements of German culture in the 18th century, that is, in the German equivalent of the culture in which she had been brought up and which had formed her thinking and her cultural values and beliefs. It is true that she visited Germany several times, that she was familiar with Vienna, that she spent time in Weimar, met everyone and made a deep impression, and that she was similarly successful in Berlin. It is also true that there is every evidence that she was personally familiar with nearly everything she discusses. And above all it is indeed the case that as one reads the book one builds up a picture, inaccurate as many of the details might be, of an extraordinary and, to France and England, an unknown culture — one that was not, as they thought, backward and even absurd and old-fashioned, but one that exhibited a vitality that France and England might well envy, and had done so for half a century. Indeed, as we have already seen, the achievements of Germany were in fact even more striking than Mme de Staël had grasped. Yet even more important than the information about Germany that the book offered was the fact that it yielded a picture, or so it seemed, of an entire culture. Nor was it the culture of a small group located in Edinburgh, or London, or Paris; rather, it seemed, as one read, to be the culture of a nation, though — and this is most important — that nation was not politically unified.

To the Romantics, emerged and emerging, such as the young Thomas Carlyle in Edinburgh, what *De l'Allemagne* first of all presented was the concept and the realization of a culture alternative to that dominant in France and England, a culture, according to Mme de Staël, given its vitality by what she identified as the essence of German intellectual vitality — enthusiasm. And this enthusiasm was the expression of individuals whose achievements were accomplished not in major cultural and political centers but in isolation, in out-of-the-way corners of a vast area of central Europe. What the book offered was the vision of an immense cultural diversity unified by a common enthusiasm, the creation of the individual's search for expression. It offered a vision of what might be accomplished by individual creativity free from organized political and cultural domination and control. In the post-Napoleonic years Mme de Staël's book appealed to the emergent Romantic culture of France as a source of ideas and literary possibilities, as an inspiration to transcend the desiccated and corrupted Enlightenment that was the Napoleonic bequest. Furthermore, in the very years in which the book was published in England, Germany organized itself into the struggle for freedom from Napoleon, a struggle ultimately successful in 1814 and solidified in 1815.

When we consider what Germany has done in the 20th century, it is difficult to grasp what Germany meant in the early 19th. One of the things it meant was that a people could rise and throw off a foreign oppressor. Germany became the emblem of a freedom which France had damaged, even destroyed for a time, for in 1813 the *Befreiungskriege,* the Wars of Liberation, and the battle of Leipzig, the Battle of the Nations, destroyed the Napoleonic control of Germany and soon led to the downfall of the Napoleonic empire. Leipzig was fought on the 16th of October, 1813, the very month *De l'Allemagne* was published in London. Mme. de Staël's affirmation of the superiority of German culture to French culture under Napoleon was vindicated on the field of battle, by the triumph of Prussia and its allies.

Yet in spite of that victory and the victory of Mme. de Staël, it was in time brought home to France and England that the Napoleonic armies had brought to all of Europe conquered by Napoleonic visions of freedom, equality, and political and social rationality that forever changed those countries most affected, particularly Germany and Italy, and that the Germany of *De l'Allemagne* was to be overwhelmed by a petty political and social repression specifically aimed at eradicating the ideas of the Revolution. The splendid and free Germany that Mme. de Staël offered Europe was in part an illusion and was to become almost entirely so. It is only with great difficulty that it was to survive the early decades of the 19th century, and with great loss. It is hardly too much to say that it was to re-emerge only during the Weimar republic after World War I, only to be again destroyed by Hitler, and at least in West Germany to struggle once again towards existence after the Second World War. But to the Romantics after 1815 *De l'Allemagne* offered a vision of a culture of the North, a culture free from the exhausted tradition of the Mediterranean, a Romantic culture, a Gothic culture, the very proof that cultural transcendence is a possibility. Yet even before the first and aborted publication of *De l'Allemagne* a new and different voice was heard in Germany.

E. T. A. Hoffman   In 1809 Ernst Theodor Wilhelm Hoffmann,
1776-1822   having begun his career as a music critic,
                          changed his third name to Amadeus, in honor
of Mozart. Born in Königsberg, the city of Kant, and coming from a family of Prussian lawyers working for the government, he prepared for a legal profession at his family's insistence, though already in the far from poor musical culture of Königsberg his passion had become music. Nevertheless he was reasonably successful in the legal profession and made steady advances, in spite of one setback — the result of his talent for caricature — and by 1804 he had a good permanent position in Warsaw, which had fallen to Prussia on the third division of Poland in 1795. There for the first time he was able to throw himself more fully into music, particularly the administrative side of it, although his amateur composing continued, moving steadily towards professional competence. In 1805 he published a piano sonata, and his *Singspiel* (roughly, musical comedy), *Die lustigen Musikanten* (*The Merry Musicians*), was performed in Warsaw.

As vice-president of a music society he remodeled and did wall paintings for its concert hall and headquarters, conducted the orchestra, and composed fairly extensively. Then, suddenly, in June, 1807, this productive and happy life was broken off by the Napoleonic conquest of Poland, which became the Grand Duchy of Warsaw, though much reduced from its size before the partitions began in 1772. Hoffmann was out of a job, and the Prussian government itself was so poor that it could neither pay his back salary nor give him another position. Then began years which were to turn him into a great writer

— almost by accident. He took the position of music director at Bamberg, a beautiful old city on the Main river in central Germany. Once the seat of a prince-bishop and with a glorious Romanesque cathedral, as the result of the Napoleonic dissolution of the Holy Roman Empire Bamberg passed in 1803 to the Kingdom of Bavaria. Unfortunately, Hoffmann's first attempt at conducting was disastrous and further difficulties developed; for several years he composed incidental music for the theater, and then in 1809 his connection with the theater was ended. Henceforth, he had to depend on teaching music for a living and on what he could gain from a new profession, music criticism.

In 1798 Breitkopf and Härtel, the famous publishers of music in Leipzig, had founded a new publication, *Allgemeine Musikalische Zeitung* (*General Music Journal*) and had appointed a fine musician and critic as editor, Friedrich Rochlitz. In January, 1809, Hoffman sent Rochlitz a strange short story, "Ritter Gluck," which was published in the February issue of the *AMZ*. This was the beginning of Hoffmann's career as a music critic, and his entry into professional writing brought him in a few years to the creation of his marvelous tales, short stories, novellas, and novels, which were to have an enormous influence on all kinds of authors from Russia to the United States. Nor did he give up composing. In 1809 he produced a beautiful *Miserere* for Würzburg, 45 miles west of Bamberg, and in the following years various theatrical works, including *Undine,* written 1812 to 1814, perhaps the first truly Romantic opera, and produced with great success in Berlin in 1816. (The burning of the opera house after fourteen performances and the destruction of all the sets and costumes prevented further performances.)

In 1813 he tried once again to be a successful music director, obtaining a post with a company performing in Dresden and nearby Leipzig, where he was during the Battle of the Nations in October, 1813. But this effort once again failed, and he returned to Berlin. This time, after an interval of severe poverty, he was able to resume his legal career, at first without pay; but in October, 1814, he became a judge of the supreme court. Thenceforth his professional duties and his writing filled his life, with little time left over for music. But to understand his stories it is necessary to grasp his attitude towards music, and it must never be forgotten that his talent for literature emerged from his talent, by no means negligible, for music and from his passion for it, and that his writing was, perhaps, a surrogate for what turned out to be his lesser talent for composition.

In "Ritter Gluck," a story about his encounter with the composer Gluck, long since dead, he introduced, though without realizing immediately what he was doing, several themes which were to play a large part in his subsequent work: the mystery of music, the revenant or ghostly return, the disparity between imagination and realization. But he did not immediately realize what he had originated. So he began what seemed to him his best opportunity, the criticism of newly published music sent to him by Rochlitz, including Beethoven's Fifth Symphony — the first appearance of what earlier in this chapter we have seen as the Romantic attitude towards music; that music is more and other than the imitation of affects, that it gives access to subjective forces and powers not otherwise accessible, and thus is the source of value and of the renewal of value. And while Hoffman was writing criticism he also played with a kind of fusion or combination of music criticism and imaginative literature. He invented a Kapellmeister or music director, Johannes Kreisler, such as he had been to a certain extent in Warsaw, had attempted to be in Bamberg, and was again to attempt in Dresden and Leipzig. The first time he used this figure was in "The Kapellmeister Johannes Kreisler's Musical Sufferings," sufferings that arose from a sensitivity to music so intense and so extreme that he was unbalanced, on the edge of madness.

But again Hoffman did not immediately realize the possibilities of what he had invented, and Johannes Kreisler was not to appear again for several years, and then as a pseudonym for various short essays on the wonders of music. Indeed, it was his editor, Rochlitz, who suggested that he write another piece in the manner of "Ritter Gluck." And so he wrote "Don Juan," published anonymously in March, 1813. As the narrator watches Mozart's *Don Giovanni* from a box to which he has unique access as the guest at a neighboring hotel, the singer of Donna Anna, Don Giovanni's victim, appears to him, and during the intermission, "She said that her whole life was music, and that often while she was singing she believed she grasped much that is secretly concealed in the inner life and which no words express." Because of her he arrives at a new interpretation of the opera, in which he understands Don Giovanni as a magnificently endowed man, destroyed by a desire to find on earth perfect realization and satisfaction, for that desire for perfection opened him to the snares of Satan. And here we find Hoffmann's emerging interest in myth, a matter to which we shall return.

The success of "Don Juan" now at last revealed to Hoffmann the potentialities of his literary talent. He wrote two longer works, "News on the Latest Adventures of the Dog Berganza," (Berganza is taken from Cervantes) the theme of which is the disparity between the ideal of art and the actuality of its realization, and "Der Magniteseur" (i.e., the hypnotist). In 1814 he collected his two published stories, six new and old essays on music, which he called "Kreisleriana," and two new works in two volumes, *Fantasiestücke in Callots Manier* (*Fantasy pieces in the Manner of Callot,* the great 17th century French engraver), which his friend Kunz published for him in Bamberg. And shortly he was inspired to write *Der goldne Topf* (*The Golden Flower* [originally *Chamber*] *Pot.*) That work he published in a third volume of the *Fantasiestücke* at the end of 1814, and in Easter, 1815, he followed with a fourth volume, which included "Die Abenteuer der Silvester-Nacht" ("A New Year's Eve Adventure"), and a second series of six "Kreisleriana," four of which had already been published in 1814. (A seventh from 1816 was added in a second edition.)

A few remarks about three contemporary works will give some notion of the literary and cultural factors in Hoffmann's situation, for all three influenced him, especially the first, Gotthilf Heinrich von Schubert's *Ansichten von der Nachtseite der Naturwissenschaften* (*Notions on the Nightside of the Natural Sciences*), 1808. By *Naturwissenschaften* is meant the Philosophy of Nature — that is, Schelling's. What Schubert was concerned with was the complement to the creative self, or will, or imagination, as illuminated by Schelling, and that complement was the destructive element. Further, he derives from Kant's notion that we know the world only in terms of human interest; and from the evidence of what man does in the world, Schubert thinks, those interests must often be anxiety-ridden, mysteriously fatal, and poisonous to human satisfaction and accomplishment. What the radical Enlightenment lost from European culture was the ancient and explanatorily powerful notion of Original Sin. Schubert revealed as a central Romantic task the restoration of the function of original sin, and with that the function of all mythology, Christian and pagan. So mythology was re-created, but now consciously so. Mythology was understood as products of and therefore insights into those aspects of the human mind otherwise inacessible — that is unconscious, but which are the true determiners of human behavior.

In order to have a clearer understanding of what the Romantics were after, we may look at mythology from a modern point of view, one which is nevertheless a continuation of Romantic thinking. Thus, myths are a creation of language. Man needs to categorize human behavior, to break it down, not merely to understand it but also to control it, that is, to normalize it, for only by constructing normative categories of behavior can he put limits on it and control it by using myths not only as modes of understanding, their secondary function, but as modes of instruction, their primary function.

The gods and spirits in any mythology are categories of behavior towards the non-human or natural world and the human world, that is, human interaction. The enormous instability of all mythologies, including the Christian, is the instability that characterizes all modes or systems of verbalization, or verbal behavior. Myths, like all language, require constant modification in order to encounter, categorize, and integrate into human cultural systems those contingencies the attributes of which make them unsubsumable by current terminology. New stories about the Gods, as well as modifications and additions to old stories, are necessary to give some stability and continuity to our comprehension of existence, just like scientific theories. And, to anticipate the developments of a century, it was the gradual recognition of the structural resemblance of mythology and scientific theory that made it possible for the Romantic tradition to arrive at a notion of exploiting the necessary instability of scientific theory, a notion which gave birth to the enormous and — let us remember the lesson of Schubert — in part *destructive* explosion of science in the 20th century. Nevertheless a secularized age cannot exist without Gods. So much today is under rational and scientific control that the one immensely important categorial function for gods is simply a generalized aggressive competence, generalized because it takes place in the world of games, a world in which nothing is at stake except competence. This is why our popular-culture gods are athletes. And for another segment of population, the mythical equivalents of athletes are artistic performers, pianists, violinists, singers. And these athletes and performers are godlike. Their normative importance becomes apparent when we realize that the norm of human behavior is incompetence, and that social control at its most general and abstract level is simply the effort to maintain as high a level of competence as possible. Thus the Christian deity is defined as (1) all-wise, (2) all-good, and (3) all-powerful, that is, totally competent. Our athletes and musical performers are closer to demi-gods, or heroes of competence under the inspiration of mythical deities — or more accurately, no doubt, avatars of the Christian monotheistic deity, itself divided into three functions.

Schubert was important for the Romantic reconstitution of mythology, a self-conscious reconstitution, at least for the more sophisticated Romantic thinkers and writers, precisely because he located destructiveness in the human psyche and not in nature. But for the adequate comprehension of these forces it was necessary to create a categorial distinction between behavior and the psychic or, more properly, cultural forces which determine that behavior. What Schubert needed, of course, was Hegel's *Geist,* the concept of culture and the subjective manifestation of culture in the personality or psyche of the individual. Hegel can be seen as synthesizing Kant's epistemology of knowledge as determined by human interests with Herder's notion of culture as the determinant.

One famous work of 1811 was important for establishing the separation between the realm of behavior and the subjective-cultural determinants of behavior. This was *Undine* by Friedrich Heinrich Karl, Freiherr (or Baron) de la Motte Fouqué (1777-1843), a minor German Romantic, a kind of pallid and sentimental (though highly popular) imitator of Tieck. In *Undine* Fouqué presented a subject that was to be repeated innumerable times in the 19th century, the water spirit who gains a soul and marries a human being. The latter subsequently falls in love with a real human and speaks angrily to the water-spirit. The water-spirit returns to her element but comes back to kill her husband with a kiss. Not only was Hoffmann attracted to this story, he persuaded Fouqué to write the libretto for his opera. The story became the subject for at least three more operas — by the German Lortzing, the Russian Dargomizhky, and the Czech Dvořák, both the latter using the name Rusalka in place of Undine.

It is impossible to interpret the story of Undine as a mere allegory, particularly since Romanticism makes a distinction between allegory and symbol, rejecting the former in favor of the latter. Allegory was, to the Romantics, little more than a picturing or emblematizing, as it were, of rational concepts. Symbol precisely gives access to and releases those powers inaccessible to reason which Donna Anna felt when she sang. And in justification of the Romantic position we today have the idea of culture, in the anthropological sense; though we have hardly more than a low-level grasp of it, so that myths are the first form of cultural anthropology, which has not done a great deal more than to use abstract terms in place of the names of gods in order to assert the identical functions of gods in different cultures. What can be said about *Undine* is that it presents in narrative, mythical form the dangers, the destructiveness of releasing the unknown and unknowable determinants of human life into consciousness — of becoming aware of these forces, just as the singer of the role of Donna Anna in "Don Juan" is destroyed by her comprehension which the mysterious music gives her both of her part and that of Don Giovanni.

The third work to reveal to Hoffmann the possibilities of literary Romanticism was *Peter Schlemihls wundersame Geschichte*, (*Peter Schlemihl's Extraordinary Story*), published in 1814 by Adalbert von Chamisso (1781-1838), another minor Romantic and friend of Hoffmann's. Schlemihl (Yiddish for a foolish, stupid, worthless fellow) sells his shadow for the purse of Fortunatus, and is execrated and shunned by everyone who sees him in the sunlight. But by giving away the purse and becoming poor he acquires by apparent accident the seven-league boots and becomes a great scientific naturalist. So the shadow merely means the attribute by which an individual is categorized by others as a member of the same category as theirs. A lost shadow means alienation. Only when Schlemihl gives up his wealth does he become indifferent to being an outcast and accepts his alienation. And that alienation releases his imagination and intelligence and is the condition for his greatness as a scientist. In "Die Abenteuer der Silvester-Nacht" Hoffmann took the idea and changed it into the loss of a reflection in a mirror. But Hoffmann uses the idea to explore the self-alienation that can emerge from erotic enthrallment. Moreover, that self-alienation involves an alienation from others; the protagonist's wife dismisses him, telling him not to return until he has regained his reflection.

Hoffmann was exploring a problem derived from Kant but not envisioned by him. We know ourselves just as we know others and know the world, in terms of human interests and culturally constructed categories. Our successful interaction with others depends upon a self-reflection, that is, a construct of ourselves. And just as the source of that construct is mysterious, so the loss of that construct is equally mysterious, or magical. In "Der Magniteseur" Hoffmann explores the reverse of this problem, the destructive effects of the entry into an ideal world, a world of pure value, uncontaminated by ordinary existence. Using the notion of mesmerism, or animal magnetism, or, as it is now known, hypnotism, Hoffmann tells of how a *Magniteseur* leads a young woman in her trances to visions of such supernal beauty that she becomes wholly dependent upon him, and dies. This is but another form of the theme of *Undine*.

The most important work in the four volumes of *Fantasiestücke* was *Der Goldne Topf*, Hoffmann's fullest exploration, so far, of the possibilities of a new mythology. The interpretations of this work have been various, yet none has been satisfactory, and for very good reason. Hoffmann here pushed his newly-discovered art to the limits. The work is designed to resist interpretation, at least beyond the obvious and immediate opposition between the ordinary world and the magical world. For the former, Hoffmann employs a typical Romantic realism, a most platitudinous picture of everyday life in a German town of the time, specifically Dresden. The magical world is in opposition to it and in many ways a structural parallel. It is a world of trans- formation, a world in which ordinary symbols of evil, such as snakes, become symbols of good — but not symbols of the ordinary moral good, like that found in the ordinary, realistically presented world. All that we can be sure of is that the student Anselmus, having suc- cessfully copied manuscripts in a language which he does not under- stand, is rewarded with Serpentina, the daughter of the archivist Lind- horst (who in the magical world in a salamander) and goes to live with her in Atlantis. Veronika, the structural parallel of Serpentina, is rewarded with what she desires, a commonplace man who becomes Hofrat, or Court Councillor. But there is no complete parallel be- tween the two worlds, so that the magical world stands in some kind of explanatory or allegorical relation to the real world. The reason is that Anselmus leaves the ordinary world and enters the magical world. Nor is it enough to label the gold pot, originally, it will be remembered, not a flower pot but a chamber pot, with the allegorical term, the imagination. Hoffmann is doing something quite different. That the magical world is the world of the imagination, or the world of forces which determine human behavior, that it is mythological is unquestionable. But Hoffmann is using mythical narrative in the way in which its advantages are most salient.

A mythical narrative implies meaning, powerful and important meaning, but unlike allegory it does not commit the author to any particular allegorical meaning or explanation, nor to any theory of the source of those interests which are the determinants of human be- havior, neither to the psyche, conscious or unconscious, or the culture, or to religious revelation. For his aim is not to provide such a theory nor to construct such an allegory but rather to release into the story, and therefore into the reader, precisely those forces that are what music reveals — forces both of value and the struggle and error and inimi- cality that obstruct the access to value. If the pot is to mean anything in particular it means precisely that value which can transform even the most debasing and repulsive aspects of human existence. In short, Hoffmann has attempted, and has succeeded, if we do not push irrelevant demands upon him, in creating the experience of meaning-fulness without committing himself or the reader to any particular limiting meaning.

Hoffmann's aim is to create in literary narrative the effect of music, the sense of extraordinarily powerful meaningfulness. Just as in his theory of music he went beyond the notion of imitative affect, so in *Der Goldne Topf* he went beyond the ordinary and traditional limits of literature to penetrate into the unlimited, which he called the in-finite, the realm of experience available, one would think, only to music; but which in fact is also the realm of the truly mythical. Thus appears once again the great Romantic theme of the incomprehensi-bility of human experience, but this time blended with the notion that value lies in the imaginative realization of that very incomprehensi-bility. Or, put another way, music and mythicized literature can convert the rationally and discursively incomprehensible into value-laden imaginative comprehensibility. Thus the experience of under-standing is separated from understanding something, the experience of meaning from particular meanings. For example, the conflict between good and evil can be comprehended without any necessarily limited and unsatisfactory commitment to explanation of the nature or essence of either. So Hoffmann has carried further the task of cultural transcendence by releasing himself as artist and the reader as well from the limiting intellectual chains of the existent culture. The experience he believes music can offer and which he is endeavor-ing to achieve in literature is precisely the necessary pre-condition of cultural transcendence.

In 1814 and 1815 he wrote a work longer than anything he had done so far, *Die Elixiere des Teufels* (*The Devil's Elixir*), published in September, 1815, and May, 1816. It is a complement to *Der Goldne Topf* and explores the possibility of the functional equivalent of myth in a different way. Medardus, a monk of somewhat mysterious origin, is put in charge of the relics of his monastic church, and is tempted to drink a relic from Satan's temptation of Saint Anthony, an elixir that gives one the sense of health, of strength, of boundless capacity and competence, of a desire to experience life free from moral limitations. It is not surprising that Hoffmann first had the idea in

1812, the year before he wrote "Don Juan," for the conception of Don Giovanni in that work is almost identical with the effect of the devil's elixir. The first effect of his drinking the dangerous brew is to become a marvelously effective and almost immediately famous preacher. As an artist he is exposed to the destructiveness of enormous artistic success. He is rebuked by his superior and is sent to Rome on monastic business.

But by a series of apparent chance occurrences he enters into secular life, a life which shortly becomes a life of criminality — hypocrisy. lust, murder — but always with the conviction that some mysterious power over which he has neither control nor of which he has any comprehension is driving him into his infamy — a wickedness which eventually terminates in something close to madness. At length a fragmentary manuscript makes available the secret of his destructive life. An ancestor, a friend and pupil and follower of Leonardo da Vinci had also drunk of the devil's elixir. In three subsequent generations, marked by an immense and almost incomprehensible network of interrelations among corrupt individuals and the innocent whom they seduce and damage, the seed of evil finally works its way to Medardus, who commits every crime his ancestors had committed. And he discovers that the mysterious other self or double, an individual who looks like him and pursues him and haunts him and even adopts his costume as a monk, whom Medardus has mistakenly believed he has accidentally killed, is in fact his half-brother, Viktorin. When Viktorin stabs Aurelia, Medardus' beloved, as she is about to take the veil, Viktorin himself is killed; only Medardus is left of the vicious clan whose seed of evil he has carried in his personality. He dies a penitent.

Die Elixiere des Teufels is literarily regressive, a throwback, and except for two or three factors hardly worth considering among Hoffmann's works. In a way it is a return to the genre which undoubtedly inspired Hoffmann in the first place but which until the writing of this work he had seemed to be quite free; and that predecessor is the Gothic novel. In many ways the work is a Gothic novel, though to be sure a superior example of the genre. The Gothic novel was a product of the late Enlightenment culture of emotional lability, a mixture of the sublime, the beautiful, and the picturesque. What Hoffmann does with it is an illustration of how Romanticism used many artistic devices of the previous cultural epoch and transformed them into something quite different, just as Beethoven transformed the elegant minuet into the powerful and even brutal and sinister scherzo.

For Hoffmann introduces two important new themes. The first is that of the double, in the Viktorin-Medardus relationship. The Gothic element remains in that the doubling is rationalized into the half-brother relationship, but at the same time when Medardus encounters Viktorin he sees himself in his own viciousness and madness. The double was to appear again in Hoffmann's works, and over and over again in the work of his imitators and those influenced by him, and is already seen in the lost reflection and the lost shadow. It depends upon the perception of oneself as other, a recognition that every individual is a social dyad — an individual who sees himself and acts upon himself as he sees and acts upon other individuals. Here begins, one may say, that analysis of the personality in all its complexity and incoherence which was to become one of the great themes of the Romantic tradition. It is no wonder that among those who felt profoundly the influence of Hoffmann was Dostoevsky.

The other factor or theme in *Die Elixiere des Teufels* is, as suggested already, a new way of achieving literarily the function of mythology. And the work is substantially a parable of how history forms the individual. Just as the theme of the double is present to show how Medardus is at once aware of his viciousness and equally aware that he does not understand it, nor why he engages in it — that he is the victim of a fate over which he has no real control, in the same way the elaborate genealogy of Medardus shows the emergence from the past and the formation of that fate, the creation and transmission of the "seed of evil" which Medardus is aware of as growing within him. That genealogy, that tribe of Medardus' ancestors and relations, is the equivalent of the mythical element in *Der Goldne Topf* and other stories. It provides not an explanation of the destructive element in human life but only a pseudo-explanation of a particular strain of evil. Like myth, it is in fact an example without an explanation. It preserves the incomprehensibility of what controls human life and behavior but does not commit either the author or the reader to an abstract explanation of that evil. It uses with splendid effectiveness the myth of original sin, but without the theological metaphysics that had been developed to justify and explain that powerful insight.

And thus obliquely and almost accidentally Hoffmann reveals one of the important functions of history in Romantic thinking. The historical approach to any problem of human life preserves that life in all its complexity and incoherence; and by doing so transcends those abstractions of the Enlightenment responsible for the Revolution and the Napoleonic tyranny, now drawing to an end, and which, therefore, had not provided adequate explanations for human life nor adequate cultural instructions to redeem its evidently inherent failure. So Medardus can redeem himself not into life but only into repentance and death. Thus history in Romantic culture performs the function of explanation while preserving the mysteriousness of the determinants of human behavior. It is another instance of meaningfulness without meaning.

Ingres — 2   Far away from Germany, in Rome, the artist
1780-1867   Ingres was evincing tendencies strangely parallel
to and convergent with some of the themes and interests of Hoffmann, though two artists superficially as different can scarcely be imagined. Yet in Rome Ingres' break with the past was as powerful as Hoffmann's, but unlike the writer, the painter was severely, even brutally, and certainly stupidly, criticized. Indeed, success and recognition did not come to Ingres until 1824 with the exhibition in the salon of that year of "The Vow of Louis XIII." In other words, though Ingres was touted as a classicist in the Parisian war between Classicists and Romanticists, a wholly adventitious and essentially meaningless fight, only with the emergence in the Paris of Romanticism did Ingres achieve recognition, at the same salon in which Delacroix and Constable created such sensations. As we have seen, Ingres' first important painting in Rome was the "Bather of Valpinçon," his first envoi, a picture a winner of the Prix de Rome was required to send back to Paris (1808). It was poorly received,

not too surprisingly, since it was beyond the comprehension of the academic critics and painters in Paris. More surprisingly, even "Oedipus and the Sphinx" of the same year was criticized, for it is very much in the manner of David, less radical than the "Bather," that is, less musical. And the first parallel between Hoffmann and Ingres is that both were musicians and that Ingres achieved a transformation of music into painting, just as Hoffmann achieved a transformation of music into fiction. The second parallel is even more striking.

In a way the most illuminating thing about "Oedipus and the Sphinx" is that it began as a mere academic study of the male nude. Only later did Ingres add pieces to the canvas in order to provide room for the Sphinx, the skeleton, the rocks. He had, it would appear, little interest in the myth he was illustrating. His next *envoi*, finished and sent in 1811, was received even more harshly, and for good reason, for it was an enormous leap from "Oedipus and the Sphinx," and even from the "Bather of Valpinçon." It was truly culturally transcendent and is, I believe it can be said with some assurance, one of the great pictures of the 19th century. Its greatness indeed has not always been recognized, and in fact it may be that only when it was cleaned and exhibited in the important Ingres exhibition of 1967 in Paris could Ingres' achievement be realized. Significantly, in 1979 it was placed at the entrace of the Museum of Modern Art in the Beauborg instead of its normal home in the Museé Granet in Aix-en-Provence, to which it had been relegated in 1834 after it had been bought by the government.

The subject is from the first book of the Iliad — Thetis imploring Zeus to favor the Trojans until the Greeks give Achilles, her son, his rights. If, as seems to be the case, Ingres turned an academic nude into Oedipus simply because his pose sugggested asking a question, "Thetis and Jove," as it is often called, was clearly conceived as a revelation of its subject. The colors of "Oedipus and the Sphinx" are typical Davidian colors, brownish, subdued, in order to bring out the sculptural character of Oedipus' body. The colors of "Thetis and Jove" are brilliant. The background of sky is a deep blue, the body of Jove is ivory and that of Thetis a lighter ivory; astonishingly, Jove's robe draped from his shoulder and across his lap, revealing his powerful naked torso, is an extraordinary pink, and Thetis' a strange green. Beyond Jove's eagle, on his left, the clouds have the reddish color of storm and sunset, and his throne is bronze. In contrast to these colors are the God's wild and magnificent black hair and beard. Most astonishingly and quite against the canons of neo-classicism is the one visible breast of Thetis. As she has knelt to Jove and leaned forward on his thigh, her breast has been pressed upward. And similar realistic details are the fold of skin across the indentation of Jove's navel and the gap between the big toe and the second toe, formed by the thong of a sandal, though the sandal he is wearing does not have that thong.

Homer presents Zeus as sitting on the highest peak of Olympus, but Ingres shows him seated on a throne the front of which is carved with Gigantomachia, his war upon the giants and their defeat, and the throne seems to be floating on the clouds boiling around its base and rising up in back of the throne so that Jove's left arm leans and is cushioned upon clouds, an indication of his immateriality. Thetis' awkward pose, her strained neck, her arm, as in Homer, thrust up to Jupiter's chin, her garments falling away from her — all indicate her passionate eagerness to move the God to her wishes. And at the left is the head of Juno, reposing on a cloud, watching with distrust; for, as Homer says, she has been berating Zeus for his aid to the Trojans, and his powerful face is brooding on the problem Thetis presents.

What is Ingres doing in this extraordinary, this glorious, this huge picture, the first sight of which is dazzling, breathtaking? (It is 10¾ by 4½ feet.) In the course of the 17th and 18th centuries in literature and in painting the gods of Greece and Rome lost their divinity. Even the marvelous evocations of Tiepolo on the ceilings of palaces in Würzburg and in Milano could hardly do more than give brilliance to what had become allegorical emblems. The cultural leap of Ingres is central to the Romantic concern, for in this picture he is endeavoring to restore Zeus to his proper divinity, to revitalize mythology. Surely without the self-consciousness and ideological justification of Hoffmann, nevertheless he was engaged in the same task, to strip myth of cultural accretions and distortions and pettiness and restore it to its pristine power and mystery. "Oedipus and the Sphinx" is an academic exercise. "Thetis at the feet of Jove" is ancient mythology

Jean-Auguste Dominique Ingres
Jupiter et Thetis
reproduced by permission of the Musée Granet, Aix en Provence

reborn into energy-laden and magnificent life. Such revitalization of classic myth was to become one of the major themes and preoccupations of the Romantic tradition, well into the 20th century.

One factor in this transcendent leap was Ingres' experience of Italy. On his way to Rome he stopped in Florence for a few weeks, and there the greatest impact was the work of Masaccio in the Brancacci Chapel in St. Maria del Carmine — the beginnings of Renaissance and modern painting; but also the great Medici collections in the Uffizi and the Pitti were available. When he arrived in Rome, he set out to master the art of that city. All this was a revelation to him, for he was plunged, as all sensitive visitors to Italy are, into a past of beauty far beyond anything he could have imagined, even though he had seen the paintings which the Napoleonic armies had stolen from Italy and which were later installed in the Louvre. It must be remembered that all he could have seen in Paris of, for example, the frescoes of Raphael in the Vatican were copper engravings. The color of these paradisaical rooms must have been a revelation to him. The point is that preceding winners of the Prix de Rome were not so affected. One would never guess, from the evidence of their paintings, that they had ever left Paris. It is instructive that the director of the French Academy at Rome granted Ingres a studio outside of the Academy buildings next to SS. Trinità dei Monti at the head of the Spanish Steps.

By the time "Thetis and Jove" had been so badly received in Paris, Ingres' appointment at the Academy had already ended. He had, evidently because of the reception of his *envois,* decided to stay in Rome, and he moved from the Academy to 40 Via Gregoriana, which runs down hill from the piazza in front of SS. Trinità. In 1812 he took a large studio in the monastery of SS. Trinità. But of course one of the deciding factors in his not returning to Paris was the fact that early in 1810 the French occupied Rome. He had already received commissions from the French king of Naples, Murat, who had succeded Joseph Bonaparte in 1807, and the latter had been in possession of Naples as of 1805.

As early as 1810 Ingres received a portrait commission from an official of the occupying French (Charles Marcotte), and a series of such commissions sustained him until the departure of the French in 1814. And he also received more important commissions. The Quirinale Palace was prepared as a residence for Napoleon, though he never came, and Ingres received commissions for two large works, "Romulus Bearing to the Temple of Jove the Arms of the Defeated Acrone" for the second salon of the Empress (1812) and "The Dream of Ossian" for the ceiling of Napoleon's bedroom (1813), a work influenced by Girodet's famous and perhaps satirical or parodistic "Ossian Receiving Napoleonic Officers," which Ingres would have seen in the Salon of 1802, as well as Gerard's "Ossian," exhibited in the Salon of 1801.

Yet one feels that in neither of these commissions was Ingres very interested. Another painting, probably of 1812, of somewhat the same character, was "Virgil Reading the Aeneid to Livia, Ottavia, and Augustus." Ingres left the picture unfinished, and it was ultimately completed by several pupils, many years later. Perhaps of 1813, or perhaps later, is another version, or perhaps a sketch for a further version, without Virgil. The most striking element in this picture is the color of the richly and intricately painted draperies. Far more important to Ingres was his decision to execute a series of paintings illustrating the life of Raphael. But only two were carried out, "Raphael and La Fornarina" (Raphael's mistress) and "The Betrothal of Raphael," the latter evidently painted in 1813 and 1814.

It has been suggested that Ingres identified himself with Raphael, and certainly he was strongly infuenced by him. However, just as important as identification (and probably more important) was the interest in the representative artist — an endeavor to explore the world of artistic feelings, to determine pictorially, using one of the greatest of artists as exemplar, what it means to be an artist. In the various versions of "Raphael and La Fornarina," La Fornarina is seated on Raphael's lap, but the artist has turned away from her and is contemplating one of his pictures; and in the background is one of his most famous paintings, differing in various versions. On the one hand these two paintings are, like Hoffmann's Ritter Gluck, an evocation of a long-dead artist; and on the other they are examples of historical realism, the determination to bring the past into existence again, just as "Thetis and Jove" was the result of a determination to recreate the power of ancient myth.

Four further paintings of these early years in Rome, all small, like the Raphael paintings, show the direction in which his interests were moving: "Paolo and Francesca" (1814); "Don Pedro de Toledo kissing the sword of Henry IV" (1814); "Pietro Aretino and the envoy of Charles V" (1815); and "Pietro Aretino in the studio of Tintoretto" (1815). When a friend and patron, Charles Marcotte, a French funcstonary in Rome, whose portrait Ingres had painted in 1810, expressed considerable reservations about the second of these when it was exhibited in the Salon of 1814 and received quite badly, Ingres defended the picture above all for its truth, that is, its historical accuracy; and various drawings preserved in the Ingres Museum at Montauban testify to his historical research and care. The two pictures involving Aretino show similar interests, not only in the also quite out-of-the-way subjects, but because of the care given to historically correct costumes and furniture. And all three reveal an interest in finding new subjects and in doing so in actual historical events, two of them involving a writer and an artist. The picture of Paolo and Francesca was possibly inspired by Flaxman's illustrations to Dante (1807) and perhaps by Silvio Pellico's play, published in 1815 but performed earlier, one of the first manifestations of Romanticism in Italy. Even before Ingres left Paris there had already appeared an interest in the Middle Ages, and in the styles of medieval miniatures and 15th-century Flemish painting. This was the *style troubadour,* particularly favored by Josephine, Napoleon's first wife. The primary inspiration was evidently Chateaubriand's *La Génie du Christianisme.* And something of that medievalism is to be found in Ingres' painting, showing further his interest in distancing himself from the Davidian tradition and from late 18th century neo-classicism.

That distancing is carried even further in the second great painting of these years in Rome before 1815. It is "La grande Odalisque," signed and dated "1814, Rome." It is over five feet long, and so the nude is, if anything, more than life size. She lies, facing away but with her head turned toward us, in a tumble of silk and fur on a Turkish divan. She holds a Turkish fan of peacock feathers; to the right is a Turkish water-pipe, in the foreground is a Turkish jewel; and her headdress with its heavy gold tassels is certainly supposed to be a Turkish shawl or other fabric. It is the first appearance of orientalism in Ingres' art, a theme to which he was to return more than once, and with some of his greatest paintings, of which this is certainly one.

However, the most salient departure from academic norms is not the rather adventitious and somewhat unconvincing Turkish properties, but rather the nude herself. This extraordinary harem creature is one of what has been called Ingres' monsters, figures of strange physiological distortions. At the time it was hardly recognized that the distortion, the incredibly long back and disproportioned hips, was not error but rather intentional, the "something more" which Ingres added to a reproduction of what he saw, that transformational element in any response which had hitherto been identified as what the artist added to reality as invention. But those inventions also conformed to either real or possible configurations. What Ingres has done is to apply the arabesque, hitherto confined to draperies, to the human form. Something of this can already be seen in "Thetis and Jove" in the long back and strange neck of Thetis, as well as the enormous chest of Jove, so broad in relation to the waist. Now in "La Grande Odalisque" Ingres carries that deliberate deformation of the human body even further, his aim being to embody in paint on canvas the transformational power of the imagination. It is not, as has so often been proposed, a matter of expression, that is, of intensifying possible emotional significance. The odalisque looks over her shoulder at us, out of the corner of her eye, but her face is without expression. The mood of the painting is certainly not one that proposes to inspire in us pity for a victim of the Grand Turk's harem, nor is it particularly erotic. Quite the contrary, and the complaints of those who objected to the distortions were fundamentally that the painting is non-erotic, that it is of frigid calm. No, the work is a Romantic hymn to the "something more," to the power of imagination, not its inventive power, as in the past, but in its transformational power. It is a picture which already hints, though only we at our distance can hear that hint, of the immense artistic transformations of the early 20th century, to what we still call modern art.

The Nazarenes   Yet of these paintings of Ingres the least typical, "Paolo and Francesca," is historically one of the most significant; for it suggests that Ingres was interested in and perhaps influenced by the ideas of a group of German painters who arrived in Rome in the summer of 1810 and settled near the French Academy and even closer to what was to be Ingres' home on the Via Gregoriana. After a few weeks at the Villa Malta, on the Via Sistina, which meets the Via Gregoriana at the Piazza of SS. Trinità, they moved to the then abandoned monastery of S. Isidoro, the grounds of which are across the street from those of the Villa Malta. Indeed, it was the Director of the French Academy who helped the Nazarenes find a place to live in the abandoned monastery. Such a location was precisely to their taste, for they were convinced that only through religion could true art be reached and German art be reborn from the moribund academies and their traditions. The path to that rebirth, they were equally convinced, lay through studying and absorbing the German painters of the time of Dürer and the Italian painters of the time of Raphael and earlier. The name by which they are now known was originally a derisive nickname, given because of their long hair, their long cloaks, and their home in a monastery, as well as their artistic hopes and pretensions and aims.

Wackenroder was one of the principal sources of their ideas, but he was not the only one. In 1802 Friedrich Schlegel went to Paris for several years, and there met the brothers Melchior and Sulpiz Boisserée, who had come from Cologne to Paris in order to study the German and Flemish medieval paintings brought there by the Napoleonic conquests. Schlegel started a journal, *Europa,* which began publication in 1803 and ended in 1804, surviving for only four issues. In it Schlegel wrote a series of articles on the Louvre exhibitions, and was persuaded by the Boisserée brothers to pay more attention to the paintings they were interested in than he otherwise would have. This art was, of course, a revelation to Schlegel, and in his later articles he extolled its beauty and importance. When he left Paris in 1804 he accompanied the brothers to Cologne and for a time settled there. It was then that the brothers began to assemble their famous collections of medieval German and Flemish paintings. The supply came from the Revolutionary and Napoleonic closing of monasteries and churches, and sometimes they even rescued important paintings from junk men. In 1814, when their collection was in Heidelberg, they persuaded Goethe to pay them a visit, and in spite of Goethe's classicism and his resistance to medieval architecture and art, the "old pagan," as he called himself, was overwhelmed by the beauty of what the Boisserée brothers had brought together, and spent days in the study of their collection. And the brothers were also responsible for what was one of the greater medievalist undertakings of the 19th century, the completion of the cathedral of Cologne.

This dual interest of the Boisserée brothers in medieval painting and architecture was more a single interest in medieval culture, and their interest in medieval painting was thus part of the larger phenomenon, usually associated with architecture of the Gothic Revival. The 18th century interest in the Gothic was of the same sort as that century's interest in Chinese decor and in Asiatic Indian, Hindu, and Muslim. It was the Rococo interest in exoticism, but an interest which used exotic materials, whether of the past, as the Gothic, or the geographically and culturally distant, as the Chinese, in order to subdue them to Rococo principals of form. And the late neo-classical period of the 18th century saw exotic styles, including the Gothic, subdued to neo-classical principles. The whole phenomenon was an aspect of what we have already seen as the late 18th century culture of emotional lability.

But in the Romantic period the Gothic revival was of an entirely different character. In the 18th century the Gothic was used for the architecture of play, garden pavilions or fantasies such as Fonthill. In the 19th century architects and in time their patrons began to use Gothic design for serious purposes; for churches, cathedrals, houses, especially vicarages; or for castles built by individuals to demonstrate their political and economic power; and, in time, railroad stations and even those classical hold-outs, banks. Above all the Gothic was seen as a Christian architecture, and there was a strong feeling that the return to Gothic architecture would mean a revitalization of the society and the culture. But there was also a perception of the Gothic as an alternative to what was thought of as an exhausted architectural academicism. Thus for both reasons an archaeologically correct Gothic became the aim. But that aim was not independent of the effort to achieve an archaeologically correct classic architecture, based upon a careful study of surviving Greek architectural monuments and fragments of monuments. And as was to become clear in time, the object of both archaeologically correct revivals was not merely the revitalization of European culture through a historical grasp of Europe's past, as all historicism was, but the determination by means of archaeology to discover and lay bare the very foundations or fundamental principles of architecture; and thus enable the development of a new architecture, an aim not to be achieved until the 20th century, in spite of the numerous efforts to do so in the 19th.

Of the various individuals associated with what came to be known as the Nazarene movement, in the period before 1815 only three were of significance, and even so their finest work lay in the future. The first two were Johann Friedrich Overbeck (1789-1869) and Franz Pforr (1788-1812). Overbeck was born in Lübeck and early in life set out to be an artist, with the encouragement of his intelligent and cultured family. When he was only thirteen or fourteen years old he was profoundly impressed by outline drawings of old Italian paintings made by a pair of minor Romantic artists, the Riepenhausen brothers. So that when he went to study painting in the Vienna Academy in 1806 he was ready to be thoroughly dissatisfied with the traditional academic training he was offered, principally the copying of plaster casts. There he met Pforr and together with a few other friends they became outspoken in their contempt for the training being imposed upon them. In 1808 the reopening of the Imperial Gallery in the Belvedere Palace made available to them such Italian painters as Perugino and the early Raphael and the school of Michelangelo. These were important revelations, for the academic training they were being exposed to was descended from the Caracci, the

Bolognese and Roman painters of the early 17th century, strained through the Baroque, the Rococo, and the Neo-classic styles. Even more important to them were the early German painters, Dürer, Cranach, Holbein. In short they came into direct contact with those painters they had read about in Wackenroder and Friederich Schlegel.

So on the first anniversay of their first meeting in 1808, on July 10, 1809, the six friends founded the Brotherhood or Order, as they sometimes called it, of St. Luke, the legendary painter-apostle. Because of the disturbed times, the Academy was closed, and when it reopened in 1810 the number of students it could accept was so limited that, quite reasonably, considering their outspoken expression of antipathy, five of the six were left out. Four of them, led by Pforr and Overbeck, decided to go to Rome, and in June, 1810, they set out. Nor was their ambition to experience the classical Rome previous artists had set out to discover. Rather, it was to find the Rome of the early and the high Renaissance, a term barely yet in use. They thought of themselves as re-discovering the source of the tradition of European Christian painting, not marked by the sophisticated complexities of the Baroque tradition, nor by the equally sophisticated, though superficially simplified, new academicism of the late 18th century, particularly that of David.

They deliberately set out to revitalize painting by returning to compositional simplicity, purity of color, and firm draughtsmanlike outlines. What indeed they were interested in doing was stripping away nearly three centuries of accumulated painting tradition in order to discover and recover the foundation, the essence, of their art, and to found European painting anew. And to be sure, something of their immense ambition arose from their perception of the political situation. To reject the academic tradition was to reject French culture, for it had come to Germany from France; that is, to reject the Napoleonic domination of Germany. What they were determined to do was to revitalize German culture from its original Italian sources, from an Italy in Dürer's time still Christian and politically independent. What they sought was the art of Italy before it came under the repressive and ultimately decadent domination of Spain, when, as has been often said, in the 16th century Spain locked Italy in a prison and threw away the key.

Even while they were still in Vienna, Overbeck and Pforr had already begun their efforts to create a new art on an old foundation. Overbeck had painted a "Raising of Lazarus" (Lübeck), which he called his first-born. It was clearly an allegory of the effort of a religious dedication to bring a moribund art once more to life. And he had started an even more ambitious painting, one which he took to Rome with him, "Christ's Entry into Jerusalem" (formerly Lübeck, destroyed in 1942). Here his originality began truly to emerge. Instead of the implied pyramid or triangle of the academic tradition, instead of the frieze-like arrangement of Davidian neo-classicism, the painting is organized around an immense implied circle or, perhaps, aerial bubble, which occupies the central third of the painting, and into which Christ rides on his donkey. Pforr had begun a series of drawings in the style of Dürer as illustration to Goethe's *Goetz von Berlichingen,* the work which together with *Faust, Part I* (published in 1808) represented to these young men the Goethe they were interested in, the Goethe who in part of his life, at least, had been interested in the culture of medieval Germany, even though he now harshly repudiated it, having yet to come under the influence of the Boisserée brothers.

Pforr's reading in medieval history had led him to the story of how Rudolf of Habsburg, while besieging Basel in 1273, was elected Holy Roman Emperor, and was received by the citizens of Basel with rejoicing. Thus Overbeck and Pforr both celebrated the entry of a religious savior and a political savior into their rightful heritages, just as they were determined to make such an entry into what they conceived to be their rightful heritage. Both paintings accompanied their own entry into Rome. It cannot be said that Pforr made any great effort to show a medieval city and medieval costumes. Rather the costumes were those of the early Renaissance, such as he found in Dürer and the important 1808 republication in lithography of Dürer's marginal decorations for the Emperor Maximilian's prayer book.

Of the two entry paintings, Pforr's is the more important, for he went far beyond Overbeck in rejecting the whole tradition of academic painting, in stripping away the accretions to painting of three centuries, so that the finished work evokes not the medieval world in a historically realistic manner, but rather the medieval way of perceiving and transforming the world — an apparent naiveté which in fact barely conceals a rich and subtle compositional complexity, one in which an overlapping confusion of backs and figures, and round heads, and horses in profile, contrasts with the cubistic angularity of the buildings. Few paintings of the 19th century so strongly suggest an alternative mode of grasping the appearances of reality. Certainly few are so profoundly original.

Almost as striking is "Count von Habsburg and the Priest" (Frankfurt-am-Main), in which this same Rudolf offers his horse to a priest bearing the sacrament to a dying man. In this picture the landscape has something of the beauty of the landscapes of Dürer and the Venetians of the early 16th century. As in the "Entry" Pforr abandons chiaroscuro and also the traditional modes of composition. The figures are disposed across the painting; from left to right are dogs, a page, horses, Rudolf, another dog, his head hidden behind the priest, and a priest's assistant. There is a very subtle and partial implication of a dome-like semi-circle that might enclose the figures, but as in the "Entry" the composition is narrational. In that picture the center is occupied by an anonymous figure on horseback; in·front of him is an empty space with a dog running across it. The Emperor is half-concealed at the right. He has to be looked for; and the official reception group of mayor and councillors consists of tiny figures at the extreme left and far in the background.

In both pictures the figures are casually disposed, as they might have been in a photograph of the event. To this degree and in this way Romantic realism enters Pforr's historical evocation. One further effect needs to be noticed. His abandonment of three centuries of principles of composition makes the observer aware (and the effect would have been more powerful in 1810) that this is a picture, not a mimesis. That is, the principles of composition had become so engrained in the academic tradition that they seemed natural. Pforr's violation of that tradition forces the viewer into the realization that he is looking at a picture, at (in a famous later formulation) a certain disposition of shapes and colors on a flat surface. His aim is neither mimesis nor expression but imaginative transformation.

Franz Pforr

Der Einzug König Rudolfs von Habsburg in Basel

reproduced by permission of the Städelsches Kunstinstitut und
Städtische Galerie, Frankfurt am Main

Friedrich Overbeck
Franz Pforr
reproduced by permission of the Nationalgalerie,
Staatliche Museen Preussischer Kulturbesitz, Berlin (West)

Among the finest and most instructive works of the early years of the Nazarenes at Rome are portraits of each other and self-portraits. Two made in 1810 are a powerful self-portrait, highly stylized, of Pforr, and Overbeck's beautiful portrait of Pforr in the German Renaissance manner, not that as yet a distinction was made between medieval Germany and the Renaissance Germany of the early 16th century – the time of Dürer, who died in 1528. In German art history all these portraits and self-portraits are known as the "Friendship Portraits," but that friendship was of particular significance in the social history of Romantic culture. The Nazarenes were a new instance of the little group of self-sustaining culturally self-alienated Romantic artists and thinkers. And the verbal undertaking with each other was witnessed to not with a published manifesto, as became common in later years, but with a device Overbeck invented to be affixed to the back of the brotherhood's pictures. The purpose of the numerous portraits and self-portraits was not merely to celebrate their friendship but, more importantly, to define themselves by costume and expression and artistic style; and the definition of each other was at the same time a self-definition so that the portraits of each other also functioned as self-portraits. In Overbeck's exquisite portrait of Pforr, for example, the young artist, who was to die of tuberculosis in 1812, is placed in an open medieval window; in the background is a young woman, a possible future wife, knitting and reading a pious book; and beyond her, through another window, is a German medieval town; and beyond that is the coast of Italy, a reference to the desire, expressed in other painting, to combine Italian tradition and artistry with German seriousness and piety. The framing window is vine-clad, a hint that the medieval world, in the thinking of the Nazarenes, is still alive.

Among these portraits is a unique double portrait, in pencil, of Overbeck and a new recruit to the Brotherhood of St. Luke, Peter Joseph von Cornelius (1783-1867), the son of the director of the Düsseldorf Gallery (Private collection, München). Like Pforr, who had come from Frankfurt, Cornelius was a Rhinelander, but unlike Overbeck, who was converted to Catholicism in 1813, Cornelius came from a Catholic family, and was all the readier to abandon the neo-

classical tradition, in which he made his first significant efforts, for a
return to German art. He was, like the Nazarenes, powerfully moved
by the 1808 lithographic reproduction of Dürer's Maximilian Prayer-
book. And in the same year he was equally moved by Goethe's *Faust I,*
which seemed to him a return to Goethe's true tradition, the German.
He set about to make illustrations to *Faust,* at first drawings and then
eventually engravings, published in 1816. He showed the completed
ones to Goethe, who objected to the "old German style," but Cornelius spiritedly replied that he had no intention of surrendering to
what he called the bad side of the spirit of the age, the very neo-
Classicism which Goethe was trying to force upon German art. Cornelius had heard about the Nazarenes in Frankfurt and Heidelberg,
where he presumably saw the Boisserée collections, and in 1811 he
set out for Rome, convinced that a study of the art there would help
him to complete his *Faust* series. On arriving in Rome he went directly to Overbeck, and was soon an official member of the Brotherhood of St. Luke, taking the place of Pforr, whom he knew only
briefly before Pforr's death. In 1813, then, he and Overbeck executed
their admirable double portrait, each drawing the other. He successfully completed his *Faust* illustrations and also did an equally remarkable series of illustrations to the *Nibelungenlied,* the Middle High
German heroic epic poem, rediscovered after a couple of centuries
of oblivion, in the mid-18th century and published in 1757. The
growing nationalism in Germany, called into existence by the Napoleonic hegemony and soon to lead to the Freedom War, turned
the poem into what, it was then felt, every nation must have, its own
national epic. (In 1807 Joel Barlow had attempted to provide the
young United States with a national epic; but *The Columbiad,* untouched by Romanticism, was a rather dismal failure.)

Before 1815 Cornelius made only one effort to create a major
painting, spurred by his 1813 visit to the marvelous Signorelli frescoes
in Orvieto. It was "The Wise and the Foolish Virgins" (Düsseldorf),
begun in that year but never finished, a work also strongly influenced
by Raphael, though it appears to be more strongly influenced by the
the 16th century mannerists than by either Signorelli or Raphael,
particularly in its acid colors and its refusal to create mimetic space.

Peter von Cornelius
Die fünf klugen und die fünf törichten Jungfrauen
reproduced by permission of the Kunstmuseum Düsseldorf

And like the work of Overbeck and Pforr it is most original in its composition, which consists of three implied vertical rectangles, disposed from left to right across the painting. Its iconography is equally original, for it presents the bridegroom as Christ himself, issuing from the doors of paradise. Not a mere illustration of the New Testament parable, it is an interpretation of it — the divine recognition of those who wait for illumination. It is perhaps not coincidental that it was begun in the year Overbeck was converted to Cornelius' faith and perhaps should be construed as an affirmation of Cornelius's solidarity with the group dominated by Overbeck, even though Cornelius was six years older.

It is likely that Cornelius abandoned the painting in 1816 because he had become ingrossed in the commission the Nazarenes had received to fresco a room in the apartment of the Prussian Consul in the Palazzo Zuccari, at the corner of the Via Gregoriana and the Via Sistina (now in Berlin, the Nationalgalerie). Jacob Salomon Bartholdy (1779-1825), the uncle of the composer Mendelssohn who was to take his second name from him, recognized what the Nazarenes had accomplished so far, though he knew, of course, that by 1815 they were more promise than accomplishment, especially because of the loss of Pforr. Nevertheless, he believed that they deserved a chance to do what Overbeck in particular most desired to do, to revive the abandoned art of fresco painting.

What Overbeck desired was commissions to fresco new cathedrals and churches in Germany, but that, at the moment, could scarcely be hoped for. Overbeck and Cornelius were aided by Wilhelm Schadow (1788-1862), in Rome in 1811, a Nazarene in 1813, and Philip Veit (1798-1877), in Rome in 1815, a Nazarene in 1816. This Nazarene accomplishment, their success, belongs to the years after 1815, but the granting of the commission needs to be recorded here, for it was a recognition that they had indeed accomplished what they had set out to do, to revive German painting by uniting the early Italian and German late medieval and early Renaissance traditions, and to do so in the name of religion. The commission was a recognition of the really daring ambition of the chief Nazarenes, in spite of what they said; for their true ambition, never spoken, was less to use religion to revitalize art than to use art to revitalize religion and the religious culture of Germany. It was the task of art, not of religion, to be the redemptive mode of a new civilization.

Friedrich — 2   In this aim they were continuing what Friedrich
(1774-1840)   and Runge had already attempted in quite dif-
              ferent ways.   Overbeck visited Runge on his way
to Vienna and certainly was strengthened for his forthcoming resistance to the neo-classicism of the Vienna Academy.   Runge died in
1810, but Friedrich in time knew of the work of the Nazarenes and
disapproved of it.   His aim was not the revitalization of an old style
and an old iconography but, as we have seen, the creation in landscape of a new system of Christian symbolism, symbols that would,
moreover, reveal new aspects of Christianity, or would offer a generalization or universalization of Christian belief.   The result was analysis
of such belief, a reduction of it to psychic or emotional or mental
generalities.   An example is a drawing in sepia done around 1810.
In this work Friedrich picked up a motive he had used several years
before, views out of the window at his studio on the Elbe, that is,
from an enclosed and almost featureless and unattractive space into
an open space filled with beauty and incident.   In this new picture
the window opens onto a park, and on the outer window sill are two
plants.   The picture has been interpreted as the vision of paradise
from the restricted earthly life, the two potted plants as emblems of
humans on the verge of entering paradise, and the poplar in the park
as an emblem of death.   All this may very well be the case, but the
picture can be responded to without reference to that Christianized
iconography.   It can be seen as a vision of freedom from a position
of repression, or like the contrast in music between minor and major,
between a world of hindrance and a world of guidance, from a situation
of deprivation to a situation the exact opposite of that deprivation,
the plants being symbols of the possibility of the movement from one
situation or world to its opposite.   That Friedrich was at the time
intensely concerned with this opposition and transition is indicated
by the fact that we have evidence of two sepia drawings and four

oils of the same subject, all six having now disappeared.

Similar are two wonderful landscapes of 1810, one of a view from the island of Rügen toward a bay and the sea beyond, arched over by a rainbow, and the other, which is larger, of a sunlit man leaning against a rock outcropping on a hilltop and looking toward a mountain scene darkened by storm and arched over by a rainbow. The second increases the symmetry of the first, for the man is almost in the exact center, while in the first the man is at the extreme right and is balanced by a tree at the left, the two configurations being connected by the rainbow. In the first picture the foreground is dark and the background light, increasingly so to the horizon. In the second just the reverse is the case. In the first there is hardly an interruption of the flat horizon line save for the upper half of the man and the top of the tree at either side. In the second, the horizon broken by mountains is interrupted in the very center by an upthrusting pyramidal mountain beyond an abyss from which mist can be seen rising. In the first a broken and dead tree is in the dark foreground; in the second a foreground rock and some live trees are illuminated. In the first the landscape contains sheep and in the distance boats on the sea and in the center a farmhouse. In the second only the man is an indication of human life; the landscape is wild and gloomy, almost a night scene in spite of the sunlit foreground. In the first the movement from front to back is from death to life, the rainbow offering a paradisaical promise in ordinary life, a position supported by the herd of sheep in the foreground. In the second, the rainbow is a promise is value or of, perhaps, religious hope and consolation in spite of the gloom and threat and terror of the background. Because of the rainbow the man can gaze away from us and into that darkness without fear and anxiety. So, relaxed, he is leaning against the rock, the emblem of faith, but in this generalized analysis of the meaning of religion, the rock is the symbol of any support to be found in life. And this second landscape with rainbow is the most symmetrical work Freidrich has yet painted; the whole picture becomes a symbol of the affirmation of the individual will to meaning.

In 1811 Friedrich painted a picture, exhibited in 1812, that carries this theme even further. It is a kind of meditation of the Tetschen altarpiece, painted after additional landscapes that moved from light into darkness and from darkness into light. (This also was purchased by Friedrich Wilhelm III.) "Morgen in Riesengebirge" ("Morning in the Riesengebirge," the mountains on the border of Saxony and Bohemia) presents a vast landscape of mountain range beyond range, emerging from mist, almost like waves in the ocean. In the sky, which occupies the upper half of the picture, is the flush of dawn, shading from pale yellow through pinks to blue at the top of the picture. At the right foreground is an immense outcropping of rock, much like that of the Tetschen altarpiece. It is surmounted by a delicate cross, embraced by a woman who has evidently led a man to this spot. Here the improbability of the Tetschen altarpiece is enormously intensified by the wildness of the landscape; and the fragility of the cross as well as of the two tiny figures is equally intesnsified. Why should there be a cross on this isolated peak, and why should a man and a woman have climbed there? The cross becomes the only possibility of hope in the immense mountainous ocean of life. There is an enormous and almost terror-struck reduction of the significance and power of Christianity, of any religion. Faith becomes an act of wild desperation. Thus religion is analyzed into a source of value in the incomprehensibility and inimicality of life, as symbolized by the stony waste of the foreground.

This sense of the inimicality of the human environment, this feeling that man exists in a world which offers him nothing of a home, continues in two paintings of 1811. Both are winter landscapes. One shows a man with a crutch alone and bent over in a landscape of snow, dead trees, and tree stumps. The other shows an even more desolate landscape with, however, a living fir tree as a background to one of Friedrich's attenuated and fragile crucifixes, and rising out of the mist in the background the towers of a fantastic Gothic cathedral. Again the alienation of man from the natural world is powerfully emphasized, and in the first is a symbol of the lost Romantic wanderer. Allied to this pair of pictures is "Felspartie (im Harz)" ("A rocky spot or glen in the Harz mountains"). Here the fir-trees, emblems of human life, emerge from the rocky and barren and desolate setting. The opposition between man and an inimical

Caspar David Friedrich
Morgen in Riesengebirge
reproduced by permission of the Nationalgalerie
Staatliche Museen Preussischer Kulturbesitz, Berlin (West)

world is not reconciled but held in a powerful intellectual suspension. It is an acceptance of the condition of human existence. Similar is another painting of 1811, showing a chapel with a minute cross in the midst of a stony mountain-top wilderness.

Affirmation of the value of existence, then, emerges through the function of religion and in spite of the early conditions of human existence, so ill-suited to human needs. In 1812, probably, appeared a picture which makes this point even clearer. As so frequently with Friedrich, the end of a sequence of related pictures is marked by an extreme symmetry. So in this picture there is again the rocky glen with dead trees, but in the precise middle is a spring, and above it a barely visible typical slender crucifix. Beyond that rise, between huge fir trees, the towers of a church, clearly, as in the earlier picture, a church of fantasy, an emblematic church. The extreme symmetry once again symbolizes the affirmative exercise of the will in creating religious significance in the midst of an inimical world.

This power of the will is even more subtly analyzed in "Oybin Ruins." Oybin is a ruined monastery east of Dresden which appears often in Friedrich's pictures. Here again is an almost perfect symmetry. The picture shows the sacristy or apse of the monastery church, its roof and the tracery and the glass in the three empty windows long broken. In the center is an altar supported by two kneeling angels. At the left is a crucifix, at the right a statue of the Madonna. In front of all three of these emblems are growing plants, even, before the Virgin, a lily. From the life in the natural world, then, man can create a realization of the functions of worn-out religious emblems and turn them into symbols of man's value-creative will. This development made it possible for Friedrich to create an entirely novel series of paintings, quite different from anything he had hitherto produced and inspired by the Freedom War against Napoleon, a series begun a year before the 1813 Battle of Dresden. Yet these three paintings show the human power to create from the resources of the natural world affirmation of the value of human existence. Two of these are of funerary monuments of an ancient hero, often known, therefore, as the "Grave of Arminius." As indicated by Kleist's *Hermannschlacht* (written in 1860-1809 but not published until 1821),

Hermann or Arminius became in the Freedom War an emblem of the German resistance to invasion, since Hermann had defeated the invading Roman legions. In the first picture are two chasseurs, in the second, one, French light infantrymen trained as scouts for the French army. Here they have come to a cul-de-sac in which they are faced by the spirit of German resistance.

In 1814 Friedrich exhibited a picture that makes this point of confrontation even clearer. It shows a French chasseur who has come to the end of the road in the midst of a dark and brooding German forest. Advance is impossible. The fir trees are symbols of the spirit of German resistance, a spirit developed from the natural world in which the Germans find themselves, a further emblem of man's power to use aspects of an inimical world for his own purposes. Even so in 1815, after the defeat of Napoleon, Friedrich in two pictures turned to a theme he had employed before. Each shows a single ship in full sail on the open sea. A ship, to Friedrich, is the creation of the human will and its power to transcend the spiritual barrenness of the world in which he finds himself. These pictures are the answer to the "Monk on the Seashore."

In all of these pictures, then, of the period 1810 to 1815 Friedrich is intensely concerned with the capacity of the individual human will to transcend the conditions of human existence by creating symbolisms of that transcendent power. By his exquisite realism that transforms reality and adds something to it, Friedrich makes the observer intensely aware that he is looking at a picture, a certain disposition of shapes and colors on a flat surface, a human creation. The picture itself as a picture becomes a symbol of the creative power of the individual human will. Once again art becomes the source for the revelation of value, and Friedrich's effort to understand the fundamental significance of religion by means of exploring the innovative symbolic possibilities of art means that art and the artist are the means whereby the true function of a lost religion can be recreated. Thus Friedrich appears to be saying that no matter what man may have lost in the Enlightenment, his creative religious power remains untouched and capable of rebirth, and art is the instrument and means of that rebirth.

Constable – 2   Friedrich returned frequently to the same scene
and the same subject, but most of his paintings
were made of combinations of scenes he was familiar with. They were
traditional in the sense that they were "inventions." His English
contemporary Constable, on the other hand, particularly in the years
we are concerned with here, 1810 to 1815, returned again and again
and again to the same scenes, a handful of places in his home country.
It will be useful, therefore, to be a little more precise about this area
to which, as we have seen, he began to return in 1808, and which in
the years from 1809 onward was almost the exclusive subject of his
landscape paintings, mostly sketches; for in these years he produced
very few finished pictures for exhibition at the annual show of the
Royal Academy. The area he devoted himself to was an oval hardly
more than four miles long and less than two miles wide.

As you take the main highway northeast of London from Colchester
to Ipswich, at Stratford St. Mary, 55 miles from the center of London,
you cross the River Stour, which for much of its length marks the
border between Essex to the south and Suffolk to the north. At the
Stratford bridge you cross from one county to the other. To the
left and close by is the village of Langham, and between Langham
and Stratford bridge are the low hills called the Combs. From the
top of these one can look down the valley of the Stour past the bridge
to Manningtree and the estuary of the Stour. Between Stratford
Bridge and Mannigtree are two villages, Dedham with its beautiful
church steeple and beyond Dedham the village of Flatford with a mill
and the cottage of Willy Lot, still standing, which Constable painted
again and again. About a mile and a half north of Flatford is East
Bergholt, Constable's birthplace and the home of his well-to-do father,
who owned, as we have seen, the mill at Dedham. Low hills rise just
south of East Bergholt and to the south of Dedham and mark the
limits of the valley of the Stour, known here as the Vale of Dedham.
To this confined area Constable devoted for nearly a decade sketch
after sketch and even a series of finished paintings, though the great
series of paintings – six-footers, as he called them – did not begin
until 1818. Most of the oil sketches were done between 1809 and
that year.

The greatest number were done at Flatford, for there was a superb subject of the River Stour flowing past Willy Lot's cottage and between tall trees into the open meadows beyond. Thus one of his subjects was a view from a confined area into an open area. Yet just as many were devoted to extensive open areas, and probably the most beautiful of the sketches and pictures of this period were views of the whole Vale of Dedham; Constable's vantage point was the Combs. And in these the most conspicuous object is the tower of Dedham Church, which appears repeatedly in other sketches, of the mill at Dedham, for one, from a lane from East Bergholt down to the river, and from Flatford up the vale towards Dedham and Stratford bridge. The viewpoints of this fascinating series of sketches of the Vale of Dedham sweep in a great semicircle from Stratford Bridge to Flatford, a semicircle radiating from the tower of Dedham Church. Is it enough to conclude that this recurrence of the verticality of Dedham Church tower, so often rising above a horizon line, was for Constable no more than a focal point for his composition? Perhaps so, but it is also to be observed how centrally many Romantics determined to resanctify the world and to do so through art. And it is also to be noted that a vertical thrust is an assertion of self, of identity.

At the least it may be hinted that the frequence of the appearance of this church tower is something of a clue to Constable's obsessive concern with this almost tiny area of England. The Vale of Dedham was not Constable's home; East Bergholt was, which lies on the slopes above the Vale and which Constable painted far less frequently than almost any of his favorite views in what is now known as Constable country. The flowing of water past the tree-formed gate at Willy Lot's house, the movement past a construction into a sunlit openness, and a vast landscape — far vaster than the reality — pulled together by an up-thrusting church tower — these are the two great themes of Constable's years of sketching, several hundred times, in the Vale of Dedham.

To comprehend this strange phenomenon it is useful to think once again of what he might have owed to Wordsworth, of what the Beaumonts had told him about *The Prelude,* and of what he himself had very probably read of Wordsworth's poetry. There too he had found

John Constable
Boat-Building near Stratford Mill
reproduced by permission of the Victoria and Albert Museum

the rewards that come from a determined and obsessive exploration of the significance of a particular landscape to the child who is father to the man, in Wordsworth's famous phrase. A further clue to what he is doing is to be found in a later remark that sketches are not of any great use for finished pictures, for they record the feelings one had when the sketches were done, or, as he put it, "one's state of mind." Yet it is equally evident that he was also concerned with understanding the natural character of the scenery he was painting — the light, the water, the fields, the old bridges and locks (the shallow Stour had been made navigable for barges by a series of locks), the mills, the boat-building yard, the innumerable shades of green in meadow and trees (which impressed Delacroix so in the 1820s), the cottages, the barges, the horses, the boys and the workmen.

By constantly painting and repainting almost the same subjects Constable was always engaged in undermining the conventions of painting. And thus though he learned much from Ruysdael, Claude, Rubens, he was also going past them. His studying by means of oil sketches the same scenes again and again brought him ever closer not only to the actual appearance of the world but also, by going past conventions, to the realization that the actual appearance of nature is in fact an endless series of appearances. And so he came to realize two modes of succession, the constantly changing landscape and the constantly changing states of mind. A painting to Constable is the accidental or random intersection of these two independent series. So a painting is at once a transformation of a flowing and of a still point in the turning world; it is the River Stour flowing past Willy Lot's house and the tower of Dedham Church in the center of the vale of Dedham.

What he mastered in these years of obsessive sketches was the Romantic interaction of reality and perception, the Romantic realization of the uniqueness of every moment. It is of such a painting, from 1815, one which he exhibited at the Academy as "Boat-Building near Stratford Mill," that his painter friend and biographer, Charles Leslie, said: "Such is its atmospheric truth, that the tremulous vibration of the heated air near the ground seems visible. This perfect work . . .". In it, we find emerging what in the next fifteen years

was to be the character of his great series of the Stour Valley, a tremendous monumentality, a grandeur of the moment of revelation,
of the interpenetration of landscape and self.

Turner — 2   While Constable was focussing on the Vale of Ded-
(1775-1851)   ham, Turner was diffusing his stylistic interests.
                    This is understandable, of course, since Turner had
long since arrived at a mastery Constable, only a little less than fourteen
months younger, had yet to achieve. Even so, the contrast is instructive; it indicates that Turner was still restlessly searching for a style
unique to his temperament and to his extraordinary talents.

As we have seen, the first indication of his stylistic dissatisfaction
was the series of Thames oil sketches, in which he quite deliberately
was seeking to transform the conventions he had mastered and to do
so in the direction of realism, or, as some critics term it, naturalism.
That line he pursued into the second decade of the century. He returned to a subject on which he had built his reputation, portraits of
gentlemen's houses, but two such portraits were profoundly different.
One was "Petworth, Sussex, the Seat of the Earl of Egremont; Dewy
Morning" (exhibited the Royal Academy, 1810). It was painted for
Turner's greatest patron and one of his closest friends. It was a friendship that was to last for decades, and Petworth inside and out was to
provide subjects for as long. Here he surpassed even his Thames Valley
sketches, incorporating everything he had learned. It is indeed a
dewy morning, before sunrise, and the sky is at once both the most
miraculous and the most realistically convincing that he had painted —
a sky equalled only by the beautiful reflections in the water in the
foreground. The great house of Petworth is only partially visible;
behind it is a spire of the neighboring village; and to the left is a
gently rising hill which is the location of the dewiness of the title.
And the title indicates exactly what Turner wanted the observer to
respond to, not a portrait of a house but a transformation of a particular morning, and of a particular kind of morning. This picture
also marks a notable change in Turner's technique. For the first time
he used in a finished picture what he had experimented with in the

Thames sketches, painting on a white ground, thus taking over from watercolor on white paper into oils on canvas a luminosity wholly new in oil painting.

The achievement of this picture is repeated and carried even further in a picture exhibited in 1811, "Somer-Hill the Seat of W. F. Woodgate Esq." This is a sunset sky, again reflected in water, with a group of ducks in the right foreground and birds hovering over the water. Beyond the water is a sloping field with cattle, and at the top of the hill is the house. Above is a sky of a luminosity like that of the preceding picture, even more marked by an apparently infinite gradation of color — yellows, oranges, red, blues, grays. In the next year, 1812, Turner exhibited "Teignmouth," one of the results of his trips in these years to the southwest and west of England. Here again is a sunset scene, the mouth of a river, a black and a white cow attended by a girl in black and white clothing, boats under construction at the right and silhouetted against the sky, a stretch of water reflecting in the foreground the sun, and beyond a vast stretch of greenish or bluish bay, and above, occupying almost two-thirds of the picture, a sunset sky that continues and surpasses the skies of the two house portraits. Only three or four preceding pictures of Turner gave so much area of the picture to the sky, but in "Teignmouth" the reflection of the sky in the water makes this truly the first picture — and many were to follow — of which it can be clearly said that the subject of the picture is the sky itself. Moreover this picture is a prediction of what was to come. With great accuracy it can be said that in this picture the true subject is not even the sky; it is color, color itself, color as the very embodiment of Turner's vision of nature as divine.

But one may go beyond such a statement to what is perhaps an even greater accuracy to say that the true subject of these three pictures is simply light itself. And that view is supported by what may be called the climax of his naturalistic or realist strain in these years, "Frosty Morning," the idea for which he got on an early winter morning when he was travelling by coach through Yorkshire (exhibited 1813). Indeed, in the distance at the left, disappearing down the road, is the coach itself. Save for a strange blue on a little girl's dress, a black horse, and a couple of black figures, the foreground of the picture is entirely a study in browns, endless shades of brown, such as make winter landscapes so beautiful. But the upper two-thirds of the picture is white sky, only tinged here and there with yellow and greenish yellows, inadequate terms, since for Turner's colors there are by this time no words. The endless shades of brown are echoed by the endless shades of white, or the infinite gradations of light itself. Moreover the composition of the painting has no precedent; it preserves the randomness of natural appearance; it anticipates the photograph.

Moreover these infinite shades of white and brown suggest something else, something which is perhaps the true, underlying, covert subject of "Teignmouth." First it is to be noted that probably no pictures lose so much in reproduction as do Turner's. The explanation is the exquisitely delicate impasto, which gives a richness and inexhaustible pleasure to the surface, and the infinite color shades which no reproduction process can hope to capture. And in these two aspects, more than in any others, impasto and color, the greatness of Turner as a *painter,* one who puts color-loaded brush to canvas, is to be found; for these two sustain one's interest, keep one's eye wandering back and forth over the surface, forever seeking new delights. Turner can sustain one's visual interest as few other painters can, perhaps no others.

And in that sustainment is to be found the covert subject, as I have called it, of "Teignmouth." In the foreground is a girl with her arms fully extended abover her head. Perhaps she is gesturing to the cows, attempting to control them. But perhaps it is the covert point that she has raised her arms in adoration of the marvelous, the incomparable scene before her. We have already discovered that one of the innovative notes that Romantics sought to embody in works of art was the ecstatic, the sustained rapture. In music and even in poetry that is possible because the artist can control, completely in music, the time the observer spends before the work. But the painter cannot. What he can do, it would seem, Turner did. By making the surface of the picture, the painterly surface itself, so endlessly fascinating he offered the observer the experience of what the picture itself signifies: precisely that ecstatic, rapturous quality of experience, that sustained

sense of value which is the antithesis to and the escape from the equally powerful sense of meaninglessness, the experience of the loss of
value. To transform in a painting the natural world into the experience of ecstasy — that was to become in time Turner's ambition.
And in that aim he was never understood, not even by one who wor-
shipped him, John Ruskin.

Extraordinary as these paintings are, they did not satisfy Turner.
Restlessly he turned in an unexpected direction. He set out not to
imitate Claude Lorraine but to surpass him in Claude's own style,
beginning with "Mercury and Herse"(exhibited 1811), and culminating with "Crossing the Brook" and "Dido Building Carthage" (both
exhibited in 1815). To these should be added the companion to the
third, "The Decline of the Carthaginian Empire" (exhibited 1817).

In 1829 in the first draft of his will Turner bequeathed both Carthage pictures to the National Gallery, with the proviso that they be
hung next to two Claudes, presumably those acquired from the Anger-
stein collection when the National Gallery was founded in 1824.
Except for "Crossing the Brook" the subjects for these pictures are
historical and mythological, and that picture, in spite of its vertical
format, has the look of Italian landscape, so marked was his challenge to Claude, even though it was on the whole quite an accurate
view of the valley of the Tamar, the border of Devon and Cornwall.
This determination to revive the style of Claude and then to surpass
it is a further indication of the restlessness of Turner in these years,
his casting about for a truly emergent style.   And in doing so, he
did what the Nazarenes were doing at the same time; he turned to
the past of his art. In exploring and recovering the source of so many
of the landscape clichés and conventions of his time he could hope,
with his newly gained mastery of color and light and naturalistic
accuracy, to transcend those conventions by giving them renewed
and emergent life and thus release his own originality. "Crossing the
Brook" is silver light; the Carthage pictures are gold. Thus this turning to Claude was yet another example of Romantic historicism. But
the strange thing is that he had already leapt to a style of astounding
originality. And it almost seems as if he did not recognize what he
had done, for it was to be years before he set out to realize and de-

velop what he had accomplished in one extraordinary stylistic transcendence in "Snow Storm: Hannibal and his Army Crossing the Alps"
(exhibited in 1812).

He had the idea for the picture as early as 1810, when he sketched
a storm at Farnley Hall in Yorkshire. At the time he told his host's
son: "in two years you will see this again, and call it Hannibal crossing
the Alps." But when it was finished and exhibited in 1812 it turned
out to be the most astounding and disturbing picture yet painted
in the 19th century. The historical part of the picture shows the attack
upon Hannibal's army by an Alpine tribe; the rocky foreground, extending from the left about three-quarters of the width of the picture,
shows murder, robbery, and rape. To the extreme right, occupying
a small area in the lower right-hand corner of the picture, is a group
of soldiers in great confusion, also evidently under attack. By implication the army extends back of the rocky foreground to the distance, a great valley filled with Hannibal's troops, an elephant in
silhouette. But all this occupies only the lower fifth of the picture.
The rest is a vision of a tremendous storm, so intense that one is not
sure that the mountains filling the right third of the picture are indeed mountains or storm cloud. And most extraordinary, the sun
is burning through the storm clouds and shedding a Niagara of light
on the army in the background, beyond which are again hints of
snowy mountains. And to the extreme left of the picture the sky
is clearing.

All this could be traditional, or at least like other storm scenes
Turner had painted, were it not for the composition of the picture.
Occupying three quarters of the surface is implied an immense oval
formed by clouds and the valley floor and the upthrust of the rocky
foreground. But the upper part and the left part of this oval are cut
off by the edge of the picture. Within that oval is something like a
three-dimensional spiral or vortex which pulls the observer's attention
irresistibly to the flood of light mentioned above. Yet at the right
edge of the picture, in contrast to the almost black oval, are white
snow showers directly above the torches of the army in the lower
right-hand corner. So there is no visual climax, no place to which
the eye is finally led, which, as in traditional composition, the pro-

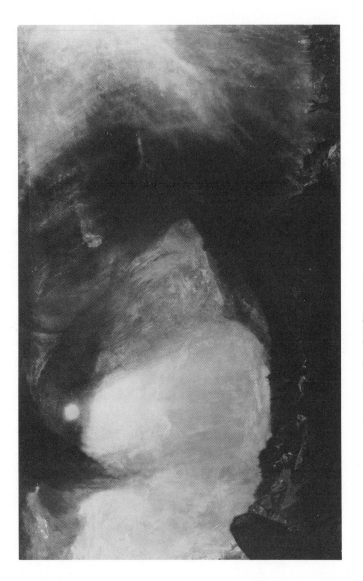

Joseph Mallord William Turner
Snow Storm: Hannibal and his Army Crossing the Alps
reproduced by permission of the Tate Gallery

cess of perception is resolved. On the contrary the eye is swept back and forth and imagines a three-dimensional space or aerial perspective into which it cannot help plunging. And that lack of visual resolution is supported by a verse-quotation in the exhibition catalogue, written by Turner himself and purportedly taken from a poem called *The Fallacies of Hope,* a poem which apparently never existed except in the purported quotations which Turner printed in catalogues to accompany his pictures and to give the observer further directions on how to respond to them.

Turner's profound pessimism now emerges for the first time, and it is perfectly possible that this picture has a reference to Napoleon and to what Turner saw as the destruction of the Napoleonic enterprise and empire, just as the Carthage pictures may also have been subtle and covert references to the rise and fall of all empires — that is, the fall of all human magnificence.

Yet stranger, indeed, than this extraordinary picture itself, a picture of absolute originality, a picture such as no one had ever painted, was the fact that it had no immediate successors. On the contrary, we have seen, it was mostly after this that the artist turned to his Claudian revivalism. We know one thing about Turner: that he always felt that he was never understood, and this is the period in which the most virulent attacks of Sir George Beaumont were being made on him. He was not to attempt to develop what he had achieved in this picture for many years, except in watercolor sketches, works of surpasing beauty and originality which he kept completely private. By 1814 only in this picture had Turner's profound alienation from his culture and his country been permitted to show itself. And in spite of the success of the picture it was to be many years before he exhibited anything like it. This picture makes his other paintings of this time, in spite of their originality, seem traditional. It is not much of an exaggeration to say that in the entire history of European painting no picture was so extraordinarily original and innovative as "Snow Storm: Hannibal Crossing the Alps." The subject is that of the first difficulties of a great enterprise, and the poetry accompanying it warns of the failure to come.

Craft, treachery, and fraud — Salassian force,
Hung on the fainting rear! then Plunder seiz'd
The victor and the captive, — Saguntum's spoil,
Alike, became their prey; still the chief advanc'd,
Look'd on the sun with hope; — how, broad and wan;
While the fierce archer of the downward year
Stains Italy's blanch'd barrier with storms.
In vain each pass, ensanguin'd deep with dead,
Or rocky fragments, wide destruction roll'd.
Still on Campania's fertile plains — he thought,
But the loud breeze sob'd, "Capua's joys beware!"

Did Turner feel that his own enterprise as a painter was doomed to failure, had he lost trust in his public, or in himself? One could almost say that in this picture, and for some time to come, Turner was a Romantic in spite of himself, an unconvinced Romantic, a Romantic so overwhelmed by the greatness of the past that he was not yet ready to achieve that stylistic transcendence of which this picture showed him to be both capable and uniquely prepared. Yet beyond that, this painting, dominated by its black storm clouds, this symbolization of the darkest pessimism — serves to provide a foil to such paintings as "Teignmouth," serves to reveal Turner's deepest purpose to be the creation of ecstatic value in order to redeem his blackness, his pessimism, his conviction of the fallacy of hope. It is no wonder that he was convinced he would never be understood.

Beethoven – 3   There is an odd similarity between the develop-
(1770-1827)   ment of Turner from 1810 and 1815 and that of
                      Beethoven, for the composer exhibits not merely
the same restlessness but also shows the same black pessimism, only in the form of a despair so deep and so bitter that serious composition becomes for a time almost impossible to him. In 1813, for example, during a period when he had become increasingly careless of his appearance — he had been something of a dandy — and even dirty, he accepted a commission to write something totally unworthy of him,

Wellington's Victory or the Battle of Vittoria, that decisive victory over the French forces in Spain which forced Joseph Bonaparte, King of Spain, to flee to France (Opus 91). The work was commissioned by Johann Nepomuk Mälzel (1772-1838) for his automatic musical instrument, the Panharmonicon, and later, at Mälzel's suggestion, scored for large orchestra. By a bitter irony no other work of Beethoven's was so popular during his lifetime. Directly after completing it, he wrote the only other work this once prolific composer accomplished in 1813. But to understand the significance of that work we must first return to 1809.

In that year Beethoven reaped the rewards of the cultural triumph of the Fifth Symphony and of the joyousness of the Sixth. In the autumn of 1809 he finished a number of superb works. First to be started, probably some time in the second half of 1808, was the Piano Concerto No. 5, popularly known as the "Emperor" (Opus 73). The work begins with a splendid assertion of the virtuoso pianist as hero and continues with a first movement full of energy, guided aggression, and pleasure. The second movement is a perfectly balanced withdrawal into sustained happiness, and leads without pause into the final movement, the main theme of which is a shout of joy. In that same autumn he finished the Quartet No. 10, Opus 74. The most noteworthy movements are the second, offering the most entranced rapture he had yet achieved, and the third, a further development of the energy of the Scherzo of the Fifth Symphony. In October of 1809 he wrote the Piano Sonata No. 24, Opus 78, turning away from the heroics of the Waldstein and the Appasionata into a withdrawn, domesticated happiness, ending with another shout of joy, and appropriately dedicated to a Countess, one of his best friends. And the end of 1809 also saw the completion of a work begun in March. Because of Napoleon's advance on Vienna, Archduke Rudolf von Habsburg, Beethoven's pupil, friend, and patron, was forced, with the rest of the Imperial family and retinue, to leave Vienna; and Beethoven wrote a delightful piece of program music, the three movements being named "The Departure," in which we hear the carriages rolling away, followed by the dreariness of "The Absence," and the anticipated joy of "The Return" (Sonata No. 26, Opus 81a). And finally in 1809 he began the overture and incidental music for Goethe's drama *Egmont* (Opus 84), first presented at the fourth performance of the revival of the play in the Court Theater on June 15, 1810. No doubt for Beethoven this complex play meant the defeat of a man struggling for freedom against tyranny, and in that defeat achieving a moral victory which was to give birth to a political one. So the overture and the incidental music end with "Siegesmusik," victory music.

All of these works, then, celebrate Beethoven's own stylistic and cultural victory of the Fifth Symphony, and from all of them, even the Overture to *Egmont,* is absent the dramatization of the titanic struggle of the great series of works culminating in the Fifth. Now suddenly a change takes place. Beethoven writes a new quartet, No. 11, Opus 95. It is certainly in the middle or second style of his career, but it strikes a new note. It is in the minor; the world is once again perceived as hindrance, as a place of restricted confinement, such as we encountered in several works of the early years of the decade. Instructively, it is not dedicated to a prince or an archduke or a count or a countess but to an old friend, a relationship dating from Beethoven's earliest years in Vienna, a man with whom he often had dinner and who, an assiduous civil servant, kept Beethoven supplied with sharp goose-quill pens. The letters to him are filled with jokes and good humor and charm, this Nikolaus Zmeskall von Donamovecz. At one time or other the work acquired the name of "Quartetto Serioso." As the dedication suggests, it is a profoundly personal work. Indeed it was not performed until 1814 nor published until 1816. Compared with the preceding works composed after the Fifth Symphony, what is missing is the almost careless and virtuosic expansiveness of those compositions. Instead, the work is short, highly compressed, brooding, at times of an almost savage temper, and in the second movement touched, more than touched, by despair. Yet the last movement summons Beethovenian energy again, though in the minor and close to hysteria. And then suddenly the coda bursts through into light, affirmation, almost, as it were, tossing off the rest of the quartet as irrelevant, a perfect symbolization of the willed effort to throw aside depression. This work was followed in early 1811 by the glorious, radiant, noble "Archduke" Trio, Opus 97, dedicated, of course, to the Archduke Rudolf, who, among other services, received and kept treasured for the future a copy of everything that Beethoven wrote.

In the summer of 1811 Beethoven wrote overtures and incidental music for two plays written by Kotzebue, the most popular of German dramatists, for the opening of the new theater at Pesth, the Hungarian capital, and he was able to give these works something of a Hungarian character (*King Stephen,* Opus 117, and *The Ruins of Athens,* Opus 113). But otherwise his productivity was already falling off. (Indeed, it had begun to decline in 1810.) However, in the autumn of 1811 he began the Seventh Symphony (Opus 92), which he finished in the summer of 1812, and immediately followed it by the composition of its companion piece, Symphony No. 8 (Opus 93). In various concerts of 1813 and after, *Wellington's Victory* and the Seventh Symphony were so popular the Eighth Symphony was more or less ignored. And that annoyed Beethoven, for he felt that the Eighth was the finer of the two works. Indeed, its last movement was the richest and most complex symphonic movement he had yet achieved.

He followed this symphony by what is probably the finest of his violin piano sonatas, Opus 96. But it is also very different, different from anything Beethoven had yet composed. The entrancing first movement is of a delicious loveliness, tinged, just barely, with melancholy. The ravishing second movement is a long meditation, close to a prayer, but intensifying the note of melancholy. And that is further intensified in the scherzo in the minor, most unusual for a work in the major. The delicate final movement, a set of variations on a theme of a gentle and almost popular character, ends with the only sustained burst of energy in the work. Two things are extraordinary about it. The first is its gentleness, unparalleled in Beethoven's previous works, and with that gentleness a sheer beauty, even though touched with melancholy, a loveliness that Beethoven had never before achieved nor tried to achieve, and never was to achieve again. And the second striking thing about it is that with this work Beethoven's serious composition comes to a sudden halt. A perfect work, it nevertheless describes a sharp decline of energy, wit, and aggressiveness. It was to be year before he wrote the work mentioned above, the only serious work of 1813, directly after the pot-boiler of *Wellington's Victory,* written because, as a consequence of the terrible Viennese inflation resulting from the Napoleonic wars, Beethoven could scarcely make ends meet; and there was as yet no hope for an end to Europe's distress.   1812 was the year of the famous letter to the "Eternal Beloved" (probably Antonie Brentano, according to the latest research).   At any rate it was the heart-broken failure of his last hope for love and domestic happiness.   At the same time his deafness was steadily becoming worse, and he was socially more isolated. Indeed, his interest in Mälzel was because of the latter's ideas for hearing aids, which were ineffective.

So the one work of 1813 which is important and beautiful is his second setting of "An die Hoffnung" ("To Hope," Opus 94), a poem by Christian August Tiedge, a poet now forgotten but then much admired, one whom Beethoven had met.   This second setting is not written in strophes to match the stanzas of the poem, as the first setting was, but in a dramatic form, almost like a solo cantata, and the second stanza, the most poignant, the most despairing, is repeated at the end.   Certainly it was written in the midst of Beethoven's unhappiness and even despair.   All symptoms point to serious depression, a crisis in life and more profoundly in art.   Certainly at this time he expressed dissatisfaction with everything he had written.

In 1814 he undertook a revision of *Leonore*; the result was *Fidelio,* the opera we now know, dramatically improved and with wonderful musical additions, but also with some genuine musical losses.   But most significantly, Beethoven was, once again, dissatisfied with the work.   Restless, unhappy, unable to engage in serious composition, he found nevertheless that the work on *Fidelio* had a revitalizing effect.   And in the spring and summer after the very successful production of *Fidelio* he was able to write a new piano sonata.

Sonata No. 27, Opus 90 in E minor, is the first indication of the onset of what has come to be known as Beethoven's third period, and the first indication that he was emerging from his depression. The work is in two sharply constrasting movements.   The first is bare in style and grim in character, but full of struggle and at moments in the development marked by a new kind of pianistic richness.   The opening theme is built on a repetition of one of the most powerful and frequently recurring motives in Western music of the last few centuries, to be used by Liszt in *Les Préludes* and César Franck in his symphony: a single bare note, a movement downward, then a movement upward a tone or two beyond the pitch of the opening note. It is a withdrawal in order to summon the energy to advance. This thematic pattern is repeated four times, and then the melody withdraws hesitantly to a pitch below the point where it started. There are two more attempts at assertion, but each time, though delivered with force, the third note of the pattern only returns to the starting note. And the opening exposition subsides into weakness followed by a sustained silence. It is the pattern of the entire movement, which ends with a repetition of that last part of the opening. The effort to overcome an inhibiting and crushing hindrance has failed. And it is of import that for the first time Beethoven gives a specific directions for how his sonata is to be played, "*Mit Lebhaftigkeit und durchaus mit Empfindung und Ausdruck*," "With liveliness and throughout with sensitivity and expression." Here is a Romantic specification and assertion of the kind of cultural instructions the work is proposing.

After this failure of assertion, the second movement is a complete contrast, beginning with a gentle and lovely and consoling theme, a beautifully balanced upward and downward pitch movement. It has something of the beauty of the violin sonata, Opus 96, but unfolds with greater ease and confidence. What can this sonata mean but a description of the depression he had been experiencing, his vain struggles to get out of it, and now an easy and fervent rejoicing that he has recovered? And this interpretation is supported by his ability to complete a much neglected and beautiful work, often called dull and uninteresting, Overture in C Major *Zur Namensfeier,* to celebrate the name day of the Emperor, an overture designed for concert use (Opus 115). Begun in 1809 and finished at last in March, 1815, it has hints of the Ninth Symphony, suggestions of the third and final style.

But even greater support for the interpretation offered here of Opus 90 is a remarkable work begun at the end of 1814 and finished in the summer of 1815, *Meerestille und Glückliche Fahrt*, Opus 112, a work for mixed chorus and orchestra, in effect a short cantata. The poem is Goethe's, and the usual translation of the title, *Calm Sea and Prosperous Voyage,* is completely misleading. Actually there are two separate poems, the first describing not a calm sea but a becalmed ship, unable to move forward, and its anxious captain. The last three lines read, "Todesstille fürchterliche! / In der ungeheuren Weite / Reget keine Welle sich." *"A fearful deathlike stillness! in the horrible emptiness no wave moves."* A more perfect metaphor for depression can scarcely be imagined. Indeed, Coleridge used it in *The Ancient Mariner* a year or so after Goethe published his poem — "Day after day, day after day, / We stuck, nor breath nor motion; / As idle as a painted ship / Upon a painted ocean." The second poem, printed directly after the first, ends, *"Es teilt sich die Welle / Es naht sich die Ferne; / Schon seh ich das Land!"* "The waves part; the distance nears; already I see the land!" Beethoven's setting is as fine as the poem, and like all great musical settings of language it adds to and intensifies the meaning. The explanation, particularly in this instance, is that the composer can regulate and control the lapse of time. Thus in repeating the last lines of *Meerestille* Beethoven can slow down the utterance and introduce pauses in a way that would be intolerable if the words were merely spoken. Thus he can intensify both by repetition and by tempo Goethe's metaphor of hopeless despair. And with the sheer volume of his chorus he can similarly intensify the relief, release, and joyousness, almost ecstatic, of *"Schon seh ich das Land!"*

And Beethoven did indeed see the land, for in the summer of 1815 he finished a pair of works begun that spring, two sonatas for piano and violoncello, Opus 102. These works mark two stages of development into his final style. In the first not only is the Beethovenian energy and aggressive will restored, together with a renewed dramatization of struggle and something of the new loveliness of Opus 96, but also emergent is a tightness of structure, and in the last movement an emphasis upon and revelation of the power of musical organization without benefit of sensuous appeal. That tightness is revealed even in the organization of the two movements, each offering a slow then fast pattern. In the slow movement of the second sonata he achieved an intensity and a profundity of feeling that was also emergent. And in the last movement he wrote the first of his third period fugues, again returning to a Baroque form in order to give weight and power to a final movement — as he had discovered earlier, a deliberate harshness and aggressive force that the more expansive and discursive sonata-allegro form cannot achieve. And here again in his typical late-period fugue the bare bones of musical composition are revealed with a transparency not to be found in the fugues of the 18th century, even those of Bach. The structure of music, "structure" in its most complete and inclusive sense, has become Beethoven's aim, to embody in music and to reveal in music the power of the organizing mind. That these works were genuinely emergent is hinted at by the execration with which they were received. But now we can see that they mark a new level of Beethoven's greatness.

What we have, then, in these years from 1809 to 1815 is a full-scale Romantic crisis, outlining in music and the absence of music the pattern which we have already seen so perfectly set forth in "The Ancient Mariner." That Beethoven's depression was not merely a personal depression — stemming from his financial difficulties, his frustrated love, and his growing deafness — but a depression involving and probably emerging from the profoundest source of his self-valuation, his musical genius — is evident in the fact that to get out of it he forged a new style. Thus he was reborn. These years exhibit with an astonishing transparency the very essence of Romanticism. When the cultural sources of value have failed, the individual must develop from his own resources his self-ascription of value; and having transcended his culture he must, sooner or later, transcend his own transcendence. In the fascinating drama of Beethoven's life, a drama that has engaged intelligent attention for nearly two centuries, no period is more dramatic than these final years of the Napoleonic ascendancy. And that reference to Napoleon is justified, for Napoleon's betrayal of Beethoven's beliefs and the vulgar and gimcrack empire he created must have had an effect on Beethoven's grasp of the world and of life. He finished his great cantata about depression and recovery and his first two essays in his last style within weeks after the battle of Waterloo on June 18, 1815.

Hegel — 2   It is one of the amusing convergences of Ro-
(1770-1831)   manticism, not at all ironic, that Hegel and Hoff-
                       mann were in Bamberg at the same time — Hegel
arriving in February, 1807, Hoffmann in the following year, before
Hegel left for his headmastership in Nürnberg, 35 miles to the south.
It is appropriate that they were in Bamberg at the same time and
that both men found their publishers there, for both were coming to
focus their attention and analytical and imaginative powers on the
purely human resources man has with which to encounter the world
and to organize his relation to it. And of course they had another
bond, even though if they met in Bamberg we know nothing about
it, in that both lost good positions because of the Napoleonic turmoil. Yet Hegel never lost his confidence in Napoleon, his justified
conviction that the Napoleonic armies carried to Europe the ideal
of rational government and freedom from the moribund social institutions with which Europe was burdened. And after Waterloo he
was convinced that there would be a radically conservative reaction,
an attempt to do what could not be done, to restore the social and
political institutions and controls that had obtained in Europe before
the French Revolution and the Napoleonic devouring and releasing
flame. And of course he was right. Yet, it will be remembered, he
was also aware that the absolute ideas of the Enlightenment and the
Revolution would necessarily end, if an attempt were made to embody them in social reality, in an outpouring of blood and human life,
as since 1815 they have done often enough. The only barrier to that
destructiveness of the absolute, he saw, lay in understanding the processes in human thought by which the destructive absolute is created.
And this task is complicated by the fact that, as was revealed by the
liberty-enhancing results of the Napoleonic whirlwind, the absolute
can also be creative. As other Romantics had realized, but none so
clearly as Hegel himself, the support for social and political liberty,
its foundations, its underpinnings, is cultural freedom. In the *Phenomenology* he had demonstrated that the fundamental character
of both *Geist* (or culture) and the individual mind is a steady movement towards such freedom, and that the cultural self-consciousness
which was the prime result of both the Kantian revolution and the

Revolutionary crisis, that self-consciousness which the *Phenomenology* was designed to bring to full awareness, was the most important step toward cultural freedom and thus toward social and political freedom it was possible to take.

In his first great work he had shown how our apprehension of the world is built up from sensory perception and is equally the product of the history of such apprehension. Now it was necessary to continue his investigation and to examine the consequence of those processes, the instruments of apprehension and control and self-awareness which man had developed. And his name for those instruments was "logic." Only by understanding what he called "logic" could the cultural self-consciousness reached in the *Phenomenology* be solidly grounded. And he gave new meaning to that word because he perceived that the traditional logics, hardly changed from Plato and Aristotle, were moribund. The subject matter of logic, he concluded, is the categories by which we apprehend and organize our relation to the world, for categories are all we have for that apprehension and organization. The weakness, the failure, of Kant's logic lay precisely in the fact that he accepted traditional categorizations without subjecting them to the analytic examination which, when performed, as Hegel proposed now to perform them, revealed their internal and external contradictions and confusions, the result of the fact that, as we have already seen, every category brings into being its negation. Traditional logic maintained, and for some conservatives still does, that there is a unitary and unified, coherent, and self-consistent structure to thought, and that that structure can be determined, codified, and taught. This is what Hegel denied, and as soon as he could after settling down in Nürnberg in 1808 and establishing himself both administratively and pedagogically as headmaster, he set to work in his evenings to write his *Wissenschaft der Logik* (*Science of Logic*). He published Part One of Volume One in 1812, Part Two in 1813, and Volume Two in 1816.

As he himself said in a notable metaphor in the Introduction, with this study we enter the realm of shadows, a metaphor that hints his convergence with the fictional enterprise of Hoffmann. And he also warns that the various titles of chapters and chapter divisions and parts, and all the rest of the paraphernalia set forth in the various Tables of Contents, are not to be taken seriously for a moment. He is in fact telling the reader that what structure the book has is merely a convenience, superficial, of no real importance, that indeed the structure of the book is what he happened to think about in the course of writing it. So her inserts "Notes" outside of that stated organization to emphasize its unimportance. To be sure, the book moves roughly from the category of Being, which, he says, is simply the category of Nothing, through the category of Essence to the category of the Notion, the world as it exists in the mind of God before the creation of man and nature — one of Hegel's more fantastic jokes: "God," "man," and "nature" being themselves categories of "logic" and belonging to the world of shadows. But that notion, in itself, is hardly more than a matter of convenience, a matter of imposing a certain control upon the flood of ideas which are not about the structure of thought but about the absence of such structure. Previous thinking about categorization, even Kant's, had been static. Hegel's is fluid, seeking out the confusion, the contradiction, the momentary coherence, the fundamental impermanence of categories, the way they slip, slide, and slither on the surface of the world. Hence in his investigation of the world of shadows he has no concern with the relation of categorization to the real world.

The subject matter of "logic" is the categories, that is, logic itself. And that is the source of the difficulty of writing and thinking about logic. To study the inadequacy of categories we must use inadequate categories. Thus we can arrive in the study of what Hegel calls "logic" at no finality, but only a heightened and self-conscious awareness of the fluidity of thought, the positive aspect of which is the fact that because of this fundamental instability of categorization, even, he says, in the physical sciences — let alone the arts and the humanities — man can constantly modify his "logic" to meet the exigencies, the emergencies, the constantly changing demands of his encounter with the world, an encounter which changes the world. It is this awareness of the true character of thinking which, for Hegel, is the third important step to cultural self-awareness, the first two having been taken in the *Phenomenology*.

There is no denying that the *Science of Logic* is enormously difficult, and equally competent people have given quite opposite judgments of it, some saying that to work one's way through it is immensely rewarding, and others asserting that such an enterprise is not worth the trouble it takes. I have accepted Walter Kaufmann's interpretation, for it is the only one that makes sense in terms of the *Phenomenology*, of which it is the necessary consequence. But Hegel has left us one tremendous clue to what he was doing and, perhaps, attempting to do. The last discourse he wrote before he died of cholera on November 14, 1831, was the Preface to the second edition, "dated Berlin November 7, 1831" in which he states, "The forms of thought are, in the first instance, displayed and stored in human *language*." The only access to the categories of "logic" is language itself, and he might as well have said that what he was writing about in his *Science of Logic* was not the imagined structures of formal logic but the actual concrete reality of natural language, of the way language is actually used to establish relations between ourselves and situations, situations which constantly require changing the meanings of our categories. What Hegel revealed in his work is that the very instabilities, the incoherences, the confusions, the contradictions of language and the categorizations it "displays and stores" are precisely the source of what success we have in our encounter with nature and with each other. Even more than the *Phenomenology*, the *Science of Logic* is the greatest initial effort to accomplish the Romantic analytic dismantlement of the cultural superstructure of human behavior.

Lord Byron   In the year in which Hegel began to publish his
(1788-1824)   *Science of Logic,* 1812, a work appearing in a
                    small edition and little regarded at the time,
except for a few professional and academic philosophers, a work which together with the *Phenomenology* was not to rescue him from his headmastership until 1816 — another literary career was begun which was to have extraordinary consequences, that of George Gordon Byron, sixth Baron Byron. In that year he published Cantos I and II of *Childe Harold's Pilgrimage: A Romaunt,* on Tuesday, March 10,

to be exact — and, in a famous phrase, "awoke to find himself famous."
That poem was superficially an account of his travels in 1809 and 1810
in Portugal, Spain, Malta, Albania, and Greece. He began to write
at Janina in Albania on October 31, 1809, and finished the second
canto in Smyrna on March 28, 1810. His travels, which had begun in
June, 1809, ended with his return to England in July, 1811. A few
statistics will give some indication of his impact not merely on England but also on the continent, in the colonies of Europe, and in some
former colonies, like the United States. By the end of 1815 *Childe
Harold's Pilgrimage* had gone through ten editions. In later years the
addition of two more cantos led to endless editions in the course of
the century. In 1813 he published the first of his "Turkish Tales,"
The Giaour, which by 1815 had gone through twelve editions. In
the same year appeared *The Bride of Abydos,* five editions by 1815,
in 1814 *The Corsair,* nine editions by the end of 1815, and in 1814
Lara, four editions in 1815. Also in 1815 appeared his first official
collected edition (there had been two pirated collected editions in
the United States in 1813 and 1814), and that was reprinted endlessly,
with the gradual addition of later poems. Moreover, by 1816 his fame
had spread to the continent, and by the end of 1820 there were numerous translations of these and later works in French, German,
Italian, and Danish. But that was just the beginning. In the course of
the century translations of his various works appeared in these lan-
guages and also in modern Greek, Polish, Russian, Spanish, Swedish,
Armenian, Bohemian, Dutch, Hungarian, Icelandic, Portuguese, Rou-
manian, Bulgarian, Hebrew, Serbian, and a synthetic international
language; and in the 1820s he became a figure in Part II of Goethe's
Faust.

When we read these poems of Byron's today, from the first two
cantos of *Childe Harold's Pilgrimage* through *Lara,* it is easy to be
at a loss to account not only for this immense popularity but even more
for the immense importance and ascription of greatness which his
works, and his figure, enjoyed and still enjoy, even though he is no
longer much read. For example, his works have provided the plots
for more than forty operas, as well as three operas about the man
himself, and any number of songs and lengthier vocal, choral, and orchestral works.

In *Childe Harold* and the heroes of the four other poems the principal character, indeed, the sole character of interest, is said to be a self-portrait. There is just enough truth in this to be misleading, and it may be indeed the case that Byron used these five figures from Harold through Lara to project a desired self-image, partially based upon his own feelings and experiences, and partly derived from the villains of Gothic novels. But these figures are not presented as villains. Rather, each is a victim, the pattern of which is set forth in the first poem, a man driven from his own country by obscure but powerful forces and feelings which cannot be satisfied at home, a man of whom it is hinted that one of the forces is guilt over an unnamed crime. And certainly that is repeated again and again. On the one hand, however, there are in *Childe Harold* and particularly in *The Bride of Abydos* realistic accounts of life in foreign climes; in the first Portugal, Spain, and Albania, and in the second Greece and its isles. One of the cultural phenomena to emerge later in the century, and partly because of Byron, was the Romanticization of Spain as a wild, half-civilized country, still steeped in its Arab and gypsy inheritance, and certainly not really part of cosmopolitan and sophisticated Europe. Late in the century *Carmen* was witness to this. Even more exotic, of course, were Albania, under the control of the infamous and fascinating Ali Pasha — theoretically subject to the Turkish Sultan but in effect virtually independent — and Greece, then still under Turkish rule. The cultures on the edge of Europe and the Muslim cultures outside of the European culture area even though actually on the European continent — these were the settings of Byron's early poems, a setting he was to continue to use into the 1820s. And of course he was to die in the effort to aid the Greeks in the re-Europeanization of that unfortunate country.

Hence, in all of these poems was the appeal of the exotic, the appeal, as we have met before in the developing Romantic tradition, of alternative cultures. Unlike the 18th century, which was interested in subduing non-European styles to a European rococo and in seeing alien cultures in the light of imagined cultural universals, Byron, highly Romantic, was interested in the differences among alien cultures, and above all in asserting the validity of those cultures in their own terms. Thus in *The Giaour,* part of the guilt of the hero lies in his violating Turkish customs and ethics, and he does so only for erotic reasons and for revenge. The relatively non-Byronic hero of *The Bride of Abydos* and the very Byronic hero of *The Corsair* are pirates. The latter is outcast from his own society and is one who preys upon Turkish society; and in *Lara* his return to his homeland in some unnamed part of Europe reveals his alienation from that society, an alienation which ends in his death. 1814, the year of the third and fourth Turkish Tales, was also, it will be remembered, the year of Ingres' *La Grand Odalisque,* in which the marvelous attractiveness of Turkish culture is hinted at, even revealed, a theme Ingres was never to abandon. But most important for Byron and his many readers and followers was the revelation that morals and behavior are a product of cultural situations and historical circumstances, not of universal and permanent human traits and morals. This geographical relativism was the equivalent in space of Hegel's similar relativism of time, a growing belief that all manifestations of the *Geist* are equally valid.

Yet this aspect of Byron's poetry was not the only aspect nor indeed the most important. The clue to deeper and more significant meaning of what Byron was up to is to be found in the complete title of his first important work, Childe Harold was on a Pilgrimage. A Pilgrim sets out to go to a spot or a temple or a church which his cultural tradition has designated as and continues to recognize as holy, that is, a place where the divine enters the human, a place, therefore, in which the value of the individual is renewed, reaffirmed, reascribed, given fresh confirmation and support. Moreover, a pilgrim sets out on his quest because the ordinary sources of value-ascription — his local parish church, the cathedral of his diocese, the holy spots of his home area, such as tombs of saints — are no longer, for him, efficacious. The length, the difficulty, the expense, the loss of normal income of his undertaking are all sacrifices which prove the seriousness of his purpose and earn for him what he is seeking. But for Harold there were no holy spots at home nor a holy spot to which he journeyed and which did for him the traditional miracle of arriving at the object of a pilgrimage. Rather, the object of his quest proved to be Greece, not present-day Greece, but the ruins of ancient Greek civilization, ruins which served to intensify his sense of isolation and abandonment. The object of his pilgrimage no longer existed.

That these heroes are indeed heroes of value, not of values, is proved by the fact that though they are pirates and outcasts nevertheless they are capable of being in love. The Corsair, for example, having seen his beloved die, simply vanishes, only to reappear as Lara, and in that poem he is inconsolable, unable to love the woman disguised as his page, the woman he had rescued from the harem of the Turk Seid, the woman who loves him. And the heroes of the of the other two poems are equally devoted and intense in their loving. Thus emerges for the first time the peculiar theme of Romantic love, a cultural tradition of the utmost importance, one which survives today in popular songs, so profoundly has it penetrated into all levels of Western culture. Our language makes a distinction between "loving" and "being in love." The distinction is subtle but of the utmost importance. We can say not only that we love a person, and mean it either erotically, or non-erotically; we can also say that we love a symphony, or a painting, or a baseball team. The importance of the objects of such loving is that they are objects of the ascription of value to others and to oneself as an other, an ascription essential to the life of social interaction. "Being in love" is quite another matter, indeed the reverse of "loving," for to be in love with a person is to be dependent upon that person for an ascription of value to oneself; it is a confession that one needs that ascription of value. It can be a factor in depression. Freud, himself, a product of the Romantic tradition, judged "being in love" to be the model psychosis. But it is also a confession of one's potentiality as a member of the human community. It is, therefore, a particular note of adolescence, a period in which uncertainty over one's own value is at its most critical. In Byron's heroes "being in love" is proof that they are heroes, not villains, but heroes of a new kind, heroes who are manifestations of an emergent cultural situation, one in which the ascription of value has failed, except for the one individual who is a source of value ascription. Their being in love is proof that their alienation is the consequence of a crisis in their culture.

All this gives us a hint about the popularity of Byron's works, which, except for Chateaubriand's, have faded more than those of any writer we have yet considered. It has been suggested at the beginning of this chapter that though the number of creative or productive figures of Romanticism were only few, a tiny drop in the ocean of Europe's population, there must have been others who responded to them and of whom, except for a stray letter or other document, we have no knowledge. The popularity of Byron attests to the existence of these individuals. What he offered was something that many had waiting for, even though they had not known it. That is, Byron's great theme is the theme of loss, the theme of the failure of one's culture, the sense of alienation, of isolation, of abandonment, of disinheritance and disenchantment. As we have seen, that is the theme which runs throughout Wordsworth, but in such a way, and so subtly, that it was not easily recognized. Evidently Byron himself did not recognize it in Wordsworth, but with his extraordinary sensitivity it is more than possible that in fact he responded to it. For even though the ancestry of his heroes can be traced to the villains of the Gothic novel, they are not villains. They are heroic figures, but individuals without a society, a cultural milieu, in which to prove their heroic attributes. They are not Mozart's conception of Don Giovanni, but Hoffmann's. They can display their heroism only by preying upon another society, just as Harold himself, an outsider in the countries he visits, is a kind of cultural parasite, and certainly a cultural outsider with no way of playing a role in those countries. Yet his journey is a pilgrimage, and a pilgrimage with a reward, for the poem reveals that in that very self-realization of loneliness, of abandonment, is to be found the source of his value. The poem is in fact a means of ascribing value to Harold — that is, to Byron — for the very reason that he has discovered that the value sources of his society have in fact failed. That is the metaphorical significance of his meditations on the ruins of ancient Greece.

And that also is the secret of the immense popularity of these poems, in spite of the fact that, by any standards, their literary merit is not very great. But that made no difference, and is of no importance. Rather, here for the first time was a dramatization and symbolization of precisely that cultural collapse which the years of Revolutionary and Napoleonic turmoil had accomplished. Byron's greatness, and the greatness and power of his appeal, lay in his extraordinarily powerful and above all accessible symbolization of the task of the then truly modern individual, the emerging Romantic, the task of responding to the loss of the efficacy of the culture's traditional sources and modes of value-ascription by recreating from his own unique resources, his unique access to and transformation of *Geist,* an innovative and emergent mode of establishing value. What Byron revealed so powerfully was the terror of realizing that loss, of recognizing that the task of value creation was the isolated individual's, and with, as yet, no notion of how to go about it. The loss was revealed in a way no one could miss. But how to recover from that loss remained a mystery. That mystery was Byron's power; that made him a genuine culture hero.

Wordsworth — 3   In these works published from 1812 to 1814
(1770-1850)   Byron metaphorically set forth and established
the syndrome of what came to be known, in time, as *"le mal du siècle."* Towards the end of the century Nietzsche was to call it Nihilism. Byron's dramatization of it and the appeal of his picturesque accounts of life at the edge of Europe and beyond gave the notion a new ease of accessibility, in part because it was not accompanied by an elaborate historical or metaphysical explanation. Thus it could appeal without hindrance to thousands and in time perhaps hundreds of thousands of Europeans — and by "Europeans" is meant here all those who were under the control of European culture — North and South Americans, Australians, New Zealanders, and innumerable educated individuals of the Indian sub-continent, even Europeanized Japanese and Africans. That syndrome was to reappear in endless avatars, as it were, and was to become one of the dominant themes of 19th century Romantic culture. Byron's greatness was precisely the fact that he struck the most sensitive nerve of post-Revolutionary, post-Napoleonic, consciousness. Yet even while he was writing these immensely seminal works, William Wordsworth was writing an extended, subtle, and frequently beautiful, but on the

whole difficult and relatively inaccessible, analysis of precisely that syndrome. It was *The Excursion,* one of the most unread and under-valued works of English, even European, poetic literature.

He began it in 1806, no doubt in the surge of self-confidence he must have felt after reading *The Prelude* to Coleridge and the Beau-monts, and continued working on it well into 1809. But then var-ious difficulties, particularly his quarrel with Coleridge, occasioned by his disappointment, distress, and anger over the addict Coleridge had allowed himself to become, interrupted the poem. After nearly three years he resumed work in 1811, writing into 1814, when *The Excursion* was published — and stupidly received by the most power-ful critic of the day, Francis Jeffrey. And in general even Words-worth's friends were not happy with it. Yet it is a wonderfully ori-ginal work; not, as it seems at first glance, as part of the great and un-writable philosophical poem, that tormenting and destructive will-of-the-wisp set loose by Coleridge, but original because of its grandly scaled dramatization of what we have just seen as the Byronic syn-drome, the sickness of the century.

It tells simply of a walk taken in a very small part of the Lake District, with a bit of southwestern England transported to Cum-berland and with the rearrangement of a few hills and valleys. The Narrator, the least developed of the four major characters, meets the Wanderer, a retired pedlar, at a ruined cottage. (Book One is simply "The Ruined Cottage" which Wordsworth wrote in the 1790s.) To-gether they go to find the Solitary, a man withdrawn in bitterness from the world. Almost against his wishes they persuade him, the next morning, to continue their excursion with them. They walk into a neighboring valley and there visit the church, meet the Pastor, hear his tales of those buried in the churchyard, have a meal with him, and then row across a lake to have a picnic with the Pastor's wife, his two children, and a friend of his son. After sunset they all re-turn to the Parsonage, and there break up, going their various ways. This is all that occurs. Nevertheless something of great importance has happened.

The focus of the poem is the Solitary, a man who has made an immense, a total moral, emotional, and metaphysical investment in the French Revolution, has been overwhelmed by its failure, has attempted to discover a new world in America; but he has found only an extension in space of the corrupt European life, and has returned to a remote valley in Cumberland. As we have already seen, the story of the ruined cottage in Book I is a metaphor for the Waste Land the Solitary now inhabits, a metaphor subtly emphasized and revealed by the great disorder of the cottage's attic room in which he lives, his needs being taken care of by a family in the rooms below. The problem the Wanderer presents, the problem in which the Narrator is deeply interested, is how to rescue the Solitary from his despondency. And each of the four characters is an aspect of Wordsworth himself. He has divided himself into four in order to analyze himself as a cultural representative of his time and in order to show that rescue from the Solitary's despondency is possible and can be accomplished. For that rescue is accomplished, and in a highly dramatic device of immense subtlety.

The Narrator is that aspect of Wordsworth which might be called his minimum position, not that of the sanctifying poet but merely of an almost characterless country gentleman who loves the landscape he lives in and is deeply interested in its people. The Solitary is, of course, the Wordsworth of the middle 1790s, the Wordsworth who had yielded up moral questions in despair. The Wanderer, a successful and retired Pedlar, is the continuity in Wordsworth's thinking of a kind of Enlightenment deism and progressivism, as well as his eternal restlessness, his role of observing outsider. The Pastor represents the traditional culture of remote rural England, a culture which Wordsworth had found consoling and supporting in the person of the aged Pastor of Grasmere. And the poem consists almost entirely of long discourses by the Wanderer and the Pastor, with occasional interruptions by the Solitary and the Narrator. The whole takes place against frequent references to the Napoleonic whirlwind, to war-torn Europe, and it is more than possible that Wordsworth, atypically, rushed into print in 1814 because Napoleon had been defeated and dethroned, a Napoleon given in this poem an almost Satanic dimension.

The modernity of the work comes out forcefully in an argument between the Wanderer and he Solitary. The Wanderer has been de-

ploring the future physical deterioration of the working class because
of the industrial revolution in the form of the emerging textile industry, the result of the mechanization of spinning and weaving, run
by water-power. To that the Solitary replies by pointing out that
the Wanderer is being sentimental, for the traditional conditions of
the English rural population have produced for centuries a stunted,
half-idiotic, and deformed population segment of considerable size.
The Wanderer admits the point, and the argument virtually confirms
the Solitary in his despondency. On the other hand, the Pastor, with
far less of religious preaching than the Wanderer's, simply tells stories
of how the dead in the churchyard — the deaf, the blind, the poor,
the victims of hunger and disease — were nevertheless able to find
value in existence, consolation for their sufferings, and frequently
recompense and a modicum of happiness. The Narrator is above
all the one who, in his narration and sometimes in his speeches, exalts
the beauty of the landscape, particularly in two ecstatic descriptions
of the two sunsets of the poem. He is the Wordsworth who has recovered value in responding to natural beauty.

   All of this is aimed at the task the Wanderer and the Narrator have
taken on themselves, to rescue the Solitary from his despondency.
And they have succeeded, not in the rescue but in creating at least
the beginning of a possible rescue. At the end, as he says farewell,
the Solitary shyly suggests that he would be happy to meet them
again and to undertake with them another excursion. And this is
the drama of the poem. The Solitary has been moved from a position
of absolute stasis. He has not been consoled, he has not accepted
any metaphysical explanation and justification of human sufferings,
or any religious theodicy, nor has he seen anything but a political
deterioration. Indeed, he cannot even accept the notion of England as the sole remaining repository of human freedom. But he
has been moved. He has found pleasure and amusement and value
in a few hours spent in intelligent and pleasant interaction with a few
fellow human beings. He has felt, though minimally and delicately,
the rebirth of the power to ascribe value to himself and to others.

   Thus, once again, Wordsworth, in offering *The Excursion* as Part
II of the proposed great philosophical poem, has shown, as he had

shown in *The Prelude,* that such a vast work of metaphysical synthesis could no longer be written.   Instead he has offered psychological analysis, and his subtlety and delicacy is revealed in the fact that here is no psychological system but, if anything, an anti-system, perhaps something like the Hegelian anti-system of *The Science of Logic.* Not the truth of anything that is said by the characters of *The Excursion* is the issue.   Their various metaphysical and religious and political positions may or may not be true.   The issue is the pragmatic effect of the utterance of these positions directed towards a suffering human being, and directed not in so melodramatic a term as "love" but merely in mild friendship and delicate concern.   The Solitary has become a little less of a Solitary.   The Wanderer, the Narrator, and the Pastor have had a major victory.   *The Excursion* is a drama on a grand scale, and that drama is barely noticeable.

Francesco José de Goya y Lucientes 1746-1828)   In the year of the publication of Wordsworth's strange poem the Spanish artist Goya painted what has been called the first truly modern picture, "The Execution of Madrilenos on the Third of May" [1808].   In March, 1808, the French, under the pretext of guarding the Spanish coasts against the British, invaded Spain. In May, with both king and heir of the country having been trapped into renouncing the throne, Napoleon made his brother Joseph king of Spain.   But in Madrid the first of the modern guerilla wars had already broken out.   On May 2, 1808, the people of Madrid attacked the French troops.   On May 3 those troops captured and executed summarily many of the rebels, but even so were forced to retire from Madrid, not returning until July 20.   Between then and June, 1813, Spain was torn by a terrible war between the occupying French and the rebellious Spaniards, aided in time by the British led by Arthur Wellesley, destined to defeat Napoleon at Waterloo.   As we have noted in discussing Beethoven, the British routed the retreating French on June 21, 1813, at Vittoria in north-east Spain, pursued them into France, besieged them at Bayonne, and finally defeated them at Toulouse on April 10, 1814.   It is possible that Goya painted the "Second

of May" and the "Third of May" on the occasion of the return of
Ferdinand IV, the former crown prince, to Madrid on May, 1814,
in order to celebrate the initiation of the war against the French.

The profound effect of the war on Goya was to turn him, in his
fifties, into a new kind of artist. In the 18th century his style had
been that of a late Baroque and Spanish rococo, tempered, of course,
by his painterly genius, and unaffected by the neo-classicism of the
late French 18th century. As he developed intellectually he became
a liberal, a man of the Enlightenment, one who hailed the French Revolution and the advent of Napoleon himself. The impact of the events
of the 1790s is revealed powerfully in the great series of 80 prints
he did in 1798 and 1799 which he called *Los Caprichos*. Not only
were they in many ways a typical Enlightenment attack upon the
failings of the traditional society, its brutality, its superstitions, its
materialism, its greed; they also were stylistically strikingly emergent,
presenting new conceptions of space and light and shadow. But the
invasion of Spain put him into a dilemma, shown on the one hand by
his attractive and even affectionate portraits of various individuals
of the occupying French administration, who, he hoped, would bring
the Enlightenment to Spain, and on the other by the horrifying *Los
Desastres de la Guerra* (*The Disasters of the War*), which, amazingly
he did not publish. Indeed they were not published until 1863. The
prints fall into three groups. The first (2-47) presents in terrible intimacy and accuracy the resistance of the Spanish and the inconceivable
brutality of the French army's response. The second group (48-64)
focusses on the misery, the deaths, the sufferings of Madrid during the
famines of 1811 and 1812. The third group (65-82), executed from
1815 to 1820, does not immediately concern us, though its subject
is a foretaste of what was to come first to Spain and then to the rest
of Europe in the years after Waterloo, the years of the legitimist reaction. In Spain already in 1814 one of the first acts of Ferdinand
IV was to abolish the liberal constitution of the government in Cadiz,
the government set up by the Spanish liberals to maintain Spanish
identity during the years of the struggle against Napoleon. This third
group is particularly aimed at the viciousness of the restored power of
the Spanish clergy and its Inquisition.

The stylistic character of these prints reminds one, first of all, of what Kleist was to say about Friedrich, that one felt one's eyelids had been cut away. Of all the pictures of the early 19th century these seem to us the most modern, the most immediately accessible, for they are pictures in which one is aware only of what is being presented. They are like photographs. It has taken us a long time to recognize that any photograph has a peculiar artistry of its own, that far from being a direct imitation or copying or uncontaminated registration of reality, photographs are as much transformations of the visible as any painting. So with these prints by Goya. Only in time does one become aware of their artistry, their pictorial character. And one reason is that Goya very nearly abandons, even more than in *Los Caprichos,* the traditional means of organizing and constructing a picture. For the composition has only one function, to force the observer's attention upon the particular horror Goya has, as he claims in the title of one of them, himself seen. This realism makes him a Romantic, for we have seen again and again that a distinct mark of Romanticism is a stylistic revolution and transcendence aimed above all at seeing the world afresh and as accurately as possible. Goya's stylistic emergence in these years is precisely congruent with and culturally convergent with Hegel's affirmation of a new cultural epoch. *The Disasters of the War* is Goya's *Science of Logic.*

But before the paintings of the second and third of May, 1808, can be examined, it is instructive to consider one very different painting of the many done in these years, *"El Gigante,"* (*"The Colossus"*). In the lower third of the painting — in a valley that stretches between hills and runs from lower left corner to what may be a town and certainly is a forest at the right — is a great crowd of tiny people, cattle, and at least one wagon. They are in turmoil. They seem to be running, lines of them, most of them out of the picture to the lower left corner, but not all of them. Indeed, cattle are running towards the hill on the right. What may or may not be the immediate cause of this uproar is the enormous figure of a naked giant, visible from just below the buttocks, three quarters turned away, the left arm raised in what may be a threatening gesture, with clenched fist. Were we to see all of him he would occupy the full height of the picture, nearly four feet. The upper third of the picture is covered with a black cloud, echoing the blackness of much of the landscape below. What does this astonishing and frightening picture mean?

There have been any number of interpretations, but it seems wise to propose no specific allegory. Rather, what Goya has given us is a transformation of the Romantic apprehension in these years, as we have seen — of the incomprehensibility of human life and experience, of the existence of forces and powers which man cannot hope to understand and encompass. All we know is that he painted it between 1808 and 1812, most probably, and that in that case he did it while he was painting a small series of pictures of the disasters of war and working on his great print series. Its greatness lies precisely in the fact that one can give it any number of allegorical interpretations — such as the presence of the French in Spain, or the war, or a new ideology, or the Revolutionary Terror, or the famine of 1811 and 1812 — and be entirely convincing. It will fit, as it were, any apprehension of illimitable terror, this fearful contrast between the enormous colossus and the minute figures of frightened humans, one of whom, in the foreground, has fallen from or been thrown from his horse. And is it not parallel to and the equivalent of the pessimism we have seen in Turner and Beethoven in these very years, and in *The Excursion*? Perhaps the picture is a great question: What has happened to civilization? Or perhaps we can say it is a symbolization of Goya's ability to face and record in paintings and prints horrors of human behavior that no artist had ever before had the courage to transform into pictorial emblems.

Certainly grasp of this picture prepares for "The Execution of the Madrilenos on the Third of May." "The Uprising at Puerta del Sol on the Second of May" has always been regarded as a lesser picture, even though both are obviously a pair, exactly the same size, roughly nine feet by twelve. For "The Second of May" from a distance seems almost and is certainly related to a typical Baroque hunting picture of the 17th and 18th centuries of the type originated by Rubens — a great mass of men and horses being attacked by other men rather than animals. That is, for all its confusion one can see its place in the tradition of European painting. But "The Third of May" is a dif-

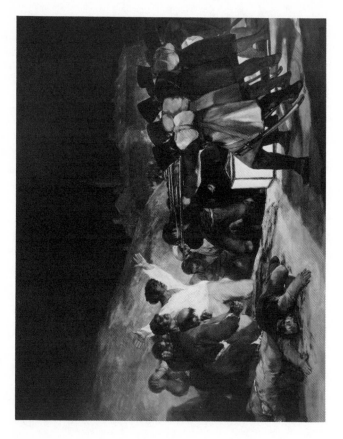

Francesco José Goya Y Lucientes
El 3 de Mayo de 1808:
las fusilamientas en las Montana de principe Pio
reproduced by permission of the Museo del Prado

ferent matter. It embodies everything Goya had learned from *The Disasters of War.* The execution of the rioters captured by the French has begun. At the lower left two or three bodies are already lying in blood. Above them is a group, waiting to be shot, monks and citizens, the pictorial focus being a man in a white shirt and yellow trousers, his arms stretched above his head in terror and perhaps pleading for mercy. Beyond him, to the right, being forced up to the place of execution, is a crowd waiting their turn to be killed. On the right is a faceless line of French soldiers, half turned away from us, thrusting their bayonetted guns toward their victims. In another moment they will let loose their second volley. In the background, against a black sky, are the buildings and churches of Madrid. The scene is so dreadful that at first we do not notice the unique, the enormously original composition. The picture is dominated by an immense implied acute triangle, thrusting in from the right side of the picture and aimed like a sword at the men about to be killed. The undermining of traditional modes of composition that Goya had accomplished, beginning with *Los Caprichos* and reaching a climax in *Los Disastres,* has yielded a new compositional device, one that is above all characterized by instability, the instability of an emergent cultural epoch.

Yet there is something more terrible in this picture than the visible murder and suffering. Just to the right of the center, at the feet of the executing and faceless soldiers, is an immense lantern. It has been brought by the French to illuminate their killing, and its light falls on the man with upraised arms, on the hill behind him, and on the already dead men in the left foreground. In *Los Caprichos* Goya did not hesitate to use puns to make his points. And here is, it would appear, the most profound and disturbing, devastating, pun of all. The Spanish at first hailed the French as liberators from the tyranny of twenty years of total royal corruption — as bringers, therefore, of light, of the Enlightenment, of, in Spanish, the *Lustracion* (the root of which is *lux,* light). We must think of everything that light has been used to symbolize in Western culture — truth, value, divinity, goodness, blessedness, intelligence, life. This picture is dominated by an immense flood of light in the darkness, a light used to facilitate murder,

murder conceived of course as justifiable execution by the occupying French army and its officers In this picture is presented the terrible diremption of the Enlightenment, its splitting apart into the rights of man and the rights of governments to execute its citizens in the name of the rights of man. What the Enlightenment, in spite of itself, took from Christianity was the syndrome of the moral justification for killing human beings, killing them not merely for something so profound as a belief but for something so superficial as an idea. Liberty that yields oppression, equality that yields tyranny, brotherhood that yields murder — these were the terrible bequests of the Enlightenment, made even more terrible by the fact that that bequest did indeed yield liberty, equality, fraternity as well as oppression, tyranny, and murder. "The Third of May" is the quintessential Romantic painting, for more than any other cultural artifact of the twenty-five years we have been concerned with in this volume it shows with the superb precision of ambiguity exactly why Romanticism had to emerge in the cultural history of Europe. Goya's great lantern of light is the Enlightenment itself.

A little more than a year after Goya painted this picture the final defeat of Napoleon on June 18, 1815, at the Battle of Waterloo promised the end of the Revolutionary and Napoleonic nightmare that was a political and cultural whirlwind; and at the same time it promised a consolidation of the immense gains for mankind that whirlwind had brought That was the terrible ambiguity, the fearful conundrum, that brought Romanticism into existence and with which, henceforth it would have to continue to struggle. And that struggle meant the utmost effort at the critical analysis of Western culture's sources of value.

Appendix I

Music and Meaning

The conviction or at least the near certainty that somehow or other music and emotion are related and that that relation can justifiably be called a mode of "meaning" goes back at least to the early Renaissance. Even so and particularly since the middle of the nineteenth century, an opposite opinion has been that music is in fact "meaningless" and that what is properly responded to in listening to music consists of formal relationships or the relations of formal elements. The deficiency of this second position is that in fact people constantly respond to music by generating verbal responses and that these verbal responses belong usually to the large family of terms of "emotion" or "feeling." A further deficiency is that the formal elements themselves may properly be called meaningful and that the relations among them may properly be related to shifts or changes or contrasts of feeling states or emotional conditions.

To be sure, one of the gravest problems of the purely "formalist" position is the vagueness constantly to be found in the use of the word "form." One reasonable meaning of that term is "perceptual determinism," and at the second level "form" can reasonably mean the perceptual determination of relationships among perceptual determinations. The deficiency of this position insofar as it is applied to works of music or in general to works of art is that this two-level perceptual process or activity can in fact not be avoided. To create a work of art merely to provide an occasion for the tension reduction involved in orienting oneself to a perceptual field seems hardly worth the trouble. Of course the justification is that such works offer a more satisfactory mode of such experience than do perceptual fields which are not works of art. Since for some individuals that may be the case and for other individuals not, it is reasonably clear that extra-artistic factors, social, or personal, or moral, as the case may be, are responsible for the fall of the individual's preference in either direction.

A further possible meaning of the term "form" is what is frequently called the exquisite or accomplished or superior filling out or obeying the rules of an established pattern such as, in music, that of the sonata-allegro movement or the fugue. Analysis shows, however, that such satisfaction, commonly called aesthetic simply because it happens in apprehending a work of art, depends upon exactly the opposite, that is, the violation of the conventions for that particular pattern, or as I have called it elsewhere, external discontinuity. (See my *Man's Rage for Chaos*, 1965.) In such cases the mastery of the composer is to be found in the raising of the tension of disorientation by not fulfilling the pattern followed by a reduction of that tension or a reorientation that comes from realizing what the pattern, or rule, is that is being violated.

What is usually taken, however, to be the most powerful objection to the notion that music is meaningful is that music cannot present "cognitive" concepts or ideas. And that is perfectly true, but for a very simple reason. Such concepts or ideas are verbal. It is not the case that an "idea" is "expressed" in a "verbal form." Rather, an idea or concept is a verbalization to begin with, whether overt (spoken) or covert (unspoken). The confusion here arises from the identification of "idea" with all modes of "thinking," but thinking can be verbal, or visual, or musical, or muscular, or spatial, or temporal, and so on. The notion that music is not meaningful simply arises from the assumption long unquestioned in philosophy and ordinary life that only verbal behavior is thought. This objection to "meaningfulness" in music is only an assertion that only words can be meaningful, that all meaning is verbal meaning, and that only verbal meaning is meaning. But that in turn depends upon the notion that meaning is immanent, that in consequence the word dictates the meaning. Now in closely politicized and policed verbal disciplines such as philosophy and many kinds of science that illusion is unavoidable. But it is an illusion, as ordinary behavior in ordinary circumstances and situations makes quite clear. One has only to meditate on the enormous amount of effort that constantly goes into restricting the responses to verbalizations to realize that the very condition of verbal behavior and therefore of verbal meaning is uncertainty. Consequently, the only acceptable conclusion about the meaning of "meaning" is that the meaning of any utterance is the response to that utterance. (For elaboration and clarification of this proposition see Appendix II.)

Now any utterance, whether a grunt, a word, or an oration is a perceptual determination or assemblage of perceptual determinations. If the response to such a verbal perceptual determination is a meaning, then a response to any perceptual determination is a meaning. (Such a determination, or configuration is a "sign," and for futher discussion of "sign" or "semiosis" — sign behavior — see also Appendix II. This discussion of musical meaning will use that term rarely, although it assumes that music is a semiotic activity.) And from this point of view the notion that music is meaningful requires no further defense. But it does need a certain amount of elaboration. For one thing it is perfectly apparent why people respond to music with verbalizations, for human beings, for whom verbalization is species specific, respond to everything with verbalizations. There remain, however, for the position that music is meaningful two serious difficulties. To put these paradoxically, the difficulties are that the verbal responses to a given work of music while dissimilar are at the same time so similar.

For example, to take a very obvious instance, the verbal responses to the last movement of Tchaikovsky's Sixth Symphony can be that it is sad, or melancholy, or depressive, or neurotic, or gloomy, or despairing, and so on. Such a range would suggest that there is little precision to the meaning of music, whatever that meaning might be. But on the other hand, it is equally clear that all these responses belong, as it were, to the same family or verbal group with similar and over-lapping meanings, that is, their own conventionally appropriate verbal responses. Whatever one may hear about this work, one is not going to hear that it is gay, or cheerful, or light-hearted. But since the verbal responses to this work of Tchaikovksy's are so much alike, why are they not more alike? Among others Mendelssohn has claimed great precision for musical meaning, but this example — and one could give endless others — certainly does not seem to support that claim. The most thoroughgoing effort to provide that precision has been Deryck Cooke's in his *The Language of Music* (1959), which has been called easier to deride than to ignore. But Cooke's effort to give precision was not so much mistaken as misdirected. His first error, of course, was to use the term "language." Unless that word is restricted to verbalization, immense confusion is bound to result. To think that music is a language is to conclude that there are immanent meanings common both to musical phrases and to words, at least to anyone who like Cooke and indeed anyone who until recently believed verbal meaning to be immanent. By studying the association of certain musical phrases and certain words in operas, oratorios, and songs, Cooke demonstrated that that association is certainly conventional, and he also opened the way to thinking that it is even more than conventional. For he shows that not only is there a similarity in the verbal response to music but also that there is a similarity in the musical response to words. Just as, however, there is only a family resemblance in verbal responses to music, so there is only a family resemblance in musical responses to words. That is, he showed, without I think fully realizing what he had done, that the conventions governing the relation of words and music in musical settings are unstable.

The factor that is responsible for the symmetrical character of the transformation of words into music and music into words, the factor that Cooke made no use of and was evidently unaware of, is the factor of interpretation. We live in an interpreted world. Nothing in that world dictates our response, nor does any other factor, such as culture or social pressure, dictate response. Response is a matter of determination and judgment. Thus, given the fundamental uncertainty in response and given the character of the human brain, that uncertainty exposes us to randomness of response. If we are to interact successfully with the world, including other people, it is necessary to control that uncertainty, to limit it. Faced with uncertainty of interpretation, what we do is to control our responses and to limit them, to protect ourselves from randomness, by surveying the situation and controlling and limiting responses by picking up clues, or controls, from configurations to which responses are of greater certainty. But these clues are also the consequence of discrimination or determination and judgment. It is simply that the uncertainty of such clues is less, ideally to the point of bare existence.

Let us consider an example not of the translation of words into music, which would be the case if music were a language, but of the interpretation of words by a composer's act of determination and judgment, an act which we may call not translation but (semiotic) transformation. A composer has chosen, let us say, to set to music a two-stanza poem. In the first stanza the speaker exults over the success and happiness of his love; but in the second he laments the failure of that love, giving us the reason why it has failed, because, for instance, of the death of the beloved. Now one composer, using the conventional distinction between major and minor, sets the first stanza in the major and the second in the minor. But another composer, controlling his interpretation of the first stanza not merely by that stanza but by the whole poem, sets the melody of the words of the first stanza in the major but the accompaniment in the minor. Criticism would no doubt call his decision the more subtle, since it suggests an awareness (so might the critic state) on the part of the speaker that his happiness was doomed to be temporary or evanescent. The first composer also concludes the setting with a minor chord, but the second composer, after composing, like the first, the second stanza in the minor, concludes with a major chord. Criticism would probably say something to the effect that the grief over the loss is resolved and that the speaker has turned from that loss to a new or at least different and more satisfying mode of existence. What Cooke has actually shown is that in the tradition of setting words to music there is a tradition of non-binding conventions according to the situation in which the particular word appears. This may vary from a single line of verse or even a phrase to the entire libretto of a lengthy opera or in the case of Wagner's *Ring* four operas. Moreover, the composer is free to do what we all do when faced with uncertainty of response and a situation deficient in usable controls; he invents or imagines a situation. And this applies to the performer as well, whose task it is to interpret a score, for a score in spite of the most extensive markings of tempo and volume and so on, does not and cannot completely dictate a performer's response. Thus Charles Panzera, the great French singer, sang Schumann's *Dichterliebe* in a light ironic tone, but the young Dietrich Fischer-Dieskau sang it in a most melancholy tone without a trace of irony. The irony, of course, came from the singer's judgment, based upon his knowledge of Heine's *Intermezzo*, that the speaker of the poem has already arrived at the conclusion that his response to the love affair was even at the time inappropriate, or at least that it is no longer appropriate, since irony merely consists of a judgment that a response is inappropriate to the situation in which it occurs.

Yet all this does not take us into the problem suggested above, that the similarity in various responses to the same music, or in composers' differing responses to the same text, is more than merely conventional: that is, that it has, as it were, a stability below the level of either kind of interpretation, insofar as such interpretation is controlled by convention or, more properly, by an individual speaker's or composer's interpretation of convention. In both cases the non-identity of response is accounted for by the individual vagaries of interpretation of situation and of convention. This is a manifestation of the general law of human behavior that no behavior, no matter how conventionalized, can be perfectly learned or perfectly transmitted. There is always loss; that is, there is always a certain element of randomness in every response, and this fact accounts for the phenomenon of drift in modes of human behavior. To get at this factor it is useful to glance once again at the verbal response to a given piece of music. The choice of a word or, in the opposite case, the choice of a musical device, is the result of the responder's interpretation of the total situation, or as much of it as he can grasp or judge relevant, in which the musical segment appears (or in the reverse case, the word). That is why one critic may call the last movement of the Tchaikovsky Sixth neurotic, basing his judgment on what he knows of the composer's life. Another may call it melancholy, since it hints, he thinks, at the composer's unconscious intuition of his death, which was to happen so soon after the first performance. Another may call it tragic, controlling his verbal response by knowledge of what has recently been asserted, that Tchaikovsky's death was suicide. This suggests that in a family of similar but not identical responses there is indeed a factor of identity. Thus each speaker controls his verbalization by a different apprehension of the situation, but at the same time each speaker is responding to the same attribute of the musical segment. In the preceding example the distinction between major and minor keys is such an attribute.

It seems clear, then, that we must examine the attributes of music and that if we consider the non-musical source of such attributes it will be possible to locate a source of similarity, or identity, in musical responses to words and verbal responses to music. For several hundred years, ever since the middle of the eighteenth century, it has been widely recognized that the source of music is the intonation of the voice when engaged in verbalization. Linguistic behavior involves both words and intonation, though these may be separated — the words in written language and the intonation in music. Musical instruments have only to modify various attributes of intonation in order to produce various timbres; and likewise just as verbal behavior can be notated so can intonation, the result being the notation of music. The difference is that the notation of words does not go much beyond what can be done vocally in words, but the notation of music can go far beyond what individual voices are capable of doing. First, the transformation of intonation into instruments and then the invention of musical notation has given the composer immense recources, far beyond what verbal notation has given the writer, even though it may be said that by now the writing of language has immensely transformed and extended the possibilities of spoken utterance, and among highly literate people constantly exposed to elaborate written language, has brought about a spoken utterance of a kind hardly to be achieved or arrived at without verbal notation and its development in written language.

And there is a further difference between verbalization and intonation, a difference which sheds a great light on the character of music as bearer of meaning, that is, as material to which it is culturally appropriate to ascribe meaning, just as words are utterances to which it is culturally appropriate to ascribe meaning. When an individual is under emotional strain his control over verbalization will ordinarily last longer than his control over intonation. That is the principle of the polygraph, the so-called lie-detector, and also the reason why that device is so easily abused. But the fundamental link between intonation and verbalization becomes clear when it is realized that a sufficient emotional disturbance can so affect verbalization that it becomes broken and even impossible, a condition which

Melville exploited in *Billy Budd.* It is this link which makes both possible and convincing the musical setting of words. It is clear, then, that the crux of the matter lies in how we are to understand, to interpret, the term "emotion."

The human organism, like any organism, is forever engaged with its environment, with manipulating it to what it judges to be its benefit. However, since that manipulation involves manipulating its own organism, its body and its responses, it would be more accurate to say that the human *brain* is forever engaged in manipulating the situation to which it is responding, a situation which includes not only what is outside the skin of the organism in which it exists but also what is inside that skin, the body itself, or, more precisely with controlling the body so that it manipulates the situation in a way the brain judges to be to its benefit (even though, at times, that manipulation may not be to the benefit of the body or even its survival). For our purposes, and perhaps for any purposes, the activity of the brain may be reduced to the initiation of instructions for controlling the situation and the judgment of whether or not those instructions are being carried out. If the judgment is that the instructions are not being carried out, are being interfered with, the result is emotion. That emotion is the result of judgment is indicated by the fact even when the body may be savagely injured there may be no emotional response. Emotion is, then, first the consequence of the brain's experiencing a hindrance in its efforts to control the situation, and second, the consequence of such efforts, as is indicated by the powerful emotional response when a hindrance is suddenly removed. Thus, basically, all we mean by emotion is a physiological change that may or may not rise above the threshold of perception.

To understand this mechanism of emotion more thoroughly it is necessary to have a term to complement the term "hindrance." That is, since the individual human organism lives in a world in which its judgments are affected by other human organisms, the brain as controller is itself controlled. And that control over brains we call "culture," or learned behavior. Culture turns behavior into action and performance. (By performance is meant the pretense of an action, that is, lying, as in the phrase "putting on an act" or "acting on a stage." The theater situation is one in which pretense is both appropriate and required. For a detailed discussion of the distinction between action and performance see my essay "Literature and Behavior" in *Romanticism and Ideology,* 1985.) Culture is the necessary protection against the brain's capacity for randomness of response, that randomness being at once the source of creativity and the source of error — the human enterprise permits on the whole only a very limited amount of either in a high degree. "Culture," which is but an explanatory abstraction from actual human behavior, guides the brain's instructions and judgments. To this must be added, for our purposes, one further factor in behavior which is readily observable in intonation. The factor in question appears as the degree of volume and as what we call intensity. Both are matters of energy level which the brain judges to be appropriate for carrying out the current instructions. The first is a matter of the level of noise the intonation produces; the second is a matter of muscular tension involved in enunciating, the result of an anticipation of hindrance, a summoning of muscular reserves in anticipation of releasing a higher level of energy. But the level of energy release is to be found not only in volume of verbal productivity but also in the rapidity of verbal execution, that is, the factor we call tempo. And there is a third factor in energy release, the factor of pitch. The more rapid the vibration of the vocal chords, the higher the pitch of the sound produced, and this increase in the frequency of vibration is the result of a greater level of release of energy, or, if one prefers, a higher level of activity, focused on the vocal chords.

In addition to these a further factor in intonation or attribute of intonation may be discriminated, the attribute of rhythm. In all behavior success in carrying out the brain's instructions is indicated by a steady outpouring of activity or energy release, steady and smooth, so that repetition of particular segments of the behavior occur at regular intervals. Any hindrance results in the interruption of the regularity of recurrence, which we call rhythm, and this "arrhythmia" continues until a new rhythmic pattern of behavior is established. ("Arrhythmia" is a term from cardiology. Its extension is justified by the fact that an emotional disturbance can affect the rhythm of the heart beat.)

All of these factors and indicators of energy release, or level of activity, are the consequence of the brain's judgment of the amount of effort needed to carry out its instructions, that is, to fulfill the imperatives of guidance or to overcome the impediments of hindrance. Emotion, or, in common parlance, that lesser degree of emotion known as "feeling" (though this is not the only meaning of "feeling") is not an intermittent activity of the organism but a constant. Thus there is no emotion without cognition, and no cognition without emotion, cognition consisting simply of the two activities of instruction and judgment of the efficacy of instruction. Consequently just as intonation always accompanies verbalization and the muscular activity of intonation always accompanies covert or unspoken verbalization, so the flow of emotion is a constant accompaniment and consequence of brain activity.

Volume, pitch, tempo, and rhythm are the fundamental attributes, the universals, of music, all derived from the intonation of linguistic behavior and transformed into various instruments. Their meaning is the level and character of energy release, of behavior of action and performance, of the effort to control the situation. A musical system becomes richer as it also develops attributes to indicate or mean or signify intensity, as for example a sudden increase in tempo without an increase in volume or with a reduction in volume to mean a greater degree of tension. That is why in Western music the trill is, as one music critic has said, always so exciting. Now if a musical system can develop a way of indicating or meaning hindrance and guidance, then it becomes even richer in its resources of significance. In the early seventeenth century that is exactly what was accomplished in Western music. Two modes, or scales (systemized selection of tones), of obvious and easily graspable and perceptible contrast became respectively the major and minor modes, the major to mean unhindered guidance, the minor to mean hindrance to that guidance. The result was an enormous explosion of music in Western culture, the development of what we call expressivity to a degree no other music, fascinating as it may have been or may be, has achieved with such precision.

For with great rapidity the contrast between major and minor was conventionalized as the contrast between hindrance and guidance, and what this meant was the introduction into music of what it had not had before and what music of other cultures does not have, a clear meaning of drama. For the dramatic consists precisely of the presentation of hindrance and the struggle to overcome it and return to guidance, a struggle frequently tragic, that is, a surrender to hindrance to the point of the agent's ceasing to release energy, to terminating activity. Thus Western music since early in the seventeenth century has come to be able to present, exactly as Mendelssohn stated, an extraordinary precision in creating *meaning constructs* of the flow of emotion, its surge and ebb, its bafflement, its smooth accompaniment of a steady flow of energy release under the instructions of successful cultural guidance, of, that is, unhindered aggression. Emotion is evanescent, fluid, rarely sustained, simply because cognition is rarely sustained. Indeed, sustained emotion is ordinarily considered to be psychopathic, whether it is depression or ecstasy, although mild or lightly sustained emotion is more acceptable. Music, at any rate, has a powerful capacity to project a *construct* of sustained emotion. And cognition is rarely sustained, for cognition is not properly understood as knowledge of reality (an unresolved puzzle for millenia) but rather as the brain's issuing instructions to the body about what to respond to, and what degree of energy release or quantity of behavior activity is appropriate, and whether the resulting manipulation should be steady and rhythmic or hesitant and arrhythmic, should increase or decrease in quantity of acitivity, should intensify or relax the degree of musical tension. And only music can equal the rapidity of the organism's emotional activity.

A further attribute of Western music, an attribute which became particularly important in the second half of the eighteenth century, is the key system. Late in the seventeenth century the establishment of equal temperament and the creation of the circle of fifths made possible the system of modulation from one key to another. (A key is a unique system of notes arranged in a scale, and from this scale are derived combinations of tones or chords.) Although many composers have particular associations with particular keys, such meanings are idiosyncratic, even though at times discernible and recoverable. But that is not the importance of keys nor why the key system has become such an important attribute of Western music. Rather, keys exist in order to be modulated into other keys. That is, a modulation from one key to another means or indicates a shift or change in the flow of constructed emotion, and the more remote the modulation the greater the change in that flow.

Music can be responded to in two ways, by an emotional response, in which the music becomes cultural directions for experiencing a particular emotional flow; or by an apprehension of its meaning accomplished by a metamorphosis of music into verbalization — or by both at the same time. Several corollaries may be drawn from this. First, one is probably justified in asserting that all verbal responses to music should be taken seriously, since, no matter how diverse or even apparently bizarre, they are invariably responses to attributes of music present in the musical flow. The second is that music is not, as is so often claimed, innocent. Like all cultural instructions, fundamentally it is political. Like all culture it offers controls for the behavior of a citizenry in a polis. Nothing could be more political than a rock concert — except a symphonic concert. And third, music abstracts emotion from behavior, and its constructs of emotion make possible a unique understanding of the character and attributes of the emotional flow, just as the abstractions of physics make possible an understanding of the physical world. And in both cases "to understand" means "to provide instruments for control."

If one wishes to comprehend how music works, one of the best places to observe it in operation is in conjunction with other semiotic systems, particularly in melodrama, spoken drama accompanied by music. At the present time the best place to encounter melodrama is in films accompanied in whole or in part by music. Since films are even more redundant than opera and currently far more accessible, the conventions of musical meaning in film are exceedingly stable, so much so that one can frequently predict the course of the action by simply paying attention to the music. In horror films, for example, the threat of the imminence of horror is almost always indicated by a minor trill in the bass, or, since that device has become somewhat worn, simply a sustained deep note on the double bass or the organ or electronic musical device. Movement upward in the major with a steady rhythm and a loud volume with an increase of tension (by a sudden speeding of tempo) quite clearly indicates a successful raising of the level of aggression under the control of the interpretation of the situation as one of cultural guidance. Just the opposite set of attributes indicates the reverse, the interpretation of the situation as one of resisted hindrance, the resistance indicated by arrhythmia. But what of music that moves down in the major with steady speed and loud volume? This combination of attributes indicates both the reduction of the level of aggression and the maintenance of the level of aggression or even, if the volume increases, the increase of the level of aggression, but under the growing control of cultural guidance. One of the most notable examples of such a combination of attributes is in the Prelude to Act III of *Lohengrin,* simply because the protagonists have entered joyfully into a highly controlled social compact, a marriage, and at the same time their aggression toward each other is appropriately increased.

I do not expect that anyone who is convinced of the meaninglessness of music will be converted by these arguments, but I hope that anyone who is willing to consider music's meaningfulness will test these proposals in his own musical experience; in the combination of words and music, in considering his and others' verbal responses to music, and in examining his emotional responses to music.

Appendix II

The Argument of Explanation and Power

The basic proposition of *Explanation and Power: the Control of Human Behavior* (New York: The Seabury Press, 1979) is that the only generally useful comprehension of "meaning" is a behavioral comprehension, the place of meaning in the rest of human behavior. Such a notion of "meaning" yields the proposition that the meaning of an utterance is the response to that utterance, *any* response to that utterance. Since successful verbal interaction does take place, meaning behavior is controlled, but not completely nor with full success. The primary means of controlling verbal meaning behavior is verbal behavior, which is thus best conceived as instructions for verbal and nonverbal behavior. A behavioral analysis of such words as "cause," "logic," "mind," "intention," shows that their use is normative and that, in fact, all utterance is normative. Examined behaviorally, descriptive sentences are prescriptive sentences. Such a word as "truth" indicates that if an utterance is said to be "true," that statement amounts to a recommendation that the utterance in question be used as a control over behavior. Behaviorally, one can only say that a response to an utterance is appropriate — more precisely, that it is appropriate only in the judgment of someone. Thus all utterance is normative.

A behavioral analysis of categorization provides the basis for understanding explanation. Behaviorally, a category in subsuming two or more words or propositions amounts to the assertion that it is appropriate to respond to such words or propositions in the same way, a response made possible only by neglecting some attributes of the items subsumed. Thus all utterance is revealed as fictive, since all terms are categorial. One acts "as if" two or more items were appropriately responded to in the same way. Categorial subsumption is itself subsumed by more inclusive categories. Explanation is built up by a hierarchy of such subsumptive levels. The hierarchy or explanatory regress can be terminated only arbitrarily. Furthermore, since meaning is not immanent in utterance, there is no necessary subsumptive relation between any two levels of an explanatory regress. Thus, given an initial act of categorization, behavior can move in any subsuming direction, terminating, for example, equally well with theistic statements or naturalistic statements. Moreover, the higher the level of regress the more instances that can be subsumed, but at the same time the less specific are the instructions to respond to any given instance. Validation and justification are behaviorally specialized modes of explanation. All verbal behavior is both normative and fictive, and there is no position which can transcend verbal behavior, such as a meta-verbal position.

What applies to responses to utterance applies also to responses to the non-verbal. The other aspect of linguistic behavior is intonation, which is used to control response to the verbal factor of linguistic behavior. An intonation of an utterance can be considered as a sign of how the utterance ought to be responded to. Hence both the verbal factor and the intonation factor of an utterance are signs. "Sign" subsumes both word and intonation. Hence "sign" can be applied as well to the non-verbal world, not only signs produced by human beings, such as gestures, but any configuration in the non-human-made world. When a configuration, or figure, is perceptually distinguished from its ground, it is then a sign. What is true of verbal signs is also true of non-verbal signs; responses to signs are both fictive and normative, for response depends upon categorial subsumption and response transfer from familiar signs to an unfamiliar sign. As the world comes into our perceptual field, the world turns into signs. Our relation to the world is a semiotic relation. From the evolutionary point of view, the puzzle is how the leap from non-verbal to verbal behavior was accomplished, that is, the leap from categorization dependent upon continuity of attributes from one sign to another (non-verbal semiotic response) to categorization not so dependent, except for the attribute of sound (verbal semiotic response). That the human brain is capable of random response accounts for this leap. From the perspective of non-verbal behavior, all verbal response is thus random. The result of the imposition of verbal semiosis on nonverbal semiosis is the enor-

mous increase of the possibilities of randomness of response, of de-
stablization of behavior, and consequently for the necessity of control
of verbal behavior if interaction is to take place, as it must for economic reasons. The complete form of that verbal control over behavior is explanation, built up initially by verbal subsumption of
non-verbal signs.

The defining attribute of human semiotic behavior, then, is that
response to signs entails the production of signs. Thus the most precise definition of human behavior is "semiotic transformation." Explanation controls behavior, and the recognition that semiotic behavior must be controlled is complemented by the recognition that
all behavior is aggressive, in that the organism has no choice but to
struggle to control and exploit the environment, including, for human
beings, the centrally important verbal environment. Two basic categories of signs can be distinguished, both most easily identified in
linguistic behavior: "performatory signs," which give instructions
on what is to be done, and "regulatory signs," which give instructions concerning the appropriate level of aggression. Semiotic behavior, including verbal behavior, thus controls both "meaning" and
"aggression." In linguistic behavior, words are performatory signs
and intonational signs are regulatory. Any configuration for which
the response has been established can be a performatory sign; regulatory signs are such matters as pitch, rhythm, volume, tempo, color,
verticality, horizontality, shallowness, depth, and so on. Regulatory
signs are interpreted to signify either guidance or hindrance to aggression. Interpretation has the same structure as explanation, is
hierarchical, and is historical, depending upon response transfer and
semiotic transformation. Interpretation is a perceptual disengage-
ment of an analogically determined recurrent semiotic pattern from
an analogically determined series of semiotic matrices.

Mythology and science are both modes of interpretation, for both
are derived not from empirical data (the world of semiotic configurations) but from preceding and less developed explanatory regresses.
Science differs from mythology in not resting on a judgment of an
explanatory regress as a stable guidance, but in exploiting the instability and non-immanency of all levels of explanation from sign con-

figurations in the natural world to that termination of explanation known as scientific theory. Thus experiment modifies explanation by generating semiotic material (or data) which the current explanation cannot successfully subsume. This is feedback. Science is merely the most complete model of the semiotic hierarchy from configuration to the termination of an explanatory regress, since it depends upon the capacity for randomness of response.

Man, then, is best understood as *homo scientificus.* But he is not so as an individual organism. Rather, the behavior that controls explanation is the kind of behavior subsumed under "society" and "culture." "Sciencing" brings out the universality of "scientific" behavior, which is of course primarily a verbal mode of behavior, and therefore both normative and fictive. The exploitation of the brain's capacity for randomness makes scientific innovation possible, but this is the model for all learning, since the acquisition of a behavior pattern is, for that organism, an innovation. Thus the factors in learning are the production of any response, the production of random responses, and the selection or validation of one of those random responses. (The brain's capacity to produce random responses is the termination of the explanatory construct of human behavior here proposed.)

To be controlled, behavior must be channelled, which is the task of any learning situation. Left to itself, the brain will produce random responses. Channelling depends first upon unreliable remembering, which must be supplemented by the constant reiteration in various semiotic modalities of the same instructions, that is, by cultural redundancy, and redundancy is supplemented by policing, the use of force. Thus meaning is ultimately stabilized by the ultimate sanctions of economic deprivation, imprisonment, the infliction of pain, and execution. In modern societies the first three are constantly used in the socialization of children, and in the past the fourth was available, as it still is in certain less developed societies. But if force fails, there is no recourse; therefore culture (or civilization) has as its principal task the maintenance of behavioral stability by circumventing the use of force. The modes of circumvention are the two basic rhetorical modes of seduction and intimidation. Thus "culture" may be defined as those semiotic, directive redundancy systems in response to which behavior is controlled, and patterns of behavior are maintained through time. But culture by itself cannot successfully channel behavior. Because culture depends upon the non-immanence of meaning and the consequent instability of meaning, it is constantly threatened with disintegration, with undermining, and with impoverishment. Culture not only channels behavior; it is also responsible for the spread of deviance into a behavior delta configuration. Controls, therefore, are set over culture. These controls are social insitutions, of which five may be distinguished: teaching-learning institutions (the family is the initial institution), value institutions (which maintain the individual's self-ascription of value, which subsumes judgments of his competence, but these judgments are necessarily, by reason of subsumption, unstable), economic institutions, governmental institutions, and ideological institutions (sciences, the arts, philosophy, scholarship). The structure of the interaction among institutional levels is the structure of explanation, for the verbal behavior within an institution is that of an explanatory regress. An institution is an explanatory regress. An ideology itself consists of the high and terminating levels of an institution. Behavior within government institutions is either of governance (the resolution of ideological incoherence), or politics, concerned with stabilizing or destabilizing governmental institutions. The tasks of ideological institutions are maintaining ideological redundancies, exemplifying them (a particular task of the arts, though not unique to them), and criticizing them, either by evaluative criticism or the critique, which is the ideological mode of undermining ideologies. The importance of ideological institutions is indicated by the fact that a revolutionary government aims as soon as it possibly can at complete ideological control over ideological institutions. Cultural levels are the levels of explanatory regress in ideological institutions. The higher the cultural levels, the greater the exploitation of behavioral instability, and the lower the cultural level the greater the behavioral stabilization. These five kinds of institutions are, in a sense, analytical abstractions, for every institution carries on all five institutional functions. Cultural history is the gradual emergence of institutions which specialize in one particular kind of institutional control over culture, using the other kinds as subsidiary and subordinate modes of control.

The argument so far can be summarized in the following rather melancholy conclusions. Culture controls behavior; culture consists of performatory and regulatory semiotic redundancy systems; words control redundancy systems; the defining attribute of verbal behavior is explanation; explanation is hierarchical, behavioral control is thus hierarchical, and all institutions are hierarchically organized; behavioral control is a matter of learning socially validated performances; performances consist of responses appropriate to the presentation of particular signs; behavioral control depends upon the meaning of those signs; and smooth behavioral interaction of any kind depends upon the illusion that meaning is immanent, but since meaning is not immanent, appropriate response can ultimately be maintained only by the application of force in the forms of economic deprivation, imprisonment, torture, and execution. The brightest spot in this picture is the capacity of science to exploit ideological instability, which is particularly noticeable in the culture of the West. In Western countries is to be found the greatest proportion of the population which experiences the life enhancement of the negative inversions of the ultimate sanctions; economic ease, the privileges of freedom and pleasure, and the enhancement of the individual's own value (i.e., human dignity). But that very individual is the cyclonic center of disturbance in the structure of human behavior, the Catch-22.

The individual as biological entity is not identical with the behavioral individual, the deposit of the organization and control of human behavior. First, the individual as persona is the selective, deceptive, and coherent semiotic interpretation of the behavioral individual, either by the individual himself or by someone else. It is an interpretation of a randomly assembled package of learned behavioral patterns. The persona construct assumes that the behavioral individual is a conjunctive category (a category in which certain attributes are found in all members of that category), but is in fact a disjunctive category (a category in which there are no attributes in common to all members, and which is a cultural and social heuristic convenience). Personality is to the individual as culture is to human behavior. Personality organizes and stabilizes the behavioral individual and ascribes value to it. From this it follows that an interest is a strategy that maintains personal stability. This is obvious in non-economic interests (though an interest can be economically functional, probably a rarity in modern society). An example is collecting. As affluence in this country increased, discretionary income and discretionary time increased. The consequence was an enormous increase in the behavioral phenomenon of collecting. This was a repetition of the collecting behavior which historically has always been a behavioral pattern of members of an affluent class. Interests are the repressive oppressor of the individual upon himself, a way of controlling and stabilizing behavior. Alcoholic or other drug addictions are further examples of interests. Agape and eros are further and almost universal modes of interest. Agape or social love resolves temporarily the tension arising from the struggle to maintain the equilibrium between aggression and control. Eros (whether sexual or mystical) resolves the tension that arises from maintaining the distinction between figure and ground and from maintaining the categorial stability of the figure so distinguished, particularly the persona as disjunctive category. Both arise from the irresolvable tension of maintaining relatively stable explanatory regresses without resorting to or being overcome by the ultimate sanctions. Agape and eros are redemptive modes, safe enough when used as vacations, but immensely destructive, as in revolutionary utopianism, when redemption is hypostatized by language into the ideal of an absolute stability, behavioral, cultural, and institutional, and an absolute freedom from the basic tensions of human behavior, the sources of organic stress. Thus redemptionism is ultimately the attempt to escape from randomness, which is, in fact, the source of human adaptability.

When this randomly assembled package of interests is introduced into an institution, the smooth working of the institution becomes impossible. Directions given from above and feedback from below (corrections of the institutional ideology from beyond the verbal frontier of the institution) necessarily threaten to destabilize the position of the individual of the institution, his "politics." Hence instructions and feedback information are both distorted, one on the way down, the other on the way up. Thus looking up, the perspective is primarily one of resentment, and looking down, one of contempt. The first regards higher levels as hindrances to aggression, the second regards lower levels as fundamentally incompetent. This increases the randomness within the institution, and paradoxically, can either destroy it or make it more viable, more adaptable.

This fundamentally unsatisfactory condition of the irresolvable conflict between individual and institution yields on the part of a few individuals the behavioral phenomenon known as cultural transcendence. The importance of the Romanticism of the early 19th century is that a few innovative Romantics discovered and established within Western culture the basic behavior pattern of cultural transcendence. This arises from the judgment of explanatory collapse (the failure of ideologies), alienation from the culture and the society's institutions, cultural vandalism, social withdrawal, reducing the interaction rate to the minimum, randomizing behavior, selecting a promising emergent innovation, collecting a little group of supporters, and propagandizing the cultural emergent or innovation or "creativity." The Romantic emergent innovation or cultural transcendence was a deconversion from hypostatized redemptionism; that deconversion led to a conversion into a permanent de-conversion. But it must always be remembered that no institution works well, whether authoritarian or democratic, for there is always a conflict, an incoherence, between the task or mission of the larger institution and the stability of the individual, for innovation always threatens dissolution of the persona. And it takes the richest possible development of the individual at the highest cultural levels to make such dissolution both tolerable and profitable. It is possible to the degree the individual regards himself as a social dyad; i.e., he knows himself just as he understands another, by observing his own behavior.

Ultimately, then, there is nothing but the individual organism, behaving, and by that device we call semiosis turning behavior into performance. The behavioral individual is the precipitate of semiosis and culture and redundancies and institutions and ultimate sanctions; he is the irreducible surd of existence, the fundamental incoherence of human life, for he cannot but strive with all his might, with all his aggressiveness, for stability; and yet at the same time he is the only source of that randomization from which issue emergent innovations — which if they cannot eliminate can at least modify, not infrequently for the better, our fictive and normative absurdities of explanation.

Explanation is the ineluctable condition, the defining attribute of human behavior, and that proposition is the termination of the explanatory regress of this theory of human behavior.*

---

*Published originally as the introduction to *Romanticism and Ideology* (Greenwood, Florida: The Penkevill Publishing Company, 1985).

Appendix III

Intention and Interpretation

Since in this and the ensuing volumes I use the word "intention," and since that is one of the more puzzling words in the problem of developing an understanding of literary and philosophical documents and of visual works of art, it will be, I hope, of some value to the reader to explain what I am doing when I use that word. The problem the word appears to offer has for many years been the occasion of various kinds of claims — that the intention of an author or artist cannot be known, or that even if known it is irrelevant, and so on. Thus some readers may very well think either that I have no right to use the word or that I am mistaken in using it, or at best that to use the word requires some justification. The present brief essay, then, is offered as a justification and explanation for my use of "intention."

The canonical texts of a culture are constantly being reinterpreted. And what is a canonical text? It is one that is used to control and limit behavior. If it is a legal text, that control and limitation are backed up by force. Attempts have been made in this country to continue an ancient tradition, to back up religious texts by force. There are certainly plenty of people in this country who would be only too happy to do so. In authoritarian countries literary interpretation *is* backed up by force. Even scientific texts are subject to reinterpretation, since in the culture of science such texts are canonical texts. But this notion can be extended further. Science is constantly reinterpreting not only its texts but the world itself. Science does not interpret any set of scientific data innocently or from scratch. That would be impossible. The very physical data science examined consists of categorial signs. Such data is not culturally naked but, as Carlyle would say, already clothed by culture. New physical data can only be subsumed by already existing categories. Only after that has been done can new categories by developed. Thus, as I said many years ago, we live in an interpreted world. The interpretation of literature is problematic only because the interpretation of

the world is problematic.   But this needs to be pursued further if we
are to develop anything like understanding of what is happening when
we engage in interpretation.

First we may notice that the examination of the history of the
interpretation of anything reveals that the most salient attribute of that
history is instability.   To be sure, that instability is frequently and
perhaps always under political control.   Thus for the past nearly forty
years the interpretation of literature has been unusually unstable
because of the widening spread of institutional demands for publication as a justification for raises, promotion, and tenure.   Since the
readiest and perhaps easiest thing to do with a work of literature
(after judgements of value, the easiest and most uninteresting thing
to do with a literary work) is to reinterpret it, economic pressure
for publication has unavoidably led to such a burst of reinterpretation as the history of the study of literature has apparently never
known.   We can be quite Marxist about this and trace the crisis in
literary interpretation directly to economic forces.   To this can be
added the fact that interpretational stability can be maintained only
by force.   That is why theocratic and ideologically committed regimes
are autocratic and oppressive.   We have at the present time the interesting situation that the normal rate of interpretational instability has
been increased by economic pressure, a step or two short of physical
force.

Now if this condition of the instability of interpretation over time
is narrowed to an actual interpretation at a given instant, the result
is to perceive a further attribute of interpretation, the attribute of
uncertainty.   And this uncertainty can easily be observed if we merely
pay attention to instances of verbal interaction and observe how
frequently the responder to an utterance asks for information about
intention or meaning or "what was in your mind."   That uncertainty
is partially concealed and easily ignored because the vast bulk of our
verbal interactions takes place in highly redundant situations.   Uncertainty of interpretation, then, is not an aberrant or anomolous
situation.   It is the basic condition of interpretation, that is, of verbal
interaction, of which the interpretation of literature is a perfectly
ordinary kind.   The only thing that marks it is the absence of the

original utterer, but that is certainly not a unique condition of literary interpretation. It is sufficient to point out that successful interpretation of an utterance is constantly taking place in the absence of the speaker of that utterance. And by successful I mean no more than successful in the judgment of the absent utterer.

Yet at this point we need a further comprehension of what makes the instability and uncertainty of interpretation possible as well as the phenomenon of emergent or innovative interpretations. Here we need to pay attention to that messy term, "meaning." Foucault's is the notion that the author is a construct "devised to limit the proliferation of meaning." I believe that notion to be defective because it implies, or certainly seems to imply, that the interpretation of literary texts is a unique interpretational problem. But every verbal interaction involves interpretation. The basic model for all interpretation is face-to-face verbal interaction, because in such interaction we learn interpretation, as children. Once we accept interpretation as constant in verbal interaction we cannot stop short of noting that all utterance is emitted by individual human organisms, by authors. That our notion of that author is a construction is, to be sure, the case, but it is a construct of something that exists or has existed. We must look, briefly, at that impingement of existent authors on the notion of meaning. Now there are two possibilities of meaning. One is that the meaning of, for example, a word is immanent and that the word compels the interpretational response. But this is obviously not the case, and even Foucault recognizes it. The other is the notion of meaning first (so far as I know) proposed by Geroge Herbert Mead nearly a century ago — that the meaning of utterance is the response to that utterance. And to this we may add the meaning of any verbal or non-verbal sign is the response to that sign. Since in theory any sign can elicit any of all possible responses and since all possible signs can elicit in a given human organism only one response, and neither of these happens, we are able to ask why they do not happen and also why they could happen. To take the latter question first, any sign can elicit random responses because the human brain as it has evolved is capable of randomness of response to culturally transmitted stimuli as opposed to genetically controlled behavior. The capacity to learn language is no doubt genetically transmitted, but the meaning of words or of non-verbal signs is not. Such meaning is learned. And learning is always marked, because of the brain, by loss and distortion. Culture itself, that is, learned behavior, may be defined as instructions that turn behavior into action and performance. Culture may be fruitfully thought of as a counter-adaptation to the brain's capacity for randomness of response, itself an adaptive mechanism. Or culture may be profitably thought of as controls over behavior. But since, as we have seen, all behavior not genetically controlled is interpretational behavior, culture can be profitably thought of as controls over interpretation. But "instruction" is better than "controls" because it better accounts for loss and distortion. And it is precisely because of that loss and distortion, from which arise innovation and creativity, that the realization that the author is a construct does not do away with the author at all. On the contrary, the notion of a real author is absolutely essential to literary interpretation.

Now, I think, we can understand what is happening when in ordinary verbal interaction we make requests such as, "What do you mean by that," "What is your intention in making that statement," and even, "What is the characteristic of your mind or your thinking that you make this statement," or "What on earth are you talking about," or "What (or whom) are you referring to?" In all such instances we are asking for further instructions on how we ought to respond; that is, we are asking for controls. But if the author of the utterance is absent we seek controls from examining the situation in which the utterance took place, and the unique culturally distorting attributes of a given author, if present, are factors in that situation. And in literary interpretation that is very frequently what we are trying to determine, what is atypical of that author's utterance in this kind of situation. That is, what is original or creative, or more precisely, what is culturally distorting. And the notion of author as more than a mere construct, as something that actually existed, is important because through our knowledge of the author we gain access to the situation, even if only by the approximate date of when he was alive, the situation from which we hope to derive controls over our interpretation. An interpretation is a response to an utterance, and what we need to be constantly aware of in thinking about the interpretational problem is that the establishment of controls over interpretational response is not only the norm of all verbal interaction, including verbal interaction with oneself, but even more that culture itself consists of controls over interpretational response, controls that are transmitted with only approximate success.

This position allows us to be a little more precise about what we are doing when we undertake to interpret a work. In seeking from the situation controls over our response what we are seeking is a determination of what the author was responding to, what controls were limiting his response, what controls he was violating, or distorting, or transcending, what controls he was originating; for we must never forget that because of the loss and distortion in the transmission of cultural instructions the individual is constantly engaged in innovating controls to make up for that loss and distortion. That is, creativity is a norm of human behavior. Or better, we validate innovating controls by calling them creative. This makes it possible to resolve the vexing problem of Freudian or Marxist interpretation. If we believe that either or both of these are universally valid explanations of the factors in human behavior, then they are part of every situation and controls over all works of literature because they are controls over all behavior. If, however, we do not accept Freudian or Marxist universals, then of course we do not consider such universals as factors in the situation, as controls over the author's response to that situation.

All this I think permits us to be a little more precise about certain puzzling terms. "Mind" subsumes variability of response. When we use that word in interpreting literary works what we are doing is controlling our interpretational response by alerting ourselves to the possibility of the author's emergent or innovative response to that kind of situation we propose he is responding to. When we use the word "meaning," we are merely asserting that we need or have created, as the case may be, what we consider for the time being appropriate controls over our interpretation. When we use "intention," we are asserting that we know or that we are asking for controls over the author's interpretation of his situation. And "reference" and "referentiality" require that we must first remember that an utterance does not refer; only speakers or authors of an utterance or a text refer. And in doing so they are indicating the factors or aspects of their situation to which they are responding, just as "reference" in general consists of instructions as to what under the circumstances it is appropriate to respond to, or what we ought to respond to, or what the speaker is responding to.

What all this comes down to is that "historical" interpretation finds its theoretical validity in the fact that it is modeled on basic, central, ordinary interpretation in face-to-face interaction. It is worth noting, in this connection, that controlled historical interpretation emerged in the fifteenth and sixteenth centuries and indeed was powerfully influenced by and grounded on historical interpretation in the legal profession. Furthermore, it emerged from the same cultural milieu as did modern science, and more than possibly it was the culture from which modern science emerged, for that science is another manifestation of what we may call situational thinking. And furthermore it is also worth remembering what those who attack historical interpretation never seem to remember: the achievements of historical interpretation of documents and artifacts in the past five hundred years have been as remarkable in their way as the achievements of the physical sciences and more remarkable than the admittedly much younger social sciences.

We must, however, also admit the limitations and difficulties of historical interpretation. And the principal limitation is that it is impossible to exhaust the possible controls for any given historical situation. Nor is scholarship mere antiquarianism, for antiquarianism is precisely that scholarly exploration of historical situations which makes possible the situationally controlled interpretation of literary texts. The mistake is to assume that a final interpretation is possible. Rather than accepting the non-existence of the author, it is far more useful to accept the inherent instability of literary interpretation, just as science progresses by accepting and exploiting the inherent instability of scientific theory. And just as scientific theory is unstable but has put men on the moon, so literary interpretation is unstable but nevertheless the interpretation of innumerable texts is more satisfactory than it was a hundred or even fifty years ago.

The lesson of this is that only historical interpretation is adequate to meet the interpretational demands of a literary or philosophical or artistic work in its situation. A systematic interpretation, a purely ideological interpretation — Freudian, Marxist, phenomenological, New Critical, structurist, deconstructionist, and so on — only turns the work into an exemplification of a theoretical system.

Appendix IV

Chronological Table

1698-1760

Political Events	Philosophy	Literature	Music	Visual Arts
			1698 Metastasio b.	1714 Wilson b.
	1724 Kant b.			1727 Gainsborough b.
				1728 Boullée b.
			1732 Haydn b.	
			1734 Metastasio: *La clemenza di Tito*	
		1736 Macpherson b.		1738 Ledoux b.
		1740 Sade b.		
	1744 Herder b.			1745-1762 Piranesi's *Prisons*
				1747 Farington b.
				1748 David b.

1749 Goethe b.

1751 Schikaneder b.

1755 Flaxman b.

1756 Mozart b.

1759 Schiller b.
Beckford b.

1760 *Ossian fragments*
1760-1767 Sterne
Tristram Shandy

1760 Cherubini b.

1761-1770

1762 Ossian *Fingal*

1762 Fichte b.

1762 Gluck *Orfeo and
Euridice*

1763 Ossian Temora
1765 Percy *Reliques*
1766 Mme. de Staël b.
1767 A. W. Schlegel b.
1768 Sterne *A Sentimental
Journey*
Chateaubriand b.

1766 Wyatt b.

1768 Schleiermacher b.

1769 Napoleon b.

1770 Hölderlin b.
Senancour b.
Wordsworth b.

1770 Beethoven b.

1770 Hegel b.

1771-1780

1771 Mackenzie *The Man of
Feeling*
Scott b.
Coleridge b.

1774 Runge b.			
1775 Turner b.			
1776 Constable b.			
1777 Friedrich b.			
1781 Fuseli *Nightmare*			
1782 Wilson d.			
1783 Cornelius b.			
1784 David *Oath of the Horatii*			
Boullée *Cenotaph*			
for Newton			
1787 David *Death of Socrates*			
1788 Gainsborough d.			
Pforr b.			
1789 David *Brutus and his*			
Dead Sons			
Overbeck b.			

1782 Metastasio d.

Hardenberg (Novalis) b.
Fr. von Schlegel b.
1773 Tieck b.
    Wackenroder b.
1774 Goethe *Werther*

1777 Kleist b.
1778 Foscolo b.

1781-1790

1783 Schiller *Fiesco*

1786 Beckford *Vathek*
1787 Goethe *Egmont*
    Iphigenia
    Schiller *Don Carlos*
1788 Schiller *Spanish Netherlands*

1775 Schelling b.

1780 Schubert b.

1781 Kant *Critique of Pure Pure Reason*

1784-91 Herder *Ideas on History of Man*

1787 Kant *Critique of Pure Reason* revised

1788 Kant *Critique of Practical Reason*

1789 Fall of the Bastille

History	Philosophy/Science	Literature	Music	Art
1790 Emp. Joseph II d. Fr. Nat. Assembly	1790 Kant *Critique of Judgment*	1790 Goethe *Faust A Fragment; Tasso*	1790 Beethoven *Cantata* on d. of Joseph II	1790 Boullée *Temple of Nature*
1791 Fr. Constitution Louis XVI's Flight		1791-1795	1791 Cherubini *Lodoiska* Mozart *Piano conc.* K595 *La clemenza di Tito* *Magic Flute* *Clarinet Conc.* K522 Mozart d.	1791-5 Tischbein *Hamilton's Greek Vases*
1791 French invade Italy				
1793 Execution of Louis XVI Marat assassinated Toulon siege	Fichte *Cont on Fr. Revolution* 1793-7 Herder *Imp. of Mankind*			1792 Boullée *Natl. Ass.* David *Marquise de Pastoret* Flaxman *Homer*
1794 Fall of Robespierre			1794 Cherubini *Eliza*	
1795 French Directory	1795 Fichte *Basis of the Entire The. of Science*	1795 Goethe *Wilhelm Meister I* Sade *Phil. in the Boudoir* Schiller *Aesthetic Education of man* Tieck *Peter Leberecht*	1795-6 Haydn Last Quartets & Trios	1795 Beckford & Wyatt begin Fonthill
		1796 Macpherson d. Coleridge *The Watchman* Tieck *William Lovell; Siegmund's Life*		
Napoleon invades Italy				

Year		Events	Philosophy/Religion	Literature	Music	Art
1797		Peace of Leoben Treaty of Camp Formio	Schelling *Phil. of Nature*	Chateaubriand *Essay on Revolutions* Goethe *Hermann und Dorothea* Hölderlin *Hyperion I* Tieck *Folk Tales I* Wackenroder *Art-Loving Monk* Wordsworth [*The Ruined Cottage*]	Cherubini *Medea*	Wright of Derby d. Flaxman *Aeschylus*
1798		Napoleon to Egypt		Novalis [*Monolog*?] Tieck *Franz Sternbald* Wordsworth & Coleridge *Lyrical Ballads* Wordsworth [*Peter Bell*]	Haydn *The Creation*	Turner *Morning among the Coniston Fells* Veit b.
1799		Napoleon returns Consulate established	Herder *Metakritick* Schleiermacher *On Religion*	Foscolo *Jacopo Ortis* Hölderlin *Hyperion II* Novalis [*Christendom or Europe; Novice of Sais*] Schiller *Wallenstein* Fr. Schlegel *Lucinde* Tieck *Folk Tales II* Wackenroder & Tieck *Fantasies on Art* Tieck *Trusty Eckbart* Wordsworth [*First Prelude*]	Beethoven *Var. on an Original Theme* WoO 77	Goya *Los Caprichos*

Year	History	Philosophy	Literature	Music	Art
1800	Napoleon defeats Austrians at Marengo and Hohenlinde	Herder *Kalligone* Schelling *System of Trans. Idealism*	Novalis [*Hymns on Night*] Schiller *Maria Stuart* de Staël *Literature and Social institutions* Tieck *Genoveva* Wordsworth *Lyrical Ballads* 2nd ed.; [*Home at Grasmere*]	Beethoven Septet Op. 20 6 *Str. Quartets* Op. 18 Cherubini *Deux Journées* Haydn *Seasons*	Runge *Achilles and Skamandros* Turner *Fifth Plague of Egypt*
1801	Peace of Lunéville Restoration of Catholicism in France		Brentano *Godwi* Chateaubriand *Atala* Hölderlin [*Archipelago; Bread and Wine*] Schiller *Aesthetic Educ.; Sublime; Maid of Orleans*	Beethoven *Piano Son.* 12-14 Op. 26, 27 no. 1&2 *Str. Quartet* Op. 29 *Piano Vars.* Op 34 & 35 *Creatures of Prometheus*	Fuseli *Sadness*
1802	Treaty of Amiens Napoleon Consul for life		Cheateaubriand *Genius of Christianity* Foscolo *J. Ortis* compl. Scott *Minstrelsy of the Scottish Border I & II* de Staël *Delphine*	Beethoven *Piano Sonatas 16-18* Op. 31; *Violin Son.* Op. 30; *Symphony II* Op. 36 *15 Var. on Orig. Themes* Op. 35; *Piano Conc. III* Op. 37	Ingres *Scene from Iliad*
1803	U.S.A buys Louisiana from France	Herder d. 1800-1803 Hölderlin [*Hymns*]		Beethoven *Symphony III* Op. 55	Runge *Die Zeiten* drawings Turner *Calais Pier*

Events	Philosophy	Literature	Music	Art
		Chateaubriand *Defence of Genius of Christianity* Kleist *The Schroffenstein Family* Scott *Minstrelsy of the Scottish Border III*		Ingres *Napoleon as Consul; Self-Portrait*
1804 Napoleon becomes Emperor Edict of St. Cloud	Kant d.	Senancour *Obermann* Schiller *William Tell* F. Schlegel *Europa* essays on Louvre ptgs.	Beethoven *Piano Sonata 21 [Waldstein]* Op. 53; 'Andante Favori' WoO 47; *Piano Sonata 22*, Op. 54	
1805 Napoleon's victories at Ulm and Austerlitz		Schiller d. Scott *Lay of the Last Minstrel* Wordsworth [*The Prelude; The Waggoner*] Brentano and Arnim *Youth's Magic Horn*	Beethoven *Piano Sonata 23 (Appassionata)* Op. 57; *Leonore* Hoffmann *Piano Sonata; Merry Musicians*	Runge *Hülsenbeck Children* *Die Zeiten* engravings Ingres *Rivière family portraits*
1806 Napoleon's Victories at Jena & Auerstadt Confederation of the Rhine established		Wordsworth [*Home at Grasmere II*]	Beethoven *Piano Conc. IV* Op. 58; *3 String Quartets* Op. 59; *Leonore Ov. No. 3*	Ledoux d. Ingres *Napoleon as Emp.* Runge *Parents* Turner *Fall of the Rhine at Schaffhausen*

	1807	1808	1809
Art	Flaxman *Dante* Friedrich *Seashore with Fisher*; *Fog*; *Dolmen*; *Summer*; *Winter*; *View into Valley of Elbe*; *Morning Mist in the Mountains* Turner *Sun Rising through Vapor*	1806-8 Turner Thames **Valley Sketches** Friedrich *Cross in the Mountains* Ingres *Bather of Valpinçon*; *Oedipus & Sphinx* Overbeck *Raising of Lazarus* Runge *Small Morning Repro. of Dürer's Prayer Book*	Constable *Malvern Hall* Friedrich *Monk on the Seashore*; *Burial of Monk*
Music	Beethoven *Overture to Coriolanus*	Beethoven *Symphony V* Op. 67	Hoffman *Miserere* Beethoven Piano Conc. V Op. 73; Str. Quartet Op. 74; Piano Sonatas 24 & 26 Op. 78, 81a
Philosophy / Science	Hegel *Phenomenology of Spirit*	Schubert *Nightside of Natural Sciences*	
Literature	Foscolo *On Tombs* Kleist *Amphitryon*; *Penthesilea* de Staël *Corinne* Wordsworth *Poems in Two Volumes*	Goethe *Faust I* Kleist [*Robert Guiscard*; *Battle of Arminius*] Scott *Marmion* Brentano & Arnim *Youth's Magic Horn II & III*	Chateaubriand *The Martyrs* Hoffmann *Ritter Gluck*
History	Napoleon's victories at Eylau and Friedland. Peace of Tilsit leaves England alone against Napoleon	Joseph Bonaparte King of Spain; Murat King of Naples	Napoleon's Victory at Wagram; Napoleon takes Pius VII

Year	History	Literature & Philosophy	Music	Art
1810	Napoleon annexes Holland, part of Switzerland and parts of Germany	Arnim *Cts. Dolores* Chateaubriand *Exmin. of The Martyrs* Kleist *Käthchen von Heilbronn*; *[Prince of Homburg]* Scott *Lady of the Lake* de Staël *On Germany* destroyed by Napoleon	Beethoven *Egmont* Op. 84; *Str. Quartet* Op. 95	Friedrich *Views from Window*; *Landscape with Rainbow* Goya begins *Disasters of War* Ingres *Port. of Marcotte* Overbeck *Christ's Entry into Jerusalem*; *Port. of Pforr* Pforr *Entry of Maximilian into Basel*; *Self-Port.* Runge *Large Morning* Turner *Petworth . . . Dewy Morning*
1811	British defeat French at Albuera	Chateaubriand *Journey from Paris to Jerusalem* Fouque *Undine* Kleist *Broken Jug*; *Tales II*	Beethoven *King Stephen* Op. 117; *Ruins of Athens* Op. 113	Friedrich *Morning in Riesengebierge*; *Winter Landscapes*; *Glen in Mtns*; *Cross in Mtns*; *Mtn. Chapel* Ingres *Jupiter and Thetis* Turner *Somer-Hill*; *Mercury and Herse*
1812	Napoleon invades Russia and retreats; British victories in Spain	Byron *Childe Harold I & II* Hegel *Logic* Vol I Part I	Beethoven *Symphonies VI & VII* (Op. 92 & 93); *Violin Sonata* Op. 96	Friedrich *Oybin Ruins?* *Grave of Arminius* Goya *Colossus ?*

	Art	Music	Literature	Philosophy	History
	Ingres *Romulus*; *Virgil reading Aeneid* Pforr d. Turner *Teignmouth*; *Snow Storm*; *Hannibal Crossing the Alps*	Schikaneder d.			
1813	Wyatt d. Cornelius *Faust*; *Nibelungen*; *Wise & Foolish Virgins* Ingres *Dream of Ossian*; *Livia, Ottavia, Augustus*? *Raphael and La Fornarina*? Overbeck and Cornelius *Double Portrait*	Beethoven *Wellington's Victory*; *To Hope*	Byron *Giaour*; *Bride of Abydos* de Staël *On Germany*	Hegel *Logic* Vol I Part II	Wellington defeats French at Vittoria; Napoleon defeated at
1814	Friedrich *Chasseur in Forest* Ingres *Betrothal of Raphael*; *Paolo & Francesca*; *Don Pedro de Toledo*	Beethoven *Fidelio* Piano Sonata 27 Op. 90	Byron *Corsair*; *Lara* Chamisso *Peter Schlemihl* Hoffmann *Fantasy Pieces I & II, III (Golden Pot)* Sade d.	Fichte d.	Napoleon abdicates; exiled to Elba; France keeps frontiers of 1792; Louis XVIII king
1815	Constable *Boat Building* Cornelius and Overbeck	Beethoven Overture *Zur Namesfeier*;	Byron *Collected Poems* Hoffmann *Fanstasy Pieces IV*		Napoleon's Hundred Days; Defeated by Wellington &

Blücher at Waterloo;
exiled to St. Helena

1816 Hegel *Logic* Vol II

1831 Hegel d.

Devil's Elixir I

1816-1830

Hoffmann *Devil's Elixir II*
1817 De Staël d.

1819 Wordsworth *Peter Bell*
& *The Waggoner* pub.

1822 Hoffmann d.
1824 Byron d.

1827 Foscolo d.

1829 F. Schlegel d.

1831-1877

1832 Goethe *Faust II*

*Calm Sea & Prosperous
Voyage*

Hoffmann *Undine*

1827 Beethoven d.

Commission for Zuccari
Frescoes
Friedrich 2 *Ships under Sail*
Ingres *Aretino & Charles
V; Aretino and Tintoretto*
La Grande Odalisque
Turner *Crossing the Brook*
Dido Building Carthage

1817 Turner *Decline of
Carthage*

1821 Farington d.

1824 Ingres *Vow of Louis
XIII*
1825 David d.
Fuseli d.
1826 Flaxman d.

1828 Goya d.

1834 Schleiermacher d.

Goethe d.
Scott d.
1834 Coleridge d.
Scott d.

1837 Constable d.
1840 Friederich d.

1842 Cherubini d.

1843 Hölderlin d.
1844 Beckford d.
1845 A. W. Schlegel d.
1846 Senancour d.
1848 Chateaubriand d.
1850 Wordsworth *The Prelude* pub.

1851 Turner d.

1853 Tieck d.

1854 Schelling d.
1860 Schubert d.

1862 Schadow d.
1867 Ingres d.
Cornelius d.
1869 Overbeck d.
1877 Veit d.

Index of Persons, Titles, and Places

Adam, 12
Aeschylus, 43
Aix-en-Provence; Musée Granet, 289
Albania, 331
Albrechtsberger, Johann Georg, 144
Alfieri, Vittorio, 181
Ali Pasha, 331
Allgemeine Musikalische Zeitung, 277
America, 105, 167, 168, 337
Amiens, 176, 228
Antony, 6, 7
Aristotle, 1, 269, 327
Arminius, 210, 308
Arnim, Achim von, *243-245*; *Gräfin Dolores,* 244
Arnold, Matthew, 170
Athens, 103
Auden, Wystan Hugh, 151
Austen, Jane, 25
Austria, 21, 88, 174, 175, 176, 273
Austrian Netherlands, 176
Avignon, 100
Babeuf, François Emile, 29, 57
Bach, Carl Philipp Emanuel, 16, 18, 19
Bach, Johann Sebastian, 325
Balzac, Honoré, *La Comédie humaine,* 271
Bamberg, 248, 277, 278, 326
Barlow, Joel, 302
Bartholdy, Jacob Solomon, 303
Bavaria, 80, 277

Bayonne, 339
Beaumont, Sir George and Lady, 221, 231, 234, 235, 310, 317, 336
Beckford, William, 46-48, 228, 229; *Vathek,* 46
Beethoven, Ludwig van, 88, *142-157,* 161, 162, 247, *254-261, 318-325,* 339, 342; "*An die Hoffnung*", 257-258, 322; Andante Favori, WoO 57, 255; Cantata on the Death of Joseph II, 145; Cello-piano sonatas Op. 102, 342-325; *Fidelio,* 259, 372; Incidental music, *King Stephen,* Op. 117, 321, *The Ruins of Athens,* Op. 113, 321; *Leonore,* Op 72, 257-258, 322; *Meerestille und Glückliche Fahrt,* Op, 112, 322-324; Overtures, Collin's *Coriolan,* Op. 62, 259, Goethe's *Egmont,* Op 84, 320, *Leonore* No. 3, Op. 72, 259; *Zur Namensfeier,* · 323; Piano concertos, No. 3, Op 37, 155, No. 4, Op. 48, 258, No. 5, Op. 73, 319; Piano Sonatas, Op. 13, No. 2, 144, Op. 22, 146, Op. 26, 147-149, Op. 27, 148-151, Op. 28, 151, Op. 31, 151-153, Op. 53, 256-258, 319, Op. 54, 256-258, 319, Op. 90, 322-323, Op. 111, 147; Piano variations, Op. 34, 151, 154, Op. 35, 154-155,

WoO 77, 147, WoO 80, 259; Quartets, Op. 18, 146, Op, 59, 258, Op. 74, 319, Op. 95, 320: Quintet Op. 29, 151; Septet Op. 20, 146; Symphonies, Nos. 2, Op. 36, 151, No. 3, Op. 55, 147, 154, 156-157, 254, 261, No. 4, Op. 60, 259, No. 5, Op. 67, 146, 259-260, 319, 320, No. 6, Op. 68, 261, 319, No. 7, Op. 92, 321, No. 8, Op. 93, 321; Trio Op. 97, 320-321; Violin Concerto Op. 62, 259; Violin-piano sonatas, Op. 30, 151, 153, 156; Op. 45, 156; Op. 96, 321, 323, 324; Wellington's Sieg, Op. 91, 319, 321, 322

Belgium, 176
Bergamo, 175
Berlin, ix, 80, 81, 190, 196, 202, 208, 277, 329
Bern, 247
Bohemia, 189, 194, 306
Böhme, Jakob, 135, 139
Böhndel, C. C. A., 182
Boisserée, Melchior and Sulpiz, 295, 296, 299, 302
Bologna, 178
Bonaparte, Joseph, 291, 319, 339
Bonaparte, Josephine, 293
Bonn, 144
Boullée, Etienne-Louis, 38, 44-46; Cenotaph for Newton, 45; Temple of nature, 45; Building for National Assembly, 45
Bouilly, J. N., 257
Boulogne, 207
Bowles, William Lisle, 219
Brandenburg, 81, 202
Brentano, Antoinie, 322
Brentano, Clemens, 202, 243-245; Godwi, 244
Bristol, 124

Brittany, 270
Browning, Robert, 115
British Library, 238
Brun, Frederike, 182
Brunelleschi, 7
Brussels, 40
Bürger, Gottfried August, 238
Burke, Edmund, 237, 272
Burns, Robert, 238
Byron, George Gordon, Lord, 114, 329-335, 336
Caesar, 6, 7
Caldara, Antonio, 26
Cambridge, 113, 124
Campo Formio, 174, 176, 177
Cape Horn, 126
Caracci, The, 297, 298
Carlisle, 238
Carlyle, Thomas, 274
Cherubini, Luigi, 32-36; Les Deux Journées, 32, 34, 35; Eliza, 34-36; Lodoiska, 32, 34, 35; Médée, 36-37
Cheviot Hills, 238
Chamisso, Adalbert von, Peter Schlemiehl, 283-284
Charenton, 60
Chateaubriand, Francois René de, 70, 102-106, 163-169, 267-272, 334; Atala, 163, 166-167; Défense du Génie du christianisme, 106; Essai . . . sur les révolutions, 102-106, 164; Le Génie du christianisme, 163-166, 168-169, 269, 293; Itinéraire de Paris à Jerusalem, 270; Les martyrs, 269-272; Les Natchez, 163; Mémoires d'outre-tombe 163-164
Child, Francis James, 239
China, ii, 250
Christ, 304
Cicero, 6, 7, 8
Cisalpine Republic, 175, 176, 177
Clement XIV, Pope, 29

Colchester, 233, 309
Coleridge, Samuel Taylor, 70, 84, 115, 116, 121, *124-130*, 131, 137, 141, 215, 217, 218, 219, 221, 223, 224, 225; *Christabel,* 240; "France: An Ode", 126, 128, 129; "Kubla Khan", 129; *Osorio,* 124, 126; *The Ryme of the Ancient Marinere,* 115, 126-129, 160, 161, 324; *The Watchman,* 124
Cologne, 295, 296
Constable, John, 160, *232-236*, 254, 288, *309-312*
Constantine, 269
Cooke, Deryck, *The Language of Music,* 347-349
Copenhagen, 182, 183
Corday, Charlotte, 39, 41
Cornelius, Peter Joseph von, *301-304*; Illustrations to the Nibelungenlied, 302
Cornwall, 315
Cowper, William 235
Crabbe, George, 241
Cranach, Lucas, 298
Cumberland, 336
Czerny, Carl, 143
Dali, Salvador, v
Dalmatia, 176
Dante, 41
Danton, Georges-Jacques, 39
Dargomizhsky, Alexander Sergeyevitch, 282
Daubigny, Charles, vii
Davenant, Sir William, 160
David, Jacques-Louis, *37-41*, 176, 197, 198, 298, 299
Dedham, 235, 309-311
Delacroiox, Eugène, 198, 288, 311
Derrida, Jacques, iii-v
Descartes, René, 10, 107
Des Knaben Wunderhorn, 243-245
Devon, 315

Diderot, Denis, 103
Diocletian, 269
Donamovecz, Nikolaus Zmeskall, 320
Dresden, 135, 182, 187, 189, 190. 208, 257, 277, 278, 284, 307
Duccio, 42
Dughet, Gaspard (Poussin), 228
Dürer, Albrecht, 80, 85, 93, 190, 295, 298, 299, 300, 301, 302
Düsseldorf, 301
Dvořak, Antonín, 282
East Bergholt, 233, 234, 309-310
Edinburgh, 237, 274
Egypt, 28, 163, 176, 250, 270
Eisenstadt, 21, 23
Elbe, 189
Eldena Abbey, 190
Eliot, Thomas Stearns, vi; *The Waste Land,* 160
England, 33, 50, 70, 103, 126, 176, 237, 264, 273, 275, 337
Eszterház, 19, 21
Esterházy, Princes, 21, 22, 23
Euganean Hills, 177, 179
Europe, 167, 168, 337
Farington, Joseph, 234, 235
Ferdinand IV, King of Spain, 340
Ferrara, 178
Fichte, Johann Gottlieb, 64, 70, *71-79,* 80, 83, 86, 107, 109, 182, 204, 247, 253; *Contributions . . . to correct the judgment . . . on the French Revolution,* 76; *Grundlage der gesammten Wissenschaftslehre,* 76-79, 80, 90
Fischer-Dieskau, Dietrich, 349
Flatford, 309
Flaxman, John, *42-44,* 186, 198; Illustrations to Aeschylus, 42, to Dante, 293, to Homer, 42-43
Florence, 6, 7, 32, 177, 178, 181, 291
Fontainebleau, 170

Foscolo, Ugo, 70, *174-181*, 182; "Dei Sepolcri", 180-181; *Ultime Letterer de Jacopo Ortis*, 174, 177-180, 181

Fouqué, Freiherr de la Motte, 202; *Undine*, 281-282

Fox, Charles James, 24

France, 5, 31, 32, 50, 113, 125, 176, 204, 264, 273, 275

Franck, César-Auguste, 323

Frankfurt-am-Main, 48, 203, 247, 301, 302

Frankfurt-an-der-Oder, 202

Frederick the Great, 81, 202

Freiburg, 135

Freud, Sigmund, 333

Friedrich, Caspar David, 182, *189-197*, 202, 154, *304-308*, 309, 341

Friedrich Wilhelm, Elector of Brandenburg, 210

Friedrich Wilhelm II, King of Prussia, 203

Fuseli, Henry, *41-42*

Gaveaux, Pierre, 257

Gainsborough, Thomas, 227

Galerius, 269

Galileo, 9, 178, 181

George IV, King of England, 34

George, Stefan, 159

Gerhardt, Paul, 243

Germany, 5, 70, 88, 119, 121, 210, 221, 264, 273-273, 288; Medieval and Renaissance, 301

Gibbon, Edward, 272

Giotto, 42

Girodet de Roucy, Anne-Louis, 167, 292

Glasgow, 237

Gluck, Christoph Willibad: *Orfeo ed Euridice*, 19

Goethe, Johann Wolfgang von, 5, 33, *48-54*, 55, 56, 67, 79, 85, 86, 139, 183, 185, 187, 205, 207, 208, 209, 247, 296, 320, 324; *Egmont*, 54, 320; *Faust*, 52, 53, 54, 299, 302; *Goetz von Berlichingen*, 299; *Hermann und Dorothea*, 52, 59; *Iphigenia auf Taurus*, 54, 86; *Propyläen*, 183; *Torquato Tasso*, 54; *Werther*, 81, 174; *Wilhelm Meister*, 49, 50, 52, 53, 67, 79, 85, 86, 139, 183, 185, 187

Gogh, Vincent van, vii

Goncourt Brothers, 90

Gontard, Susette, 160

Gorizia, 175

Goslar, 121

Göttingen, 130, 243

Goya y Lucientes, Francesco José de, *339-344*; *Los Caprichos*, 340; *Los Desastros de la Guerra*, 340-341

Graham, Martha, 97

Grasmere, 12, 120, 122, 133, 224, 337

Gray, Thomas, 47, 207

Greece, 42, 158, 161, 165, 205, 247, 250, 270, 331, 332

Greifswald, 182, 189, 190

Gretry, André, 35

Gros, Baron Antoine-Jean, 40

Hakluyt, Richard, 126

Hamburg, 182, 184

Hamilton, Sir William, 43

Hardenberg, Friedrich von; see Novalis

Haydn, Joseph, *15-24*, 25, 32, 35, 88, 144, 146, 150, 161; *The Creation*, 23; Piano Sonatas, 23; Piano Trios, 22-23; *The Seasons*,

23; String Quartets, 22-23; Symphonies, 22-23
Hector, 181
Hegel, Georg Wilhelm Friedrich, 69-70, 106, 158, 212, *245-254*, 263, 281, *326-329*, 332; *Phänomenolgie des Geistes*, 246, 253, 261, 326-329; *Wissenschaft der Logik*, 327-329, 339
Heidelberg, 296, 302
Heine, Heinrich, 349-350
Helvetic Republic, 125
Hemsterhuis, Franz, 135, 139
Herder, Johann Gottfried von, *1-15*, 34, 49, 51, 55, 64, 70, 71, 77, 158, 243, 281
Highlands of Scotland, 238, 242
Hobbes, Thomas, 160
Hoffmann, Ernst Theodor Amadeus, *276-288*, 326, 327; *"Der Abenteur der Silvester-Nacht,"* 279; *"Don Juan"*, 278-279, 286, 334; *Die Elixiere des Teufels*, 285-288; *Fantasiestuecke in Callots Manier*, 229; *Der Goldne Topf*, 279, 283-285; "The Kapellmeister Johannes Kreisler's Musical Sufferings", 278; *"Kreisleriana"*, 279; *Die Lustigen Musikanten*, 276; *"Der Magniteseur"*, 279; *Miserere*, 277; "News of the Latest Adventures of the Dog Berganza", 279; *"Ritter Gluck"*, 277-278, 292; *Undine*, 277
Holbein, Hans, 298
Hölderlin, Friedrich, 116, *157-163*, 179, 247; "Bread and Wine", 161; "Celebration of Peace", 161; *Hyperion*, 159; "Patmos", 161; *"Der Rhein"*, 161
Holy Land, 270
Homer, 42-43, 165, 198, 269, 289

Hungary, 19
Hutchinson, Sara, 217
India, 250
Ingres, Jean-Auguste, -Dominique, *197-202*, 228, *288-295*
Ipswich, 233, 309
Istria, 176
Italian Republic, 176, 177, 180
Italy, 49, 70, 145, 179, 198, 201, 203, 264, 275, 291, 298, 301
Japanese Heian culture, ii
Jeffrey, Francis, 336
Jena, 55, 64, 70, 76, 79, 130, 135, 243, 247, 248
Joseph II, Emperor, 27, 29
Joyce, James, vi
Kaufmann, Walter, 249, 329
Kant, Immanuel, ix, *1-15*, 47, 54, 55, 61, 64, 70, 71, 74, 75, 76, 78, 107, 204, 205, 247, 248, 251, 252, 253, 276, 279, 281, 283, 326, 327; *Kritik der praktischen Vernunft*, 1, *der reinen Vernunft*, 1, *der Urteilskraft*, 1, 74
Keats, John, 114
Kelso, 239
Kingdom of Italy, 180
Kleist, Heinrich von, 196, *202-215*; *Amphitryon*, 207-208; "The Beggarwoman of Locarno", 212, 214; "The Duel", 212, 214; "The Earthquake in Chile", 212-214; "The Engagement in Santo Domingo", 212, 214; *Die Familie Schroffenstein*, 206, 207; "The Foundling", 212, 214; *Die Hermannschlacht*, 210, 307; *Das Käthchen von Heilbronn*, 210; "Michael Kohlhaas", 211-212; "Die Marquise von O. . .", 212-214; *Penthesilea*, 208-209; *Phöbus*, 206, 208, 212; *Prinz Fried-*

rich von Homburg, 210-212; Robert Guiscard, 205-206; "Saint Cecelia and the Power of Music", 212, 214; Der Zerbrochene Krug, 207
Königsberg, 5, 74, 207, 208
Kotzebue, August von, 321
Kreutzer, Rodolphe, 156
Lamb, Charles, 170, 218
Latin America, v
Lauffen, 158
Ledoux, Claude-Nicolas, 38
Leibniz, Gottfried Wilhelm von, 107, 136, 138
Leipzig, 64, 130, 135, 275, 277, 278
Leoben, 175
Leonardo da Vinci, 85, 93, 286
Leonburg, 106
Leopold II, Emperor, 26
Leslie, Charles, 311
Leyden, 90
Liège, 198
Ligurian Republic, 178
Liszt, Franz; Les Preludes, 323
Livorno, 32
London, 18, 22, 23, 32, 124, 245, 270, 272, 274, 309
Loos, Adolf, i
Lorraine, Claude, 228, 229, 230, 311, 315
Lortzing, Albert, 282
Louis XIV, King of France, 49
Louis XVI, King of France, 30
Low Countries, 22, 50
Lowlands of Scotland, 242
Lübeck, 299
Lucas von Leyden, 90, 93
Lucretius, 215
Lunéville, 176
Luther, Martin, 85, 87, 90, 92
Lycurgus, 104
Lyons, 170

Mackenzie, Henry; The Man of Feeling, 33
Macpherson, James, 42
Machiavelli, 178, 181
Malta, 221, 234
Mälzel, Johann Nepomunk, 319, 322
Mantua, 32, 175
Marat, Jean Paul, 39-41, 291
Marcotte, Charles, 292, 293
Maria Teresa, Empress, 29
Martel, Charles, 100
Marx, Karl, 252
Masaccio, 7, 291
Matisse, Henri, i
Maxentius, 269
Mazzola, Caterino, 27
Mead, George Herbert, 369
Mendelssohn-Bartholdy, Felix, 17, 303, 347, 355
Mérimée, Prosper, 331
Metastasio, Pietro, 26, 27, 49
Meyer, H. H., 183
Michelangelo, 39, 41, 85, 90, 92, 93, 178, 181, 297
Michelet, Jules, 270
Milan, 174, 175, 176, 178, 290
Milton, John, 41, 42, 117, 219, 228, 269; Paradise Lost, 216, 228
Molière, Jean-Baptiste Poquelin, 207
Monet, Claude, vii
Montaigne, Michel de, 170, 172
Montauban, 197
Moses, 44
Mozart, Wolfgang Amadeus, 23, 25-32, 35, 88, 144, 147, 150, 161; Clarinet Concerto, K. 622, 25; La Clemenza di Tito, 26, 27, 30; Così fan tutte, 25, 26; Don Giovanni, 25, 334; Piano Concerto, K. 595, 25; Die Zauberflöte, 25-32, 50
Murray, John, 273
National Gallery, London, 315

Naples, 43, 291

Napoleon, 14, 27, 32, 36, 46, 60, 163, 164, 166, 168, 174, 175, 176, 178, 180, 198, 200, 203, 204, 210, 228, 247, 272-275, 288, 291, 293, 295, 307, 308, 317, 319, 322, 325, 326, 334, 337, 339, 344

The Nazarenes, 295-304

Netherlands, 90

Neubrandenburg, 189

Newton, Sir Isaac, 45

Niagara, 105

Nice, 174, 175

Niethammer, Friedrich, 248

Nietzsche, Friedrich, vi, vii, 335

Novalis, 63-71, 114, 135-142, 243; "Die Christenheit oder Europa", 137, 140; Heinrich von Ofterdingen, 138, 141, 142; Hymnen an die Nacht, 140-141; Die Lehrlinge von Sais, 139-140; "Monolog", 64

Nürnberg, 80, 90, 248, 326, 327

Octavius, 6, 7

Orcagna, 42

Orvieto, 302

Ossian, 42, 44

Overbeck, Johann Friedrich, 297-304

Oxford, 23

Pacific, 126

Padova, 177

Paer, Ferdinand, 257

Panzera, Charles, 349

Parini, Giuseppe, 178, 181

Paris, 22, 30, 32, 34, 36, 37, 145, 170, 181, 197, 198, 201, 228, 257, 272, 288; Museum of Modern Art, 289

Passage, Charles E., 137

Pater, Walter, 202

Peckham, Morse; Explanation and Power, v, 358-366; "Literature and Behavior," 353; Man's Rage for Chaos, 346; Romanticism and Ideology, 353

Peene, 184

Pellico, Silvio, 293

Percy, Bishop Thomas, 239; Reliques of Ancient English Poetry, 238, 243

Perugino, 297

Pforr, Franz, 297-302; Illustrations to Goethe's Goetz von Berlichingen, 299

Picasso, Pablo, i

Piero di Casimo, 85

Pindemonte, Ippolito, 181

Piranesi, Giambattista, 41

Pitz, 243

Plato, 1, 251, 327

Plutarch, 177

Po, 174, 176

Poland, 32, 34, 203, 273, 276

Pomerania, 182

Ponte, Lorenzo da, 27

Pope, Alexander, 132, 216

Portugal, 29, 331

Potsdam, 203

Pound, Ezra, vi

Poussin, Nicolas, 228

Prague, 26

Prussia, 163, 182, 201, 203, 204, 275, 276; Crown Prince of, 196

Purchas, Samuel, 126

Racedown, 126

Racine, 48

Raphael, 85, 90, 92, 187, 291, 292, 295, 297, 302

Richardson, Samuel, 80

Riepenhausen Brothers, 297

Riesengebirge, 189

Riga, 5

Ritson, Joseph, 239

Robespierre, François-Maximilien-Joseph, 14, 28, 32, 35, 37, 39, 44, 57, 113

Rochlitz, Friedrich, 277, 278

Rome, 32, 94, 165, 176, 201, 269, 288, 291, 292, 295, 298, 299, 301, 103; Sack of, 175

Rorty, Richard, iv, v

Rosa, Salvator, 228

Rosen, Charles, 146

Rousseau, Jean-Jacques, 47, 61, 138, 203

Rovigo, 178

Rubens, Peter Paul, 311, 342

Rudolf von Habsburg, 299, 319, 320

Rügen, 189, 305

Runge, Daniel, 182

Runge, Philipp Otto, 182-189, 202, 254, 302

Ruskin, John, 229

Ruysdael, Salomon von, 311

Sade, Marquis de, 59-62; Aline et Valcour, 60-62; La philosophie dans le boudoir, 60-61

Sainte-Beuve, Charles-Augustin, 170

St. Gottard Pass, 176

St. John the Apostle, 162

St. Petersburg, 272

Salomon, Johann Peter, 22

Sand, George, 170

Sassali, Angelo, 174

Savoy, 174

Saxony, 306

Schadow, Wilhelm, 303

Schelling, Friedrich Wilhelm Joseph von, 70, 106-112, 121, 123, 125, 132, 137, 139, 158, 182, 196, 245, 247, 253, 279; Ideen zu einer Philosophie der Natur, 107-109; System des transcendental Idealismus, 109-112, 223

Schiller, Friedrich, 54-59, 60, 62, 70, 86, 97, 159, 160, 205, 206, 238, 247; Die Braut von Messina, 59; Don Carlos, 55, 144, 145; Fiesco, 55; Die Horen, 56; Die Jungfrau von Orleans, 59, Über die aesthetische Erziehung der Menschen, 56-58; Über das Erhabene, 56-59; Wallenstein, 59; Wilhelm Tell, 59

Schikaneder, Johann Josef, 27, 28

Schlegel Brothers, 70, 125, 130-145; 144, 182, 243, 273, 295; Athenäum, 137; Europa, 295; Lucinda, 131, 141, 242

Schleiermacher, Friedrich Daniel Ernst, 70

Schoenberg, Arnold, i, ii, vi, ix

Schubert, Gotthelf Heinrich von, 205; Ansichten von der nachtseiten der Naturwissenschaften, 279-280, 281

Schumann, Robert, 267; Dichterliebe, 349

Scotland, 167, 236-240

Scott, Sir Water, 236-243; The Antiquary, 240; The Lady of the Lake, 240, 242; The Lay of the Last Minstrel, 240-241; Marmion, 240-241; Minstrelsy of the Scottish Border, 239-240, 243; Sir Tristram, 240; Waverley novels, 241, 271

Senancour, Etienne Pivert de, 169-174; Aldamen, 174; Obermann, 170-174

Shakespeare, William, 33, 34, 35, 41, 42, 100, 205; The Tempest, 144

Shelley, Percy Bysshe, 114, 141

Sicily, 167

Signorelli, 302

Sockburn-on-Tees, 121, 123, 221

Sophocles, 252

Southey, Robert, 70, 218

Spain, 29, 271, 298, 319, 331, 342

Sparta, 104

Spee von Langerfeld, Friedrich, 243
Spinoza, Baruch, 51, 107
Staël, Madame de, 272-276; De l'Al-
   lemagne, 273-276; Corinne, 272;
   Delphine, 272; De la litterature,
   272
Strasbourg, 33
Stein, Gertrude, vi
Sterne, Laurence, 33
Stockach, 177
Stoddart, John, 240
Stour, River, 309-312
Stratford St. Mary, 309
Stuart, Prince Charles Edward, 237
Stuttgart, 158, 247
Suffolk, 309
Switzerland, 113, 163, 170, 173, 203,
   228-272
Tasso, Torquato, 269
Tchaikovsky, Peter Ilyich, 347, 350
Tennstedt, 64
Tetschen, 194
Thames Valley, 225, 227, 229, 233
Thomson, James, 228, 235, 241
Thun-Hohenstein, Franz Anton von,
   194
Tieck, Ludwig, 70, 80-102, 105,
   111, 117, 182, 202, 210, 243,
   282; Die beiden merkwurdigsten
   Tage aus Siegmunds Leben, 97; Der
   blonde Eckbart, 98; Franz Stern-
   bald's Wanderungen, 84, 89-96,
   111; Der gestiefelte Kater, 98-99;
   Der Geschichte des Herrn William
   Lovell, 80-83, 99, 104; Leben und
   Tod der heiligen Genoveva, 100-
   102; Liebesgeschichte der schönen
   Magelone and der Grafen Peter von
   Provence, 98; Peter Leberecht, 97;
   Die verkehrte Welt, 98-99
Tiepolo, Giambattista, 290   290
Tischbein, Wilhelm, 43

Titian, 229
Toulon, 174
Toulouse, 197
Tours, 100, 257
Trakl, Georg, 159
Tübingen, 106, 157, 158, 159, 247
Turner, Joseph Mallord, William, 225-
   232, 312-318; Bequest, 226; The
   Fallacies of Hope, 317-318
Tuscany, 177
United States, 126, 131, 302
Updike, John, 96-97
Vaihinger, Hans, vii
Valla, Lorenzo, 8
Varennes, 30
Veit, Philip, 303
Venice, 32, 175, 176, 179
Ventimiglia, 178
Verona, 175, 176
Vesey, 170
Vico, Giambattista, 10
Vienna, 1, 18, 23, 26, 144, 175, 203,
   257, 274, 297, 319; Academy,
   297, 298, 304
Vincennes, 60
Virgil, 269
Vittoria, 319, 339
Vittoria Amadeo II, King of Sardinia,
   174
Voltaire, 269
Wackenroder, Wilhelm, 70, 80-89, 182,
   202, 295; Herzensergiessungen
   eines kunstliebende Klosterbruders
   84-88; Phantasien über Kunst, 88-
   89
Wagner, Richard, vii, viii, 141; Lohen-
   grin, 357; Die Meistersinger, vii;
   Der Ring des Nibelungen, vii, 349
Wales, 223
Warsaw, 276, 278
Washington, George, 30
Waterloo, ix, 325, 339, 344

Weimar, 5, 55, 207, 274; Duke of, 48
Weissenfels, 64, 135
Wellesley, Arthur, 339
Whistler, James Abbot MacNeil, 229
Wittenberg, 64, 135
Wolgast, 182, 184
Wordsworth, Dorothy, 70, 121, 217, 218
Wordsworth, Mary, 121, 133, 217
Wordsworth, William, 70, 84, *112-124,* 125, 126, 127, 129, 131, 133, 134, 137, 146, 180, *215-225,* 227, 230, 235, 236, 247, 265, 310, 334, *335-339;* "Alice Fell", 218; *The Borderers,* 116; "The Brothers", 120; "The Complaint of a Forsaken Indian Woman", 118; *Ecclesiastical Sonnets,* 222; *The Excursion,* 115, 124, 224, 335-339, 342; *The First Prelude,* 114, 121, 216, 218, 221; "Her eyes are wild", 117-118; *Home at Grasmere,* 115, 123, 225; "The Idiot Boy", 118; Lucy poems, 119-120; *Lyrical Ballads,* 115, 117, 119, 221, 235; "Michael," 120-121; "Ode on Intimations of Immortality. . ." 219; "Personal Talk", 218; *Peter Bell,* 118-119; *Poems in Two Volumes,* 218, 225, 235; *The Prelude,* 113, 121, 216, 221-223, 225, 234, 235, 310, 336, 339; "Prospectus to *The Recluse*", 124. 224; *The Recluse,* 115, 123, 217, 224, 225; "Resolution and Independence," 218; *The River Dudden,* 222; *The Ruined Cottage,* 114-117; "Ruth", 120; "Salisbury Plain", 116; "The Tables Turned", 118; "The Thorn", 117; "Tintern Abbey", 117, 119, 122, 235; "The Waggoner", 265-266; "We Are Seven", 117

Wilson, Richard, 227
Wright of Derby, Joseph, 227
Württemberg, 116
Würzburg, 247, 277, 290
Wyatt, James, 44 *46-48;* Fonthill Abbey, 46-48
Yorkshire, 316

Index of Paintings: Titles and Locations

Constable:
  Boat-building near Stratford Mill, London, Victoria and Albert
    Museum, 311
  Malvern Hall in Warwickshire, London, The Tate Gallery, 233
Cornelius:
  The Wise and the Foolish Virgins, Düsseldorf, Kunstmuseum, 302-303
Cornelius and Overbeck:
  Double Portrait, Munich, Private Collection, 301
Cornelius, Overbeck, Schadow, Veit:
  The Bartholdy Frescoes, Berlin, Staatliche Museen Preussische Kulturbesitz,
    Nationalgalierie, 303
David:
  Brutus and his Dead Sons, Paris, Louvre, 38
  The Death of Marat, Brussels, Musées Royaux, 39-41
  The Death of Socrates, New York, Metropolitan Museum, 38
  The Marquise de Pastoret, Chicago, The Art Institute, 38
  The Oath of the Horatii, Paris, Louvre, 38
Friedrich:
  An Abbey in an Oakwood (Burial of Monk in an Oak Grove),
    Berlin, Verwaltung der Staatliche Schösser und Gärten, Schloss Char-
    lottenburg, 196
  Ausblick in das Elbtal, Dresden Staatliche Kunstsammlungen, Gemäldegalerie,
    193, 195
  Chasseur in a Wood, Germany, Private Collection, 308
  Cross in the Mountains (Cross in a Fir-Forest), Düsseldorf, Kunstmuseum,
    307
  Das Kreuz im Gebirge (Tetschener Altar), Dresden, Staatliche Kunstsamm-
    lungen, Gemäldegalerie, 194-195, 305-306
  Dolmen (Hünengrab) in Snow, Dresden, Staatliche Kunstsammlungen, Ge-
    mäldegalerie, 306
  Felspartie (im Harz), Dresden Staatliche Kunstsammlungen, Gemäldegalerie,
    306
  Fog, Vienna, Kunsthistorisches Museum, 192
  Grave of Arminius, Hamburg, Kunsthalle; Bremen, Kunsthalle, 307
  Landscape with Rainbow, formerly Weimar, Kunstsammlungen, stolen in
    1945, 305

Morgennebel in Gebirge, Rudolstadt, Staatliche Museen, Schloss Heidecksburg, 194, 195

Morning in the Risengebirge, Berlin, Verwaltung der Staatliche Schlösser und Gärten, Schloss Charlottenburg, 306

Mountain Landscape with Rainbow, Essen, Museum Folkwang, 305

Oybin Ruins, West Germany, Private Collection, 307

Seashore with Fisher, Vienna Kunsthistorisches Museum, 192

Ship in Full Sail on the Open Sea, Hamburg, Private Collection; Chemnitz (Karl-Marx-Stadt), Städtische Kunstsammlungen, 308

Summer, Munich, Bayerische, Staatsgemälde Kunstsammlungen, Gemäldegalerie, 193

The Monk on the Seashore, Berlin, Versaltung der Staatliche Schlösser und Gärten, Schloss Charlottenburg, 195-196, 308

View from the Studio of the Artist, Left Window and Right Window, Vienna, Kunsthistorisches Museum, 304

Window Opening on a Park, Leningrad, Hermitage, 304

Winter Landscape, Schwerin, Staatliche Museen, 306

Winter Landscape with Church, Dortmund, Museum für Kunst und Kulturgeschichte, Schloss Cappenberg, 306

Winter (Monk in the Snow), formerly Munich, destroyed in the Blaspalast fire of 1930, a temporary exhibition in which a number of Friedrichs were burned along with several Runges, 193

Fuseli:

Loneliness at Dawn, Zürich, Private Collection, 42

A Nightmare, Detroit, Institute of Arts, 47

Silence, Bern Private Collection, 42

Goya & Lucientes:

El Gigante, Madrid, Museo del Prado, 341-342

The Execution of Madrilenos on the Third of May, Madrid, Museo del Prado, 342-344

The Uprising in the Puerta del Sol on the Second of May, Madrid, Museo del Prado, 342

Ingres

Charles Marcotte d'Argenteuil, Washington, National Gallery of Art, 292

Don Pedro de Toledo Kissing the Sword of Henry IV, lost; 2, 1818, Paris, Private Collection; 3, Oslo, Private Collection; 4, 1831, Paris, Private Collection, 293

La Grande Odalisque, Paris, Louvre, 293-294, 332

Mademoiselle Rivière, Paris, Louvre, 199-200

Marie-Francoise Beauregard Rivière, Paris, Louvre, 199-200

Napoleon Bonaparte, First Consul, Liège, Musée des Beaux-Arts, 198-199

Napoleon I on the Imperial Throne, Paris, Musée de l'Armée, 200-201

Oedipus and the Sphinx, Paris, Louvre, 289

Paolo and Francesca, Chantilly, Musée Condé; 2, Angers, Musée; 3, Paris, Private Collection; 4, Bayonne, Musée, 293, 295

Philibert Rivière, Paris, Louvre, 199-201

Pietro Aretino and the Envoy of Charles V, Belgium, Private Collection; 2, 1848, lost, 293

Pietro Aretino in the Studio of Tintoretto, Belgium, Private Collection; 2, 1848, Paris, Private Collection, 293

Raphael and La Fornarina, Riga, disappeared during the German invasion in 1941; 2, 1814, Cambridge, Massachusetts, Fogg Art Museum; 3, 1814, U.S.A., Private Collection; 4, 1814, Columbus, Gallery of Fine Arts; 5, U.S.A., Private Collection, 292, 293

Romulus Bearing to the Temple of Jove the Arms of the Defeated Acrone, Paris, Ecole de Beaux-Arts, 292

"Scene from the Iliad" (Achilles and Patroclus with Ulysses, Ajax, and the Envoys of Agamemnon), Paris, Ecole des Beaux-Arts, 198

Self-portrait at Twenty-four Years, Chantilly, Musée Condé, 199

The Betrothal of Raphael, Baltimore, Walters Art Gallery, 292-293

The Dream of Ossian, Montauban, Musée Ingres, 292

Thetis and Jove, Aix-en-Provence, Musée Granet, 289-291, 293

Virgil Reading the Aeneid to Livia, Octavia, and Augustus, Toulouse, Musée des Augustins; Brussels, Musées Royaux, 292

Woman at the Bath, La Grand Baigneuse, La Baigneuse de Valpinçon, Paris, Louvre, 201, 202, 288

Overbeck:

Christ's Entry into Jerusalem, Lübeck, destroyed 1942, 299

Franz Pforr, Berlin, Staatlilche Museen Preussische Kulturbesitz, National-galerie, 301

The Raising of Lazarus, Lübeck, Museen Für Kunst und Kulturgeschichte der Hansestadt Lübeck, 299-300

Pforr:

Count Habsburg and the Priest, Frankfurt-am-Main, Städelisches Kunstinstitut, 300

Self-portrait, Frankfurt-am-Main, Städelisches Kunstinstitut, 301

The Entry of King Rudolf von Habsburg into Basel 1273, Frankfurt-am-Main, Städelisches Kunstinstitut, 299

Runge:

Achilles and Skamandros, Hamburg, Kunsthalle, 183

Der Grosse Morgen, Hamburg, Kunsthalle, 185, 188, 189

The Hülsenbeck Children, Hamburg, Kunsthalle, 183-185

Der Kleine Morgen, Hamburg, Kunsthalle, 185, 188, 189

The Parents of the Artist, Hamburg, Kunsthalle, 183-185

Rest on the Flight to Egypt, Hamburg, Kunsthalle, 294

Die Zeiten, Hamburg, Kunsthalle, 185-189

Turner:

Calais Pier, with French Poissards Preparing for Sea; an English Packet Arriving, London, The National Gallery, 229

Crossing the Brook, London, The Tate Gallery, 315

The Decline of the Carthaginian Empire, London, The Tate Gallery, 315-318

Dido Building Carthage; or The Rise of the Carthaginian Empire, London, The National Gallery, 315

Fall of the Rhine at Schaffhausen, Boston, The Museum of Fine Arts, 229

The Fifth Plague of Egypt, Indianapolis, Museum of Art, 228

Frosty Morning, London, The Tate Gallery, 313-314

Large and Small Thames Sketches, London, The Tate Gallery, 225, 230-231, 312, 313

Mercury and Herse, England, Private Collection, 315

Morning amongst the Coniston Fells, London, The Tate Gallery, 228

Petworth, Sussex, the Seat of the Earl of Egremont: Dewy Morning, Petworth House, 312

Somer-Hill, near Tunbridge, the Seat of W. F. Woodgate, Edinburgh, The National Gallery of Scotland, 313

Snow Storm: Hannibal and his Army Crossing the Alps, London, The Tate Gallery, 316

Sun Rising through Vapour: Fisherman Cleaning and Selling Fish, London, The National Gallery, 230

Teignmouth, Petworth House, 313-315, 318

Subject Index

abandonment, 115, 117, 165, 333, 334
absolute, 253; destructiveness of, 326
absolute justice, 212
absolutism, 56
abstract expressionism, 231, 232
abstraction, 248, 249, 250, 251, 253, 254
"academic," 43. 298, 300
aesthetic drive, 57, 58, 59, 62
aesthetic experience and artistic situation, 75
affekt, 16, 17
affirmation, 258
aggression, 16, 37, 110, 146, 150, 152, 154, 155, 192, 199, 209, 255, 260, 322, 357
alienation, 69, 70, 74, 110, 112, 127, 128, 153, 167, 177, 195, 224, 251, 261, 266, 283, 317, 333, 334; from nature, 306
allegory, 126, 193, 292, 284, 342
alternative cultures, 81, 88, 193, 202, 266, 331; history and, 90
American Revolution, 81
analogy, 103-104, 123
ancien régime, 246
antiquarianism, as cultural anthropology, 240
arabesque, 200, 201, 202, 294
archaizing, 44
architecture; domestic, 59; exotic, 34
art, 74; additive organization of, 132; as alternative to religion, 265; and aesthetics, 57; creation of sacred, 85, 132; creative of value, 111, 245; and cultural transcendence, 81, 94; equivalent of divine grace, 112; as expression, 35, 311; finish, 39; foundation of 298; as highest of activities, 111, 245; and ideology, 75; as imitation, 201; meanings of, 111; modern, 197; moral justification, 89; new birth of, 188; normative notion of, 131-132; organization of, 135; as path to religion, 87; realization, 279; as realization of value, 95; religion of, 112; religious, 85, 304; response to, 86, 132; Romantic, 132, 135; task of, 245; test of, 86; validity, 59, 85; universality of, 245
artist; as central figure of Romanticism, prophet and priest, 66, 67; free and independent, 24
arts, hierarchy of, 267

asociality, 61, 72, 208, 209
atheism, 28
audience, 21
authoritarianism, 29
authority, 32
avant garde, 157
ballads, 238, 239
baroque, 19, 27, 80, 90, 255, 298, 325, 340,342; monasteries, 88
Bastille, Fall of, ix, 60, 102
beautiful, 19, 231, 241
behavior, 251; analysis of, 215; civilized, superficiality of, 209; color and, 232; control of, 46, 65, 106, 171, 281; drift in, 350; genetically controlled, 68, historical determinants of, 288; incompetence as norm of, 281; learned, 68; normative categories of, 280; symbolism of, 232
behavior, explanation, and power, Appendix II, 358-366; categorization, 358; culture, 361-362; explanation, 358-359; individual, 363-365; institutions, 362; interpretation, 360; mythology and science, 360-361; non-verbal meaning, 359; Romanticism, 365; signs and semiosis, 360-361; summary, 363, 365-366; verbal meaning, 358
being, category of, 250, 251, 254, 328
Bible, 6, 165; New Testament, 303; Old Testament, 44; Pentateuch, 44
bibliothèque bleu, 96
Bildung, 49, 51, 52
Boniface, Saint, 100
boredom, 171
bourgeois culture, 99
brain activity, 352-353
bureaucracy, 180
categories, 6, 9, 14, 78, 327-329; inadequacy of, 328
chance, 98
chapbooks, 92
child, power and violence of, 184
Christian church, 6
Christianity, 106, 110, 164, 165-167, 169, 247, 269, 270, 271; and Enlightenment, 126; as mythology, 195; reduction of, 306; rejuvenated, 140, 196; secularization of, 125; universalization of, 304
civilization, 41
classicism, 44, 86, 185
classic style, 16, 25, 44, 52, 133, 144, 145, 151, 229
cognition and music, 346-347
cognitive energy, 19
coherence, willed, iii

color, 313; and behavior, 232; and light, 232; meaning of, 231
community, 127, 160, 161, 224
compassion, 181
concrete, 252, 253
consciousness, 77, 251; post-Revolutionary and post-Napoleonic, 335
composers, Romantic, 24
conflict, 251
construction, verbal and will, iii
Consulate, 163, 176
contradiction, 251
conventions, 230-231; of words and music, 348-350
creation, act of, 57
creativity, 66, 201, 231, 264, 353; individual, 275
cultural anthropology, 225
—conflict, 242
—collapse, 334
—convergence, i, v, vi, 180, 223
—crisis, ix, 73, 116
—dislocation, 237
—diversity, 274
—cultural emergence, viii, 131, 333
—epoch, 157
—failure, 81
—norm, 26, 69
—relativism, 5
—renewal, 181
—shock, 118, 119
—support, 217
—transcendence, 6, 8, 65, 66, 69, 70, 79, 81, 114, 129, 134, 140, 141, 142,
    150, 162, 154, 179, 181, 218, 230, 245, 249, 254, 255, 264, 276, 285, 325;
    heroic, 257; planned, 186; precondition for, 151; in visual arts, 183
—universals, 331
—vandalism, 79, 91, 127, 129, 134, 231
culture; channelling of, 69; control over, 29; customs of, 252; definition of, 10,
    150, 352; different, 238; European, analytic dismantlement of, viii; failure
    of, vi, 64, 103, 114, 118, 120, 248; impact of Kant on, 2; pattern of, viii;
    questioning of, viii; secularization of, 12; as guidance and hindrance, 16, 17,
    352-355, 357; history, ii; as instructions for behavior, 16; learned behavior,
    68; love and value ascription, 120; Mediterranean, 47; modification of, 16;
    Muslim, 331; of a nation, 274; natural, 13; and nature, 16; new birth of, 188,
    189; Northern, 47; of the past, 237, 244; theory of, 16; transmission of,
    180; Turkish, 332; Western, ii

cubism, i, vi
cyclical form, 218, 220, 222, 227
deception, 206, 208, 209, 210, 211
deconstructionism, iii, iv, v, vii, ix
deism, 28, 96
depression, 149, 216, 320, 322, 325
desire, loss of, 172
despair, 318, 320
despondency, 337
destructive element, 279, 281, 282
deviancy, 67-69
dialectic, 252
Directoire, 36, 37, 107, 163, 175
discourse, coherence and incoherence of, iii
disillusionment, 171
divine, conception of, 160
double, theme of the, 287
drama, 206, 339; musical, 88, 355
drives, 56
duty, 54, 55
ecstasy, 95, 123, 149, 154, 314, 315, 318, 338
Edict of St. Cloud, 180
education, 115
egalitarianism, 62
ego, *see* self
emotional lability; culture of, 13, 33, 80, 81, 119, 171, 191, 228, 241, 272,
    286, 296; dramatic factor in, 88
emotions, 13, 352-355
Empfindsamkeit, 18, 19
Enlightenment, 24, 39, 44, 83, 110, 146, 198, 203, 204, 229, 239, 241, 247,
    253, 275, 280, 286, 308, 326, 340, 343, 344; abstractions of, 288; as Age
    of Reason, 6; bequests of, 344; culture, i, ix, 10, 87; demogoguery, 48; des-
    pots, 27; *Encyclopédie,* monument of, 103; failure of, 58, 103, 139, 171,
    221, 246; ideal of, 28; feminism, 272; ideologies of, 29, 37, 245, 344; in-
    coherence of, 6, 11, 48, 54, 55, 58, 59, 62, 344; language of, 65; liberalism,
    272, 274; political ideal of, 23, 113; primitivism, 238; and Renaissance, 132;
    Scottish, 237; sexual puritanism in, 31; Spanish, 343; stylistic character of,
    15, 66, 142
empathy, 251
empiricism, 266
encyclopédistes, 103
energy, 255; outpouring of, 151, 256, 257

ennui, 171, 172

epic, 269-270, 271

epistemology, 10, 107, 136, 281

eroticism, 252, 272; as sacred, 133, 141

Etruscan tombs, 43

excitement, 150-151

explanatory collapse, 67, 106

expressionsim, vii

fable, 142

fact-value distinction, 137, 139

faculties, 4

faith, 306

feedback, 253

feeling, 13, 33, 52, 78, 92, 98, 123, 171, 345, 354; projections or materializa=-
     tions of, 191; religious, 192

fiction, 242, 271

folk-tales, 86

forbidden, desire for, 168

"form", 57, 142, 345-346

freedom, 5, 24, 42, 106, 141, 255, 275, 338; absolute, 246, 251; of action,
     172; cultural and political liberty, 169, 254; Enlightenment concept of, 79;
     escape from, 173; in Europe, 24; execrable, 178; and French Revolution,
     107, 246; individual, 24; intellectual, 247, 273; and necessity, 110, 112

French Academy, 291, 295

French Revolution, 6, 14, 22, 24, 27, 28, 29, 32, 34, 35, 36, 39, 64, 71, 76,
     79, 83, 103, 106, 107, 112, 113, 125, 138, 142, 145, 158, 163, 164, 168,
     203, 212, 221, 245, 246, 257, 267, 272, 334; allegory of, 159; Committees
     of Public Safety, 14; failure of, 337; ideals of, 248, 254, 273, 275, 288, 326;
     ideologies of, 71; and Jesuits, 29; Legislative Assembly, 30; lesson of, 14;
     radicals, 46; religious effect of, 166, 296; revelation of, 37, 59, 60, 140;
     Terror, 14, 15, 32, 35, 36, 37, 39, 41, 42, 44, 55, 56, 64, 107, 113, 138,
     342

gardens, 13

Geist, 244, 245, 251, 252, 253, 332, 281, 326; as custom, 253, 260, 263, 335;
     history of, 253

geneology, 287

genius, 111

genre painting, 232

genres, 130

Girondins, 39

God, 3, 122, 253, 281, 328; and nature, 51, 58

Gothic architecture, 33

—novel, 41, 80, 241, 286, 287, 331, 334
—revival, 47, 296, 297
government, 106
grace, substitute for, 216
Greek and Roman tradition, 6, 52
Greek vases, 43, 186
guilds, 50
Holy Roman Empire, 248, 277
hermeticism, 135
heroism, 24
historians, 6; emergence from Romantic culture, 90
historical novel, 91, 242, 243, 270
—process, 2
historicism, 90, 91, 101, 103, 198, 241, 266, 270, 271, 297, 300, 315
history, 110, 253, 287, 288; as construct, 242; into culture, 243, purpose in, 3, 5
history painting, 226, 232
humanism, 8
human relations, inimicality of, 206
human unity, 57
hypnotism, 283
iconography, 185, 187, 188, 290, 291, 304
idea, 251, 346
idealism, 266
ideology, 29, 37, 75, 110, 111, 206; dominant, 29; end of, viii; innovation of, 29
Illuminati, Society of, 28, 29, 31, 70
imagination, 3, 52, 59, 78, 86, 87, 90, 110, 138, 222, 223, 233, 279, 284; as activating force, 139; analogical, 123; and art, 85; cultural independence of, 201; and cultural transcendence, 66; and erotic, 133; free creation of, vi; and innovation, 66; and interpretation, 58; poetic, 220; *vs* realization, 278; release of, 283; as sacralizing, 122; transformational power of, 294, 300
imaginative life, 222
imperialism, 125
impressionism, vii
incoherence, 271, 272
incomprehensibility of life, 94, 106, 116, 117, 118, 127, 128, 131, 132, 177, 195, 205, 209, 212, 213, 214, 265, 285, 287, 306, 342
individual, 3, 125, 162, 177, 253; formed by history, 287; isolated, 105; and masses, 45; relation to his culture, 127; value of, 332, 335
individuality, creation of, 134
industrial revolution, 338

infinite, 130-131

inimicality of life, 306, 307

innovation, i, 10, 66, 101, 231

Inquisition, Spanish, 340

Institute Nationale de Musique, 34

interests, iii, 3, 6

interpretation, 7, 8, 58, 348-349; natural control of, 11; situational, 7, 8, 10, 11; theory of, 367-372

intonation; and emotion, 351-352; and verbalization, 351, 352

intuition, 3, 52, 138; and interpretation, 367-372

invention, 3, 10, 23

Iranian Revolution, 24

irrational, 48

isolation, 121, 122, 173, 195, 261, 333, 334

Jacobins, 35

Jesuits, 28, 29, 30, 83

Judeo-Christian tradition, 6, 44, 69, 158

judgment, 3

landscape painting, 226, 332

language, 348; and adaptation, 65; and cultural transcendence, 65, 66; and culture, 56; emergence of, 12; as expression of thought, 64; Herder's conception of, 4,5; and illusion of reference, 65; maladaptive, 72; morphological commitment of, 65; as negation of itself, 65; philosophical, 249; as representation, 136; thought and, 329; transcendental, 72; unreliability of, iv

laudanum, *see* opium

liberty, 60, 104, 125; absolute, 212; political into cultural 146; political and cultural freedom, 169, 326

life, affirmation of, 265

light, 313; and color, 232; symbolism of, 343

linguistic systems, 63

literalism, 185

literary rhetoric, 97

literature; German 238; oral, 239

logic, 72, 327-329

logocentrism, iii

loneliness, 334

loss, 335

love, 339; and lust, 133; as revelation of value, 95, 120; and sex, 142; sex as highest mode of; as source of value, 178, 333

mal du siècle, le, 335, 336

man, 328 as enemy of society; and nature, 171, 266

man of feeling, 18, 171

manners, 57

Märchen, 98

Masons, 28, 29, 30, 31, 51, 70, 83

mathematical systems, 63, 114

"matter", 57

meaning, 8, 17, 288; creation of, 220; immanent, 346; moments of, 122; and music, *see* music and meaning; musical intensification of, 324; as response, 346-347; source of, 123; transformation of sensation into, 86; verbal, 346-347

meaningfulness, 266, 288; experience of, vii, 285

meaninglessness, 87, 137, 315

medievalism, 42-44, 90, 132, 244

medieval theory, 6

memory, 162

metaphysics, 71, 106, 122, 123

mind, 4, 224, 251; and world, 15, 249, 266

Modernism, i, ii, vi, 295; emergence of, viii; as Romanticism, ix

moment, uniqueness of 311

monarchy, absolute, 27, 30

morality, 121, 207; *vs* sensibility, 48

Moral tradition, 13, 17

music, 289; centrality in Romanticism 85, 267; as constructs of emotion, 355; as emotional drama, 88; as entertainment, 2; as interpretation, 16; intonation as source of, 17, 351; key systems, 19, 20, 355-356; major and minor, 17, 19, 349, 350, 354-355; and meaning, 17, 24, 345-357; melodrama, 356-357; as model art, 202, 285; mystery of, 278; response to, 356; structure of, 325; as supreme art, 96; universals of, 353-354; value of, 85

mysticism, 135

mythology, 98, 114, 122, 138, 158, 194, 219, 179, 280-285, 290, 291

narration, 98, 100, 101, 126, 285

nationalism, 125

natural laws, 12

natural man, 31

nature, 52, 107, 110, 177, 289, 348; absence of man, 96, 105; category of, 328; comprehension of, 139; as enemy of man, 179; Enlightenment notion of, 91; existence of, 250; human, 11; metaphysical attitude towards, 135; physical, 10; powers of, 122; response to *vs* mimesis of, 235; slavery to, 60

nature philosophy, 139

nature and reason, *see* reason and nature

negation, 251, 281

neo-classicism, 44, 66, 86, 227, 290, 293, 296, 299, 312, 340

neo-Platonism, 135

neurophysiology, 250

night, 141

nihilism, 335

Northern Europe, culture of, 44

Northern Gothicism, 44

Northern Romanticism, 44

nothing, category of, 328

occult tradition, 135, 136, 137, 138, 142

oil sketches, 233

opera, 17, 19, 22; aria, 20, 27; libretti, 26; *opera seria,* 27, 36; rescue, 32; situation, 158

opium, 124, 130

order, human tendency to, 173

organicism, 131, 132

orientalism, 294

original sin, 4, 12, 62, 265, 280

paganism, 269, 270

painting; brush stroke, vii; expression *vs* mimesis, 233; idealism *vs* naturalism, 186; lives of saints, 7; and music and poetry, 233; new way of, 8, 341; semiotic system, vi; Venetian, 300; Western, i

particularity, 236, 242, 243, 299; topographical 270, 271

papacy, 28, 140, 163, 166

Passion, 27, 60

past, as alternative possibility, 177

patriotism; and history and cultural renewal, 181; and Romanticism, 179

patterned effect, 200

perception, 250, 311; innovative, 231; as interpretation, 16, 58

perceptual energy, 20

personality, 281; analysis of, 287; construction, 49, 55; as work of art, 49, 52

perspective, 7, 9; scientific, 8, 136

pessimism, 317, 318, 342

phenomenology, 252

philosophers, 3

Philosophes, 103, 104

philosophical systems, 250

philosophy, 64, 111, 253; consequences, 76; Copernican Revolution, 2, 71; cultural mode, 78-82; current state, 2; dethroned, iv; end of, 71; and language, 72, 73; of Nature, 279; perennial, 135; and science, 10; stabilization, 73; system of, 123; vision, 73-74

photography, 341

picturesque, 33, 46, 47, 52, 59, 95, 119. 228, 231, 241

Pietism, 51, 81; subsumption of, 194

play, 56

poem, long, 215, 220
poet; as mediator between divine and human, 158; as priest, 225; as redeemer, 138
poetry, 51, 111, 123; and emotion, 235; symbolic *vs* didactic, 161
post-modernism, v, ix
portrait painting, 232
poem; philosophical 215, 217; synthetic, 218
pragmatism, iv, vii, 266
Prix de Rome, 197, 198, 201,288
problem exposure, 21
progress, 5; inheritance of Enlightenment, 104
prose poem, 169
protestantism, 28, 85, 140
psychology, 224, 225
puritanism, 31
pyrrhonism, 178
radicalism; Christian and Enlightenment, 125
randomization, 91, 172
randomness, 68, 84, 252, 253, 314, 348; culture as protection against, 353; source of creativity and error, 353
rapture, 154
rational explanation, 123
rationalism, 103, 136, 140
realism, 90, 91, 117, 183, 202, 215, 266, 270, 290, 306, 308, 313; historical, 266, 292-293; hyper, 192; linguistic, 97, 180, 249; natural, 233; philosophical, 266
realistic novel, 91
reason, 3, 10, 52, 91; enemy of, 25; failure of, 55, 113, 114; power of, 12; pure, 3; regulative, 58; slavery to, 60; triumph of, 30; and unity of thought, 54
reason and nature, 4, 5, 11, 12, 28, 31, 60, 62, 69; irreconcilability of, 15, 48, 52, 55, 56, 64, 79, 91, 113, 138, 139, 158, 246
redemption, 112, 138, 215, 253; secular, 123, 272
reductionism, 134, 146; metaphysical, 126
redundancy, 69, 70
Reformation, 24, 90
religion, 64, 73, 189, 253; and art, 304; death of old, 193; Enlightenment secularization of, 224; evidence of value-creating power, 317; failure of, 196; hatred of, 137; lost, recreation of, 308; Romanticism and, 265, 266; substitute for, 224; tradition of, 12
Renaissance, 7, 8, 9, 33, 90, 132, 244, 291, 345
Renaissance-Baroque-Rococo tradition, 43
repression, 13
research, 242

resolution, temporary, 251
response; appropriateness of, 350; as transformation; 349, uncertainty of, 343
restlessness, 171
revenant, 278
revolution; causes, 104, permanent, 61
Revolutionary Convention, 39
Rococo; exoticism, 296, 331; Spanish, 340
role model, 51
—playing, 83, 99
Roman Catholicism, 23, 83, 87, 140, 301
Roman Empire, 6, 7
Roman Republic, 6, 7
"Romantic"; eighteenth-century sense of, 52, 59, 66; Enlightenment use of, 33
Romantic crisis, 325
Romanticism, 11, 273; arrival, 101; analytic, 218; anti-metaphysical, 267; birth,
    ix; culture, 276; emergence, 344; and Enlightenment, 6; French, 170, 275,
    288; friendship, 84; general contours, 263; German, 183; history, 69; Italian,
    293; style, 146; tradition, viii; visual arts, 183
Romantics, 15, 143, 273; artistic styles, 66; bizarre, 67; composers, 267; En-
    lightenment contemporaries, 67; German, 247; obsessions, 66-67; task, 37, 83,
    139, 186
Romantic tradition, 215, 329, 333, 344; analytic dismantlement of Western
    culture, viii; equated with Modern, 130; paradox, 263
Royal Academy, 226, 228, 229, 233, 234, 309, 311
sacred, 67, 112, 123, 130-131, 132, 133, 265; psychology and anthropology
    of, 225; as pure disinterested value, 133
sanctification, 122, 123, 224, 225, 235; non-Christian, 138, 186
satire, 97
Schein, 56
scholarship; humanistic, 9; philological-historical, 8-10
science, 3, 9, 64; eighteenth-century notion, 76; experimental method, 9; hypo-
    thesis, 9; imagination, 139; intuition, 138; mathematical tools, 9; and nature,
    10
scientific method, 68
—theory, 180
scientist, 283
seascape painting, 227
self, 66, 82, 92, 110, 111, 131, 132, 134, 139, 140, 142, 148, 162, 201, 231,
    235, 258, as act, 77-79; affirming, 265; assertion of, 310; vs not-self, 79;
    Romantic preoccupation with, 67, 123
—consciousness, 56, 110, 111, 242, 244, 249, 250, 253, 281, 326
—creation, 51, 93

self (continued)
—discovery, 2
—display, 54
—esteem, *see* value, ascription of
—transcendence, 79, 110
—transformation, 151, 256
semiotic systems, vi, 347; music, 17; non-verbal, 254
senses, 13
sensibility, 3, 13, 25, 52; *vs* morality, 48
sentences, iii
sentiment, 33
sentimentalism, 25, 133, 171
sexual behavior, 62, 68
sickness of the century, *see mal de siècle, le*
sign, *see* semiotic systems
situation, 7, 92, 349; limits 15, 150
situational thinking, 9, 77, 91, 213, 135
skepticism, 172, 266, 270, 271
slavery, 252-253
sociability, 4
sociality, 207
social management, tools of, 211
—withdrawal, 70, 266
society, 12
sonata style, 16; form, 19, 20; last movements, 23
"spots of time", 123
stimulus field, 16
Sturm und Drang, 238
style, 169
stylistic transcendence, 168-169, 318
style galant, 16
style troubadour, 293
subject and object, 15, 266
sublime, 19, 58, 231, 241
surrealism, v
symbol, 282, 308
Symbolists, vii
symmetry, 191
symphony, nineteenth-century, 260
thought, 327, 346; musical, 346
tonality, vi
tone-poem, 259
Toryism, 237

Trasncendental Ego, *see* self

transformation in response, 294

truth, 63, 106; belief, iv; error, 205

Turkish rule, 331

tyranny, 30; absolute, 246, 251

unconscious, v, 78, 110, 111, 128, 205, 209, 222, 263

understanding, 3, 251, 285

utopia, 12, 48, 57, 61, 158

value; creation, 87, 95, 96, 111, 123, 128, 161, 162, 264, 315, 338; establish-
    ment, 335; instability, 162; loss, 113, 119, 222; maintenance, 218; moments
    of, 122, 216, 222, 227, 235; psychology, 225; pure, 283; renewal, 278;
    revolution, 29; sexual metaphor for, 124; sources, 123, 161, 215, 278, 284
—ascription of, 23, 67, 120. 274, 325, 333, 338

values, 110

variations, musical, 147

verisimilitude, 241

virtuosity, 154, 156, 319

wanderer, 84, 120, 128, 167, 172, 266, 306, 336-338

Wars of liberation, 210, 275, 307

Waste-Land, 120, 115, 125, 265, 337

Wedgwood pottery, 43

Weimarian classicism, 48, 52, 59, 142, 183

Weimar Republic, 276

will, 55, 110, 111, 121, 146; artistic, 132, 248, 191, 192, 202, 206, 222, 224,
    258, 259, 260, 279, 308; to meaning, 305, 307; unconscious, 223, 233

women, 31, 60

World War I, vi

World War II, 184, 276